GOD'S CH

Books by Walbert Bühlmann
published by Orbis

The Coming of the Third Church
Courage, Church!
The Missions on Trial
The Search for God

Walbert Bühlmann, O.F.M. Cap.

God's Chosen Peoples

TRANSLATED FROM THE GERMAN BY
ROBERT R. BARR

ORBIS BOOKS
Maryknoll, New York 10545

The Catholic Foreign Mission Society of America (Maryknoll) recruits and trains people for overseas missionary service. Through Orbis Books, Maryknoll aims to foster the international dialogue that is essential to mission. The books published, however, reflect the opinions of their authors and are not meant to represent the official position of the society.

Originally published in German as *Die auserwählten Völker*

First published in English as *The Chosen Peoples* by St. Paul Publications, Middlegreen, Slough SL3 6BT, England

U.S. edition 1982 by Orbis Books, Maryknoll NY 10545

Typeset in England and printed and bound in the United States of America.

Library of Congress Cataloging in Publication Data

Bühlmann, Walbert.
   God's chosen peoples.

   Translation of: Die auserwählten Völker.
   Includes bibliographical references and index.
   1. Salvation outside the church. 2. Election
(Theology) 3. Salvation outside the Catholic Church.
4. Christianity and other religions. 5. History
(Theology) I. Title.
BT759.B8313 1982   261.2   82-12635
ISBN 0-88344-150-0 (pbk.)

CONTENTS

Chapter 5
THE CHURCH'S ASSOCIATES IN HISTORY

Chapter 10
THE OTHER RELIGIONS

Chapter 11
EVANGELIZATION

Abbreviations of Frequently Cited Sources

AA   *Apostolicam Actuositatem.* Decree on the Apostolate of the Laity (Vatican II).

AAS   *Acta Apostolicae Sedis* (Vatican City, 1909 seq.).

AER   *African Ecclesiastical Review* (Musaka/Eldoret, Kenya, 1959 seq.).

AG   *Ad Gentes.* Decree on the Missionary Activity of the Church (Vatican II).

AIF   Agenzia Internationalis Fides, Rome (Italian edition).

DH   *Dignitatis Humanae.* Declaration on Religious Liberty (Vatican II).

DV   *Dei Verbum.* Dogmatic Constitution on Divine Revelation (Vatican II).

EN   *Evangelii Nuntiandi.* Apostolic Letter of Paul VI (1975) on evangelization in the world today.

GS   *Gaudium et Spes.* Pastoral Constitution on the Church in Today's World (Vatican II).

HK   *Herder-Korrespondenz* (Freiburg, 1946 seq.).

JEE   *Jeevadhara.* A Journal of Christian Interpretation (Alleppey, India, 1971 seq.).

KM   *Die Katholischen Missionen* (Freiburg, 1881 seq.).

LG   *Lumen Gentium.* Dogmatic Constitution on the Church (Vatican II).

LThK   *Lexikon für Theologie und Kirche* (Freiburg, 1957-68).

MS   J. Feiner and M. Lohrer, eds., *Mysterium Salutis,* vols. 1-5 (Einsiedeln, 1965-76).

NA   *Nostra Aetate.* Declaration on the Relationship of the Church to the Non-Christian Religions (Vatican II).

NZM   *Neue Zeitschrift für Missionswissenschaft* (Schöneck/Immensee, 1945 seq.).

OE   *Orientalium Ecclesiarum.* Decree on the Catholic Eastern Churches (Vatican II).

OR   *Osservatore Romano* (Vatican City, 1849 seq.).

ORI   *Orientierung.* Katholische Blätter für weltanschauliche Information (Zurich, 1936 seq.).

PMV   *Pro Mundi Vita.* Centrum Informationis (Brussels, 1964 seq.).

RH   *Redemptor Hominis.* Encyclical of John Paul II (1979).

SC   *Sacrosanctum Concilium.* Constitution on the Sacred Liturgy (Vatican II).

SM   K. Rahner and A. Darlapp, eds., *Sacramentum Mundi,* vols. 1-4 (Freiburg, 1967-69).

UR   *Unitatis Redintegratio.* Decree on Ecumenism (Vatican II).

ZMR   *Zeitschrift für Missionswissenschaft und Religionswissenschaft* (Münster, 1911 seq.).

Foreword

Not just resentment, but a sense of justice and human worth raises its hackles when one person or people is preferred to another as a matter of course. This is all the more true when it is done by "divine authority" — allegedly. Something is out of joint when one laughs and the others "go empty away." It is either old-fashioned mythology, or a narrow ethnocentrism, to interpret the Old and New Testament idea of a "chosen people" in a way that involves the second-class status, perhaps even the rejection, of other peoples.

What if election does not mean a privilege of some but hope for all? What if it means not monopoly but model? That this is indeed the case is my central thesis. By the time the reader reaches the end of this book it will be crystal clear that although God wished to demonstrate, historically and authentically, in one particular people, how much he loved them — nevertheless, being God, he loves all other peoples as well, and in the same way. All peoples are "his" peoples, all are "chosen peoples". (Which is what the peoples, the Christians, regarded as nonchosen have thought all along!)

There is abundant literature available on the biblical theme of election. The present book, however, is the first interdisciplinary study of the subject. Just as a modern satellite, using different instrumentation in successive orbits, can determine now the weather, now the distribution of natural resources, and now the presence and movement of troops, so in this book I have orbited the theme of election several times — four, to be exact — examining it first of all from the *biblical* point of view, then from the *historical*, then from that of the science of *comparative religion*, and finally from the standpoint of *theology*. Much had to be abbreviated (not, I trust, falsified), else we should have ended with four monographs instead of the synthesis that we have. What was needed was a bird's-eye view, and a synthesis can give us that.

An interdisciplinary solo is risky. Our only chance of a successful flight was to keep in close contact and useful conversation with the leading experts of our four fields, and we acknowledge their great assistance in our notes. Special thanks is due to the scholars who undertook to read and check the parts of the manuscript that correspond to their respective fields of expertise: Karl Jaros, professor of Old Testament studies at the Oriental Institute of the University of Vienna; Hugo Huber, professor of ethnology at the University of Fribourg, Switzerland; Richard Friedli, professor of missiology and comparative religion, also at Linz; and Dietrich Wiederkehr, professor of fundamental theology at the Theological Faculty of Lucerne.

The breadth of our theme has precluded the possibility of an exhaustive bibliography. There were simply too many points to synthesize. On the other hand I have not been sparing in my citations and references, and this for two reasons: to demonstrate that my assertions are based on the most recent theological scholarship, and to offer the reader the opportunity to pursue further the avenues this book may open up.

The many ideas, judgments, and suggestions that have found acceptance in my earlier writings need not be repeated here, any more than they need to be retracted. What is important is that the fundament from which we move remains the same — a spirit of unconditional honesty and self-criticism. This evangelical attitude must never be allowed to die out in the church. And it will never harm the church.

There are many authors today who are occupied with a Christian interpretation of the world. But recent books about faith fly at a lofty height. Karl Rahner's "course" in the faith, Josef Ratzinger's introduction to Christianity, Hans Küng's *On Being a Christian*, the new book on the faith by J. Feiner and L. Vischer, exhaust their topic. The present work does not. But who knows? — perhaps by flying closer to earth we shall be able to smell the scent of the earth, and sink our roots in history (including present history). Thus perhaps we shall be able to verify more immediately, and more experientially, the common assertion of theologians: that being human, in spite of all, has meaning and promise.

God's Chosen Peoples

Part One

How the Chosen People Came to Be

A Biblical Précis

Chapter One

The Peoples and the People

§1 *Planet Earth*

Human beings have always come under the spell of the sea. Wherever they may experience its enchantment — the Bahamas, the Seychelles, Hawaii, or the long continental shores — they unconsciously feel their lives to be inserted into the measureless and mysterious framework of nature and history. More than the firm and rigid land, it is the coming and going of the ocean waters, their striking and silent retreat, day and night, for thousands of years, millions of years, that recalls the rhythm of those other seas — the seas of peoples that surged in waves across the face of our planet, washing it to its appointed and suspenseful destiny.

But before human beings could move across this earth, the planet itself had to come into being. For us, the earth is the most important celestial body. But in the star world it is like a speck of dust. The five thousand stars that we can see with the naked eye comprise but one-ten-millionth part of the Milky Way, and the Milky Way itself floats through a universe of some one hundred billion other star systems of similar kind and magnitude.

Some thirteen billion years ago, a primordial explosion occurred in the fiery, fluid mass of the universe, shooting its splinters as stars into the All. Then, some four-and-one-half billion years ago, our planet spun away as an independent satellite in the solar system. Three billion years ago, the earth's crust hardened. One billion years ago — somewhere, somehow — with the appearance of the first algae, the "leap to life" was achieved. The fish appeared four hundred million years ago, the first insects and reptiles three hundred and fifty million years ago, and the first mammals two hundred and twenty million years ago.

Our knowledge of those primordial times, even with all the scientific progress of the last decades, remains misty and contradictory. We are dealing with millions of years, and we must settle for the scientists' estimates, unless we wish to lay out a whole kaleidoscope of different opinions.

It is the same with the origin of the human species.[1] We are dependent upon hypotheses. Each new fossil that turns up can correct, or shake to their foundations, previous reconstructions. Because of the series of generations listed in the Old Testament, it was long believed that we had to reckon the age of humanity at a scant six thousand years. St. Augustine puts his own great authority behind that figure: "Erroneous are those irresponsible writings that speak of many millennia in the history of our ages, when we can calculate according to Holy Scripture, just under six thousand years since the creation of humankind."[2]

But fifty years ago the Biblical Institute in Rome certified that there was now no longer any way to escape a calculation of at least forty thousand years. And today it is thought that hominization was complete between one and three million years ago — that is, that hominoids, humanlike creatures, had evolved into *homo habilis* (who could use certain tools), *homo erectus* (who walked upright), and finally *homo sapiens* (who gradually developed art and writing).

But is there really any clear line of demarcation between brute animal and human being? Paleontologists speak of human beings when it can be established that they handled certain instruments, used fire, and buried their dead. Theologically, we should have to add, when they were distinguished by self-consciousness and openness to transcendence (see §8, below).

Whether this hominization occurred in one place (the theory called monogenesis), or at different times in different places (polygenesis), remains an open question. The probabilities are leaning more and more toward the latter theory. Since the investigations of R. Darte and L.S.B. Leakey, one is no longer inclined to place humanity's cradle in Asia, but in Africa, where the original nomads then drifted toward Europe and Asia. The great researcher's son, R.E. Leakey, remarks with dry humour that if those hunters had unwittingly moved camp just ten miles in the same direction every generation, in less than fifteen thousand years they could have made their way from Nairobi to Peking.[3] Time, at any rate, they had in abundance.

Of the one to three million years that human beings have existed, at least ninety-nine percent was spent in the most primitive nomadic life, a hand-to-mouth existence of foraging and hunting and sleeping in caves or under windbreaks. Seemingly, a meaningless existence. Only our fantasy might attempt to tell us what it was like, and only our romanticism can discern anything meaningful in those dark shadows. But for those men and women it was not only their daily round, it was their life and their history, which they apparently took as seriously as we take ours.

Only eight to ten thousand years ago did certain of those groups begin to settle down and engage in farming and animal husbandry. They built permanent houses, villages, and cities. Later they developed writing, and thus finally ushered in the period about which our history books have something to say.

One bit of information about the human beings of that era, betrayed by skulls that have been discovered, seems worthy of note in our own days of violence and terrorism. Among the bones found in the Transvaal by Professor Darte, going back perhaps a million years, were baboon skulls (a species of large ape) bearing all the signs of having been killed intentionally. Not far away lay the weapons: the lower jawbones of antelopes, with their sharp teeth. It would seem that the first tools, those telltale traces of the dawn of humanity, were used precisely as instruments of murder. Even the skull fragment of the Pre-Sinanthropus, which L.S.B. Leakey found in 1960 in Oldowaital, Tanzania, bears marks that would lead one to suppose a violent death.[4] So we were ever the same! If these chance discoveries lead to such a conclusion, what must have been the total extent of the violence and warfare in those dark rooms of our prehistory?

If we wished, then, to lay out the history of life on our planet in a book, with one page for every million years, our book would have a thousand pages. Of course they would be nearly all blank. And the history of humanity would appear on the last one, two, or three pages. Most of that would be blank too. So instead of representing the history of all life, let us imagine a book that starts with the beginning of human life, a million years ago. Now each of our thousand pages will have only one thousand years to cover. But we will still be confined to the last ten pages to record all the ages since we first abandoned our nomadic life and became farmers. And the whole of modern history, from the development of steam power barely two hundred years ago, and continuing through that of electricity one hundred and fifty years ago, then atomic energy thirty-five years ago (1945, Hiroshima, the first atom bomb explosion), the first Soviet satellite (1957), the first cosmonaut, the Russian Yuri Gagarin (1961), the first person on the moon, the American Neil Armstrong (1969) — all modern history will have to be condensed into eight lines at the foot of page 1,000. How tiny our present age against the broader span of time! And the ocean waves beat relentlessly on, day and night, age in, age out.

§3 The People of Israel

Out of this sea of peoples, one projects like an island. It is here that we shall now turn our attention. The history of the people of Israel, the "Chosen People," is of no mere national significance. Its meaning is universal.

The traditional division of Israel's history into the age of the patriarchs, the sojourn in Egypt, the exodus, the time in the promised land, and the era of the judges, will do insufficient justice to the complex process of Israel's development and nationhood.[5] We shall sketch here the broad framework of that history, as a help in ordering the sequence of events and understanding them in the light of today's critical studies, which use not only the Bible but other sources as well.

Abraham's emigration, today, appears not to have been an isolated event, but evidently is to be located in the matrix of the Amoritic emigration of around 1800 B.C. After wandering about in Palestine, and perhaps as far away as Egypt, Abraham's clan settled down in the south of Palestine, as also did the clans of Isaac, Jacob, and Joseph. These tribal forefathers are generally recognized today as historical figures, only they were not related by blood. The family relationships are legendary, constructed retrospectively in view of the eventual amalgamation of the tribes.

In need of sufficient land for habitation and pasture, Joseph's clan seems to have emigrated to Egypt about 1350 B.C. At first, his people found favour with the people there. But under Ramses II (1290-1224), Egypt's pro-Semitic politics altered. The Hebrews became cheap labour for building the Pharaoh's cities.

It was during this time of oppression that Moses stepped forward, devising escape plans for the Hebrews. Moses himself was probably not of Joseph's clan, but a Midianite. He had had a religious experience, as a result of which he felt himself driven to organize the flight of the Hebrews and other dissatisfied elements of the population. The escape was scarcely a sensational one in the eyes of their masters. Egyptian sources have nothing whatever to say about it. But for the little group that fled, it was the devisive experience of their history. And it was evidence that Moses' god Yahweh was the truly mighty god.

The flight can be dated around 1230 B.C. Moses led the group over the caravan routes, through the Sinai into his Midian homeland, and there obliged them to do homage to his god Yahweh. Then the group took to the road once more, to return to central Palestine, where they had also settled long ago. Jericho was not destroyed on this occasion; it had long since lain in ruins. Joseph's tribes then united with the clans of Israel and Jacob, already in place, and converted them as well to the cult of Yahweh. The next two hundred years witnessed an intensive process of settlement, of transition to an agrarian way of life, of the development of the clans into tribes, and of increasing consciousness of community based on identity of language and on the common cult of Yahweh.

In order the better to avert the danger from the Philistines, as well as to unite the people still more closely, a monarchy was established, with Saul as first king. After Saul's death David managed to come to power overcoming Jerusalem with a single blow and making it his capital. David extended the kingdom from Damascus to the Red Sea. Under Solomon more poet and businessman than king, there were uprisings, and severa provinces broke away. The result was the schism into the northern and southern tribes. Now the history of the kingdoms of Juda and Israel went their separate ways. The northern state, Israel, fell in 722-721 to the Assyrians, who deported its upper classes in several successive waves.

In Juda, in the region of Jerusalem, David's dynasty still ruled. The prophetic promises of Nathan had lent it such religious reinforcement that it was in no inner political danger. But the Babylonians destroyed Jerusalem in 587-586, and brought the Judean upper class to Babylonia. When Cyrus II, king of Media and Persia, crushed the Babylonian empire, he allowed the exiled Judeans to return to their homeland (538) and rebuild their temple. The temple was completed and dedicated in 515, but Juda remained a Persian province.

It was during this period that Judaism proper was born. It was now that its messianic and eschatological thinking sprang up. But at the same time the primitive breadth of the Old Testament succumbed to a book-and-law religion, with all the intolerance that goes with such a religion.

In 331 the Hellenistic period began, under Alexander the Great. In 64, under Pompey, the Roman period began.

Against the background of such an anguished, weak, and wounded history, Israel held its faith aloft: Yahweh journeyed with his people. And this filled their history with meaning.

§4 *The Yahweh-Faith*

When we consider the religion of Israel at its inmost core — the Yahweh-faith — we see the same picture as for the political history of Israel, indeed for the whole history of the earth and of humanity: nothing has fallen in full bloom from heaven. Everything has a long history of becoming.[6]

In nomadic times the Hebrew tribes had no knowledge of Yahweh at all. Each tribe simply honoured its own "father-god". This was a very transcendent deity, who only seldom interfered in humans' lives, demanded no sacrifices, and was linked to no sanctuary. He simply journeyed with his tribe of nomads. Now and then he would appear to someone in a dream. He was paid the homage of an unreflective basic trust.

As they came in contact with more civilized peoples, especially in Canaan, the Hebrews came to know other gods and sanctuaries, especially Baal, the fertility god, and El, the highest god, the latter evincing many similarities to the father-deities. Then as the tribes melded, the deities of each were generally adopted, rejected, or mutually identified, depending on the case.

Yahweh, the god adopted by Joseph's tribe in Midian, also corresponded to the father-gods in many respects. Only he showed himself to be more jealous, more exclusive. His cult was linked to the holy mountain of Midian, a volcano — hence the fiery circumstances of his apparition. Now, thanks to the authority of Joseph's tribe, the other tribes too adopted the worship of Yahweh. In so doing, they were not questioning the existence of the other gods. But from now on, for the Jews, Yahweh was the only god who counted. He united in himself the traits of the gentle father-deity, the jealous Yahweh, and the more universal El.

When the nomads became farmers in Canaan, a new problem arose. From time immemorial, it was Baal who had always answered for the fertility of the soil. Was there a way out of this dilemma? Elijah, one of the greatest of Baal's opponents, originated the elegant solution of transferring Baal's attributes to Yahweh. Yahweh, Elijah explained, took care of rain and fertility too. Then further attributes were concentrated in Yahweh, and the Yahweh faith soaked up everything like a sponge.

Next the new people directed the light of this faith back in time, and the last chasm was bridged magnificently: Yahweh was represented to have said, from the burning bush, "I am the god of your father, the god of Abraham, the god of Isaac, the god of Jacob" (Exod. 3:6). Thus the father-god of the patriarchs, the Canaanites' El, and the Midianites' Yahweh are in the last analysis not diverse deities, but expressions of the recognition, now developing at high speed, that the god the Bible calls Yahweh had been the companion of Israel's forebears from the very beginning — and the companion of all other human beings as well, though under diverse names.

Let us summarize. In the Bible, under the influence of the cultures and religions of their environment, and under the leadership of God, human beings conjured up the picture of God that indeed comes closest to representing what human speech generally means when it says "God". The fact that so many peoples, cultures and religions, with all their various creative talents and abilities, could cooperate in the fashioning of this image of God, is evidence that God is indeed close to all peoples, and that this picture of God can be the right one for all cultures. The Bible itself, then, leads us along a path of the most generous tolerance. It by no means directs us toward any religious fanaticism.

§5 *Origin and Development of the Hebrew Bible*

There is a third series of questions that exhibit a historical character — namely, the origin and development of the Hebrew Bible. We draw all our information concerning the chosen people of Israel from the Bible, and so we ought to read a detailed introduction to the Old Testament.[7] Here we can only draw the main lines, and in an abbreviated and fragmentary fashion.

In the beginning there was the oral tradition of the sagas, genealogies, legal formulations, and so on — the property of each tribe. As the tribes

8

came together, the oral material coalesced. The first great compilation appeared in the time of David and Solomon, primarily from the oral material of the southern tribes. It was called the "Jahwist" history, because God was usually called Yahweh in that tradition.

After the separation of Israel from Juda, there appeared in the court of Samaria a compilation drawing on the oral material of the northern and central Palestinian tribes, called the "Elohist" history — because the name given to God here is Elohim. Later the two sources were placed side by side, but at the same time they were still being elaborated. Then during the exile and afterward, the so-called priestly writings came into existence. They elaborated cultic prescriptions in all their extensive connections and applications.

The so-called Deuteronomist made use of this material around 560 B.C. in writing the history of Moses and of the period from the occupation of the promised land to the end of the kingdoms of Israel and Juda. In the post exilic period, the books of Genesis, Exodus, Leviticus, Numbers, and other books finally came into the form in which we have them today.

The first of the prophets came on the scene in the eighth century: Amos, Hosea, Micah, Isaiah. The great prophets were very little accepted in their own time. What they said was recorded only by disciples and friends, and handed on. Only in the post exilic period was it recognized that the prophets had been right with their criticism and their warnings, and that the court sycophants had been wrong. Then began the publication of the prophetical books, in the course of which the prophets' assertions were often expanded, adapted for liturgical use, and updated. By about the first century before Christ the prophetical books were in the form that we have them today.

The third group of books of the Old Testament, the "writings", as they are called — Psalms, Proverbs, Ecclesiasticus, the Song of Solomon, and so on — reveal widely varying dates of composition. In today's psalter, a post exilic compilation, very old passages are to be found next to very late ones, all chosen from different earlier collections.

The books of the Hebrew Bible were available in Jesus' time as we have them today. But not all of them were counted as books of Sacred Scripture. The Sadducees recognized only the Pentateuch. The Pharisees on the contrary, and probably Jesus as well, acknowledged most of the books of today's Old Testament.

The genesis of the Old Testament, and its recognition as Sacred Scripture, entailed a process that lasted a thousand years. Any responsible explanation of it must do justice to this long process. It must take full account of the word of God as the word of human beings also. In Sacred Scripture human beings speak of their own experiences, with themselves, with one another, and with God. And yet in the last analysis these human beings have no wish to be understood in their human quality alone, but in the attracting and compelling appeal of God to themselves. Only when we fully accept the Bible as the word of human beings can we also understand it in faith as God's word to us.

In the following pages we shall not always have need to fall back upon these literary and critical considerations. As a general rule we shall be able to take the Bible and understand it as it actually served the life and faith of the synagogue and the church. But it is good always to keep in mind that there is such a thing as scientific biblical criticism.

Chapter Two

Election and Covenant in the Old Testament

The Creation Covenant

§6 *First Beginnings*

At first the people of Israel lived entirely on the promise, on hope, on the future. In the time of the patriarchs, they journeyed toward the new land. In the service of Egypt, they persevered in the hope of liberation. In the desert, they believed in the God of the covenant and in the land of promise. As nomads they experienced God as one who journeyed with them and saw to it that they survived the dangers of a risky life like theirs. This is why the entire first phase of the historical writing of Israel is centred upon the God of the covenant, who, with Abraham of old, then in the exodus and in the Sinai, made history with his people.

Only later, as the nomads settled in the land of Canaan to become farmers and shepherds, at nature's mercy for weal and woe, did it occur to them to inquire into the foundations of this nature with its blessings and its terrors. And so the question arose about first beginnings, about creation. Now the Hebrews, in their religious thinking, proceeded from the God of history to the God of creation. The Old Testament we read today begins with creation, and to us it seems evident that it ought to. But we should know that the creation documents were prefaced to the covenant history only later, both as reflection and as introduction.[8]

And indeed the past and the future, like the present that lies between them, belong jointly to the totality of history. Without the firm foundation of first beginnings there can be no dependable future, and thus no courage to face the present. History's bridge has to be anchored at either end, or it will not hold up.

Perhaps we, along with the Jews, have too long overemphasized the covenant with Abraham — as if God had only then begun to intervene in history, as if he had only then given someone a name and calling — Abraham.[9] Had he not called Adam and Eve by their names as well, and promised to make them into a people too? The later covenants are no grounds for ignoring the covenant of creation. Without the creation account it would be unclear just who *is* the God of Abraham, Isaac, and Jacob, the God of Jesus Christ, the God of all humankind.

11

In order to construct this reflection on their first beginnings it was of no use to Israel to fall back on its own tradition, which was a kind of national memory or recollection. And evidently there was going to be no light from on high to reveal to them, as if in a movie flashback, "the way it was". Today, thanks to our improved acquaintance with the creation myths of Israel's neighbours — the Egyptians, Sumerians, Hurrites, Hittites, and Canaanites — we know that the widely current image of Israel as some sort of cultural and religious island in a sea of pagan peoples does not correspond with reality. Israel was altogether a part of the ancient Eastern world, and naturally lived and thought within the framework of the life and thinking of its time.

Thousands of years before the biblical creation account, similar myths were already circulating in the East. Of course they were permeated with polytheism and with exaggeratedly anthropomorphic notions of God. Strife and jealousy reigned among the gods. The primordial void seems to have been an emanation from the divine substance. Everything revolved on its own axis, in cyclical rhythm. Here the Israelite authors, inspired by the spirit of God, have done some correcting. They have excised elements that were too human. In particular, they drew a clear line of demarcation between creator and creation, handling them as realities closely related to each other, but at the same time unyieldingly distinguishable.

It is significant that Genesis calls the sun the "great light" and not *shamash*, which means both "sun" and "sun god", and calls the sea "the waters" instead of *yam*, which could have meant either "sea" or "sea god". Finally, the Genesis account leaves no time for useless nostalgia about a paradise lost, but posits a point of departure, sets in motion a linear historical evolution, and sends human beings along the road to meet their future.[10]

Not only in the Mesopotamian world, but in India, Africa, and America as well, we find astonishingly similar myths of creation, paradise, and fall[11] (see Part Three, §6). Are they recollections of real occurrences in the prehistory of all peoples? Or rather are they a projection into the past of the urgent questions of the present?

In any case, today, after thousands of years of uncritical acceptance of the myths of the Bible and of other peoples, we have to face the question of the relationship between myth and science, between myth and faith. How can we reconcile faith in creation, as it is handed down in Scripture, with the theory of evolution and with the findings of the other sciences?

First of all, we must distinguish between the content of a proposition or statement, and its form. There is absolutely no need to understand the six days' creation story literally. It is not the report of a journalist on the scene. Nor is it that of a prophet who had it whispered into his or her ear by God in so many words. The creation account has no intention of communicating scientific data. It does seek to give our life a deeper meaning by faith. Or to put it more precisely, the creation account does contain science, but it is the science of the time in which it was composed. It is the task of theology in every era to subsume the science of its time in theological reflection. One may not engage in theology without incorporating science.

We have made a great deal of progress today in the etiology (from the Greek, *aitia*, "basis, cause") of the creation myths.[12] Human beings seek an explanation for their ongoing experiences of the history of salvation and perdition, for their unfulfilled longings. What happens always and everywhere must have a basis in something that happened in the very beginning. And so we have myths, our primitive models of this primordial occurrence. They are the mirror of our daily life today. In them we rediscover human beings as they have always been. Such myths are useful and helpful. They explain something that is hard to explain in any other way. But one has to see through the myth, to try to understand the meaning behind it.

Farmers of all times, regions, and religions, constituting the overwhelming majority of humanity before the industrial revolution, lived within a totally mythological conception of the world. One by one, in whatever order they came, rain and drought, health and sickness, good harvests and poor ones, were all understood as gifts or scourges, just as they are today. Through prayers and sacrifices to God or gods, to angels or spirits, to saints or ancestors, persons thought they could render this upper world benevolent and turn the course of human and natural events in a better direction.

Today this concept of the world collapses before the advance of science. The world is governed by laws of its own, and may be improved through technology, medicine, agricultural science. The Second Vatican Council recognized the autonomy of earthly reality (GS 36, 41, 59). But it would be disastrous to abandon the process of explanation and demythologization to atheists. Not only would religion be delivered from myth (legitimate secularization), but human beings would be delivered from their religion — that is, robbed of it (illegitimate secularization — see EN 55). The faithful — "believers" — are therefore to be initiated into this new worldview cautiously. The baby is not to be thrown out with the bathwater. That is, in demythologizing the Bible we must be careful not to reject what is meant along with what is not meant.[13]

§8 *Permanent Substance of the Creation Account*

We have to ask ourselves what may be the permanent substance of the creation account.[14] Creation, in today's understanding, means that God's thought and will became creative — that behind a world so

13

drastically broadened by the spatial rearrangements of Copernicus and the temporal ones of Darwin, however the sciences may see that world and its genesis, there stands a sovereign God, and that therefore this world is to be understood as planned and meaningful. Creation means that humanity in particular was not a random product of evolution but was expressly known and willed by God, with all its gifts, with its bisexuality ("male and female he created them"), with its longing for the joy of life (paradise).

Creation means that the human being is not merely God's work but God's "image", God's partner, and that therefore one need not hesitate to deal with God in all familiarity. But creation also means that this immediate access to God has to be exercised in inner conflict (heredity) and in exposure to the menacing forces of this world (environment), so that when they sin, human beings may be brought low with guilt — and yet never lose hope.

Finally, creation means that human beings have a task of worldwide dimensions. In executing it they must not cramp themselves to the parameters of the titanic works of technology, but should also give themselves to repose, to leisure, and to celebration (the Sabbath). Human beings are to "lord it over the whole creation" — minerals, plants, beasts — which may be permitted to miss their immediate purpose, but not the human being, ever. For the human being is in God's likeness, and when men and women stand before God in the consciousness of being the pinnacle of his creation, far from failing their last end, they are fulfilling it.

Thus capsulized in its essential propositions, the creation story still carries a very meaningful message for today. We understand Genesis better today, now that it has been demythologized.

As to precisely *when* humankind began, scholars may continue with their disputations. Theologically what is important is that what makes a human being human is the experience of transcendence. We are continually bumping up against the frontiers of our being. Everything within us makes us want to cross over them. But of ourselves we are never able to bring this about. Then we hear an invitation. We sense an opportunity and a call to initiation into the ultimate mystery — God. On God's initiative we can open wide enough to receive "the something more", but "in grace". To put it another way, human beings become human beings in that "instant" when they begin to know themselves and, in crossing the Rubicon of that frontier, to know God too.

In Part Three we shall see that all human beings of all cultures have actually made this step. Were evolution ever to turn around and proceed so far in reverse that human beings no longer wondered about their first beginnings and last end, then, as Karl Rahner puts it laconically, they will have reverted to being merely resourceful animals again and human history will therefore have come to a close[15] (see Part Four, §§18, 22).

14

It is not only in its tendency toward God, in its powers of theological interpretation, that this humanity appears as creation's crown and a mysterious work of wonder, but in its biological make-up as well. The primordial elements that give a child the gift of life — the father's spermatozoon and the mother's ovum — each contain twenty-three chromosomes, carrying countless genes, which in turn code an enormous multiplicity of interrelationships, hence inheritable traits. Once seed and egg have united, a new life process begins.

From the very start, within the tiny fertilized egg, all but invisible to the naked eye, is housed the whole background programme of action for each hour, each day, each year of the physiological course of this new life, together with the inherited mental aptitudes, just as a computer at Cape Canaveral regulates (rather more expensively!) the whole program of an expedition into space. A human being's genetic code counts billions of molecular symbols, each one having its own specific function. If one wished to transcribe the information contained therein into modern scientific language, the result would be a library of thousands of volumes.[16]

Does God stand behind such a human being, and such a world? The Christian can answer a confident yes. Of course at the same time he or she should be clear about one thing: this yes is a faith assertion. It cannot be scientifically proved. Of course it cannot be scientifically disproved either. Biblical faith in creation, and modern unbelief, share one insight: the intrinsic meaning of the world phenomenon cannot be proved. For biblical faith, of course, this is only one side of the coin. The other side, which only faith can see, is God's care of the world and of every individual human being within it.

All persons must decide for themselves with which answer they will pronounce themselves satisfied: whether they will interpret the wondrous phenomenon of evolution as the work of happy coincidence, or as the product of a mysterious, divine word of power looming in the background.[17]

§9 The Creation Covenant

In view of all that has now been said, we are surely justified in designating the creation event as a creation covenant. The designation has not long been customary. The covenant with Abraham used to be celebrated to such a point that one seldom spoke of a covenant with Noah, let alone a creation covenant. At best, creation was the beginning of the "natural order"; supernatural revelation, and the covenant of grace, began with Abraham.

But it is impossible to exaggerate the importance of the creation. It contains God's endorsement, providence, and definitive affirmation of the world and of all human beings. Each individual human being is

"Adam" (Hebrew for "human being"); is created by God just as much as the first Adam was. Creation's mystery is repeated in each of us.

Israel was to be "a sign for all peoples" (see §13, below); hence the Jahwist concluded that all peoples must already have been blessed. He therefore redacted the universal primordial history of the world in the first eleven chapters of Genesis and inserted it as an introduction to the history of Israel. Ultimately the gracious covenantal reign of God over all humanity dates from the creation, and prevails because of the creation. We must therefore conclude to the radical continuity and unity of all the covenants.[18] It is said of individual prophets that they were "fashioned and called from the wombs of their mothers" (Jer. 1:4-8; Isa. 42:6, 49:5). All humanity as well, and every member of it, has been willed and called by God from the very beginning.

Of course we are dealing here with a covenant, or contract, only "improperly" speaking. Not only did one of the parties, God, remain mysteriously hidden in the creation covenant (as in all the other covenants), but human beings, in this case, did not even exist yet. One of the parties to the covenant came into being through the covenant itself. Thus it was without being asked about it that human beings were inserted into the unalterable *fait accompli* of being under contract with God — basically as happens to every child through birth, with respect to its mother. And yet both of these "improper" contractual relationships have proved themselves stronger than any "proper", mutual, contract. A mother never really gives up her child. And even if she should forget her child, God never abandons his people, his humanity, every person (cf. Isa. 49:15). Our whole life, like the totality of human history itself, is lived out in the framework of this unwritten contract.

How vain is the basic fear, mistrust, and compulsion to self-destruction of so many contemporary men and women. It must surely be said, to their exoneration as well as by way of psychological interpretation, that they evidently have never experienced the protective love of a mother, and hence lack the natural prerequisite for believing in the still greater security they have in God.

The latter is not a matter of "natural" relationship between creator and creature, in contradistinction with what is called "supernatural". The "supernatural" is not to be thought of as a sort of second level, built later atop nature and after the fact. Creation, even as such, can and must be conceived of as an act of God's self-communication. It is not an act by which God makes something other than himself and sets it apart from himself, but as the act whereby God bestows on another the gift of his own reality.

Now, if the world arises as an instance of God's self-communication, then, however transcendent God may be, there is an immanence of his that is bestowed, corresponding to what Christian theology calls personal grace, or the divine indwelling, in the spiritual creature. But then this

16

indwelling is no random occurrence; it is a foundational relationship between God and the human being as such. Hence we cannot speak merely of grace bestowed on sinners. We must also reckon with an order of grace vis-à-vis created reality as such. There is no neutral zone in the realm of creation.

Creation in its totality is dependent upon God, accepted by God, and drawn toward God. But inasmuch as God is ever a God of grace, even the altogether "natural" things, the things that happen to us every day — our longing that is never fulfilled, the tragic experience of human greed and lust, the dilemma between the joy of living and the fear of dying — even these quite "natural" things are already within the sphere of influence of the "supernatural", are within the framework of a "supernatural existential" right from the start. Even what we call "natural" stands within that concrete mode of being that God, in free and loving choice, but from the very beginning nevertheless, has bestowed upon the human being.[19]

But to say grace is also to say Christ. The experience of the crucified and risen Jesus occurred historically only later, but in retrospect it enables us to understand the Christ event itself as the long intended climax of God's self-communication to the world. The Christ happening is not something that just happened on the stage of the world at some moment or other. It was the point toward which all world evolution was striving from the very start. Thus we can speak of a "hidden christocentricity", a "christocentricity in mystery", of the whole creation, and of a "cosmic Christ".[20] Two of Christ's ardent disciples, John and Paul, opened up this grander view of Christ for us.[21]

A theology that does justice to creation, nature, history, cultures, and religions is one of the principal demands addressed by the theologians of the Third World to the theology of Europe.[22] The common bond we all have in the covenant of creation gives the lie to the many exclusivisms and antagonisms that have marred our ways of thinking.

Thus the creation covenant — the election of the first human beings, and in them *all* human beings, to a meaningful and graced life — proves to be the presupposition and anticipation of all covenants to come. The later ones only confirm and explicitate what has already been laid down in the creation covenant. Salvation history began when humanity began, and in spite of all sin and all calamity, "the outcome is now no longer in doubt. The history of the world is basically determined, and it is determined for weal,"[23] not for woe.

The Covenant with Noah

§10 Sin

In our confident delineation of the creation covenant there was an element we mentioned only in passing. But it is something that will have to be taken more seriously. That element is sin. It suddenly stands out like a shrill, false note in the harmony of paradise. It must have been there from the beginning, for it reappears everywhere in history, and not only as a possibility but as a mysterious fact of grave consequences.

N. Lohfink has shown that the account of the creation and fall did not come into being after the account of the covenant with Abraham and Moses, but forms an altogether substantial part of the theology of covenant itself. The first sin is presented as the classic prototype of breach of covenant. Just as he would later do with Israel, Yahweh made, called, and chose Adam and Eve, led them into a special land, and gave them his commandments as conditions of a covenant. If they kept them, they would live and prosper. If not, they would die. But they transgressed the command, just as Israel would ever be doing.[24]

The sin of the parents was followed by the sin of their child — Cain — and of their children's children. Sin rolled on like an avalanche, so that God "repented" humanly speaking, of having made human beings at all. Genesis underscores it twice (Gen. 6:6-7). The holy God cannot endure sin. Human beings had broken the creation covenant; God determined to break it too, and radically. Five distinct verses repeat his decision to "exterminate" humankind (Gen. 6:7, 13, 17; 8:4, 23). And so he did. The great flood would be a "lesson" once and for all! The fall back into chaos (*tohu wavohu*) and the primordial flood at the beginning of creation (Gen. 1:2) were simultaneous.

§11 God's Renewed Salvific Activity

And yet fall and flood would be seen to have been only the dark backdrop of God's renewed salvation activity in favour of all peoples. Hard on the heels of the original sin followed the primordial message of hope, the so-called *protoevangelium*, the protogospel — the announcement of the serpent's destruction (Gen. 3:15). The literal meaning of the original text is far from clear, but in Christian tradition it acquired a christological and mariological interpretation; it signifies the definitive conquest of evil in Christ.[25]

The catastrophe of the great flood was followed by the covenant with Noah (Gen. 9), like a new creation after a second chaos. The fivefold threat of "extermination" is now replaced by the fivefold promise of the covenant between God and the survivors, as well as with their "descendants", or "all living beings on the earth", or "for perpetual generations" (Gen. 9:9, 12, 15, 16, 17). The presence of Noah, then, the

18

just man of faith in a world of disbelief, sufficed to snatch the world from total annihilation. The fate of the cosmos depends on the saints.

The universality of this covenant is further emphasized by the reference to Shem, Ham, and Japheth, who were Noah's sons, "and from them stems the entire race of humankind" (Gen. 9:19). A literal interpretation of this verse is no longer tenable in view of modern advances in prehistory and ethnography. In those days it was thought that the whole world lay between Mesopotamia and the Mediterranean Sea. Thus in Joseph's time it was said that the famine had spread "over the whole earth" (Gen. 41:56). The *substance* of the matter is Israel's faith that Yahweh is the covenant God of all peoples for all times. G. von Rad comments: "Thereby the concept of the oneness of humankind by its very creation is expressed with a clarity without parallel in the whole ancient world".[26]

It is not necessary to accept the literal historicity of this flood and the ark. Similar myths enjoyed broad currency in the East, as on other continents, and perhaps indeed they hearken back to the actual experience of such a primordial flood (although the peoples of those primordial times surely could not have built such an ark!). But perhaps they simply constitute a mythological magnification of all the floods that had occurred so often in so many places. One thing is very clear: the author of this chapter adopted, as in the case of the creation account, certain myths that he had at his disposal, and refined them so as to make a theological statement in images to which the people would be responsive: that God does not allow the just to perish; that he shows understanding and mercy even to sinners; and that henceforth he no longer wishes to exterminate them, on account of "the evil the human heart is inclined to from its youth" (Gen. 8:21). It is simply astounding how the meaning of great truths comes to life in mythological images!

Concretely, the covenant itself consisted in three parts: God's assurance that he would never again send such a flood, human readiness to accept a minimal list of prescriptions and prohibitions, and the rainbow as a sign of the covenant.

Once more, then, God has embarked on a venture with men and women. And men and women have embarked on a venture with God. The history of ill was never to gain the upper hand over the history of salvation. And it never will. Sin is never to have the last word. But more: in the covenant with Noah, the oneness of all humanity that was established in the creation of Adam ("human being") but left unexpressed is confirmed and explicitated. From this point of view the covenant with Noah can be considered the formalization and conclusion of the history of the creation. All peoples stand within the salvation order of God. It is inconceivable that there ever be, or ever has been, a time when any people of this world had no salvation history.

There is one more thing to note. In Noah we meet a person who was not a member of the people of Israel — still less of Christianity — but of one of those religions that would later be labelled "pagan" and disparaged. And yet Noah "found grace in the Lord's eyes", was "a just man and perfect among his contemporaries, and walked with God" (Gen. 6:8). He is rightly reckoned among the "saints of the Old Testament", along with Abel, Henoch, Job, Melchizedek, Lot, and the Queen of Sheba.[27]

In Noah, then, and in the covenant with Noah, we discern a legitimation of all non-Israelite religion that goes back to God himself. For the author of this account, both the peoples of the covenant with Noah — the "pagans" — and the people of the covenant with Abraham — Israel — come within the scope of God's salvific will, albeit in different fashions. In both, God has acknowledged all peoples as "his" — and even to our own day makes the rainbow rise over them all as a sign of ever new hope after the storm.

The Covenant with Abraham

§12 *Change of Scene*

In chapter 12 of the First Book of Moses (Genesis) there is a sudden and surprising change of scene. Up to this point everything has been happening on the stage of literally a world theatre. From the dawn of creation, it is the peoples, *all* the peoples, who march through the millennia. Generation succeeds generation. Yahweh has ever been the God of one, whole humanity.

But now the field of vision narrows abruptly. Now everything turns on one man, Abraham, and his posterity. Beginning here the Old Testament no longer tells us about anything but the history and religious experiences of the people of Israel. The other peoples disappear from the scene.

One might be inclined to see the calling of Abraham as a totally new beginning, the start of God's entirely unique entry into the history of a particular people, the point of departure of a special salvation history.[28] But the sudden appearance of so much that is new must not tempt us to forget the fundamental continuity and unity of all the covenants.[29] Whatever happens now we must always see against the background of creation, and the world of the peoples, of the first eleven chapters of Genesis.

The final redactor of the Pentateuch placed those eleven chapters at the beginning for a purpose. He considered them necessary for situating the history of Israel in its broader context once and for all. Then, to use an analogy from modern technology, it is as if he sighted one person and one people in his lens and "zoomed in" to pull them up close. But this should not afford us any pretext for overlooking what is in the background.

The special history of this particular people will, one day, reach its goal, and then the field of vision will open up again to the ends of the earth. Then the connection with the first eleven chapters of Genesis will reappear:

> In speaking of Israel, and of the meaning of its history of election, one had to begin with the creation, and seek to understand Israel in the universal picture of the world of peoples. No more modest framework exists for the questions that arise concerning the election and vocation of Israel.[30]

And yet this particular instance is interesting enough in itself. Israel was the first people to publish a written history in the proper, if not the modern, critical, sense of the word. More importantly, Israel is the first people to have seen the liberating action of God in all its history.[31]

§13 Abraham and Melchizedek

In our reading of the text, there are certain elements we shall want to single out in connection with our theme of covenant and election. Let us first listen to the brief, classic report of the calling of Abraham, and his answer:

> The Lord spoke to Abram: "Go out from your homeland, out from your family, and out from your father's house, into a land which I shall show you. I will make you a great people, and bless you ... In you, all generations of the earth shall be blessed." Abram set forth, as the Lord had commanded him (Gen. 12:1-4).

Total eradication from the mother soil, total sacrifice of everything that makes life protected and secure, to wander uncertainly into the uncertain — to a land that God will reveal only later. But Abram undertook his journey toward the unknown goal more surely than one who knows for sure where one wishes to go. The word of the Lord gave him total security.

And yet, as if Abram's faith would have been overtaxed by having to respond to a single, brief illumination, "God speaks" to him anew, confirms and clarifies to him time and again that he wishes to "strike a covenant" with him (Gen. 15:18; 17:2, 7), that his posterity is to be as numerous "as the stars of the sky and the sand on the seashore", and that through them "all peoples of the earth will be blessed" (Gen. 22:17ff.), that God will give to his posterity, after a certain time in foreign parts (obviously a *prophetia post eventum*, a historical retroprojection) "the land from Egypt's river even to the great river of the Euphrates" (Gen. 15:16-18).

Their signs of the covenant is to be that all male children will be circumcised. This strikes us moderns as odd, especially for the decisiveness with which the sign is demanded: "My covenant in your flesh shall be an eternal covenant: an uncircumcised boy, who is not circumcised in the flesh of his foreskin, shall be torn up from this people, for he has broken my covenant" (Gen. 17:10-14).

And so Abram sets out, under the star of promise. Now he leads the life of a homeless nomad, with all the surprises, suspense, and risks of that life. History has more fascination for nomads than for farmers. One is not "established". One experiences continual beginnings, continual journey, continual questions about a new day and a new land. Later, when Israel became a sedentary people, it felt a quiet nostalgia for nomadic times. Many of its usages and ways of thinking can be explained only by the nomadic identity of the patriarchs, and the years in the desert.[32]

The hardest test of faith for Abram — whose name God had meanwhile changed to Abraham (Gen. 17:5) — consisted in the command to sacrifice his son Isaac, born of ninety-year-old Sara (Gen. 17:17). Once again the message is brief and drastic:

> And God said: "Take your only son, whom you hold dear, go out to the land of Moria, and take him there to a mountain which I shall show you, and make a burnt offering of him." Abraham rose early in the morning, saddled his ass, and took with him both of his servants and his son Isaac (Gen. 22:1-3).

What is this? His only heir, the bearer of the promises, is to disappear? And he, the father, is to be the one to kill him? No such questions. Abraham obeyed like a soldier. He heard the order, accepted it, and stretched out his hand to slaughter his son.

Suddenly there was another way. For "the Lord sees" (Gen. 22:14), and foresees — and does not wish human sacrifices as did the other gods of those days.

Then, very suddenly again, this journeying Abraham is met by Melchizedek, king of Salem. Melchizedek emerges and disappears like a meteor (Gen. 14:17-20). He offered a sacrifice of "bread and wine", for he was "a priest of the most high god". He blessed Abraham in the name of this god "who has made sky and earth", and Abraham returned to him the tithe of the gift.

And so Melchizedek — not one of the chosen people, but a Canaanite — ranks higher than Abraham. He is recognized by Abraham as a priest, and not only by Abraham but by the God of the covenant too, so that this mysterious figure remains, for all times, even for Jesus, the model and norm of priesthood (Ps. 109:4; Heb. 7:17). The "God of Abraham, Isaac, and Jacob", then, is still the God of all peoples, just as he was before.

Melchizedek's appearance at the beginning of the election history of Israel clearly portrays the same teaching as the Noah event at the close of the history of the creation (§11, above): the universality of the one God. Melchizedek stands there as the prototype of *oikoumene*, as the counterpoise of all exclusivity in matters of religion.[33] This teaching must never be allowed to die out.

Abraham was "one hundred seventy-five years old" when he died (Gen. 25:7). His history unfolded between the nineteenth and seventeenth centuries B.C. But he still lives in his corporal and spiritual posterity — in Jews as the father of Israel, in Muslims as father of Ishmael, and in Christians as father of their faith (Rom. 4:16). He lives too in the memory of all pagans and sinners, for he sought, out of love and solidarity, to intercede with God, "the judge of the whole world", in favour of the sinful cities of Sodom and Gomorrah (Gen. 18:25).

§14 *The Theology of Abraham*

Later a genuine theology of Abraham sprang up. He is the only person in the Old Testament to be called "friend of God" (Isa. 41:8; 2 Chron. 20:7; Deut. 3:35; see also James 2:23). In the New Testament this exclusive title is broadened to include all the disciples of Christ: "I have called you friends, for I have made known to you everything I have heard from my Father" (John 15:15). It was Abraham, then, who was the pioneer, the forerunner, the prototypical figure. It was he who beat the path that the whole of humanity was to follow.

In late Judaism Abraham became the towering figure that cast all other personages of the Old Testament, not excluding Moses, into the shade. Being the children of Abraham was Israel's greatest pride. It was also its undoing, for Israel presumed a certitude of salvation based on biological descent from Abraham, which Jesus and Paul opposed fiercely — if unsuccessfully (§§30, 32, 34, below).

The church fathers interpret Abraham's life allegorically. They see it as prefiguring three "sacraments", three mysteries. Abraham's covenant is the prefiguration of the new covenant. Isaac's miraculous birth points to the virgin birth of Jesus. The marriage of Isaac and Rebecca represents the bond of Christ with the church.[34]

For all times, Abraham is the one to whom "the gospel was preached in advance" (Gal. 3:8, in the Greek text), and in whom all the peoples of the earth will be blessed. For nearly four thousand years now, humanity lives in promise and expectation!

23

The Sinai Covenant

§15 *The Exodus*

God has time. God can wait. God makes us wait. Abraham's posterity lived in Egypt for what seemed an endless time of waiting. The seventy persons who were originally deported there with the elderly Jacob had become, in the Bible's exaggerated arithmetic, six hundred thousand men, plus the women and children (Exod. 1:5; 12:37). It seemed to be all over with the dream of election. Here they formed a slave class, and eked out a livelihood at forced labour.

Then at last there was a sign. "God heard their groaning. Now God remembered his covenant with Abraham, Isaac, and Jacob. God looked down and saw the children of Israel and knew . . ." (Exod. 2:24ff.). Moses, who had actively committed himself to the rights of this people, now had to fly before the vengeance of the Egyptians. He moved to the land of the Midianites, married the daughter of the priest Jethro, and served his father-in-law by tending his flocks. One day he drove his herd to the holy mountain of Horeb. There he saw a burning bush, and heard coming from it the voice of God, who announced to him his intention "to liberate (Israel) from the hand of the Egyptians, and to lead them out of that land into a land beautiful and broad, flowing with milk and honey" (Exod. 3:8).

Henceforward this exodus from Egypt will be the new starting point of history. The memory of this event, with its wonders and mighty works of God, will never more grow dim. That night, at Moses' behest, the Israelites slaughtered and consumed a sacrificial lamb, for the Lord was "passing over" (*passach*), sparing his people, but destroying the firstborn of the Egyptians. This night would be forever solemnised and celebrated "for coming generations" as an everlasting institution (Exod. 12:11, 14). No less wondrous was the crossing of the Sea of Reeds, and the annihilation of the Egyptians who were in hot pursuit. Today we must trim away much of the story as legendary accretion. But Israel believed that the Lord had showed himself mighty in that night.

§16 *Yahweh*

"The Lord is a war hero! Yahweh is his name!" So sang the Israelites after the drowning of the Egyptians (Exod. 15:3). Now they had to believe that God had really appeared to Moses, and that he was a mighty god indeed. Even Moses had had his doubts at first: "Who are you? How can I make the people believe that you really sent me?" God answered Moses, "Yahweh, ['I am who I am']." And he continued, "So shall you address the Israelites, 'The "I am" has sent me to you'" (Exod. 3:14).

Much has been pondered and written about God's self-description as Yahweh.[35] There seems to be no exhausting the implications of this name. Philosophers extract from it the eternal identity of the highest Being. They see it as the formula for a metaphysical conception of God. Mystics can ecstatically plumb this ultimate Being who has no beginning or end and dismiss all historical events as insignificant. But God has revealed himself precisely as the God of history — not a God of speculation or mysticism, but of action (which does not exclude speculation or mysticism). The Hebrew word *Yahweh* expresses an active presence. Ever since Buber, one is inclined to translate, with him, "I am there, I shall be there [for you], I am the one who helps." And so it is stated that human beings will experience God's accompanying, assisting presence and being. They need only perseveringly abandon themselves to this promise.

We ought to substitute "I shall be there [for you]" for "Yahweh" wherever it occurs in the Old Testament. Only then will the breadth and depth of this name be realized. It is not a matter of God's essence, then, but of his "assistance," his standing by. The name of Yahweh is not a theology lesson but a proclamation, not a credal proposition but a historical experience. The people will realize who Yahweh is when they walk with him.

We are not exactly dealing here with a new revelation of the name of God. Yahweh was already the tribal god of the Midianites. It must have suddenly occurred to Moses that this God corresponded to the God of Abraham, Isaac, and Jacob as well. To the generic name "God" or "Lord" a proper name is now added, which admits of a much more intimate relationship than does a family or generic name.

Yahweh, the god of the Midianites, now becomes the God of the people of Israel, and through this people the God of "all the peoples of the earth", as had been promised to Abraham. And so, as Moses arrived with the people in the land of the Midianites after the flight, and the priest Jethro offered his god a holocaust and sacrifices, it posed no problem whatever that "Aaron and all the elders of Israel came forward to celebrate a sacrificial supper before God with the father-in-law of Moses" (Exod. 18:12).

Once again, as with Noah and Melchizedek (§§11, 13, above), we are confronted with an *oikoumene* that transcends all religious bounds! It is in their placing all peoples under one and the same God that the core of these authors' kerygma can be seen.

§17 *Mount Sinai*

The victory song of the Sea of Reeds (Exod. 15: 1-21) would not be long in the singing. Three short verses later it is reported that "the people murmured against Moses" because they had found no water in three days of looking (Exod. 15:24). A little later they murmured again, sighing for the fleshpots of Egypt (Exod. 16:2ff). Still later they all but mutinied, grumbling against Moses and even against God. "Is the Lord really among us or not?" (Exod. 17:7) they wondered. Yahweh's name, "I shall be there [for you]," hung in the balance.

At last they came, after the flight, to Mount Sinai.[36] Here Moses must have had an extraordinary taste of what today is called the "desert experience." Apparently he felt the need to withdraw somewhat from his "hard-necked people" (Exod. 32:9; 33:3, 5; 34:9), so he ascended the mountain alone. There he felt something that overwhelms all Sinai pilgrims, even today — the spell of the desert, its stillness, in which you can hear God speak. The ocean of sand, vaulted by the blue heaven by day and the crystalline tent of stars by night, the dunes drenched by the setting sun in brilliant yellow, then crimson, then shadow black, make this desert all one needs to lose touch with everyday cares and noise and busyness.

Moses stayed forty days and forty nights on the mountain, "with the Lord; he ate no bread, and drank no water" (Exod. 34:28). He gained insights that came in one way or another from God, and he shared them with the people as the will of God. And the people doubted not a whit that God had actually spoken with Moses "mouth to mouth" and "face to face", as one speaks "with a friend" (Exod. 33:11; Num. 12:8; Deut. 34:10).

§18 *The Sinai Covenant*

Through the mediation of Moses, God's covenant with his people had now reached its full stature. This is the same covenant that had begun with the patriarchs. But it was now no longer a contract with individual human beings but with the people as such.[37] The Sinai covenant now becomes the Old Covenant pure and simple.

Let us keep in mind that the writings that report the covenant were written centuries after the fact (§5, above), so that the whole theology of the covenant represents largely a retrospective projection. What we have is not a historical description, but a category of living theological thinking.

This covenant is portrayed in the Second Book of Moses (Exodus) in the following manner. First, God cites his mighty deeds just performed, and thereby places a deposit in trust: "You have yourselves seen what I did to the Egyptians, how I have borne you on eagles' wings and carried you to myself." Then he proposes the covenant: "If you listen faithfully to my voice, and keep my covenant, so shall you be my special property among all peoples. For mine is the whole earth! You shall be for me a kingdom of priests and a holy people!" The unanimous response of the people is, "All that the Lord has said, let us do!" (Exod. 19:4-8). Finally,

God details his will in the ten commandments and numerous prescriptions for the rectitude of daily living, for health and hygiene, and for worship (Exod. 21-30).

A similar structure, still more detailed, is to be found in the Fifth Book of Moses (Deuteronomy 5-11) — historical prologue, moral and ritual prescriptions, blessing or curse for each. These are the great core chapters of Holy Writ, the constitution of the covenant itself, the passages that will be read aloud again and again in the liturgy of the great pilgrimages and at passover.

The Hebrew word for covenant is *berith*. It occurs in the Old Testament 286 times, often qualified by additional descriptives such as love, following, loyalty, or by the metaphors of king, bridegroom, father. *Berith* denotes essentially a relationship, a personal relationship with God, not loyalty to a law. (Granted, out of this relationship of mutual belonging grow rights and duties, thus also a law.) The Old Testament covenant God is not a *deus ex machina* who comes to the rescue at the last moment, but a God who always takes the first step, who always anticipates. Before he lays down the law he places a human being within his grace, and this makes observance of the law both meaningful and possible.

This covenant far surpasses the creation covenant in point of being explicit. Still it is not a bilateral contract in the proper sense. God is not a party to it as the human being is. God's presence as party to the contract must be taken on faith. And yet it was believed that this mysterious nearness of God could also be experienced. Troubadours sang, "Where might you find so great a folk, whose gods were near to it, as the Lord our God is near, how so often we call to him?" (Deut. 4:7).

Faith in Yahweh as king gave this people a new orientation, one that reached out beyond all tribal mentality. It gave it its proper unity and identity. No longer did blood descent stand in the foreground, but a common historical experience with Yahweh. It was Yahweh who finally made these tribes not only *his* people, but *a* people in any sense at all. The whole basis of the existence of this people lies in its covenant with God. Were the people to break it, there would be nothing for the Lord to do but "ship them back to Egypt", where they would be "auctioned to their enemies as slaves", but no one would buy them (Deut. 28:68). There they would pine, without masters and without bread, their last state worse than before Yahweh ever noticed them.

§19 *Election*

Most intimately bound up with the concept of covenant is that of election.[38] The expression "chosen people" occurs in the Old Testament only rarely. However, the verb "to elect, to choose" occurs 164 times. Israel's election is spoken of in order to indicate all the privileges the Old

27

Testament ascribes to it: the divine calling, the adoption, the inheritance, the special dwelling of God among his people. The whole thinking of this people was governed by the notion of election. The crowning text appealed to was "You are a people consecrated to the Lord your God, that of all the peoples on the earth you may be to his possession" (Deut. 7:6). The prophets never tire of recalling to the Israelites that they are "his people", that they are the "people of God".

Of course they should certainly not puff themselves up on account of it. "Not because you are greater than other peoples did the Lord become attached to you and choose you — for you are the least of all peoples. No, it was for love of you ... " (Deut. 7:7ff). God does not *seek* worthiness, he *bestows* it. Except in the time of David and Solomon, Israel was of no significance politically. It was merely a buffer zone between Assyria, Babylonia, and Egypt, and increasingly became these nations' football. Nevertheless Israel lived in the unshakable conviction of election, in the unconquerable consciousness that it was chosen.

Of course there was another side to this matter of election. It seems to imply the rejection of anyone not elected. How is this to be reconciled with the creation covenant, and the covenant with Noah — with God's universal love? This will have to be explained later (§§22, 25-26).

§20 *Possession of the Land*

Likewise bound up with the covenant is the concept of possession of a land. It is painful to be homeless, to be a "person without a country". Everyone strives to have a piece of solid land where he or she can be "at home". Genesis 1-11 contains several histories of land and expulsion: Adam, Cain, Babel. In Genesis 12-50 the patriarchs are sent to wander in search of a country. Waking and sleeping, they are strengthened ever anew in their hope for this homeland (Gen. 28:13, 35:12). Then came the experience as foreigners in the land of Egypt; then the nomadic life in the desert to the point of desperation (Num. 14-16). But at last came the glorious occupation of the celebrated land. All Israel's thinking clustered about two poles, Yahweh and the land. For Israel, the land was what Jesus would be for Christians: the content of the promise.

But the land had always to be considered Yahweh's gift. Hence the many regulations for just administration of land. Land might never be sold definitively: "it belongs to me! You are only foreigners and guests in my country" (Lev. 25:23). Every fifty years in the Year of Jubilee, all mortgaged land had to be restored free and clear to its original owner (Lev. 25). Later on, the kings would begin to dispose of land as if they were its proper lords, and then prophets would come to the fore. When the prophets' efforts were of no avail, landlessness and exile were the result. Jeremiah was the great prophet of land and landlessness.

According to his teaching, possession of land was a sinful act, and landlessness was an act of faith in a "new land" to come (Jer. 24:4-10). The dialectical tension between these two concepts of land — possessing it, you possess it not — will be resolved and transcended only in Jesus. "Happy the meek, for they shall receive the land as their possession" (Matt. 5:5). And this new land will again be a gift of Yahweh — but it will be a test of faith at the same time, and for many, a scandal.[39]

§21 Prescriptions of the Law

As in the case of the creation covenant (§8, above), there is some demythologizing to be done here too. We have two series of propositions to consider.

The endless prescriptions of the law in the Five Books of Moses — the Jewish Torah — regulating life down to the smallest detail and all set forth as the will of God, are placed directly on God's lips. Today they are known to be comprised one and all of loan material from Israel's neighbours. The covenant with God in its entirety must be understood by analogy with the feudal contracts of the ancient East, whereby lesser kingdoms allied with a great king in return for his promise of protection.[40] Scholars today hold that only the very general lines of a covenant with Yahweh were drawn in the Sinai, and that the whole "law of Moses" consists of later interpolations. This applies even to the revelation on Mount Sinai and the Decalogue, the ten commandments, which came to have a special place in the Christian moral proclamation. The Decalogue betrays various editorial stages, and hence scarcely belongs to the original Sinai material.

No, the originality and genius of the Old Testament authors consisted in this that, although they took over the civil laws of other peoples, they placed the whole of life under the absolute authority of Yahweh. Granted, God's *generosity* finds scant reflection in the application and interpretation of these laws, instead it is replaced by a decadent, petty legalism. Schalom Ben-Chorin conjectures that Paul's liberal interpretation of the Law with the Christians inevitably brought about a relativization in the rigorous, typically Jewish concept of law[41] (but see §33, below).

§22 Yahweh's Exclusivity and Brutality

It is even more difficult to find the right thing to say about the exclusivity and brutality attributed to Yahweh. So many texts portray him more as a God of war than of peace, and more as the tribal god of Israel than as God of all peoples.[42] One can understand that God might command his people to live "cut off from all peoples of the earth" (1 Kings 8:53), not to mingle with other peoples, not to speak their gods' names (Josh. 23:7, 12ff.). But when he goes further it raises questions: "You shall break up their altars", he commands, "smash their sacred stones, hack down their sacred poles, and burn their idols, for these are a horror to the Lord your God" (Deut 7:5,25). Where are tolerance and *oikoumene* now (see §16 above)? Nor is this all. They shall not even have to conquer the land; Yahweh himself does it for them: "This is how you shall know that a living god is in your midst, who will absolutely certainly drive before you Canaanites, Hittites, Hivites, Perizzites, Girgashites, Amorites, and Jebusites" (Josh. 3:10). After all, he is the "Lord of hosts", of armies (2 Sam. 7:22, and elsewhere).

There is still more. He commands the extirpation of all these peoples: "All the peoples that the Lord your God delivers to you you are to exterminate, showing them no mercy" (Deut. 7:16). And so they did, in city after city: "But Israel had killed all the people of Ai. Every one fell in sacrifice to the sharp edge of the sword." The same thing in Hazor: "Every living being within it fell to the sword. Nothing was left alive" (Josh. 8:24, 11:11). Can later history show us colonialism more cruel than that? Did the Christians not appeal to the wars of the chosen people in their own "holy wars" against Saxon, Moor, and Turk?[43]

The only answer we can give to these questions lies in an appeal to the literary genre. The author neither wished to transmit "divine truth" here, nor could have transmitted it. He was only writing a heroic epic, with all the exaggerations expected of him in the East at that time (as also in later chauvinistic historical compositions — see Part Two, §2; Part Three, §§25, 27). His purpose was to encourage the people by recalling God's mightly deeds for their fathers of old.

Every Eastern people was proud of its war god. In Babylonia it was Marduk, in Assyria Ashur, with the Hittites Ea, and so with others. Israel wanted to "show all these gods up", so to say. Doubtless the land fell to the chosen people not nearly so gloriously or so cruelly; it took place by gradual penetration, by intermarriage, together with minor insurgencies. Our information on these and many other questions about the origin of Israel is still incomplete. In many points we are dependent upon provisional hypotheses.[44]

The church fathers' allegorical interpretation of these passages as all-out war against evil is no longer convincing today. Instead we have simply to accept such texts as ideological exaggerations of history — as the expression of a historical mentality that we (it is to be hoped) have overcome today. The decision was well taken to omit the psalms of vengeance in the new edition of the Divine Office.

§23 *The Davidic Covenant*

Among the various remaining covenants in the Old Testament — with individuals, with the Levite class, and the like — the covenant with David merits special consideration. The prophet Nathan assured David that the Lord was with him, that he would grant him peace in the sight of his enemies, and would treat him like a son. "He will build a house to my name, and I shall make his royal throne forever strong . . . Your house and your kingdom will stand before me always. Your throne will be firm for eternal time" (2 Sam. 7:10-16).

Then the covenant with David is sung and elaborated by the troubadours in the various royal psalms, especially: "I struck a covenant with my chosen one — swore to my servant, David, 'I grant your tribe eternal continuance, and erect your throne for all generations'" (Ps. 89:4). The prophets then take up the idea and apply it, in their messianic expectancy, to the eschatological shoot, or sprout, of David (Isa. 11:1ff.; 16:5, 55:3; Jer. 23:5). The evangelist Matthew, who wrote his Gospel for the Jews, was very concerned to demonstrate that Jesus was descended from the house of David through Joseph (Matt. 1:16, 20). The people often called Jesus "Son of David" (Matt. 9:27; 12:33; 15:22; 21:9).

Thanks to the monarchy, Israel was now on the verge of firm possession of the land and of a mighty nationhood. But all too suddenly a new danger appeared: the worship of God might become a cult of the king, the covenant with David would be celebrated more religiously than the Sinaitic covenant, the central royal power would degenerate into a tyranny. In the later Books of Chronicles, David appears as the ideal, lordly figure of a religious past in full glory, to which the present would do well to look. But this is a false picture of the reality. Israel was great when it was small. When it imagined it was great, it headed toward fall and ruin:

> The real actors in this provincial theatre of world history were not the kings and the priests, but that handful of simple little lost shepherds and farmers who had followed the voice of their God and spoke with him as they spoke with their peers.[45]

The Prospect of a New Covenant

§24 *The Prophets*

Yahweh's covenant with his people struck a resonant sympathetic chord with his people, and its glories were sung by prophet and psalmist. But this subtracts nothing from the tragedy of the covenant: God's calls, his enticements of love, were unfailingly solemnized in celebrations and words of troth — but then they were soon answered with doubts, murmurs, and disloyal deeds.

Only a few persons dealt seriously with the covenant concept and held the Yahweh-faith pure down through the centuries. Among them were the prophets. The prophets experienced God, as a light one looks at and yet does not see, as air one breathes and yet does not feel. They spoke as Yahweh's mouthpiece. But their voices were not gladly heard by the leaders of Israel — or else they simply ignored them entirely ("a voice in the desert" — Matt. 3:3). And still the prophets proclaimed God's message to the people, ceaselessly, as if "in volcanic eruptions" (W. Eichrodt), from sheer inner tension.[46]

They did so at first as unwanted heralds of warning. Hosea's drama is heartrending, both in his person (God commanded him to beget children of a prostitute!) and in his proclamation:

> As Israel was yet a little lad I held him dear, and I called my son out of Egypt... With tether of tenderness drew I them to me, and with cords of love. I was to them like a mother and father who lift their baby to their cheek; I bended me down to him, and reached him food ... But the more I called them the farther they withdrew from me, making offerings to the Baals and setting their incense pots before idols. Curses spread, lies, murders, thefts, adulteries ... Rejoice not, O Israel. You whored your way from God [Hos. 11:1-4; 4:2; 9:1].

And Jeremiah: "Back they went to the sins of their ancestors, who refused to hear my words. They too ran after other gods, to do service to them. The house of Israel, and the house of David, broke my covenant, which I struck with their fathers" (Jer. 11:10).

In accelerating tempo, the prophets become clairvoyants and proclaim a new covenant:

> Of a truth — spoke the Lord — the days are coming and I shall strike with the house of Israel and with the house of Juda a new covenant ... I shall lay down my law in their innards, and write it into their heart. I will be their God and they must be my people (Jer. 31:31, 33).
> I shall give them a new heart, and lay a new spirit in their innards. I shall remove from their body the heart of stone and give them a heart of flesh ... Then they will be my people and I shall be their God (Ezek. 11:19ff).

All this is to happen in the "day of the Lord", which will be at once terrible and consoling, a sentencing and a new beginning: "The sun will change to darkness, and the moon to blood, by the day of the Lord — the great and fearful day. But each that calls on the Lord's name will be saved" (Joel 3:4ff.; see Isa. 13:6, 9; 30:26; Zech. 12).

But the champion of them all is Daniel, apocalyptic prophet of the Old Testament, who sketches horrid visions of the fall of the world's empires and the victory of the kingdom of the Messiah. No other prophet had the influence on the New Testament that Daniel had. When Jesus speaks of the last days, he uses and updates Daniel's prophecy (Matt. 24).And so it is Daniel who links the Old and New Testaments. His proclamation of the victory of the Son of Man and of the kingdom of God is thematic in both testaments, and unites them in one common hope and expectation.[47]

But the people and their leaders no longer cooperated. Since the return from the exile, the mentality called Judaism had arisen[48] — a defensive, ghetto attitude, with the exteriorization and absolutization of legal observance. The law, the Torah, was now no longer seen as an instruction and gift of God to his people, but as a means of finding oneself just. A hundred new commandments were added, to be followed scrupulously and casuistically and laid as a burden on others. Will Jesus, with his spirit of freedom and childlike trust in the Father be able to change anything here?

The People and the Peoples

§25 *Particularism and Universalism*

Before we move on to the New Testament we ought to look back and ask ourselves what the "chosen people" of the old covenant thought about the other peoples. We have seen that one people was singled out from among the many peoples to begin its own unique history. To what purpose? Only self-interest?

This raises the question of particularism and universalism, a pair of concepts that of its nature is charged with tension. How will this tension be discharged? In one of two alternative directions, so that one has to choose between exclusive nationalism and the surrender of one's identity in love for others? Or can there be a synthesis instead? *This question will be the central issue of our entire book.*

A reading of the sacred texts yields no unambiguous answer.[49] And this is understandable for a book that took a thousand years to write and is the work of so many different authors. There is no need to return to the first eleven chapters of Genesis, from which it is clear that God has all peoples ever before his eyes. Nor do we need to rehearse the messages of the priest Melchizedek (§13) and the priest Jethro (§16).

We find a further important text in Malachi: "From the rising of the sun to its setting, my name is great among the peoples, and in every place is incense offered, and pure sacrifice, for great is my name among the peoples" (Mal. 1:11). Even if it is permissible to understand this in a more profound sense — to be fulfilled later in the Eucharist — still it is immediately intended for the current time of those other days. The prophet wishes to say that Israel should assume no airs as a result of its gifts and sacrifices, but that "the religious life of all humanity, whatever names it gives to God, and whatever cultic acts it performs, is ultimately directed to God, and that God sees his name revered in it."[50]

Several other scattered texts point to the equality of all peoples. "The Lord of armies will speak: 'Blessed be my people Egypt, Assur the work of my hands, and Israel my inheritance'" (Isa. 19:25). "'Are you not of the same worth to me as the Cushites, you sons of Israel?' spoke the Lord. 'Have I not led Israel out of the land of Egypt, but also the Philistines out of Caphtor and the Aramaeans out of Kir?'" (Amos 9:7).[51]

But these are isolated texts. The universalism typically stated in any context having to do with the peoples is a universalism expressly centred on Israel:

> All you peoples, sound applause! Shout to God with sound of jubilee! For the Lord is awesome, the highest one, a great king over all the world. *Before us* he struck down peoples, cast tribes beneath *our* feet. He chose *our* land of inheritance *for us*, the glory of Jacob whom he loves (Ps. 47:2-5).
>
> Praise the Lord, all peoples! All nations sound his praises! For almightily reigns his goodness *over us*; the Lord's troth lasts forever' [Ps. 117].

Psalm 100 is similar although Psalms 96 and 97 make admirable exceptions. Generally, then, the peoples are at the service of Israel. Indeed, they can become instruments of God for blessing or cursing Israel (Amos 6:14; Hos. 10:10; Isa. 5:26-30).

The crowning point of Israel's outreach to the other peoples is Isaiah. "All the peoples will make pilgrimage to the mount of the Lord's house. Jacob's God will teach his ways to all peoples, so that they beat their swords into plowshares and war will be no more" (Isa. 2:2-5).

There are especially beautiful passages to be found in chapters 40 to 55 ("Deutero-Isaiah"):

> Turn round to me, be saved, all ends of the earth! For I am God, and no other is! [Isa. 45:22]. Hearken to me, you peoples; you nations, listen to me. For I give you direction. I make my rightness to shine out as a light for the peoples. My goodness is near, my salvation is forthcoming, my arms direct the peoples. The islands trust in me, and hope in my arm [Isa. 51:4ff].

Then comes the prophecy of the suffering servant of God — who gives up his life, who bears the sins of the many, and comes to the defence of the faithless (Isa. 52:13 - 53:12).

But these passages all but founder in the ocean of sixty-six chapters of threat and encouragement directed toward Israel. Isaiah may have been called from his mother's womb "as the light of the peoples, that my salvation may reach to the world's end" as well as to "straighten up again the stalk of the tribes of Jacob" (Isa. 49:5ff.); but one cannot escape the fact that he did far less justice to the former task than to the latter.

In the Old Testament, then, there is no ideal solution to the question of universal salvation, neither theologically nor pastorally. The notion was received by the "chosen people" with more antagonism than anything else. They always returned to themselves. All who did not belong to the chosen people were called, contemptuously and with disgust, *goyim* — "peoples" or "pagans".

To this extent the prophet Jonah was typical of the people of Israel. He would rather have escaped his mission to the pagans. Then, when he must go nevertheless, he is disappointed that Nineveh is converted and hence does not perish. The lesson of history! God alone has care and love for the multiplicity of these human beings — *all* human beings (Jonah 4:11).

H. Gross summarizes:

> This consciousness of Israel's that it alone is a chosen people prevents any form of missionary activity during the period of the Old Testament revelation. And indeed Israel will find it easy to look for an excuse to consider itself in a deviant, constricted understanding of this distinction — to think of itself as the sole, esoteric community of God, to the extent of being permitted to overlook and set aside the original assignment addressed to them in the election proclamation (Exod. 19:3-8) to exercise the office of priesthood for all peoples ... And so, as is easy to see in the historical development of Israel, in the Samaritan secession, in the Qumran community's break with the mother community of Jerusalem, the road of election is fraught with the constant risk of being viewed by the elect as the road of separation and narrow-mindedness, instead of the way to breadth and universality. The original divine intention thus can easily be blocked at any moment.[52]

§26 *Theological Reflection*

Even if a simple reading of the texts is not very satisfactory, a theological reflection nevertheless makes it clear as day that Israel's election occurred only and solely in view of the peoples, the gentiles. In the concrete case of the one people, all peoples were chosen. If Yahweh decided upon precisely the most wretched of peoples to elect, it was only that he wished to show that his love embraced all peoples — even the lowliest, especially the lowliest.

The choice of Israel is not to be understood exclusively but inclusively. Israel's is the special case in which the election of all peoples is to become visible and tangible.[53] Just as it was for the sake of the people that the patriarchs and prophets received their vocation, so Israel was called for the sake of the peoples, who are always on God's horizon.

Passages that run counter to this proposition must, again, be considered in their literary genre. For example, when the sacred author places in Yahweh's mouth "Jacob I loved, but I hated Esau" (Mal. 1:2ff.), this anthropomorphic manner of speaking does not actually militate against the unfathomable love of God that ever embraces all human beings — including those whose "reprobation" is here humanly dramatized. Thus it was not because God had no care for other peoples that he chose Israel, but precisely *because* he cared for other peoples. Israel was not elected to a privilege but to a service: to reveal God's affection for all peoples.

Israel's temporary separation from the peoples was obviously for pedagogical reasons. The purity of monotheism and the hope for a Messiah should, after, be temporarily borne through history by the people among whom the Messiah was to arise. This one people would also have the practical experience of what it means to belong to God, to belong to a history to which God yields up his own name. And so Israel had both the burden and the grace of election to bear, that a universal salvation might dawn at last for all:

> The Jewish claim to election is . . . intended neither as racist nor as chauvinist nor as isolationist, but as a salvific and vicarious function in favour of all persons, and as obedience and loyalty in the name of them all, and in spite of everything else. It has a note of dynamic universality.[54]

Chapter Three

Election and Covenant in the New Testament

Jesus Christ

§27 *Research in Christology*

In the Old Testament, God revealed himself by his proper name, Yahweh ("God is there [for us]"). As the New Testament opens he confirms and strengthens this name in Jesus ("Yahweh rescues, Yahweh is salvation"). But he goes beyond names this time, and reveals himself in the form of the bearer of the name.

God among human beings. What a drama, what a risk! And then of all things this Jesus had to go and let himself fall into the hands of just those who would scourge him and crown him with thorns, as also, later on, of those who, for centuries, would implement inhuman attitudes in the name of Christianity (see the whole of Part Two), or consolidate the ugly division of the world into rich Christian lands and poor non-Christian ones. Or how, instead of taking Jesus and his teaching seriously he was made a training ground for scholastic philosophy, and cast in the irons of academic propositions, theses, and formulas.

In recent years we have been witnessing a new resurrection of Jesus. Jesus films fill the movie houses: Pasolini's *The Gospel According to Matthew*, Norman Jewison's *Jesus Christ Superstar*, Zeffirelli's *Jesus of Nazareth*. The Jesus movement has changed the names of our city streets. But most of all, *comunidades de base* of all kinds — grassroots ecclesial communities — are multiplying on all continents. They seek and hope to renew their life, form their community, and inspire their witness, from the gospel. Jesus shines as light and strength in the hearts of believers.

Modern research on the historical Jesus has bent its efforts, through form criticism and other critico-historical methods, to lay bare an original, authentic picture of Jesus.[55] This is not to say that, thanks to the number of exegetical and dogmatic books we have about Jesus, everything is now transparent. Jesus Christ comes completely to no one — not to the disciples and apostles of long ago, not to the bishops and theologians of today, not even to mystics and saints. But one comes a little nearer to him when one distinguishes — not as opposites, but as distinct aspects of a single reality — the historical Jesus as he unpretentiously walked and lived in days gone by, preaching his message, from the Christ of faith as his disciples saw him after the first Easter, and preached him accordingly.

Similarly, there is an unavoidable distinction to be made between the "authentic Jesus material", or *ipsissima verba Christi*, and the texts that were elaborated and inserted by the evangelists in the recollection of Jesus and his spirit. One must not forget that the Gospel of Mark was written only shortly before the destruction of Jerusalem in the year A.D. 70, and that the other gospels were written even later, when a "literal" report of the words of Jesus would no longer have been humanly possible.

Depending on which of these two aspects of Christ one keeps uppermost in mind, we can have a "low christology" (of the historical Jesus) or a "high christology" (of the Christ of faith and of the later dogmas). Or we can even have an "inward christology", which limits itself to a theological viewpoint, and an "outward christology", which attempts to reconstruct the ancient historical context that helped form our image of Christ.

One finds a wide variety of representations of Jesus through the centuries, in art as in theology. In the time of the persecutions Jesus was the good shepherd in the catacombs; in the mentality of the Eastern Empire he was the Pantokrator, Ruler of the Universe, in the golden dome of the apse; in medieval popular piety he was the suffering Lord; and so on.

The New Testament, like the creation account and the entire Old Testament (§§5, 7, above), is neither a critico-historical study nor sensational journalism. It is a committed and engaging faith-witness, the book of life of a believing community.

§28 *The Lordship of God*

Of modest origin — like all Israel! — Jesus, having prepared himself for his office by John's baptism and by fasting, unexpectedly appeared, in Galilee. With him God appeared in history in an altogether new way of being experienced, and brought his enterprise to its climax.

He spoke these words: "The time is accomplished: The kingdom of God has come near. Be converted, and believe in the gospel" (Mark 1:15). Thus in two concise sentences the evangelist sums up the core of Jesus' message. What is central is the kingdom of God, the lordship of God.[56]

Jesus' meaning becomes clearer in Luke. One day in Nazareth Jesus went to the synagogue for the Sabbath, as usual. But now he rose for the first time and read from the Scriptures. What he read was this passage from Isaiah: "The Lord's spirit is on me, for he has anointed me. He sent me to carry good news to the poor, to announce to prisoners that they are to be freed, to the blind that they shall see, to the oppressed that they shall be released, and to declare the Lord's year of grace" (Isa. 61: 1-2). Then he rolled up the scroll, and to the astonishment — and offence — of his hearers he gave this text a most up-to-date interpretation. "Today," he said, "this passage has been fulfilled, right before your eyes" (Luke 4:16-22). (It is worth noting that Jesus broke off reading just before the verse about the "Lord's day of vengeance"!)

Thus Jesus proclaims a new world order, which is now become reality through him, where the hopeless receive the gift of hope and salvation, where the lordship of God will burst brilliantly into the world. The synoptics speak of the lordship of God in nearly a hundred places. It starts, they say, in the person of Jesus. And the fulfilment it promises is a new cosmos.

Strikingly, in all his activity Jesus never speaks of a covenant, either new or old (except in the words of institution of the Eucharist, which we shall be considering shortly), and one wonders where he might have found the idea of the lordship of God. Of course, he could speak in underived fullness of power; he had no need of borrowing his authority elsewhere. Nevertheless it is a fact that the notion of the "day of the Lord" that would set everything topsy-turvy, of the "kingdom of God" that was to succeed the kingdoms of the world (Dan. 2:44; see §24, above), was blowing in the wind, and occupied the minds of the Jews of that time. The baptist, too, John, had seen his mission as that of preparing human beings for the "kingdom of Heaven" that had drawn near (Matt. 3:1).

We have already noted above (§18) that covenant denotes nothing else but the personal relationship of the individual and of the people with Yahweh. What Jesus calls the "lordship of God" therefore coincides perfectly with the notion of covenant. "New covenant and kingdom of God are correlative concepts,"[57] just as are "kingdom of God" and "life," or "attaining life," or "entering into life" — expressions Jesus often used.

But his contemporaries did not entertain these theoretical considerations. What was important to them was how Jesus actually embodied the lordship of God in his person and in his teaching. They saw how he altered the spiritual and psychological climate of the country in no time at all. His challenge spread across the countryside like a tornado. Everyone wanted to see him, hear him, touch him. He spoke with power and authority.

A force went out from him that healed everyone. He showed his favouritism (breaking all the rules of better society) to the poor, the oppressed, sinners, tax collectors, prostitutes, the possessed — what we would today call "marginals". He walked with them, dined with them, showed his solidarity with them. He did so not in order to exclude the others, but to make it understood that what was important was not wealth and prestige, but human worth and the universal human longing for salvation that is stronger and more evident in outcastes. Jesus wished to show — and he did show — that "with the coming of God, the crippled human being is restored from his or her multiple handicaps and is full of life again — clean, seeing, hearing once more."[58]

Everyone was comfortable around him — except the self-righteous, the Pharisees, and those for whom law and establishment were of more value than freedom and human worth. Jesus was strangely harsh — very harsh — with them: a protester, a demonstrator, in the best sense. One gets the feeling that he went out of his way to heal on the Sabbath in order to provoke such groups.[59]

But with the others, he worked to instill courage and hope, especially by his parables. (Are we looking for "authentic Jesus material"? Here it is.) No one could ever be worse off than the prodigal son, and even he came out all right — very much all right! We would do better to call the parable "the prodigal father" instead of "the prodigal son," for that is its proper statement, and its surprise. The parables of the lost sheep and the lost coin (Luke's whole chapter 15) run along the same lines.

Jesus taught us to call this father, who is what these parables are all about, not just "Father," but *Abba* — "Daddy, Papa," a pet name. The fact that Jesus used this term even at the moment of his greatest abandonment, on the Mount of Olives (Mark 14:36), speaks volumes. And so we ought to stop fabricating our own conceptions of God. We ought to *pray* to the God that Jesus has revealed to us, a God who disarms us in compassion and love, forgives all our sins, and stays with us even in our inevitable death. With the word *Abba* Jesus unleashed a revolution in the history of spirituality.[60]

In this attitude of spirit, in unconditional trust in the Father, in awaiting the lordship of God, one finds it possible to devote oneself to the following of Jesus. One even finds it possible to try to fulfil the (humanly speaking) impossible demands of the Sermon on the Mount. The following of Jesus was by no means restricted to the twelve apostles or to the other disciples. It was openly advertised, loudly proclaimed — but relatively few dared to come forward, and they were "the chosen" (Matt. 20:16; 22:14).

The following of Jesus is on the same plane as a teacher-pupil relationship. It can be explained only by Jesus' primary, underived messianic fullness of power. He acts in the place of God. As Yahweh summoned the Old Testament prophets in sovereign authority, so Jesus sovereignly calls his disciples. Under condition of an unconditional break with all conditions, he inserts those he calls into a community of life and destiny with himself, and thereby into the service of the enterprise of God's lordship. Consequently there is an intrinsic and immediate connection between following (discipleship) and mission.[61]

40

Jesus' teaching and public ministry had a socio-political character.[62] It is not that he analyzed conditions or mapped out programs of action. He elaborated case by case, whenever he met a human need. Nor would one have expected him to take a position in favour of the Old Testament theocratic system, where the civil and the religious are amalgamated, and both realms are administered by God-sent leaders such as Moses, or by priests. Religion under these conditions necessarily becomes totalitarian and intolerant. It avails itself of means unsuited to its nature. It comes as no surprise that Jesus distinguished and divorced the two realms, and his answer to the Pharisees was quick: "Then give Caesar what is Caesar's and God what is God's" (Matt. 22:21). And to Pilate he declared, "My kingdom is not of this world" (John 18:36).

Statements like those have at times led some to the conclusion that Christians have only heaven to be concerned about. And this in turn — in theory if not in practice — led to a division of the single, integral salvation that God wished to bring to human beings in Jesus. Salvation became spiritualized and eschatologized. The imperfect Old Testament, it was said, had looked for its recompense in the form of *material* weal, but the perfect New Testament now promised a *heavenly* reward. Nothing could be more inhuman, more un-Christian, more ungodlike, and hence more terribly false.

No, Jesus took the whole human being seriously, coming to his or her assistance in every need and aspiration. It is true he exercised no authority over the world or the political scene, and spurned the opportunity to become king (John 6:15). But he *interpreted* the world and politics, and he inspired them. And he committed himself to the world. He saw this domain, too, within the framework of the kingdom of God. Not even everyday matters such as physical growth, the falling of a hair from one's head, or the determination of the length of one's lifetime, occur outside the purview of God's kingdom (see Matt. 6:27; Luke 21:18).

It cannot be ruled out that Jesus had indirect ties with the Zealots,[63] a group that today would be called political terrorists, somewhat like the IRA or the Basque ETA. The Zealots were hoping to be able to liberate their land from the rule of the Romans. In itself surely this was a legitimate endeavour! It would not have been normal for Jesus as a Jew not to feel a certain sympathy for them. And why is it so flauntingly stated in Luke 6:15 that one of his disciples, Simon, was a Zealot? The so-called Proto-Luke, an earlier document that was incorporated into the gospel of that name, contains a whole series of verses concerned with the political liberation of Israel (Luke 1:68, 74; 2:38; 24:21). The reason why this political side of the gospels is not further developed may be simply that by the time they came to be written, after the destruction of Jerusalem, the whole question had become outdated.

But it is clear that what had first priority in Jesus' mind was the radical cure of evil — not just a change of government, but the conversion of human beings. Without this, you could change all the scenery you wished and it would still be of no help. Roman oppression, as a matter of fact, was less discouraging than that of the Pharisees and Sadducees, who laid burden and scorn alike on human beings in the name of religion. That was something Jesus could not endure.

§30 *Restriction to Israel*

It is striking that Jesus at first limited his activity and that of his disciples to Israel (Matt. 10:5; 15:24). And yet he had made it expressly clear, especially in the parables, that the lordship of God that he was announcing brooked no constriction to the limits of Israel. But oddly and tragically, opening the kingdom to all peoples is tied to the rejection of Israel. How difficult it is, in practice, to harmonize election and universalism! "But I say to you, many will come from the East and West and recline at table with Abraham, Isaac, and Jacob in the kingdom of heaven, while the children of the kingdom will be cast out . . . " (Matt. 8:11ff.; similarly Matt. 21:43; Luke 14:23ff; Mark 12:1-9).

And Jesus showed, though with reserve, a notorious love for men and women who were not of the chosen people but who demonstrated a faith to shame Israel, such as the Roman merchant (Matt. 8:10), the Canaanite woman (Matt. 15:28), and the Samaritans (John 4:39-41), who in Jewish eyes were worse than pagans. Such a behavioural pattern is not to be overlooked.

It becomes clear that Jesus' restriction of his ministry to Israel was not nationalistic but strategic. Evidently Jesus hoped to bring Israel, by enticements and warnings, under the lordship of God first, and then open the way to others.

The first real breakthrough occurred only after, and because of, the resurrection. Now there was a new situation in salvation history. Now the historical Jesus, who had so unassumingly passed through the land, was certified by God, and proclaimed "Lord most high" (Phil. 2:11). Now the long announced reception of pagans into the kingdom could become reality, and the dynamic mission to that purpose might commence. Now the distinction between the people and the peoples was lifted and nullified, for "all peoples" are to be disciples of Jesus (Matt. 28:19).

The word *goyim* — Gentiles, pagans — must now give up its discriminatory character. Now the "far" become the "near", in the blood of Christ who is our peace, and who draws back the sundering partition (Eph. 2:13). Now the circle of the aboriginal, comprehensive community of creation is closed once more. Now a new phase in the evolution of religion is under way, and the world, previously split into many peoples, each with its own deities and religion, is finding its way home again to oneness.

The basic unity of all human beings is one of the most fundamental concepts of Christianity. It pertains to its very essence, for God, who has revealed himself in Jesus, is himself but one. Now, of the tribal religion of the Jews, the religion of the whole world is born.[64]

The historicity of the missionary mandate in the last chapter of Matthew is fiercely disputed. It is pointed out that Jesus had never before used a trinitarian formula, and that he had conditioned salvation only on the acceptance of the kingdom of God, on conversion, not on rites (baptism) and commandments. Then there is the complexus of problems concerning the mode and manner of the "apparitions" of the resurrected Lord. Why, if the command had been given as it stands on the gospel page, did the breakthrough to pagans encounter such vehement opposition? And why was its chief protagonist — Paul — someone who had not been there to hear the mandate?

However one may attempt to solve these specific questions, the missionary commission of Matthew's Gospel is better understood as the consequence, rather than the basis, of the missionary dynamic that was launched with Jesus' apparition on that occasion. Anyone who takes Jesus and his proclamation seriously will hand the message on. With or without Matthew 28:19 there will be mission. Even the conciliar decree *Ad Gentes*, in establishing the theological and scriptural basis for the missions (AG 2-9), makes only passing reference to the Matthean pericope (AG 5).

§31 *Who is Jesus Christ?*

The whole question becomes: Who is Jesus Christ? How could such a movement have started with him? "Who do people say the Son of Man is?" (Matt. 16:13). Who do we Christians say Jesus Christ is? The catechisms took care to teach children the answer as if it were no problem. He is true man and true God. This is one of those mighty statements that ought not to be taken lightly, lest it remain a rote formula and nothing more. It can only be the *last* word — it can be pronounced only as the last try after a long struggle with it. Even Peter evidently found his way to his profession, "You are the Messiah, the Son of the living God" (Matt. 16:16), only after the Easter experience, even though it was then projected in redaction back to the public ministry.

In this central question of the meaning of Jesus Christ,[65] exegesis and theology must go hand in hand. If we approach the texts of Scripture purely exegetically and then attempt to draw conclusions for understanding our faith today, we will be like the disciples during the years before the resurrection. Jesus cannot be explained without the

43

Easter experience and the faith tradition of the first Christian community. Christ's apostles and disciples, who had walked with him, were in the best position, in the light of all their interior and exterior experiences, to interpret his being and his intentions. And the primitive Christian community was *their* community. It is this special character of the first Christian group — that of being the community that had eyewitnesses for members — that forms the basis of its unique and non-negotiable importance for all believers as the projectory of the faith. When all the studies are over, the moment comes when the question of trust imposes itself. It must be answered.

Jesus did not practise metaphysics on himself. He did not enter into an introverted self-examination. He submitted no apologia for his divinity. He sought no reverence or adoration. For him the only thing that mattered was to show human beings the image of a loving God and Father. But he prayed, spoke and acted out of an experience of God that, for his disciples, was utter mystery. He did not simply proclaim a message as had the other prophets. His message was entirely his own. He was himself the message, God's self-communication, the unique salvation bearer, the eschatological salvation event. His disciples were drawn into the new relationship with God through him, but Jesus always expressed himself out of his primordial relationship to the Father.

Then the postresurrection community, under the influence of the risen Jesus, alive again, expressed its memory of this man — who had once walked with some of them — in such words as: he is "the Messiah, the Son of the living God" (Matt. 16:16), "he is the Word that was with God from the beginning" (John 1:1), "the image of God, the firstborn of all creation . . . everything has been created through him and toward him" (Col. 1:15ff.). He is the support or the bridge that carries humankind from creation to completion.

The two churches — Eastern and Western— have centred their interpretation of the life of Jesus Christ on two distanced poles. The church of the East concentrated on the incarnation — the assumption and divinization of human nature — as the decisive salvation event. The Western church centred almost exclusively on the crucifixion, interpreting it as a sacrificial and atoning death. And the life of Jesus between the incarnation and the crucifixion? It was presented merely as the model of virtuous behaviour.

Today we are trying to see the salvation event in the totality of his life as a unity. From the very beginning it had been proclaimed, "Today a saviour is born for you" (Luke 2:11). The saviour's death, then, was to be at once the logical end and the climax of his life, which would receive its uniquely new and enduring dimension in the resurrection.

Before he died, Jesus celebrated the last supper with his disciples. According to the oldest report, this is what took place:

> The Lord Jesus, on the night on which he was betrayed, took bread, gave thanks, broke it, and spoke: "That is my body for you. Do this in my memory." Likewise after the meal he took the cup as well, and spoke: "This cup is the new covenant in my blood; do this, as often as you drink from it, in my memory."

And Paul, who wrote this report in his First Letter to the Corinthians, adds:

> For whenever you eat this bread and drink this cup you proclaim the death of the Lord, until he comes [1 Cor. 11:23-26].

But even this text was written some twenty-five years after Jesus' death, and various questions can be posed by way of textual criticism. Certain authors believe the idea of a "new covenant", a clear reference to Jeremiah 31:31-33 (§24, above) — the only reference to this text in Jesus' entire preaching — is a Pauline interpretation and interpolation. They go so far as to say that the supper was but a farewell meal, and Jesus' death was simply the death of a prophet, without further meaning for salvation — a death that Jesus distressfully anticipated rather than foresaw as part of his task.

Here again one must approach the primitive Christian community. And we read that "God has given up his son for us" (Rom. 8:13ff.), that "he has made him into sin for us" (2 Cor. 5:11). His death *was* interpreted as a means of our salvation, and his life, death, and resurrection were the means of the insertion of the lordship of God, the new covenant, into the world.

"Jesus' name is the Archimedean point from which a movement is launched from the unredeemed past to the salvific future."[66] Past and future, of course, are not to be taken temporally — as if there had been no salvation before Christ — but theologically, inasmuch as all salvation, from the beginning of creation onward, is Christ's salvation (see §9, above).

What is decisive for Christians is not the simple repetition of an act of worship "in his memory", but the retroactive fulfilment of what that act of worship celebrates: self-surrender for the sake of others. Over against the selfishness imbedded in the nature of the human being, hence transcending the bounds of all the eras of human history, is the hope arising from the life of Christ: that other-directedness can indeed *be*, and therefore can be demanded. It is ever a test of the church's vitality whether the Eucharist is understood simply as the fulfilment of a Sunday obligation and urged with more or less success, or as the life-giving celebration of an "existence for others" intended to bring dynamism and bravery into our lives, until he comes.

If Jesus is the beginning, and the content, of the new covenant, then we ought to enquire into his position in relation to the Old Testament. First we must state the obvious. Jesus was Jewish. He took the name, language, writing, culture, and religion of Judaism. He was circumcised. He made pilgrimages to the temple while a boy. He prayed the Psalms, he celebrated passover. He knew Scripture — the law and the prophets — and used it all his life, as is seen especially from Matthew, whether in prayer (Matt. 27:46), in determining his course and behaviour (Matt. 4:4, 6, 7), in describing his task (Matt. 11:4, 29; 12:20; 13:35; 23:39; 26:31, 64), in instructing others (Matt. 5:21-43; 6:6; 8:4; 12:37-41ff.; 13:32, 43; 15:4; 18:16; 19:19; 22:37ff.; 25:46), in prophesying (Matt. 24:6-10; 15:31), in defending himself (Matt. 13:3-7; 19:4ff.; 21:13-16, 42; 22:32). And he not only knew it and used it, but "laid claim to it, as someone who approaches an old inheritance."[67] True, he was astonishingly free in his interpretations and adaptations.

Jesus — a Jew! If there had been modern census forms in those days, when Jesus came to "religious preference" he would have written not "Christian", but "Jewish". Do we not have to admit that later, in the long history of anti-Semitism (see Part Two, §§5-7), we were ashamed of him? Have we not made him un-Jewish, uprooted him, prettied him up, Europeanized him? From the time of Emperor Constantine onwards, Christians systematically burned Jewish texts that treated of Jesus. They wished to have only "their" Christ of faith, not the Jesus of sources outside Christianity. This is part of the reason why we in fact know so little about the historical Jesus.[68]

Today we are on the point of overcoming our complex, and we are undertaking research into Jesus in cooperation with Jewish scholars. We cannot love Jesus *and* despise his people. We ourselves, through Jesus, belong to this people somehow. In our new sympathy for each other we shall both be able, together, to come closer to Jesus[69] (see Part Two, §8).

But Jesus' relationship with the Old Testament goes deeper. The Old Testament bears him witness, certifies him, through Moses and Elijah (Matt. 17:3). He has come not to abolish the law, but to fulfil it (Matt. 5:17), in fact to take full sovereign charge of it — "You have heard that it was said to those of old . . . But I say to you . . ." (Matt. 5:21-44).

The New Testament is shot through with the pathos of persons' astonishment that something new could be dawning, of their overwhelming consciousness that they were being placed at the beginning of something from which totally new horizons of the divine salvation activity have come in sight. The kingdom of God is here![70]

Now everything has to be read in reverse, from this new horizon. For all of us, as he did for the disciples on the road to Emmaus, Jesus must "open up our minds" (Luke 24:45), to understand from the Scriptures the new situation in salvation history.

The Old Testament concerns us Christians only through Jesus. Were it not for its connections with him, the Old Testament would be "just another sacred book", as in any other religion — sacred for the members of that religion. Yes, it is finally possible to recognize the Old Testament for what it actually, properly means: it leads and points to Jesus. Ultimately the unity of the two testaments is rooted in the unity of the one Yahweh in both — however new be his way of revealing himself in Jesus, surely unforeseeable as such from the standpoint of the Old Testament alone. Hence the standpoint from which we can see both continuity and discontinuity between the two testaments: the Old Testament is fully understandable only in Jesus; and Jesus can be seen in his deep roots in the first beginnings of the world, as well as throughout all history, only in the Old Testament. We Christians cannot read the Old Testament simply as a document in and for itself.[71]

The Apostles

§33 Paul

Among the Apostles, a special place is to be assigned to Paul. Paul had not known Jesus. He had not walked with him as had the Twelve. But he experienced him perhaps even more inwardly intensely than they. "Fanatical proponent" of the Jewish traditions (Gal. 1:14), enemy of Christ and Christians, he must have been overwhelmed by a sudden, violent interior experience — perhaps comparable to the sudden conversion of a Giovanni Papini, a Douglas Hyde, or an André Frossard — and he knew as if in a flash of lightning that "God singled me out from my mother's womb, and called me, by his grace, to experience his son within me, in order to spread the news of him among the pagans".

It was less by way of instruction "than through a revelation of Jesus Christ", perhaps especially during his sojourn in the Arabian desert, that he had come to know the gospel (Gal. 1:11-19). And he became the mighty messenger of the New covenant to all peoples. What Christ had brought about in spontaneity and enthusiasm, Paul would expound theologically. And at the same time he would manage, over such opposition, to force acceptance of his project of opening the new covenant to all peoples.[72]

And so Paul never tired of emphasizing and repeating that Jesus is the mediator of the new covenant, that the church is the New Israel. He calls the covenant the "testament" (in Greek, *diatheke*, "dis-position"), as had the Septuagint before him. There are thirty-three occurrences of this word in the New Testament, and seventeen of them are in the Letter to the Hebrews. It is important to notice Paul's shift in emphasis. A covenant is a mutual contract; "testament" puts the emphasis on the disposition of a testator — in this case God — who has left us a gift out of sheer gratuitousness.

Just as all human beings without exception have fallen victim, in Adam, to the situation and condition of sin and death (Rom. 3:9, 12), "all are also brought to life in Christ" (1 Cor. 15:22; Rom. 5:17). Our new justice in Christ was certified in advance, "attested to, by the law and by the prophets" (Rom. 3:21), for Christ was present throughout the whole Old Testament. Everything is his prototype — for example, the rock from which water gushed forth in the desert (1 Cor. 10:4), or the son of Abraham born of the free woman and not of the slave girl (Gal. 4:22-25).

The law had the function of a precursor. It surged "toward Christ" (Gal. 3:23). And yet it is just because of those many laws that we became transgressors of laws (Gal. 3:19) and this led finally to "slavery" (Gal. 4:24). But now Christ is "the end of the law", and "unto justice for each that believes" (Rom. 10:4; Gal. 3:25). He is the high priest who

> entered once for all into the sanctuary not with blood of goats and calves, but with his own blood, and gained a redemption lasting eternally . . . Wherefore he is the new covenant's mediator, so that through his death — which served as ransom from the sins that occurred in the first covenant — those who are called may receive the promises, for the eternal inheritance [Heb. 9:11-15].

Paul was not acquainted with the Roman Christians at all. But he must have known their legal mentality, which was owing partly to the presence of the many Jews among them and partly to the spirit of Roman law itself. Hence it is especially in the Letter to the Romans that he sings the paean of liberty — not liberty to sin, but liberty from the law and freedom for life in Christ. For even Abraham was not justified through his works, but through the faith (Rom. 4:3ff.). "The one that loves his neighbour is the one who has fulfilled the law" (Rom. 13:8). We even have hope that "it too, creation, will be freed from the forced labour of the past, to the freedom of the glory of the children of God (Rom. 8:21). (Was he altogether successful in liberating the Roman community from legalistic thinking for all time?)

Those within the New Covenant are called as a group the "body of Christ", or simply "Christ". In Christ, these many persons make up but one body (1 Cor. 12:12, 27). The body of Christ, in turn, is coextensive with the church (Col. 1:18, 24). The faithful of this church are the true circumcision (Phil. 3:3) — they represent the twelve tribes of Israel (James 1:1), and they are God's new children and heirs (Rom. 8:17).

There is no distinction of class or race in this community, "for we are all baptized in one spirit to one body, whether we are Jews or Greeks, slaves or free" (1 Cor. 12:13; Gal. 3:28). All those who thus live "in Christ Jesus" are addressed by Paul as "beloved, called, holy, chosen" (Rom. 1:7, 8:33; 1 Cor. 1:2; Col. 3:12; Eph. 1:4).

If Paul thinks so highly of the Christians, those who are baptized in Christ, what does he think of the Jews and pagans?

§34 *The Jews*

In his letter to the Romans, chapters 9 through 11, Paul develops his theology of the history of his own people, the Jews — in solidarity with whom he too would like to be "someone cut off, far from Christ". He does not proceed very rectilinearly, however, but dialectically, appealing continually to Old Testament texts in support of his own intuitions. His most important ideas run as follows.

On the one hand, the Jews "are Israelites, and they possess the status of children, the glory, the covenantings, the giving of the law, the worship of God, and the promises". On the other hand "not all who come out of Israel are actually Israel as such", for carnal descent from Abraham no longer means anything (Rom. 9:1-7).

One must not forget Israel's stubbornness, for the Lord himself says of them, "All the day long I reached out my hands to a stubborn and refractory people" (Rom. 10:21). And yet they are by no means rejected by him. There is still "a remnant, according to the election of grace . . . but the others were obdurate". Then this depressing statement is tempered by the appearance of a brighter horizon: "Through their obduracy, salvation came to the pagans". But if their rejection occasioned the world's salvation, what will be the wonderful result of their acceptance? For this obduracy came only "over a part of Israel, until the full number of the Gentiles should have entered in", for "God's gifts of grace, and his calling, are irrevocable". Truly, "how unfathomable are the decrees of God, how unsearchable his ways!" (Rom. 11:1-36).

It is edifying and instructive to compare all this with No. 4 of the decree *Nostra Aetate*, with its heavy reliance on the Pauline theology. But not even the council actually found a way out of the dilemma. "Jerusalem knew not the time of its visitation"; on the other hand, Israel is "still loved by God". It is stated emphatically that one can lay the passion of Christ "to the account neither of all Jews then living, without distinction, nor to that of the Jews of today. Surely the church is the new people of God; nevertheless one cannot represent the Jews as having been rejected or confounded by God".

Well, then, are there two chosen peoples, one succeeding the other? It would surely be more correct to say that the Jewish people retain their legitimate claim, so that there can in no way be really "another" chosen people — but only two versions of the one people, each of itself existing alongside of and for the other, representing a tension of mutual obligation and service, until the day of the Second Coming reveals, and brings about, their full unity.[73]

§35 The Gentiles

Paul, the apostle of the Gentiles, developed his theology of history not only for the Jews but for the others as well. Mighty partisan of his own people though he may have been, he nevertheless breaks out, charismatically and radically, through all the frontiers of a narrow political and religious nationalism.

In that large, universalist view of his, he speaks about all human beings — we all find ourselves in the same order of sin and grace. "All sinned and were in need of God's glory" (Rom. 3:23). "God grouped them all together in disobedience so that he could show them all mercy" (Rom. 11:32). "As all died in Adam, all shall also be brought to life, in Christ" (1 Cor. 15:22). "The grace of God has appeared, as salvation for all human beings" (Titus 2:11).

These tremendous texts, proclaiming hope for everybody, stand in curious contradiction to other passages of the same apostle where he speaks of those "who are being lost". He says "the word of the cross is foolishness to those on their way to being lost; but to us, who are being saved, it is the power of God" (1 Cor. 1:18). "We are the good odour of Christ before God, among those who are being saved and among those who are going to their ruin" (2 Cor. 1:15; cf. 2 Thess. 2:10; Phil. 1:28). It is just the same as with Paul's theology of the Jews. There is an unresolved dialectical tension here. Paul has not yet thought it through to synthesis. The question has been a challenge to Christian thinkers of all times.

Thus while the question of salvation for everyone remains an open one theologically, pragmatically Paul permits himself generalizations and repudiations that, with all his advocacy of the pagan peoples, betray a typically Jewish sense of superiority, his "*goyim* mentality", which he has still not overcome. He remained a child of his time when he presupposed without distinction that "pagans live in the idle aimlessness of their feelings" (Eph. 4:17), that they stagger about in "passionate lust", because after all "they do not know God" (1 Thess. 4:5).

The same thing is maintained further, and carried to the point of the grotesque, in Paul's well-known "catalogue of vices" in his Letter to the Romans: those who, in spite of their better insight, do not serve God, are "filled with all injustice, malice, lechery, evil, greed, jealousy, murder, strife, treachery, and spite. They libel, they slander, they are God's enemies. They are rude, arrogant, and boastful — resourceful in sin, disobedient to their parents, without understanding, honour, feeling, or mercy" (Rom. 1:29-31).

Does he mean all the pagan Romans? Then this is truly no *captatio benevolentiae* on that nation. Doubtless it was morally corrupt in certain circles, but surely not so bad as all that. (Indeed is there anyone that has all these vices, and nothing but vices?) These texts stand as blemishes on the countenance of the great apostle.

For the rest, Paul committed himself to his mission to the pagans with matchless zeal and constant openness to the Holy Spirit, so that in the course of twenty years he succeeded in setting up a network of communities that stretched from Jerusalem to Rome. They would live on as churches of Christ, and would change the Roman Empire from the inside out.

Once upon a time the Lord most high said of this man, "He is my chosen instrument for bringing my name before peoples and kings, and before the people of Israel", and "I shall show him all he must suffer for my name's sake" (Acts 9:15ff.). These sufferings are portrayed in the Acts of the Apostles, from chapter 13 to the end of the book. They came not least from "false brethren" (2 Cor. 11:26), who had never learned to stomach the mission to the pagans, and bitterly resented that Paul had had no wish to impose the Law and circumcision on everyone.

§36 *Peter*

Paul did not have to wage the battle for freedom from the law entirely by himself. In the Council of the Apostles the other apostles shared his view (Acts 15). In this affair Peter had an especially painful lesson to learn.

Perhaps it was in the year 64, hence toward the end of his life's pilgrimage, that Peter addressed his first letter to the various communities of Asia Minor, in which the singularly beautiful words appear

> But you are a "chosen people" [Isa. 43:20], "a royal priesthood, a people sanctified" [Exod. 19:6], "a people that was acquired for the purpose of proclaiming his deeds of renown" [Isa. 43:21] "who has called you out of the darkness into wondrous light. Once you were no people. But now you are a people of God" [Pet. 2:9ff.].

Peter here applies the classic texts of the chosen people's covenant theology to the communities of the church of Christ composed of Gentile Christians. For it has appeared in the meantime who the new people of God are. Those who had been a nonpeople have become a chosen people (see also Rom. 9:25ff.; 10:19). This was something that had by no means been clear from the beginning.

As would happen in history again and again, those of the circumcision school were unable to reconcile themselves with the sudden irruption of new ideas, with a new situation in salvation history. They went about sowing discord among the Christians, to the effect that the law and circumcision were not to be surrendered (Acts 15:1, 5). Paul was especially reproached with "teaching secession from Moses" (Acts 21:21). Peter continued to live as a prisoner of the law. Then God intervened.

The hungry apostle saw, in a trance, certain unclean beasts, and a voice told him, "Rise, Peter, slaughter and eat". But Peter said, "Never, Lord, not ever. For I have never eaten anything vulgar and unclean". But the voice persisted: "What God has made clean, do you not call unclean". This happened thrice. But Peter still did not grasp what was meant. Just then some men entered the house and bade him come to where the centurion Cornelius, "a just and god-fearing man", was staying. Now it dawned on Peter that it was these "alien tribesmen" whom he was not to call unclean — that indeed "God looks not to the person, but in every people the one who fears him and practises justice finds acceptance with him". And the ice was broken: while Peter was instructing Cornelius' whole family, "the Holy Spirit came upon all who were hearing the Word". And so all were baptized (Acts 10:9-48).

But on a later occasion Peter lacked the courage of his new insight. He was on the point of joining some pagans in Antioch at table, when certain members of the traditionalist circle of James approached. Kephas pulled back at once, out of opportunism, out of fear of the members of the circumcision clique, and separated himself from the pagans. Paul found out about it and flew into a holy rage. He "stood up to him to his face, for he was in the wrong" (Gal. 2:11). And this act of correction, this humiliation of the chief of the Apostles, made the rounds. Paul publicly spoke of it, and it entered Holy Writ as a lasting memorandum and admonishment to all Peters, little and great, not to allow themselves to be too much captivated by traditionalists — and to all big and little Pauls to stand right up to the Peters to their face whenever necessary.

The Christians

§37 *Jewish Christians*

What the apostles had received from the Lord, and were now proclaiming, was being lived out in Christian communities. But Jesus was a Jew, and had not actually founded a new religion but had fulfilled the old covenant in the new.

Most of the first Christians, too, were Jews, and continued to live as believing Jews. These so-called Jewish Christians[74] took part in the temple worship — with ardour (Acts 2:46; 5:12) — as if it were self-evident that they should. They observed the Jewish hours of prayer (Acts 2:46; 3:1). They kept to the dietary prescriptions (Acts 10:14). They celebrated passover and kept the Sabbath (Acts 16:13). They had their children circumcised (Acts 21:21).

And yet they considered themselves members of the new covenant. They had been received into it through faith in Christ and baptism (Acts 2:38, 41). They assembled for the common repast (Acts 2:42-46), which on certain days presumably included the Eucharist. They even began to celebrate Sunday as the day of Jesus' resurrection (Acts 20:7; 1 Cor. 16:2). And they all called each other brothers and sisters (Acts 14:2).

There were various other subgroupings in Jewish life — Pharisees, Sadducees, Essenes, the Qumran community. Christians were just one more group, and at first they caused no sensation whatever. But gradually they came to public attention as a group of a different sort, and were soon labelled a "sect", a "heresy" (Acts 24:5, 14; 28:22). Still the Christians were convinced that they could be disciples of Christ without ceasing to be Jews. In fact they were convinced that anyone wanting to be a real Jew, and true to the prophets, must become a Christian. They felt that one did not fall away from Judaism in doing so, but were simply drawing its ultimate consequences.

It is surely a pity that these Jewish Christians failed to gain the insight that perhaps this notion of theirs could be valid for the members of other religions too — that perhaps they too should not have to recant their religion, but rather could bring it to fulfilment in faith in Christ.

With all their openness to Christ, most Jewish Christians remained, basically, narrow-minded representatives of exclusivist Judaism. This was their downfall. They sank more and more into isolation and lost their leadership role. Their case demonstrates once and for all that the Christian decision, once taken, can be endangered not only from the side of moral laxity, but just as easily from the side of moral rigorism.

§38 *Gentile Christians*

The tension concerning circumcision and the law, which Paul and Peter had to work their way through, visibly lessened in proportion as the so-called pagan Christians, or Gentile Christians, who had come to faith in Christ from Hellenism, gradually gained the upper hand. The years from the destruction of the temple (A.D. 70) to the insurgency of Bar Kochba (A.D. 135) were distinguished by the break of Christianity with its Jewish roots. The Jewish Christians had had to flee Jerusalem along with the other Jews in the political turmoil of the day, and they then eked out their sorry lives wherever they found themselves and finally sank into the sea of history. But the pagan Christians survived, rose more and more to a position of supremacy, and spread from city to city. They thought of themselves as heirs of the community of the people of God in the desert (Acts 7:38; see also Deut. 18:16), heirs of the primitive community of Jerusalem, the new chosen people (§33, above).

The terms "lordship of God" and "kingdom of God" came to be used less frequently; in their place there appeared the expression "church", in Greek *ekklesia*, the band of the elect or chosen ones of God (Acts 11:26; 14:23-27; 15:3, 41; 16:5). The purpose of the terminological reform was to emphasize the break with the synagogue, the detachment of Christianity from Judaism. The Christians became a "third people", as it were, alongside the Jews and the Pagans — or at least a new people, which would henceforth be the one to determine history.

§39 A Look Back

A look into one's beginnings always has an animating and inspiring effect, like the memory of one's first love. It was those Christians of the earliest times who must have known best what it really meant to be Christian — and perhaps not exactly what Christianity later made of itself.

For a certain length of time, while the Twelve, the Lord's witnesses, were there for contemplation and honour, what stood at the centre of the "Jesus movement" was simply the figure and message of Jesus. No additional structures and laws were needed — only the all-animating power of Jesus' Spirit, who fostered the growth of the young church (Acts 2:47; 6:7), sped the missionary journeys of Paul (Acts 16:9; 19:21), and crowned his deeds with success (Acts 19:11; Cor. 2:3ff.; Rom. 15:17ff.). This same Spirit also issued certain regulations for the life of the community (1 Cor. 3:9ff.; 2 Cor. 12:19; Eph. 4:12-16). The community endorsed this. It saw no contradiction here with the free activity of those who possessed charismatic gifts: the regulations and the charisms both came from the same Spirit. Enthusiasm and order went hand in hand, even if Paul had to address certain warnings to those filled with the Spirit (1 Cor. 14).

Only in the second and third generations — as the immediate experience of Jesus paled with time, and it became evident that the expected lordship of God was not just around the corner after all — did the various ministries arise, likewise in the Spirit of Jesus. Now there was a great deal more emphasis on authority. Laws were framed, the community was organized, and there arose what certain authors call "early Catholicism."[75]

Circulating among the fixed communities were wandering disciples, preachers, and prophets, who wished to live Jesus' invitation literally, and so went without homes (Matt. 10:23), families (Luke 14:26), goods (Luke 6:24ff.), or protection (Matt. 5:41), and this is the way they proclaimed the message. Later the same function was performed by traders and soldiers, especially, who bore witness to their faith wherever they might go, as if this were quite the natural thing to do. Then too the communities themselves attracted others by radiation — recruiting simply by being themselves. "See how they love one another", was what others said when they saw those Christian groups. Their community life, in which even all one's goods were shared (Acts 4:32-37; 2:42-47), had the effect of a shock therapy on those around it. It presented an alternative lifestyle worth pursuing. It had the effect of a question mark and an exclamation point at the same time.

The unbaptized, even the merely curious, were allowed to take part in the liturgy of the word, and they listened and were astounded. Gripped with excitement, they said, "Truly, God is among you!" (1 Cor. 14:25). And so there was a mission without a mission, simply in the testimony of Christian living, in Christian contagion. The church did not seek to persuade, but to invite — to let others come and see.

Of course it would not do to idealize those days, either. There were tensions then, too, for various reasons. Paul expressed his concern about it in the First Letter to the Corinthians. But basic unity reigned in spite of everything — in the hearing of the word of the Lord, in the possession of the Holy Spirit, in the belief in the one Lord, and in community with the other churches.[76]

They drew much from Judaism, those Christians, and much from Hellenism. But they also presented something creatively new. They had come mostly from among the poor and lowly, and yet their brilliance shone even in the houses of the rich and mighty. They formed minority groups, yet they worked as a leaven in the whole of society. They were periodically persecuted with open violence, and yet they continued to expand.

After the conversion of Constantine, the church all too often relied not on the power of the Spirit, but on baldly human means, for its security and propagation. The parallel with today's situation thrusts itself upon us. True, providence has not decreed that our church be catapulted back into the time before Constantine. It has shot us forward into the post-Constantinian era instead. From many viewpoints, our situation bears similarity to that of the first centuries: antipathy toward exaggerated structuring, the appearance of charismatic movements, confrontation with new cultures, our minority situation, and restrictions on religious freedom in the political systems of both left and right to the point of persecution. A look back at our roots can help us bear up under the loss of certain positions and status — the better to interpret, and courageously come to terms with, the present time.

We have gathered many impressions in our first survey of the biblical terrain. Let us summarize the findings.

The church of Christ lives the belief that Yahweh chose for himself a people in Old Testament times — and that he wished to show that people his special favour and care, but always with *all* peoples in mind. That church further believes that this same Yahweh, now recognized as the Father of Jesus Christ, gathers to himself a new people in the new covenant. That new people is the church. Gathered from among all peoples now, its purpose is to proclaim and mediate the salvation of Jesus Christ to humankind as a whole.

Strangely, on its way out to the peoples during the first centuries, the church composed no "church history". Salvation history was *lived*, not written down. That was enough. Later, lists of bishops began to be put together in order to demonstrate their continuity in the world that came after. But only in the fourth century, when the church began to step out as a kingdom and a power and began to boast of its history, did historical writings appear. As weighty a historian as Baron H. von Campenhausen therefore wonders whether this beginning may perhaps have coincided with the beginning of a heresy in the area of salvation history.[77]

This question — this indictment — challenges one to take up the history of this new chosen people, and to examine how it has understood and conducted itself down through the course of the centuries. And this is what we shall do in Part Two.

Notes to Part One

[1] Muschalek, *Urmensch*; Overhage and Rahner, *Das Problem der Hominisation*; Leakey, *Origins*; Toynbee, *Menschheit - woher und wohin?*

[2] *Der Gottesstaat* 2:246.

[3] Leakey, *Origins*, pp. 120ff.

[4] Kaufmann, *Afrikas Wege*, pp. 44-62.

[5] See de Vaux, *Histoire ancienne d'Israël*; Bright, *Geschichte Israels*; Metzger, *Grundriss der Geschichte Israels*. See also: Jaros, K., *Die Stellung des Elohisten zur kanaanäischen Religion* and *Aegypten und Vorderasien*. For this summary (§§3-5) I am greatly indebted to Prof. K. Jaros of Linz.

[6] See Schmidt, *Alttestamentlicher Glaube*; Eichrodt, *Religionsgeschichte Israels*; Jaros, *Die Stellung des Elohisten*.

7 See the three books of Eissfeldt, Fohrer, and Smend, respectively, each entitled *Einleitung in das Alte Testament.*

8 Schmid, *Die Steine und das Wort*, pp. 28ff.; Schoonenberg, *Covenant and Creation* (Introduction).

9 This is what P.G. van Breenen does in his very popular *Called by Name* (New Jersey, 1976).

10 Schmid, *Steine;* Fesforazzi, *La Bibbia*, pp. 168-79; Bultmann, *Das Urchristentum;* Schult, *Urgeschichte;* Eliade, *Die Schöpfungsmythen* (pp. 227ff.), *La nostalgie des origines* and *Le mythe de l'éternel retour*. See also the whole of Part Three.

11 Zimmer, *Indische Mythen;* Baumann, *Schöpfungsmythen;* Eliade, "The Yearning for Paradise in Primitive Traditions," *Daedalus* 88:255-67 (Cambridge, 1959).

12 K. Rahner, "Aetiologie," LThK 1:1011ff.

13 P. Houée, "Développement rural, libération humaine et salut en Jésus-Christ," in de Surgy (ed.), *Recherches et réflexions*, pp. 37-60.

14 J. Ratzinger, "Schöpfungsglaube und Evolutionslehre," in H.J. Schultz, *Wer ist das eigentlich - Gott?* (Lucerne, 1970), pp. 232-45; Rahner, in Overhage and Rahner, *Das Problem der Hominisation*, pp. 13-90; Thielicke, *Wie die Welt begann*, pp. 17-48, 111-27. For a contemporary explanation of original sin see M. Flick and Z. Alszeghy, *Il peccato originale* (Brescia, 1972).

15 Ranher and Imhof, *Ignatius*, pp. 37ff. See K. Lehmann, "Transcendenz," LThK 10:316-19.

16 B.O. Küppers, "Wie die toten Moleküle einst den Sprung ins Leben lernten," *Die Welt*, June 2, 1979.

17 Gollwitzer, *Krummes Holz*, pp. 211-28; S. Jaki, *The Road of Science and the Ways to God* (Chicago, 1978).

18 Pfammatter and Furger, *Judentum und Kirche*, p. 20.

19 K. Rahner, "Über das Verhältnis von Natur und Gnade," *Schriften* 1:323-45; "Christologie im Rahmen des modernen Selbst- und Weltverständnisses," *Schriften* 9:227-41; "Erlösungswirklichkeit in der Schöpfungswirklichkeit," *Sendung und Gnade*, pp. 51-87; Schoonenberg, *Covenant and Creation*, p. 109.

20 K. Rahner, "Schöpfungslehre," LThK 9:470-74; "Die Christologie innerhalb einer evolutiven Weltanschauung," *Schriften* 5:183-221; Maloney, *The Cosmic Christ.*

21 Johannine Prologue, John 1; hymns to Christ, Col. 1:15-20, Eph. 1:3-12.

22 *Europäische Theologie herausgefordert durch die Weltökumene* (Geneva, 1976).

23 Rahner, "Erlösungswirklichkeit," p. 68.

24 The account of the fall in Lohfink, *Das Siegeslied*, pp. 81-101; cf. Böckle, *Fundamentalmoral*, pp. 133-42.

25 See J. Michl and K. Rahner, LThK 8: 822-34; Comblin, *Theologie des Friedens*, pp. 162-72.

26 Von Rad, *Theologie des Alten Testamentes*, 1:175.

27 Daniélou, *Die heiligen Heiden des Alten Testamentes*, esp. pp. 73-90; cf. Schlette, *Die Religionen*, pp. 77ff.; O. Biehn and H. Junker, "Sintflut," LThK 9:787-89.

28 Daniélou, *Le Mystère de l'Avent*, pp. 29-32.

29 See Pfammater and Furger, *Judentum*, p. 20; Keel and Küchler, *Synoptische Texte*, pp. 25-27.

30 Von Rad, *Alten Testamentes*, p. 178.

31 S. Hermann, *Storia d'Israele*, pp. 57-60.

32 De Surgy, *Recherches sur l'espérance chrétienne*, p. 26; M.S. Seale, *The Desert Bible: Nomadic Culture and Old Testament Interpretation* (London, 1974).

33 See Petuchowsky, *Melchisedech, Urgestalt der Ökumene.*

34 Daniélou, *Avent*, pp. 29-59; J. Schmid, LThK 1:57ff.

35 Eichrodt, *Theologie* 1:178-205; Keel and Küchler, *Synoptische Texte*, pp. 25-27.

36 For our purposes it is unnecessary to go into the many repetitions and differences in Exodus and Deuteronomy. The covenant is struck now at Mount Sinai (Exod. 19, 34:2), now at Mount Horeb (Exod. 17:6, 33:6; Deut. 5:2). For the desert theme see G. Greshake, *Die Wüste bestehen* (Freiburg, 1979).

[37] The works of Eichrodt, de Vaux, McCarthy, von Rad, Schoonenberg; Lohfink, *Siegeslied*, pp. 11-43; McKenzie, *The Two-Edged Sword*, pp. 133-55; Bright, *Geschichte Israels*, pp. 133-39; H. Caselles, "Bund," SM 1:642-52; V. Hamp, "Bund," LThK 2:770-74. I had a very useful conversation on this part of the material with Prof. R. Koch of the Alphonsianum in Rome.

[38] The books by Rowley and Stuhlmueller; Comblin, *Theologie des Friedens*, pp. 137-73; R. Schnackenburg, "Erwählung," LThK 3:1061-63.

[39] Thoughts from Brueggemann, *The Land*, and Gottwald, *The Tribes of Yahweh*.

[40] See the work by McCarthy; also K. Baltzer, *Das Bundesformular* (Neukirchen, 1960).

[41] Schalom Ben-Chorin, *Die Tafeln des Bundes* (Tübingen, 1979), "Vorwort." On the whole matter see Böckle, *Fundamentaltheologie*, pp. 167-84; Lohfink, *Siegeslied*, pp. 151-73; R. Koch, "Vers une morale de l'Alliance," *Studia Moralia* 6:7-58 (Rome, 1968).

[42] See Comblin, *Friedens*, pp. 84-110; Schwager, *Brauchen wir einen Sündenbock?*, pp. 64-80; H. Frederikson, *Jahwe als Krieger* (Lund, 1945); P. Volz, *Das Dämonische in Jahwe*.

[43] M. Villey, *La croisade: Essai sur la formation d'une théorie juridique* (Paris, 1942), pp. 25-27; Seifart, *Der Gott der politischen Theologie*. See also the whole of Part Two.

[44] Gottwald, *Tribes*, pp. 191-235, 660.

[45] Bright, *Geschichte Israels*, pp. 215-20.

[46] R. Koch, "Die Gotteserfahrung der Propheten," *Studia Moralia* 15:323-44 (Rome, 1977).

[47] Schedl, *Alten Testamentes* 5:386ff.; von Rad, *Alten Testamentes*, the whole second volume.

[48] J. de Fraine, "Judaismus," in Haag, ed., *Bibel-lexikon*, pp. 890-92.

[49] W. Vogels, "Covenant and Universalism," ZMR 57:25-32; Stuhlmueller, *God in the Witness of Israel's Election*.

[50] Petuchowsky, *Melchisedech*, pp. 33ff.

[51] There are further such loci in E. Mveng, "Afrikas Beitrag zum Universalismus in der Bibel und im Koran," in Falaturi, ed., *Drei Wege*, pp. 207-17; M. Greenberg, "Die Menschheit, Israel und die Nationen in hebräischer Überlieferung," in Nelson and Pannenberg, eds., *Um Einheit und Heil der Menschheit*, pp. 23-48; Keel and Küchler, *Synoptische Texte*, pp. 25-27.

[52] H. Gross, "Der Universalitätsanspruch des Reiches Gottes nach dem Alten Testament," in *Kirche und Bible: Restschrift E. Schick* (Paderborn, 1979), pp. 105-19, esp. 108ff.

[53] "The choice of Israel is not an exclusive, but an inclusive one. She is chosen because all are being chosen. . . ." (Moran, *The Present Revelation*, p. 248). Cf. Giblet, *The God of Israel*, pp. 3-22; J. Jeremias, *Jesu Berheissung für die Völker*.

[54] C. Thoma, in Pfammatter and Furger, *Judentum*, p. 108. Cf. J. Neuner, in Hölbock and Sartory, eds., *Mysterium Kirche* 2:830-34.

[55] See Küng's survey of these works in his *Christsein*, pp. 137-57. D. Wiederkehr, "Kontexte der Christologie," in Pfammatter and Furger, eds., *Zugänge zu Jesus*. *Theologische Berichte* 7:11-62 (Zurich, 1978) presents and evaluates the christologies of E. Schillebeeckx, H. Kessler, J.B. Metz, J. Moltmann, H. Küng, K. Rahner, and W. Kasper.

[56] Kümmel, *Theologie des Neuen Testamentes*, pp. 24-35; Schnackenburg, *Gottes Herrschaft*; Nolan, *Jésus avant le christianisme*, pp. 37-46. 63-120.

[57] J. Guhrt, "Bund," *Theologisches Begriffslexikon* (Wupperthal, 1967), 1:159ff.

[58] Wiederkehr, *Glaube an Erlösung*, p. 37.

[59] Further elaborated in Bühlmann, *Wo der Glaube lebt*, 2pp. 166-69, "Kontestation in der Kirche"; (English edition: *The Coming of the Third Church*, St Paul Publications, Slough/Orbis Books, Maryknoll N.Y.).

[60] J. Jeremias, *Abba: Studien zur neutestamentlichen Theologie und Zeitgeschichte*

(Göttingen, 1966); *Die Gleichnisse Jesu*, (Göttingen, 1956); K. Herbst, *Was wollte Jesus selbst? Die vorkirchlichen Jesusworte in den Evangelien* (Düsseldorf, 1979).

[61] M. Hengel, *Nachfolge und Charisma*, pp. 96-99.

[62] Wiederkehr, *Glaube*, pp. 27-38; Nolan, *Jésus*, pp. 123-33; de Surgy, *Recherches*, pp. 187-233.

[63] S.G.F. Brandon, *Jesus and the Zealots* (Manchester, 1967).

[64] Klingler, *Offenbarung*, p. 215; J. Schmid, *Das Evangelium nach Matthäus* (Regensburf, 1959), pp. 390-97, "Der Missionsbefehl des Auferstandenen."

[65] Wiederkehr, *Glaube*, pp. 39-43; Kümmel, *Neuen Testamentes*, pp. 52-76; K. Rahner, "Kirchliche Christologie zwischen Exegese und Dogmatik," *Schriften*, 9: 197-226.

[66] C. Maurer, "Die Einheit der Menschheit in biblischer Sicht", in Nelson and Pannenberg, pp. 49-74, esp. pp. 73-74; H. Schürmann, *Jesu ureigener Tod* (Freiburg, 1975), pp. 56-65; Moltmann, *Der gekreuzigte Gott*, pp. 228ff.; Kümmel, *Neuen Testamentes*, pp. 76-105.

[67] Von Rad, *Alten Testamentes*, p. 348.

[68] Communication from Prof. L. Alvarez Verdes of the Alphonsianum, Rome.

[69] C. Thoma, *Christliche Theologie des Judentums* (Aschaffenburg, 1978).

[70] Von Rad, *Alten Testamentes*, p. 349.

[71] Ibid., pp. 339-412.

[72] Kümmel, *Neuen Testamentes*, pp. 121-226; K.H. Schelkle, "Israel und die Kirche im Neuen Testament," in R. Schnackenburg, ed., *Die Kirche des Anfanges*, pp. 607-14.

[73] See K. Jaros's commentary on the French Bishops' Declaration on the Jewish Question of April 16, 1973, in *Theologische-Praktische Quartalschrift* 123:56-58 (Linz, 1975).

[74] Kümmel, *Alten Testamentes*, pp. 111-21; J. Blinzler, "Judenchristentum," LThK 5:1171-74; Papa, *Tensioni e unità*, pp. 235-40.

[75] K. Kertelge, *Gemeinde und Amt im Neuen Testament* (Munich, 1972); Y. Congar, *Un peuple messianique* (Paris, 1975); Goldstein, *Paulinische Gemeinde*; G. Theissen, *Soziologie der Jesus-Bewegung*; F. Hahn, "Das Problem des Frühkatholizismus," *Evangelische Theologie* 38:340-57; Schmitz, *Frühkatholiizismus*; Schnackenburg, *Gottes Herrschaft*, pp. 181-245; D. van Damme, "Gottesvolk und Gottesreich in der christlichen Antike," in Pfammatter and Furger, eds., *Judentum und Kirche* 157-68; K. Hruby, "Die Trennung von Kirche und Judentum," ibid., 135-56.

[76] *Tensioni e unità*; Jacquemont, *Le temps de la patience*, pp. 60-94; Daniélou, "Das Christentum als missionarische Religion," in Toynbee, *Auf diesem Felsen*, pp. 293-99; Bultmann, *Das Urchristentum*, pp. 191-205, "Das Urchristentum als synkretistisches Phänomen."

[77] H. von Campenhausen, "Die Entstehung der Heilsgeschichte: Der Aufbau des christlichen Geschichtsbildes in der Theologie des 1. und 2. Jahrhunderts," *Saeculum* 21:189-212, esp. 211-12.

Part Two

The Chosen People's Self-Image

A Historical Investigation

Chapter Four

Preliminary Considerations

§1 *The Outward Aspect of the Church*

Nearly two thousand years have gone by since the New Testament people of God started down the road of history. At once the question arises: How has this people looked upon itself through the course of time? How has it lived? Has it kept true to the high ideal to which it was called, or are we about to find still one more instance of history's tragedy — that divine impulses, once in human flesh, become all too "humanized" indeed?

Before we begin, we must emphasize that it is not the *inward* aspect of the church to which we now turn our attention. Volumes have been written on that — on the rich symbolism in our churches and cathedrals, from Romanesque to Gothic to baroque to modern; on the world of theology, from patristic to scholastic to postconciliar; on the saints, from the holy popes, kings, and monks to the many real Christians who have not been canonized and nonetheless are saints because they are holy; and on all the enterprises of education and the works of mercy. All this is already there, standing in history like a monument.

No, what interests us here is the outward aspect of the church — how this church has appeared to others, or how these others (the "unchosen peoples") have experienced the church. Election always implies a relationship to others. Neither the Old Testament people of God nor its New Testament counterpart was chosen for its own sake. Each was chosen as a sign for others. We are inquiring not merely into the fate of the others, but into the church's own understanding of itself.

Let us then make a journey through history with each group of "others" who have been the church's partners in that history. We shall attempt to discern the shape of the church's relationship with each of them in turn.

§2 *Triumphalistic Historiography*

First we must take into account the fact that history sees and judges many things differently since the advent of scientific criticism. Church and state used to practise an expressly triumphalistic historiography. Heroes of bygone days were idealized. Their failings were glossed over, their achievements were gilded and magnified. Compromising documents were suppressed, flattering documents were forged. Everything served the purpose of presenting church and state to posterity as something so great that one owed them unconditional dedication.

It was church history, especially, that pursued this apologetical aim. The divine institution of the church was to be demonstrated from its wonderful expansion, its holiness, and its victories over its enemies. Church history seemed a prolongation of the Old Testament, with wonders heaped upon wonders.

We find a typical example in a work of the Camaldolese Fra Mauro, later Pope Gregory XVI: *The Triumph of the Holy See and of the Church over the Onslaughts of the Moderns*,[1] published in 1799. Everything in the book is geared to repulsing these onslaughts and defeating them. There is never a question as to whether perhaps the church might have something to learn from the "moderns". This would have been an attack on its very essence, "as if the Church could be exposed to any deficiency!" It is only to the wicked world that the call of conversion can be addressed. Nor did Fra Mauro abandon this attitude later, when, as pope, he undertook the struggle against these "modern errors" with *Mirari Vos*, and began to lead the church into its lamentable ghettoization.

Theological justification was found for everything. Even when church expansion was anything but evangelical, when the conditions of that expansion were all too frankly human, a pseudo-sacral superstructure was erected upon it and anyone who objected was suspect of heresy. Disturb the peace and order of that superstructure and you were forthwith expelled for blasphemy.[2]

Today that kind of church falls under suspicion of the manufacture of ideology. It stands accused of seeking to justify situations and attitudes of pure self-interest on seemingly factual and even theological grounds. F. Châtelet and G. Mairet have devoted a two-volume work to the investigation of the whole history of the West from the viewpoint of ideology. Secular and ecclesiastical history alike get their share of bad marks.[3]

Meanwhile we have learned to admit that not everything that occurs in the church is *eo ipso* justifiable. We now allow ourselves to take a critical position on both past and present questions. Free speech reigns in the church.[4]

A historic turn occurred early in the Second Vatican Council when Bishop E. de Smedt spoke on the provisory schema on the church, on

December 1, 1962. De Smedt said that the schema was clericalistic, inappropriately juridical, and thoroughly triumphalistic, and that this was typical of the whole Roman style. That the life of the church should be presented as the triumphal march of the church militant, said de Smedt, was out of step with modern thinking as well as with the gospel. The applause that filled the conciliar hall helped to keep his words from being forgotten.[5]

And surely, not to be able to admit to shortcomings in the church — hence, to reject all criticism — is to be guilty of a kind of monophysitism, as if there were no elements in the church that were not divine. Confession of a fault redounds to the credit of the person at fault and the confession of sins honours Christ as redeemer, even if the sins are those of the head and members of the church.

The position enjoyed by historians in the church has surely changed. During the Modernist era (see §18, below), they were branded as chief among the heretics with their critical questions. Today they enjoy complete liberty. Even when historical facts touch a sensitive spot, no authority objects any longer to their divulgation.

One of the protagonists of this unconditionally honest church historiography was Lord Acton (1834-1902), the first Catholic in England with the title of lord, and a private observer at Vatican Council I.[6] Passionate partisan of the values of liberty, conscience, and truthfulness, he knew that non-Catholics reproached Catholics with being afraid of the truth. One should not react to the accusation emotionally, Acton held, but should throw open the archives, pull out the documents, and tell the whole truth about the church. Christians are not to be exempted from the burden of history. History offers no escape; you must come to terms with it. Lord Acton studied the Inquisition and the flaws of the papacy with consternation; but when all was said and done, as he confided to a friend, he could look back on the whole thing as just a horrible nightmare, from which he could awaken with sunshine and peace in his soul.

§3 *A Theological or Nontheological Discipline?*

But to undertake not only to present the church's attitude toward other historical groups factually, but to judge it from a modern (dare we say evangelical?) standpoint as well, may well seem to the academic historian something of a heresy. Since the turn of the century there has been an attempt to incorporate church history into profane history, and minds are still divided on whether church history is a theological or nontheological discipline.[7]

Conzemius, Küpisch, and Kohler, for example, plead the empirical and profane character of church history. The historian's task, they hold, is to establish the genesis of the facts, to understand the intention of human beings. All other judgments are, "from our point of view", clerical arrogance. Is ours, after all, the fullness of insight? Will historians a hundred years hence not have to pass judgment on the views we hold today? If we consistently take the gospel as church history's final standard, does this not

> open the door to all manner of frivolous moralizing? Now we can pillory Christians' failure in history. Now we can take the trendy stance of the one who tells all, and reveal their treachery . . . A self-consciousness tantamount to masochism sharpens its quill. The better judges here will be historians not involved with the church, or indifferent to it, because they will have no need of expending so much of their energy in an effort to divorce themselves from their past. Peter's cock must surely have crowed itself to death long since over the misery of Christendom, for it is simply a joke how far from Jesus' program for living are its weak implementations — we may as well say it, the caricatures, disguises, and distortions which refer to his followers.[8]

None of that is supposed to be any business of the historian. The moral pathos of the judge too easily stifles the ethos of the researcher.

Others — Jedin, Grotz, Kempf, for instance — hold that although church history is a part of historical science in its methodology, in its subject and its ultimate viewpoint it is part of theology. Purely profane methods will never sound the deepest essence of the church. From its foundation to the *parousia* — hence, in all its history — the church is an object of faith. It is therefore legitimate to do one's thinking and judging on two different planes, the historical and the metahistorical or theological. Thus for example one can extract the positive side of the Crusades as the expression of a deep piety, and still say that these campaigns were contrary to the core of the gospel.

In the interests of the church, which is always involved in a process of learning and theological growth, I choose the second of these positions. Besides, church history as a purely objective discipline awakens little interest today. It means little to learn facts in isolation. But learning from the facts to respond better to the gospel can have a stimulating effect on committed Christians. In contrast with the historian who strives to interpret, and thereby to comprehend, all the affairs of his or her "clients", even any misconduct on the part of the church, in their inner causes and outward connections, in conformity with the purpose of this book I place myself on the side of the others — who have been touched by this misconduct, who have suffered under it, and hence become its quiet or loud accusers. This taking of sides in favour of the weak and suffering can surely not be called unevangelical or unecclesial, even if it does not always do the church great honour.

§4 The Kingdom of Christendom

Before we focus on the church's encounter with its historical partners, we must consider a certain form this church took without which much else would be unintelligible. The church did not always remain the vital community it was in its beginning. Having christianized the Roman Empire from within, having become a state religion, having received privileges and lands, the Jesus-movement (and the following assertions are intended only positively, not exclusively) became an institution. The open city placed on a mountain (Matt. 5:14) became a fortress, with walls and moats. The bark of Peter sailing on the high seas became Peter's rock-hard shore, where waves smashed to foam. The church in mystery became a church in empire, became the kingdom of christendom.[9]

The notion of covenant and of people of God, which had receded into the background even in the preaching of Jesus (see Part One, §§28, 31), all but disappeared in the church fathers, owing to the opening up of the church to all peoples. But it came back upstage as the church identified with the world of the Germanic peoples and their feudal system.

Charlemagne saw himself as the new David, and had his throne in Aachen modelled after the throne of Solomon. The little flock had become a great church, and a Christian empire. It used civil structures for its own ends. The two summit leaders of Christendom, the pope and the emperor, took up the two-edged sword, the spiritual and the secular, respectively. But it was the prerogative of the pope to crown emperors and kings ("by God's grace") — or depose them. By the eleventh century the papacy was in clear ascendancy over the empire. The eschatological hope that was the sign and power of the church when it was young retreated, in favour of the kingdom of God anticipated on earth.

Whoever lived within this empire must accord it fealty without reserve. Whoever dared murmur against the Catholic faith was considered the enemy of the empire, and was dealt with accordingly. Beyond the empire's visible frontiers was but barbarism and the realm of Satan — hence, no tolerance, no compromise, only conflict. Proclaiming salvation meant spreading the empire and incorporating all others into the empire and the church. True, not everyone approved everything that occurred within state and church, and a cry for reform echoes down through the medieval centuries. But when it came to defending Christendom, there was no dissent. Everyone stood like a wall, protecting it by every means.

Today one can well characterize this confounding of church and state as corruption, as a deviation from the gospel idea. But one can also point to the grandeur and solidarity of this medieval polity, where, under papal leadership, kingdom and priesthood became the visible expression of the people of God. Of course, there were certain disadvantageous consequences for those who stood without. But from the positive viewpoint the Middle Ages represent a stage of the church's development that, understood in the context of its own time, one can only marvel at. Above all:

Alongside this imperial image of the Church one may not overlook that other aspect, standing with, in, and under it, and gathering ever greater and greater momentum: the image of the poor, servant church, which sees its reflection in the human Jesus, in the passion and cross, and grasps anew at the spirit of martyrdom. Above and beyond the image of the church without blemish or wrinkle is the image of the church of the saints, the church that lives hidden in the hearts of human beings, in their piety, their prayer, their self-effacement. And all the while it is taking a critical distance from the concrete church of its time, and storing up thrust and strength for its renewal.[10]

Thus it is not only the inward and outward aspects of the church that can be distinguished. Within the former there are two different faces, hence two different series of judgments. Militant laicists see the medieval epochs as a brutish state of obscurantism. Christians see them as somehow the expression of the deep faith of a people. Both are right.

Chapter Five

The Church's Associates in History

The Jews

§5 *Early Centuries*

The Jews were the church's first partner. The church itself is the outgrowth of Judaism, and Paul developed a powerful theology of its relationship to the Jews, to which he kept true even after his people had delivered him to the Romans. Arrived in Rome, he called the leading men of the Jewish community together to tell them: "I am here on account of Israel's hope!" (Acts 28:16ff).

This is the attitude that first prevailed in the earliest centuries. Christian communities evince the influence of Jewish thought over a rather long period of time.[11] Of course it is impossible to ignore the tension between the two communities. This tension is expressed, and probably exaggerated, in the gospels, which were written between A.D. 80 and 100, in the recorded disputes between Jesus and the representatives of the synagogue (e.g., John 5:18; 7:1, 32; 8:30-59).[12]

Then, as the mission to the Jews enjoyed little actual success, the theology — no, the ideology — of reprobation was developed: the obduracy of the Jews had resulted from their rejection of the Messiah. To boot, the Jews were now no longer of any theological importance; it was the church that was the true Israel now. And, to draw out this line of thinking still further, inasmuch as God himself had rejected them, Christians too could scorn them, and should. A rich literature *Adversus Judaeos* sprang up ("Against the Jews"). According to Augustine they should not be killed, in spite of their misdeeds, for this people must wander through the world as "witnesses of their transgression and of our truth". And so there arose the legend of the wandering Jew.[13]

§6 *Middle Ages*

The Middle Ages developed the same thinking even further. Now the Jews "must" remain obdurate, to the end of time. All of them were guilty of "deicide". True, the synagogue was portrayed on the portals of the Gothic cathedrals as a noble lady; but she was blindfold, and held a broken lance, to show that this people had failed its calling, and in its stubbornness had called down upon itself and its children the blood of the Messiah (Matt. 27:25).[14]

This theology justified the means employed by the secular arm. Jews were excluded from public office, prohibited from employing Christians as domestic servants, and, beginning in the late Middle Ages, required to live in walled ghettos. In the context of the Crusades it came to out-and-out persecution. Before one freed the Holy Land it was thought in place to eliminate "Christ's enemies" from one's own land. Greed was abundantly present as an ulterior motive — one could plunder their houses and shops in good conscience.

From the thirteenth century onward the pogroms grew to terrible proportions, as Jews were accused of sacrificing Christian children in their rites, desecrating hosts, and poisoning wells. Outbreaks of mass hysteria resulted. In the fifteenth century the Jews were almost eradicated from the Rhineland and from many cities in the south of Germany.

In Rome cruelty to Jews was carnival entertainment. To be sure, bishops and popes repeatedly took Jews under their protection, but they never called into question the principle of the discrimination itself.

Surely there were times of more peaceful Judaeo-Christian coexistence, but Hans Küng is not mistaken when he says, concerning the church and the Jews, that "the church in this age killed a good many more martyrs than it produced from its own ranks".[15] And H. Kühner:

> Never have so many hated so few so long and so groundlessly. This is the sorrowful side of church history. No less than ninety-two general and provincial councils passed laws against Jews between the fourth and the sixteenth centuries. Israel was stripped naked, and deprived of its inheritance.[16]

It must be added that the Reformation changed nothing here. For his part, Martin Luther wrote a very caustic work *Against the Jews and their Lies*. Expositions of the faith worked out by Catholic theologians and preachers were just as bad. They were pugnacious harangues; their solitary purpose was to triumph over the Jews, not to try to understand and win them over.

For their part the Jews continued to consider themselves as they had before, in spite of all they were made to suffer. They were the authentic proprietors of the biblical covenant and the divine revelation. Their conviction that it was they who were the chosen people was sharpened to the point of readiness for martyrdom. Their experience of exile of old helped them bear up under this new exilic situation as well, and to give it a religious significance.

Today one can only stand in awe of their deep faith. The few who for one reason or another passed over to Christianity were considered by the others as apostates, or simply as unbelievers. And so the Jewish-Christian relationship remained always the same: we did not understand them, and they did not understand us.[17]

We shall soon have to repeat, for the other partners of the church in history, what we have had to say in this first case. It is tragic that it was not out of any religious insight, but only later, through the secularism of the Enlightenment, that persons would gradually come to dismantle their religious fanaticism and acknowledge their common ground in a .single humanity.

§7 Modern Times

In modern times we have experienced the ultimate and most repulsive paroxysms of anti-Semitism, together with its universal denunciation.

It will not be necessary to review here the catastrophic events under Nazism in Dachau and Auschwitz, as well as in hundreds of cities and villages. The cruelty to the Jews in their last agony is beyond comprehension. The film *Holocaust* has recalled it to memory.

Christians will never be able to find an alibi for what was perpetrated on Jews for centuries on the basis of an appeal to the gospel. The leaders of the Third Reich actually based their procedures on an appeal to Christian practice, even though their own ideology of course rested on altogether different grounds. T. Fritsch's *Handbook of the Jewish Problem*, which saw its forty-fifth edition in 1939, adduced judgments and statements from Catholic and Protestant churches. The highest official of the "final solution", Julius Streicher, attempted to justify his actions before the Nuremberg court with the theological authority of Martin Luther. Today we shamefully confess that "at the time, the church offered amazingly little official protest against the persecutions of the Jews" (Cardinal J. Höffner).[18]

After the war we awoke as if from a delirium. One could not believe what had happened to the Jews. The World Council of Churches, convening in its plenary meeting in Amsterdam in 1948, confessed, "The churches, in times past, have cooperated in allowing an image of the Jews to be built up as the one and only enemy of Christ, thus furthering anti-Semitism in the secular world . . . Anti-Semitism is a sin against God and against humanity". And still a real dialogue with the Jews was years in coming. Since 1962, however, there have been official contacts between Jewish organizations and the World Council.[19]

At the same time, the prophetic pope, John XXIII, saw that the enmity between Christians and Jews was overdue for burial. He caused the Good Friday prayer *Pro Perfidis Judaeis* ("For the Faithless Jews") to be struck from the Roman Ritual, and initiated the thrust that has led to a total revision of the question of the Jews. His express wish was that the council would take up this theme. But the first draft of a decree proved to be "too friendly to the Jews", and was withdrawn under pressure from Arab countries. Then a way had to be found between Scylla and Charybdis. What was finally approved was very tame, and the Jews were disappointed in all their expectations. It is true that Article 4 of *Nostra Aetate* sketches a positive theology of the relationship between the church and Judaism. And for the future, Catholics are forbidden to speak of the Jews, in catechesis or preaching, as rejected by God. But for the past, the council lukewarmly "lamented" all outbreaks of hate, persecutions, and manifestations of anti-Semitism directed against the Jews by anyone at any time. How easily we bought our way out of this monstrous guilt! How quickly we allowed the grass to grow over the paths of history! The 1975 Guidelines for the Christian-Jewish Dialogue have in some measure compensated for the weaknesses of the conciliar decree.

§8 *The Future*

What can we say about prospects for the future? The churches of Geneva and Rome each have their own work groups for dialogue with the Jews. On October 22, 1974, Pope Paul VI established the Commission for Religious Relations with Judaism and placed it under the Secretariat for Christian Unity. The task of this commission is one of education, giving bishops' conferences encouragement and aids for dialogue.

On the directly ecumenical level, the International Committee for Communication was established for the purpose of organizing a dialogue between the Roman commission and the International Jewish Committee for Interreligious Consultations. Just as among the Christian churches, so also between Christians and Jews a joint effort is under way toward a better understanding and interpretation of Holy Scripture in the context of its own times. Many Jewish scholars are beginning to see Jesus in a new light, and Christians can no longer properly study Jesus without being familiar with the pertinent Jewish literature.[20]

Many local churches have seized the initiative as well, bringing Jews and Christians nearer to one another, or at least working toward mutual understanding. South Africa has a movement fostering the "Jewish identity" of persons who wish to pass to the Christian faith without having to enter the structure of an existing "gentile church". It is hoped that such persons will be able largely to retain their Jewish traditions, as did the "Jewish church" of nearly two thousand years ago (see Part One, §§37, 38), crowning those traditions with faith in Christ and with the sacraments. We are but on the threshold of a new development, which bids fair to be a very desirable one.

72

Of course there are abundant voices warning us not to be too euphoric, and interpreting the new attitude of the church as a simple reaction of fear. The church, it is said, speaks at the moment out of tolerance tactics, because it needs tolerance for itself in Marxist and other countries. As long as the "Christian era" was on solid footing, we are reminded, other religions were oppressed by every means. Only now, in the "post-Christian era," as the church finds itself living in more and more of a minority situation, one begins to hear of religious freedom and dialogue. Jews are warned not to be too ready to forget history, but to see and evaluate the new Christian attitude in its true, opportunist, context.[21]

Mighty Christendom's collapse turns out to have been a salutary event. Positions of strength are never a good point of departure for dialogue. But the same holds true for Israel. Jews, too, will have to redimension their consciousness of election and superiority — as one of the most important of today's Jewish theologians, Rabbi Petuchowski of the United States, says very well:

> I mean, salvation history, and human or world history, are interconnected. I mean further, there will be no redeemed People of Israel and no redeemed land of Israel without a redeemed humanity. There are no redeemed enclaves within an unredeemed world.[22]

This reflection points straight down the path we take throughout this entire book.

The Heretics

§9 *Sacred Scripture*

Life is grand and beautiful, but it is also full of tensions. It begins in the pangs of birth, develops in the maturity crisis, and ends in death spasms. Communities of human beings, too, are as a general rule characterized by tensions. When two human beings bash their heads together, or two peoples make war on each other, we shudder and wish there were no such thing.

Not even the church escaped this fate. It was not only with its partners on the outside that it had to reckon in the course of history. Within its own community, as well, splinter groups, called heresies, formed, and threatened or destroyed its unity. There are interesting bits of information about this phenomenon as early as the days of Sacred Scriptures.[23] The Christian communities themselves were looked upon as sects and heresies by the Jews (Part One, §37). On the other hand, the particular quality of those communities' faith — their conviction that it was nothing less than the word of God that they had to safeguard and proclaim — prevented them from speaking about it calmly, factually, scientifically. They could only speak with conviction, emotion — and in no case was any disagreement or murmuring permitted. "Whoever believes and is baptized will be saved, whoever does not believe will be damned" (Mark 16:16).

This formulation may not have been actually spoken by Jesus. What characterized Jesus' proclamation was the justification of sinners, not their damnation.[24] But it does clearly express the spiritual attitude of the Christians of that time. The same conception penetrates the synoptic, the Johannine, and the Pauline traditions.

Speaking of Paul, the pitched battle he waged against every kind of heresy demonstrates that even in those days Christian communities enjoyed no simple and uninterrupted peace, but felt threatened, insecure, and torn. Paul thinks this is unavoidable. But he also sees it as a test: "After all, there have to be divisions [*haireseis*] among you, so that it may become evident who it is among you that are trustworthy" (1 Cor. 11:19).

He warns his community in advance to be courageous in the face of these divisions: "In later times many will fall away from the faith, and turn to deceitful spirits and demons' teachings" (1 Tim. 4:1). He advises them "not to let yourselves be drawn into disputes about words. This does no one any good. It only harms those who overhear you" (2 Tim. 2:14). He does not refrain from calling such seducers of the communities "devils, godless, homicides, perjured, dogs, damned", and attributes to them every moral defect possible (1 Tim. 1:6;10, 20; 4:1ff.; 2 Tim. 1:16-18, 26; 3:1-9; Titus 1:10-16; 3:9-11; Phil. 3:2; Gal. 1:8).

Paul thinks he sees, in this tension and opposition, the last act of the apocalyptic drama, the last desperate assault of the Antichrist before the Lord Jesus definitively annihilates him (2 Thess. 2:8).

Hard words! And the consigners of heretics to eternal flames will be appealing to these words for endorsement throughout the coming history of the church.

Of course we must know that this heresy polemic was customary in all camps in those times. What is important is whether such discourse is good or bad for the matter at hand and the persons involved. What does the history of heresy say to that?

§10 *Nestorianism*

In the first three centuries, staunch as the New Testament people of God stood against persecutions from without, there was no lack of tensions within, including heresies (gnostics, Donatists). But these turned out to be temporary divisions. Then, as Christianity became the state religion, and thereby established and secure from without, disputes arose inside Christianity over the trinitarian and christological formulas, and these usually ended in schism instead of reconciliation.

The councils that were held on the occasion of these difficulties entered history as general, or ecumenical, councils, and were adopted by all the churches as second in authority only to Scripture as the basis of the faith.

On closer examination, these ecumenical councils can be seen to be church synods that were almost entirely Eastern. They were composed as follows:

(1) Nicea I (A.D. 325): 318 Eastern, 3 Western bishops
(2) Constantinople I (A.D. 381): 150 Eastern bishops
(3) Chalcedon (A.D. 451): 600 Eastern, 5 Western, 2 African bishops

Translated into modern concepts, it was as if a vital regional church, Latin America for instance, numbering half the world's Catholic population, were to hold a council, and afterwards this council were approved by the pope and accepted by all the other churches. What life and movement that would bring into the church universal!

We shall take up here only one instance from that period of struggles over the faith — that of Nestorianism. Nestorianism has a special importance as the first schism in the church that lasted up to our own day.[25] Two great archbishops of those days, Nestorius of Constantinople and Cyril of Alexandria, rose up against each other in a fierce exchange of correspondence, while clerics of each of the two cities complained to the archbishop of the other city about the unorthodoxy or bad conduct of their own archbishop. Pope Celestine I attempted to effect a reconciliation but failed. And so a synod was convoked at Ephesus for Pentecost 431.

Ephesus decided against Nestorius. He was accused of not accepting the "hypostatic union" — that is, he was accused of holding that divinity and humanity in Jesus Christ exist as separate entities, so that Mary could only be called "Mother of Christ" and not "Mother of God". Nestorius was condemned and banished. He died in exile in 451.

The friends of Nestorius were unwilling to submit to this decision. There were political motives, too. And so the Nestorian Church came into being which later produced a vital monasticism, and carried on a brisk missionary activity in Arabia, India, and even China. In later centuries several groups of Nestorians united with Rome. The church not in union with Rome numbers some one hundred thousand members today.

For fifteen hundred years the case was left precisely there. But as the prototype of heresies, Nestorianism has received renewed attention during the last fifty years. It has recently been asserted that the Council of Ephesus was right to condemn the doctrine it condemned — but the doctrine it condemned was not that of Nestorius. In other words, Nestorius was not a Nestorian, and herein lies the tragedy of this prototype.

A. Grillmeier has made of it a kind of case study in heresiology, and this is his conclusion: persons of that time were not in a position to approach a fundamentally inexpressible mystery from two opposite sides in the consciousness that both sides belong together, that only *together* could each side escape the imputation of one-sidedness. Instead, each absolutized its own view, and made its partner an opponent. Cyril and Nestorius should have combined their knowledge, with the humble realization that the contribution of each could be only a fragment of the whole mystery of God. Then they could have set them into the whole like complementary stones in a mosaic.

We must also take into consideration the fact that clerics in those times were not yet well enough versed in theological language to be able to express themselves unambiguously, and so they talked *past* each other. Hence it was unjust of the Council of Ephesus to brand Nestorius a heretic. The first heresy was manufactured, when it could have been avoided. Coreligionists split along the lines that seemed to divide them, instead of fraternizing in what actually united them.

This is a new insight, the fruit of modern critical historical research. Unfortunately, it is of no help in undoing the repetition of the structural faults of this Nestorian prototype in so many other cases throughout history.

§11 *Anathema Sit*

It was at this same time — in its synods and councils — that the church began not only to declare certain doctrines false, erroneous, and heretical, but, based on Galatians 1:9, to impose upon those who espoused them the solemn curse, *anathema sit*. As late as Vatican Council I, twenty-one anathemas were dealt out.[26] Practically speaking, it meant excommunication — exclusion from the sacraments and from the life of the church, with the additional recommendation that the person be "damned".

It would not be right to ignore the great care for *koinonia* — community, union — that is at the source of this condemnation. After all, one who abandons correct teaching places themself outside the church even without any condemnation. Nevertheless one feels rather ill at ease with the frequency and readiness with which this evil wish was uttered.

Simone Weil wrote in 1942 that because of these two words, *anathema sit*, she could not cross the threshold of the church, but preferred to remain in solidarity with those others who, because of these same two words, would also stand before the church door. The daughter of a Jewish physician in Paris, she was deeply committed to the relief of human needs, especially that of uprooted men and women. She relinquished her position as professor of philosophy and took a job as a mill worker at Renauld: she wanted to stand on the lowest rung of the social ladder, at one with all who were poor and deprived of their rights.

In a church in Assisi she was cast to her knees by a higher power and she surprised herself by praying. She began to read the New Testament, and was deeply affected by it. Interiorly, she was altogether captivated by Christ, but at the same time she felt a strong repugnance for the empirical church. She was convinced that God also endorsed the good there was outside the church, otherwise it would not be there. A church that said *anathema sit* betrayed a totalitarianism that could not be from God.

And so Simone preferred to remain in the courtyard of the church, with the great host of the expelled, and in this way profess that the divine is not bound to the institution. In spite of her ecclesial homelessness she lived a life of deep mysticism. She died in the summer of 1943, only thirty-three years old. Since then she has exercised a great influence upon French intellectual circles. She is a representative of a new type of sainthood — for if we could not suppose that there are saints among "outsiders", the world would be very poor in saints today![27]

Only against the background of the fifteen-hundred-year history of the anathema is it possible to appreciate Pope John XXIII's intuition and inspiration in refusing to set before Vatican II the task of discussing dogmatic formulas and condemning erroneous doctrines. Instead he directed it to renew the church, to show the world a new face, to offer human understanding and pastoral assistance to those gone astray. He expressed this in various addresses, especially in his opening speech to the council, which drew so much attention.

He explained the reason for this new approach. The history of the councils was a glorious one, but a cloud of bitterness and pain accompanied it through the centuries. The church had the obligation to pass on the teaching it had received — but not as a lifeless treasure. The teaching had to be presented in such a way that it really addressed the problems and lifestyles of today's world. These teachings are not something to have disputes over, but something to be carried joyously to the world.

The first task of the magisterium is pastoral. In former times, the church condemned errors, and with all severity. Now, it prefers to apply the balm of mercy instead of reaching for the weapons of harshness. It would rather simply lay out its teaching, in all its mighty brilliance, than fight off errors. Errors will condemn themselves, by the fruits they bear. With the council, a bright new day is breaking on the church, and we already see its rose-tinted dawning.[28] The world has drawn a deep breath. A new day, a new spring!

But we have not yet reached this point in our study; we are still deep in the Middle Ages, an era replete with real or supposed heretical movements.[29] This was the name applied to those who held what the church considered to be errors of faith, whether they were individuals or groups (sects). The heretics were always distinguished from the unbelievers, the infidels — that is, the Jews and the pagans — who aroused less concern because they stood on the outside. Best known of the pre-Reformation heretics were the Waldenses, the Albigenses, and the Hussites.

Desperately the church defended itself against this constantly looming danger. Here was something against which one could not be too much on one's guard. And so one studied the catalogues of the heresies, found each on the chart, and sought with the help of the state to convert or eliminate the guilty. One appealed to the church fathers, especially Augustine, who thought that Jesus' words, "Make them come in" (Luke 14:23), justified and abetted the tormenting of heretics. It is a pity that the "Doctor of Grace" could have gone so far astray on this point.

Various popes took various positions. Alexander III, more on the lenient side, followed the principle that it was better to free the guilty than to punish the innocent. But his successor, Lucius III, took a much more energentic stance and made it the duty of bishops to examine the faith of their subjects by means of an oath. Whoever refused the oath should forthwith be deemed a heretic. All such procedures are given the name "inquisition", a word that has retained its connotation of cruelty down to our own day.[30]

From the end of the twelfth century onward, what was prescribed for the purpose of safeguarding the purity of faith was no longer mere excommunication, but trial by fire, banishment, torture, imprisonment, confiscation of property, the cutting out of the tongue, hanging, and burning alive. The church decided cases in its own tribunals, over which Gregory IX had principally placed the Dominicans in charge in 1232, and handed over the guilty to the secular arm with the plea that their lives be spared. (Of course the plea was a pure formality, and anyone who hesitated to execute the death penalty would himself come immediately under indictment of heresy.) The denunciation of suspected heretics was declared to be of the strictest obligation in faith, and heretics' profession of that faith was often elicited by torture.

It is true that practice varied from place to place and from time to time, so that we should not generalize. Not a few bishops eschewed every form of torture. But the masses were hardened to it by now, full of faith and eagerness for a spectacle, and not infrequently sang "Holy God, We Praise Thy Name" while the flames sprang up around the heretic. It is said that the Inquisition sacrificed as many as ten million human beings.[31] This is a gross exaggeration. But there is no exaggerating the cruelty of the institution, nor any justifying it, nor even any glossing over it. The only explanation is the grossly misled spirit of the times. The real heretics, the real traitors to the gospel, were those who conducted the affair!

By way of a particular example, let us take a well-known one, that of Joan of Arc (1412-1431). Inspired by inner voices, this girl demanded a political role, for she wished to liberate the North of France from English occupation. And she succeeded. But then she was taken prisoner and, unmistakably for political reasons, brought before a tribunal under indictment of heresy. Admission of false teachings were wrung from her. She immediately recanted them, and so was treated not only as a heretic but as a recidivist. What happened to her next is recorded in the official document:

> Wherefore We, Peter, by God's mercy Bishop of Beauvais, and Brother John le Maistre, Substitute, for this trial, of the Illustrious Doctor John Graverent, Inquisitor for Heretical Deviancy, do declare You, Joan, generally called "The Maid", an apostate, idolatress, and cultist of Satan.
>
> But as the Church never closes her bosom against one who returns, We believed that You had truly turned from Your errors and offences, as You did on that day recant them publicly and did vow not to fail in Your resolution. Nevertheless, driven by the father of all apostasy and heresy, who has stormed Your heart to lead it astray (alas!), You have returned to them as a dog returns to its vomit: Instead of recanting in upright and orthodox conviction, it was in the hypocrisy of Your heart and in words alone that You recanted your mendacious inventions, as is demonstrated on grounds of most clear evidence.
>
> Thus have We declared You to have fallen anew under the excommunication with which you had laden Yourself, through recidivism into Your former errors and heresy. With this judgment which We have to pronounce upon you, We hereby proclaim that You are expelled from the unity of the Church as a limb afire, and ripped away from her Body lest You infect the other members, and that You are hereby delivered over to the secular arm. We beg the secular justice to moderate its sentence upon You and not kill You or mutilate Your members. And if a sign of true remorse becomes evident in You, the Sacrament of Penance is to be administered to You.
>
> Conformity with the original certified by G. Boisguillaume, G. Manchon, N. Taquel, Notaries.

Immediately after the reading of this document the condemned girl was delivered to the executioner. She mounted to the stake and was burned alive.

Unlike what happened in most cases, this was not the end of the affair. As early as 1449, Charles VII ordered a review of Joan's trial and her innocence came to light. She was canonized on May 16, 1920, and a milestone was reached in the history of heresy: freedom of conscience. Before we address ourselves to this new aspect, we should note that even the Reformers practised the principle of a single religion for every state, and sometimes even reinforced it, especially in Calvinism. Only in humanist and mystical circles was freedom of conscience always taken seriously.[32]

§13 Vindication of Heretics

For years now, research has gone on, investigating the history of heresy systematically and *sine ira et studio* — without hostility or prejudice — not only to bring the real facts to light, but also and especially to illuminate the background of the whole phenomenon. Above all, the accused have had the posthumous opportunity to speak for themselves, the better to explain their intentions. The result is almost necessarily the vindication of the heretics.[33]

Until recently, only polemical literature was written on heretics, and it was always against them. Their own writings were practically unknown or unstudied. A disinterested presentation of the history of heresy was simply not possible for the Middle Ages. Only since the eighteenth century has history gradually begun to be investigated factually instead of ideologically.

Today the prevalent view is that, with certain exceptions, there were no heretics in the Middle Ages who did not wish to be Christians with all their heart. Indeed they explicitly claimed to be good and true Christians, and appealed to the Bible in evidence of it — even though some of them drew erroneous conclusions from the Bible — for example, in the matter of predestination or of dualism. But in many cases their teaching was misinterpreted by others. Thus, for instance, John Hus, burned to death in 1415 by order of the Council of Constance, has been largely reinstated today.

Others simply wanted to live according to the gospel in poverty and dedication, perhaps in community. We are immediately reminded of today's ecclesial *comunidades de base*, the grassroots communities. It was precisely in this evangelical lifestyle of theirs that certain "heretics" were a thorn in the flesh of the rich and mighty church, which therefore could not leave them alone.

A happy exception was Francis of Assisi, whose simplicity and devotion to the church won grace and acceptance with the mighty Innocent III. His Franciscan brothers and sisters in France and Germany, however, were often accused of being heretics. We must not forget that Innocent was the same pope who not only excommunicated the Albigenses but convoked a full-fledged Crusade against them, devastating southern France for twenty years.

80

The way and manner in which Francis was able to renew the church *from within* stands as a model for all times. Without protest, and simply by the witness of his life, he called the wealth of the church into question by his own poverty, its narrowness by his acknowledgement of all as sisters and brothers, and its juridicism by his evangelical orientation.

A specialist in his life and times, A. Rotzetter, thinks we can draw the following conclusions for our own times, for we too are caught in an acute tension between the evangelical and the ecclesiastical, with more and more men and women appealing to the gospel but expecting to have to get along without the institutional church:

(1) We should give credible expression in our lives to the compatibility of a lifestyle according to the gospel and a devotion to the church, and should work out a theology of this relationship. We should strengthen ties with today's charismatic movements, without underplaying the importance of their relationship with the church.

(2) We must always be critical of the church, but the best way is through our own lifestyle — a "living critique".

(3) A verbal critique may also be necessary — but never by threats, and always in the love of brothers and sisters.

(4) This last conclusion is especially important with regard to the papal office — without, however, any affectation of a "cult of the pope".[34]

We are not suggesting that other "reformers" who, unlike Francis, failed to find acceptance and were expelled as heretics, had nothing to contribute. The bare fact that in spite of the risk of ending at the stake there were always "heretics" appears to say that this is a phenomenon that is rooted in the very life of the church itself. The evangelical ferment in the church has never died out and never will. Hence today we seek to do better justice to the aspirations of the "heretics" of old. Their history used to be written only by their mighty conquerors, and of course triumphalistically. But another picture emerges when we consider the situation from the viewpoint of the vanquished, and of their honest intentions. Now church and heretic no longer stand in simple antithesis, but as each other's necessary complement. They belong together, and much more than either is willing to admit.

As a rule, heresies have arisen partly through the fault of the church — out of neglect of certain truths and values within the church. Heretics function as alarms. They should occasion self-criticism on the part of the church, and from this self-criticism the forces of renewal should then proceed. Victory over "heretics" cannot simply be equated with victory over false doctrine. Very often it was the vanquished who later turned out to be right, and they became the forerunners of new ideas.[35]

A special instance, and the climax, of the conflict with the "heretics" was the Reformation — that passionate attempt to renew the church from within, which then unhappily led to the division of the church. It is not the history of the conflict that we wish to present here, but only the way and manner in which it occurred.[36]

Anyone in the church with his or her eyes open could see that a reform had to come — a reform in head and members. The Catholic expert on the Reformation, J. Lortz, acknowledges that conditions looked so desperate that a revolt in the church was to be expected. He speaks of the "dangerous necessity of turning the church inside out" — a church "that surely would have declared primitive and ancient Christianity anti-Christian."[37] The Reformers would today be called "committed Christians", who suffered under those conditions, and wished to see the church more evangelical — wished to cleanse its structure, its theology, its discipline, of their scandalous elements.

Instead of taking those legitimate aspirations seriously, Rome reacted in self-righteous self-defence, repulsing the "attacks" on the curial system. Various papal bulls shored up the traditional teaching on the primacy of Peter, indulgences, purgatory, and so on, with an unbiblical scholastic theology, condemning a series of propositions of Luther that had been excerpted more or less at random from various sources, and that more often than not had nothing essentially to do with the matter at issue. The actual intentions of the reformer were altogether ignored. In our own times the Protestant dogmatic historian P. Lohse has written that the officials in Rome, and later in Trent, totally failed to grasp Martin Luther's intentions.[38]

Nor was the vehement reaction confined to Rome. Battle was joined in Germany too, with the famous disputations and polemical writings of Dr. Eck, Johannes Cochlaeus, and Thomas Murner, in which the purpose was not to make peace with the adversary but to overcome him. Even saints, such as Robert Bellarmine ·and Lawrence of Brindisi, sought to demonstrate the falsity of the new teachers' doctrine, and heaped expressions such as "apostates, whoresons, devils's spawn" upon their heads. Any admission of one's own fault was disastrously lacking.

The humble mystic Thomas of Olera (1563-1631) constitutes something of an exception. Not that his tractate *Against the Heretics* shows the heresiarchs themselves any quarter. But Thomas considers their followers to be but innocent sheep led astray, and he addresses them as his "heretical brothers".[39]

And of course the other side was no less discourteous, repaying in kind. Martin Luther gave the good example, in his *Against Jack Sausage*, for instance, or his *Sermon to an Army about to Do Battle with the Turks*, which abound in vulgarisms. Luther sees the Turks as the

Antichrist storming into Christendom from without and the pope as the Antichrist raging about in the interior of Christendom who, with his curia, worse than Sodom and Gomorrah, calls down upon the church the wrath of God. One can only say, in slight exoneration of both sides, that coarse talk like that, and the annihilation of one's opponent at all cost and by every means, belonged to the style and tone of the time and afforded pleasure to devotees in both camps.

Internally, the Council of Trent initiated a great renewal. But vis-à-vis the Protestants it became mired down in a typical Roman "counter-reform". Whatever the reformers questioned was forthwith flaunted. Once more the day was saved and the enemy vanquished, it was thought.

One of the expressions of this feeling was the baroque style. The Catholic Church was frequently represented as a woman riding her triumphal chariot forth to victory, with the false teachers raging impotently beneath the wheels, or brandishing her sword over serpents and heretics writhing at her feet. Her victory is represented as the victory of God, and as proof clearer than day that the church has the truth. The legitimate aspirations of the reformers — the acknowledgment of the dignity of the people of God vis-à-vis the hierarchy, Holy Scripture vis-à-vis scholastic theology, the vernacular vis-à-vis Latin — were won only in the Second Vatican Council, four hundred and fifty years late.

§15 *The Catholic Image of Luther*

It will be instructive to concretize the attitudes we have been portraying by examining the Catholic image of Luther.[40] Even in ecclesiastical documents, sixteenth-century Catholic polemicists unhesitatingly referred to Martin Luther as "a scoundrel, a dog, Satan, a beast, a hopeless alcoholic drunk every day, the enemy of all chastity who leads the life of a swine, the worst filth hell ever expelled. . . "

Beginning in the seventeenth century, the tone moderated. Toward the end of the nineteenth century, Catholics even endeavoured to construct a new interpretation of Luther, but their efforts suffered a heavy blow in the two famous standard works of H. S. Denifle and Hartmann Grisar, which set the tone for fifty years to come. One could have hoped for something creatively new from a scholar as familiar with the sources as was Denifle, and yet the character, teaching, and writing of Luther remained completely closed off to him. He exhumes the old caricature, with its hedonism and haughtiness, its thirst for power and its hypocrisy. His polemical attitude toward the reformer blinds him completely to the value of this man so important for world history.

Grisar dissociates himself from Denifle's loutish tone, but sees his main task just as Denifle had — to do battle with Luther, to annihilate him, to be done with him once and for all. Only instead of taking a moral tack he takes a psychological one. For Grisar, Luther is a psychopath and that explains everything. Pius X, in his Encyclical *Editae Saepe*, on the occasion of the canonization of St. Charles Borromeo, May 26, 1910, tendered Denifle his official attestation. Grisar's English and Italian editions were warmly welcomed in the *Osservatore Romano* as late as 1950 and 1956, respectively.[41]

Only with Schmidlin, Pribilla, Algermissen, and especially Lortz and Jedin, does a just estimation of the Reformation and of Luther manage to see the light of day in Catholic circles. Here is how Lortz summarizes his judgment of the matter:

> One can stand before Luther with reverence, but one may not be blind to his faults. . . More than any other trait that characterized him, he was a religious man . . . The core of Luther's religious substance is what we call God. . . To the end of his life one finds meaningful expressions of humility, of a Christian abandonment to the will of the Father. . . It is altogether unsatisfactory and completely unjust as well, to dismiss all of Luther's exaggerated outbreaks of snorting rage as of no moral and religious value. Some of them, with all their agitated and immoderate style, are the gripping expressions of an unselfish, religious, "prophet's wrath."[42]

At last we have come to see that only a factual and just presentation of the history of the Reformation establishes an atmosphere in which, instead of strife, conversation can become possible between the confessions.

§16 *Ecumenical Breakthrough*

Once a factual level of discussion had been accepted among scholars, ecumenical contacts were made here and there for conversation and prayer. Then there followed the "springtime of Good Pope John" and an ecumenical breakthrough even from the side of the official church.

Again, this has to be seen against a background not only of the remote past, but even of recent times. As late as 1925, on the occasion of the canonization of Peter Canisius, the *Osservatore Romano* placed the new saint in outright contrast with Luther: "These two names are to each other as light and shadow, truth and heresy, obedience and rebellion, true scholarship and false".[43] Even in 1939, in his inaugural encyclical *Summi Pontificatus*, Pope Pius XII was still painting in black and white, saying that all modern errors were the fault of the Reformation, whereas the Chair of Peter had at all times preserved the truth, educating and ennobling the masses. The October 20, 1939, instruction *Ecclesia Catholica* of the Holy Office admonished Catholics to exercise the highest degree of caution with regard to the ecumenism just then beginning to stir: one was not to exaggerate the shortcomings of the Catholic Church and understate the guilt of the reformers.

The temper at the grassroots twenty years ago is evidenced in the bitter commentaries that were made as the possibility arose of a Catholic in the White House. Many Americans were convinced that a Catholic would be incapable of being honest enough for this office, that there would be a hot line to Rome instead of to Moscow, and that the Protestant churches would be closed as in Spain and Colombia.[44]

The great figures of John XXIII and Cardinal Bea altered this whole climate. Everything else followed like a hot knife through butter. In 1960 the Secretariat for the Unity of Christians was established,[45] and the conciliar decree *Unitatis Redintegratio* was adopted in 1964. There followed the sensational Roman visits of the heads of the Orthodox and Anglican churches, and the pope's visit to Constantinople and Geneva. Theological and practical teams were formed on an interchurch level. In a letter of February 23, 1979, Pope John Paul II expressed to the Rome-Geneva committee for common effort his wish "to see a strengthening of efforts, so that the restoration of the unity of all Christians can be hastened".

Before the council, Catholics pictured that unity very simply: the others had to return to the bosom of the true church and accept a strict Roman uniformity. Now they realize that all the churches must move nearer to Christ, and so necessarily come closer to one another as well. They see that even within the Catholic Church there must be much more collegiality and regional autonomy, for that church is a six-continent church now;[46] hence all the more important in case of an across-the-board union with other churches. Geneva dreams of a new council, one of all Christians — Vatican III or, better, Jerusalem II — that would spell out the minimal but unconditional grounds for union, then recognize a church of unity in diversity for the acceptance of all.[47]

After all that has happened in the last twenty years, there is certainly hope for the years to come. Meanwhile, as recommended by a document from the Roman secretariat in 1974, it is important to foster ecumenism on the local level. There must be a heightening of consciousness at the grassroots, lest — should the official churches decide to take new concrete steps toward unity — passive or active opposition arise among the faithful.

§17 *The Missions*

The ecumenical (or unecumenical, as the case may be) situation in what was the missions — today's "young churches" — deserves special mention. In contrast with what had happened in Western lands, the various mission churches did not stand off against each other in historical blocs and wage pitched *battles*; theirs was a running *war*, and the fighting was in the open. One mission would try to steal another's members, catechists, and school installations — even burn down their schools and chapels. The history of the missions fairly teems with such examples, heavily underscoring the council's assertion that such "divisions among Christians are a scandal to the world and an injury to the sacred enterprise of proclaiming the gospel to every creature".[48]

85

The classic nineteenth-century mission histories of T. W. M. Marshall and H. Hahn, each in several volumes, are ardently and acrimoniously devoted to vilifying the character of Protestant missionaries, demonstrating their greed and immorality, and the total failure of their missions — and highlighting the brilliance of Catholic missions by contrast.

Even in our own century, the two leading German missiologists, Protestant G. Warneck and Catholic J. Schmidlin, went at each other like a pair of roosters. Then there was a period of mutual neglect; in the mission histories of J. Richter (Protestant) and J. Schmidlin and A. Mulders (Catholic), there is simply no mention of the other side at all. Then K. S. Latourette, a Protestant, made the breakthrough in a seven-volume general history of the missions. He offers a very good presentation even of the Catholic side, and is full of admiration for the accomplishments of Catholic missioners.[49] Today Protestants and Catholics of the young churches know one another, pray together, and learn from one another.

The young churches sponsor many groups devoted to work and prayer in common. Some countries have a joint Christian Council, confronting the state as a single church, and undertaking common action not only in the political and social sphere but even in the proclamation of the gospel. As recently as thirty years ago Protestants did not even know that there were Catholic translations of the Bible in the languages of the missions. And Catholics for their part would burn a Protestant Bible that fell into their hands. Today in the Third World there are some one hundred and fifty interconfessional projects for the cooperative translation, printing, and distribution of the Bible.[50]

§18 Antimodernism

But we must now backtrack to the dour era of antimodernism. This time the issue was not so much overt conflict with heresy as it is the inveterate Catholic suspicion of heresy,[51] naturally always explainable by a solicitude for the purity of doctrine.

The most competent representatives of the Catholic Church had sought to align theology with modern science, as far as possible and necessary. They had sought to apply the critico-historical method to the origins and history of Christianity, and accordingly called into question certain myths of traditional doctrine and certain structures in the modern church. Their intentions were justified, even if, for lack of proper nuances and distinctions, they caused dangerous confusion in certain circles, and indeed occasionally landed in heretical territory. Keen minds discerned the dawn of a new age in these projects. But official church circles scented risk and ruin. The new movement was to be resisted by every means. It was called the "modernist plague", and there was talk of a "*mania* for the rapprochement of faith and science".

Instead of coming to an honest and scholarly confrontation with their accusers, the accused indulged in a bitter reaction against authority. And so in 1907 the Holy Office issued the decree *Lamentabili*, condemning sixty-five "modernist" theses, arranged in an illogical order. A few months later Pope Pius X published the encyclical *Pascendi*. Both documents are remarkable for their purely negative character. They seem unable to grasp the genuine and timely aspirations of the whole movement, and they generally betray a purely superficial knowledge of the authors and their ideas. *Lamentabili* plucks statements out of context and often falsifies them. *Pascendi* draws a caricature of modernism that the pope was certainly justified in condemning as irreconcilable with the Catholic faith, but it did not correspond to the historical reality. Most of the authors submitted — that is, they dissociated themselves from *this* representation of a modernist system.

But both documents drew a cry of jubilation from the integralists. Once more the conservatives had triumphed. Then, by way of cure and prevention alike, they introduced the Oath against Modernism, strengthened the Commission for the Index, and, through the *Sodalitium Pianum* under the leadership of Monsignor Umberto Benigni (1862-1934), developed an out-and-out Gestapo operation.

This prelate of humble origin and brilliant intellect was reckoned as a leftist politically, a socialist, and he enjoyed the high esteem of Gramsci, the secretary general of the Communist Party. But in the church he was an ultrarightist — a fascist, a typical example of those who see everything good about themselves and everything bad about everyone else — who condemn and persecute, without any inner conflict, anyone who thinks otherwise than they. Benigni had as many as a thousand agents and sleuths, working under a high command of some fifty persons in all the countries of Europe. No one knew who was a spy. Anyone who expressed or wrote any new ideas risked being denounced in Rome and summarily removed from his ecclesiastical position, without a hearing or discussion.[52]

Even Father Angelo Roncalli, later Pope John XXIII, nearly forfeited his career. As a young professor in the seminary at Bergamo, he was highly esteemed by his bishop, Radini-Tedeschi. But Father G. Mazzoleni, a priest who, as Roncalli himself remarks, "belonged to those zealots that no diocese lacked in those days", reported Roncalli's seemingly dangerous thinking to Rome. Cardinal de Lai responded with a warning, "which could have devastated me", wrote Roncalli, "but which did not disturb my inner peace". Later, as pope, he was shown the documents of the case from the archives of the Holy Office, and found written next to his name the annotation "suspected of modernism".[53] What a consolation for many, of those times and these!

J. Schmidlin may have been ever ready for a feud, but he is still reliable when he calls this antimodernist kettle-boiling "a declaration of war on the modern spirit", a "well-poisoning network of heretic hounds and hangmen", a "miserable world conspiracy".[54] No amount of antimodernism solved any problems. It only postponed them, until, like anything dammed up too long, they broke with all the more violence over the heads of others at Vatican Council II.

§19 *The Congregation for the Doctrine of the Faith*

The whole history of the suppression of heresy is bound up with that of the Inquisition (§12, above), or its successor the Holy Office, since 1965 called the Sacred Congregation for the Doctrine of the Faith. In his motu proprio of December 7, 1965, *Integrae Servandae*, Pope Paul VI remarked, "Henceforth the defence of the faith will be better served by the promotion of the faith", and assigned the congregation a role more of theological promotion than of defence.

Methods have plainly improved, but past memory is not easily extinguished. The gloomy old castle, long in need of a thorough housecleaning within and without, is groping for continuity with the good old days. One of antimodernism's many victims, E. Buonaiuti, wrote an incisive description of this palace, where, "for centuries, in the stillness of dark and mystery, the cruellest dramas of modern spirituality have been played out".[55]

That the church has authority to safeguard the purity of doctrine is beyond question. Before the council Karl Rahner wrote a most earnest article on the gravity of the heresies, which, he says, in their untruth present a much more serious threat to human existence than anything else. Anyone without an understanding of the church's passion for truth, and without a feeling for the mortal seriousness of the decision whether a given assertion corresponds to the truth or not, will naturally be incapable of appreciating the Christian view of heresies. Rahner even speaks of "disguised heresies" slithering about in our day, infecting every Christian in today's world like bacteria. Even if one fails to fall ill — that is, even if one does not become a heretic in the express and full sense — one must nonetheless keep aware of the danger and apply the necessary prophylaxis.[56]

Rahner himself, it is true, later wrote repeatedly of a legitimate theological pluralism, and warned against automatically viewing anyone who departs from traditional scholastic theology — that is, who attempts to develop it further — as suspect of heresy. The International Theological Commission took up this question as its theme for the year 1973, and concluded that an openness to theological pluralism, always under the caution of fidelity to the basic content of the faith, is necessary and useful.[57]

May we return no more to the preconciliar age, when theologians who pursued the important aim of keeping theology from coming into contradiction with science, and who attempted to express it for the men and women of their day, were cast under suspicion, deprived of their teaching offices, placed on the Index, harassed with intrigues, and stabbed in the back.[58] On November 8, 1963, at the sixty-third session of the council, Cardinal Frings delivered his electrifying address on the reform of the Roman Curia in general and of the Holy Office in particular. Frings demanded, as a minimum, that henceforth no one be condemned without having had the opportunity to explain, defend and then, if need be, correct himself or herself.[59]

There has been much improvement but, unfortunately, not enough. There is still much that transpires in anonymity, in secret proceedings, and in the condemnation of propositions, instead of in the thoroughgoing investigation of the whole context. There is still much that is handled without the due cooperation of the International Theological Commission, which was established in 1969 at the instance of the first Synod of Bishops, and which, after all, was to have assisted the Vatican in delicate theological questions. But this commission has shared the fate of other, similar, Vatical commissions. It was put in place, but it never had any influence.

And so it comes about that, in spite of the plain lesson of the long history of heresies, "the mistakes of the past are repeated with discouraging regularity"[60] even in our own day. The reason is that there is still a doughty band of the old guard, with a great deal of influence, among the officials and consultors of the Congregation for the Faith, keeping the newer elements out of the action. For them the only valid yardstick is still the old scholastic theology. Thus theology is done at two different levels in the congregation and members talk past one another instead of conversing.

The transformation of an old apparatus can be very sluggish. The structure seems stronger than the persons within it, and so resists timely efforts at renewal. Once more the historical principle is confirmed: Rome can wait. Rome is always on the side of law and order. Rome does not allow itself even the *appearance* of a radical renewal.

But in the meantime the situation of world and church have changed radically. Hence the current tension, to the point of dismemberment. Today it is no longer necessary to expel individuals from the church; they leave it of their own accord and in great numbers. Not a few of them appeal to the gospel, which they see as strangled by church structures. Today Rome can no longer reckon with an automatic following. Roman documents, not altogether without their own fault, have suffered a sharp loss of authority. Less cognizance — unfortunately — is taken of the good ones, and the less good ones raise a storm of indignation. A double prudence will be necessary if Rome is to recoup this loss of credibility.

89

Rome has lost the central command position it enjoyed in the Middle Ages, when the Christian West and the church were coextensive. During the decade just past, the church became a church on six continents (counting the Americas as two), and the centre of gravity of the Catholic world has shifted to the Third World. Quite a new situation, after two thousand years! The balance tipped in 1970. In that year 51.86% of Catholics lived in Latin America, Africa, and Asia. By 1976 the proportion had climbed to 55.71%. By the year 2000 it will be about 70%.[61]

Europe no longer enjoys theological hegemony. Today it is on all six continents that there are theological institutions of higher learning, theologians whose names are respected, a theological output that cannot be ignored, and theologies that can no longer simply be measured against the standard of scholastic theology. The Congregation for the Faith is simply overtaxed and will continue to be, unless it undertakes a radical renewal in personnel and performance.

Meanwhile the congregation continues to take actions that vex today's Christian and damage the image of its own authority. Item: even recent documents are still written in a style and tone, and with a theological bias, that make one simply shake one's head.[62] Item: even in the new procedure for the investigation of doctrine there are still such transgressions of fair treatment of the accused that one has to ask oneself why it goes on and how much longer it will last.[63] Item: even today, proponents of new ideas are still often blacklisted without previous factual confrontation, and care is taken through their nuncios and bishops that they be not invited to speak anywhere.

One might hope that the Congregation for the Faith would perform its role of leadership more as Paul VI wished it to — less fearful of possible "pusillanimous scandal", and with less exclusive attention to the "needs" of those who do not wish to have "their" faith disturbed, but more intent instead upon making the faith acceptable and livable for the mature persons of today who influence the world. One might hope that the congregation would do less braking, be less suspicious, and act with less belligerence toward the theologians, who, after all, may and should always keep ahead of the magisterium. One might hope that the congregation would direct its activity on a kind of Cape Canaveral model, correcting programs as need be, less anxious about every separate case in the whole world and more generous with local churches with respect to the long overdue freedom they need, challenging the bishops and theologians of these churches to expand the dialogue and be their own watchdogs.

There have been heretics in the church in every century. Many of them became heretics for lack of dialogue. These unwelcome admonishers and disturbers of the peace were often discriminated against and even eliminated, at best by stopping their mouths, at worst by killing them without any attempt on the part of their persecutors to examine their own heart and mind, and to understand the heretics' message. Now the time has come for these methods to be practised no longer. The fact that Jesus himself was a heretic in the eyes of the synagogue, and died on the cross for his "heresy" should shock us and give us pause. The realization that Jesus himself is a "heretic" is a step toward speaking about this category of believer in the church in a new language. Then we shall be able to close the door on a long, sorrowful chapter in the history of the church,[64] and a truly new morning can dawn (see §11, above).

The Schismatics

§20 *Fraternal Divorce*

Schismatics, as distinguished from heretics, are those who have not fallen victim to a false doctrine, but have refused obedience to the papal office, and have for one reason or another separated themselves from the unity of the Catholic Church. The greatest and most tragic instance of this is the Eastern Schism.

When a marriage is hopelessly in shambles, the result is often not simply separation from board and bed, but formal divorce as well. In like manner the relationship between the Eastern and Western churches worsened over the centuries, not so much because of formal theological questions as because of questions of rite, and especially because of the involvement of both churches in politics, and real divorce, or schism, was the result. The exact moment of its beginning can be placed in various deeds and contumelious documents, but an absolutely new stage was clearly reached on the occasion of the mutual excommunication by the papal delegate and the patriarch of Constantinople in 1054. But although in a broken marriage the two partners may well leave one another in peace, in the case of the two separated churches there was no neutral *modus vivendi*, but only new harassment, mutual interference, strife, and even attempts at union — all of which says that the churches really belong together. Like the heretics' story, this is not a glorious page out of the history books.[65]

The nadir was reached during the period between the councils of union of Lyons (1274) and Florence (1439). Rome lacked all readiness to oblige the special character of the church of the East in any way whatever. The Holy See itself has published the documents. W. de Vries, a specialist in the area, points out that "it only redounds to its honour to admit to the mistakes and deficiencies of this time".[66]

What Rome was interested in in those days was its absolute central authority. The goal was to bring the Eastern church simply and plainly under Latin domination. Even crusades were considered and demanded as a means to union. Pope John XXII encouraged Prince Stephan of Bosnia to a crusade to "pull up the pestilence of heresy by the roots". Crusaders reported to Urban II, "We have vanquished the Turks and the pagans, but have been unable to overcome the heretics — the Greeks, Armenians, Syrians, and Jacobites".

God was thought to be pleased at these wars against the schismatics — against these "unbelieving servants of Satan, sons of corruption, deceived by the Devil's fraud". Schismatics were considered as outlaws without rights. In spite of a whole millennium lived in all diversity of rite, theology, and discipline, but in a single community of faith and love, the church now saw unity only in the centralist, juridical, uniform, Latin sense. There was certainly no space for this "damned rite of the Greeks".

Men like Cardinal Nicholas of Cusa (1401-1464), however, were free spirits, and spoke their mind without hesitation. Nicholas took the occasion of the fall of Constantinople in 1453 to publish *On Peace and Unity in the Faith*, in which he expressed his conviction that there was but one religion, and that it lived in the various usages not only of the many churches, but also of the many religions. "May it therefore be deemed sufficient to confirm the peace in faith and in the prayer of love, while tolerating the differing usages on both sides ... To wish to strive for exact uniformity in all things is only to disturb that peace". In all religions, says Nicholas, it is the true God and Father of Jesus Christ who is supreme, and that includes Allah[67] (see Part Four, §§13-15).

During the time of the Counter-Reformation the screws were tightened once more. Rome wished to force the Eastern churches not just to the same faith but to the same abstract doctrines of the faith, such as were expressed for instance in the catechism of Cardinal Bellarmine. This must have been like a fist in the eye of the mystical Eastern theology of divinization.

The establishment of the Congregation *de Propaganda Fide* brought about an improvement. A basic step was taken toward a spirit of breadth and openness with the principle that reverence for the Eastern rites would be a precondition of union. Still, missionaries lacked the necessary preparation, and often exhibited an offensive sense of superiority. They carried on a spiritual latinization of the East, introducing the Latin breviary, Western catechisms, devotions, and relics. Individuals or groups who allowed themselves to be "converted" were often required to burn their beloved books.

The whole affair was a meandering one. Popes made repeated concessions, but the high procurator of the Russians, Pobedonostsev, refused to take them seriously. "Popes die", he quipped; "The Roman Curia does not". A highly qualified spokesman of the Eastern churches (in union with Rome), Patriarch Maximos IV Sayegh of Antioch, declared his mind as Vatican Council II opened:

Today it is much better than it used to be. But even today many think of the Eastern churches as nothing but a gracious concession of the Holy See, a privilege, an exception. Because you cannot make them altogether Catholic — that is, Latin — you put up with them as a kind of second-class Catholic. Some take no notice of us. In other cases it still comes to fighting, to real enmity.[68]

§21 *The Road to Reconciliation*

More recently, the problem has been favoured with a more factual approach. Now both sides are striving for a rapprochement because both sides have come to realize that it is not so much considerations of faith that have been at the root of all the strife, but power claims, prestige, and politics.[69] A decisive turn for the good occurred with Pius IX. On the other hand this pope, in a circular letter of April 8, 1862, says the Holy See never sought to make any changes in the Eastern rites or to latinize the Eastern churches. Hence the patriarchs should step forward to give the lie to this slander. Such a disavowal of the facts of history is scarcely the way to overcome the burdensome past and promote peace.[70]

When we compare the declarations of Vatican II,[71] once again largely inspired by Pope John XXIII, and the attitude of Pope Paul VI, with the attitudes of centuries gone by, the contrast is like day and night. On December 7, 1965, the day before the closing of the council, it was announced in Rome and Constantinople simultaneously that the mutual excommunication of 1054 had been lifted, and the heads of both churches made a declaration in common accord:

● They deplored the contumely, the unjust accusations, and the reprehensible behaviour that characterized and accompanied the lamentable events of that time.

● They likewise deplored, and extinguished from the churches' memory, the pronouncements of excommunication that followed them, whose recollection raises obstacles to a rapprochement in love even to our own day.

● Finally, they deplored the regrettable behaviour and further events that, under the influence of various factors, including a mutual misunderstanding and mistrust, eventually led to an actual split in the ecclesial community.[72]

The first encounter between Pope Paul VI and Patriarch Athenagoras, in Jerusalem in 1964, had preceded. The pope's visit to Istanbul in 1967 followed. In 1975 Pope Paul knelt to kiss the feet of Orthodox Metropolitan Meliton in the Sistine Chapel. On the feast of Saint Andrew, in 1979, Pope John Paul II went to Istanbul, where, among other important statements he made, he asked the question, "Have we still the right to remain divided?" When will this question be answered with concrete deeds?

As a kind of appendix to our treatment of the church and the schismatics, let us consider a case of narrower dimensions but greater contemporary moment: the Chinese schism. Under pressure of the communist government, a Patriotic Priests' Movement was formed in 1952. In 1957 the Union of Patriotic Catholics was established, and in 1958 two Patriotic bishops were ordained, without Rome's permission, with the express intention of forming a kind of national church. Eventually there may have been as many as fifty such bishops, and perhaps about a thousand priests. During the Cultural Revolution, many of the priests and bishops disappeared. Several of the popes expressed themselves on the matter, and sought to reestablish unity.[73]

Today China is manifesting a readiness for greater openness toward the West, and for greater religious freedom. It would be most appropriate now for Rome to enter into completely frank and open conversation with the government of this largest nation on earth. But there are two prerequisites, and without them negotiations will simply not be possible — breach of relations with Taiwan, and recognition of the Patriotic bishops and priests.

On the first point the Vatican hoped to regularize the affair with a compromise — by substituting a chargé d'affaires for a nuncio in Taipei. On the occasion of the pope's visit to the United Nations on October 2, 1979, it was hoped that he could at least have shaken hands with the Chinese delegate, especially inasmuch as, fifteen years earlier, Pope Paul VI had shown the unprecedented courage of breaking a lance for China's entry into the U.N. But no, the Chinese delegate was conspicuously absent when the Pope gave his address. China knows no compromise.

With regard to the second condition, Rome would gladly consider the possibility of a recognition of the Patriotic bishops and priests, for it is always a good thing to heal a schism. But now the tragedy. Chinese Catholics who have remained true to Rome, coming up from the underground, will not hear of a reconciliation. They avoid the "apostate priests" like poison. It would be unbearable for them to have suffered persecution and prison so long "for nothing". Persons in the church who had wished to make contact with the Patriotic group and establish friendly relations have had to change their minds in the face of the attitude of Chinese Christians.

These Christians are hard in their judgment of the "schismatics", as hard today as they had to be thirty years ago. They have no experience of the "springtime of Good Pope John". So the first question is going to be how to manage to attract these Christians, render them more reconcilable, bring them to the point of being able to see the schism of a generation ago somewhat differently today, and help them understand that it ought finally to be overcome, even at the price of certain concessions. Should a new attitude fail to be forthcoming, those valiant Christians will find themselves suddenly cast in the role of the brother who was vexed at his fathers' attitude toward the Prodigal Son. And what a tragedy of history, and of psychological captivity, this would be.

The Pagans

§23 *Different Interpretations of Paganism*

Alongside the two successive "chosen peoples" — the Jews and the Christians — the great mass of humanity has always consisted of the so-called pagans, or gentiles. We have already demonstrated with what great simplicity and absence of prejudice the Old and New Testaments sometimes speak. Sometimes, however, their attitude is very poor indeed (Part One, §§9, 11, 22, 25, 30, 35). This ambiguity is prolonged through the patristic era. Depending upon the time and the theological school, we encounter different interpretations of paganism. Here is a classic case of theological pluralism. Truth is complex. It is grasped by the human mind only gradually.

In the early post-apostolic era[74] the church had the pagan literary polemic to repulse, and did so through the apologists. The best of them accomplished their task not just negatively, — by repulsing the assaults — but by taking the offensive, and interpreting paganism itself in a new, prophetic manner. Justin, Origen, Clement of Alexandria, spoke of the *logoi spermatikoi*, or *rationes seminales*, a "participation in seed" in the divine word hidden in the practical reason of human beings, "seminally" present and active in the world even before the coming of Christ — in creation, in the prophets, in pagan philosophy. Clement and his school went even further, refusing to accept the popular opinion that paganism was an invention of the Devil, and insisting instead that it had actually been willed and planned by God — as the law of the Jews had been — in guise of a *paidagogos*, or slave who leads the truth-seeker to Christ.[75]

This comparatively positive approach was soon overshadowed by an emphasis on the reality of original sin, and of the role of the visible church in salvation. Outstanding among the proponents of this new view was Cyprian of Carthage. It was Cyprian who coined the motto, "Outside the church there is no salvation", and many fathers after him understood the maxim as literally as he had. Today Catholic theology interprets it less harshly: it is what is called a "real" principle as distinguished from a "personal" one, and means that all salvation, even that of persons outside the church, nevertheless comes in one way or another through the church, through Christ.[76]

But it was especially the "Doctor of Grace", St. Augustine, who thought he could becomingly present the full gratuitousness and shining grandeur of grace only against the dark backdrop of human sin and reprobation. In his battle with the Pelagians, who undervalued grace as if it were a natural gift, Augustine teaches that human nature has been corrupted by original sin — that the sin of Adam, passed on by the process of generation, is imputed to the whole human race. Alone, the human being cannot break free of this vicious circle of evil. Only God saves him or her, out of pure grace. And this gratuitous rescue, which in the elect redounds — with such credit — to God's grace, in the nonelect leaves only the cruel words, *massa damnata*. "The situation is this," writes Augustine; "The reprobate mass of humankind lay, or rather wallowed, in evil, reeling from woe to woe, and paying, along with that portion of the angels who had sinned, the penalty they had earned by their ungodly fall."[77]

Augustine is unquestionably under the influence of the popular notion that humanity had been outsmarted by the Devil. For him it is clear that the "city of God" is built of the chosen and the saved, whereas those fallen to the Devil are bewitched by the city of this world. In this conception we are all children of sin and of the Devil, and can be saved only rectroactively, through God's grace. Theology today takes God's universal salvific will more seriously, holding that all, though only by God's unmerited grace, are in the grip of salvation from the very start, and can only lose it later by their own fault.

It is true that Augustine also admits the possibility of salvation in pre-Christian times and in extra-Christian milieus. With other fathers, he speaks of a "church since Abel" (not since Adam, because the duality of sin and reprobation finds better expression in Cain and Abel), and holds that all the just of the Old Testament and of paganism already belonged to Christ. But evidently he is speaking of the exceptional case. Of Job, for example, he writes, "I doubt not that divine providence has so proceeded that we may learn through this man that in other peoples too there have been persons who lived according to God, and who possessed God's favour as citizens of the spiritual Jerusalem".[78]

The Augustinian pessimism has had deep effects, from early times all the way to our own. It appears in the sermons of St. Caesarius, bishop of Arles, for example. Eagerly citing St. Augustine for support, he declares: "Through our first birth, we were vessels of God's wrath. Our second birth gave us grace to become vessels of mercy. The first birth set us on the road to death, the second has recalled us to life. Before baptism, O most dearly beloved, we were all the Devil's temples. After baptism, it was given to us to become the temples of Christ."[79]

Another of Augustine's pupils, Bishop Fulgentius of 'Ruspe, formulated it even more radically, and his statement is the one adopted professes, and proclaims, that no one who lives outside the Catholic Church — not only pagans, but also Jews or heretics and schismatics — can become participators of life eternal. They all go to the 'eternal fire prepared for the devil and his angels' [Matthew 25:41] unless they be joined to her before the end of their life". In fact, "even if he has given ever so many alms, and even shed his blood for Christ, if he has not lived in the unity of the Catholic Church he cannot be saved".[80]

§24 The Struggle against Islam

Then for several centuries there was not much concern about pagans. The West was visibly Christian now, and there was no notion of the other continents, or at best a vague one. However, a new confrontation occurred, and one of an altogether novel kind in contrast with that of the first three centuries. The Muslims had occupied North Africa, Spain, and the Near East, including the Holy Places. A veritable wall had been built around the West. Now the two blocs came face to face — Christendom, the city of God in this world, a closed social, political, and religious system; and Islam, an equally closed social, political, and religious power structure. And instead of an objective discussion, the battle against Islam was what developed, both a direct one, in the spirit of defence of the true religion, and an indirect one, in the form of the Crusades against the Muslims.

The idea of the Crusades was officially launched by Pope Urban II at the Council of Clermont in 1095. One could no longer abide, cried the pope with his French rhetoric, that Christian states and the Holy Places be occupied by pagans. One must go to war. "God wills it!" cried the mass of clergy and people. This was no bonfire the pope had lit. He had let fly the burning idea that would inflame the West for some two hundred years. The knights had crosses sewn on their garments — after all, were they not "taking up the cross" to follow Christ? (see Matt. 10:38) — and set off on their armed pilgrimage, fascinated by the challenge of wresting the holy sepulchre from the infidel, and drawn by the promise of indulgences and the prospect of lands as their reward on their return. And if they fell in battle with the Arabs, several popes had guaranteed them eternal life. A holy war if ever there was one!

Even today there is no consensus on how this undertaking ought to be judged.[81] The believing Christian can say, "The Crusades are a glorious memory, and the best Christians will always read those pages on the holiness and heroism of the crusaders with reverence and enrichment".[82] Seen from a strategic standpoint, however, the enterprise was a great defeat. In the Children's Crusade of 1212, when thousands of children and young persons from the Rhineland and from France, wishing to reach Algiers and hoping for God to lead them dry-shod across the Mediterranean from Genoa, all finally boarded ship, but only a few shiploads survived to reach the slave markets of North Africa. But the other Crusades, as well, failed to contribute anything toward the strengthening of the West beyond closing Christendom in upon itself.

Culturally, the Crusades opened certain new mercantile contacts with the East, but to speak of a cultural osmosis is a gross exaggeration. The crusaders led too closed a life. They learned no Arabic, and had no interest in Islam as a religion.

From the religious standpoint, the chance was missed to bring Christendom and Islam into dialogue. Islam had called Christianity's self-awareness into question for the first time since the conversion of Constantine. A sensitive nerve had been touched. But this shock, this challenge, was not met in the spirit of the gospel. The response was ideological: that other religion was simply the work of the Devil. Mohammed was vilified. For hundreds of years the West froze in a negative political and religious stance. True, one may not overlook the new Western concern with Arabian and Jewish Aristotelian philosophy, which M. Grabmann terms "the most profound event in the history of medieval theology", and in which the writings of Aristotle, Avicenna, Averroes, and Moses Maimonides came to be known and studied in translation, and incorporated by Aquinas into his synthesis of Christian Aristotelianism. But otherwise Islam remained for centuries the model case of a failed confrontation with another religion. The Christian West could not bring itself to take up a conversation with another religion, but automatically cast it in the role of a declared enemy.[83]

"Pagan dogs, Saracen swine" was what Christians of those days called the Muslims. Before the Cathedral of St. Stephen in Vienna stands a statue of St. John of Capestrano (1386-1456), the "Apostle of Europe", one of the saints who fired the Christian troops against the Turks. At his feet lies the body of a Turk. The inscription reads, "Light of the Orthodox Faith, Scourge of Heretics, Lightning Bolt against the Turks in the Might of the Most Holy Name".[84] And yet in the cathedral itself, behind the high altar, reposes St. Stephen, who did not strike his enemies down but who was himself struck down by their stones! Thus the same cathedral enshrines two fundamentally different "Christian" attitudes. Primitive Christianity spread more by its weakness than by secular might. Later, Christendom believed it had to make might right, and the church great, through human power.

The crusader mentality was evident in other forms of holy war as well. After the renowned subjugation of the Saxons and Hessians and the subsequent baptism of the people, the spotlight fell on the conversion of the Slavs. St. Bernard of Clairvaux's call for a Crusade reverberated far and wide, but the Saxon princes declared that there were heathen aplenty on their own frontiers for taking up the cross against, and the saint allowed himself to be persuaded. He drew up a plan for a "Conversion Crusade", and wrested an encyclical from Pope Eugene III. Bernard encouraged the princes to take holy vengeance upon the heathen, to uproot them from Christian soil — that is, either to convert or to annihilate them. The pope was not in favour of this cruel set of alternatives, and the execution of Bernard's plan was less radical than its conception.[85] Still, this is the way in which many understood the *compelle intrare* of Luke 14:23.

It is scarcely surprising that the Crusades, the Middle-East war of the Middle Ages, aroused scant sympathy for Christianity among the Muslims. Arabs saw in Christians a horde of barbarians, speaking an unintelligible language, and lacking in all customs or culture. They little doubted their own superiority in all areas of life, culture, and religion. "Christian dogs", they called them. Missioners of that time, with some exceptions, practised an apologetics of polemics and dispute[86] — or else kept to the care of their fold of Christian foreigners. And so it continued up to very recent times, in Turkey, Arabia, and North Africa, with a major exception in the case of the White Fathers. Most missioners were utterly unprepared, in language or in knowledge of religion, for a dialogue with Muslims.

Only very recently have we begun to discover the "ninety-nine most beautiful names" of the good, merciful, and almighty God of the Koran, to admire the Muslim mystics, or to further any dialogue (see Part Three, §§19-21).The Second Vatican Council, in a beautiful declaration, recognized Islam's positive value, then added:

> In view of the many instances of discord and enmity between Christians and Muslims over the course of the centuries, this holy synod admonishes all to lay aside the past, to strive in uprightness toward mutual understanding, and to make common cause for the defence and furtherance of social justice, moral goodness, and, not least, of peace and justice for all human beings [NA 3].

There is a new climate abroad. Many things are seen differently now. C. Schedl claims that the many differences remaining between the Isa of Mohammed and the Jesus of Christians can largely be reconciled within a framework of theological pluralism.

Alongside of, and antedating, Greek and Latin Christianity, says Schedl, there was a Semitic Christianity, which is still living underground in Islam. Here Jesus is not yet acknowledged as Logos, Law, or Son of God, but especially as the Way to the Father. A detached investigation would suddenly and unexpectedly allow new points of common doctrine to shine through. For Christians, too, the first Christ-formula was not *Kyrios* but the Servant of God (Acts 3:13, 26; 4:27, 30; Phil. 2:7). This, says Schedl, is the apostolic cornerstone of the Koran's formula too. And so, he concludes, what we ought to do is thrust aside all the polemical works, mostly written to the tune of clashing arms, and extract new starting points from the Koran.[87]

In the context of the spread of Christendom we must say something about that earnestness in the profession of the faith that developed into a full-blown spirit of martyrdom.[88] Christ had foretold opposition and persecution, and no better way was known of demonstrating the highest pitch of love for and loyalty to Christ than martyrdom. Today, in critical retrospect, we are constrained to say that all too many of the martyrs not only proclaimed their faith in the Spirit, but attacked other religions, and expressed themselves so harshly that they occasioned the "righteous" wrath of their adversaries.

Without impugning the love of Christ that impelled the martyrs of the first centuries, we are forced to recognize that their judgment of Roman paganism was clearly too negative. They saw the Roman civil authority as God's great enemy, and considered the cult of Caesar and of the gods as demonolatry plain and simple, something to be sneered at. The Blessed Proconsul Carpus put it this way: "I worship Christ. I offer these idols nothing. Do with me what you will, but it is impossible for me to make offering to these humbug devil-images. Those who sacrifice to the gods are made equal to the demons — nothingness — and go to their ruin, in hell."[89]

St. Boniface is another typical example. His great accomplishment is immortal, for his missionary means are classic — the proclamation of the faith, the erection of churches and monasteries, the destruction of pagan temples. In the last-named endeavour his activity was in the spirit of his times. The Frisians, Saxons, and other tribes considered their deities as helpers in life; when the Christian God proved stronger, they were ready to attach themselves to him. The destruction of their temples, without the gods' wreaking vengeance, served as proof of the impotence of those gods and the superiority of Christianity.

It was in this spirit that Boniface forded the Danube at Giesmar in 724 and destroyed, as had Pirmin and Willibrord before him, many a sanctuary. Of course, not every Frisian was convinced by this line of argumentation. Many were offended and indignant, and the assault on Boniface's camp in Doccum can be understood as these pagan peoples' spontaneous reaction. As Boniface and his companions awaited their new Christian converts for a solemn celebration on the morning of June 6, 754, they were set upon. They died for the faith they had proclaimed, in a way that was not altogether correct.[90]

A beautiful example of the spirit of martyrdom is to be found in St. Francis and his early companions. He devotes an entire chapter of his Rule to those who, "out of divine dedication, wish to go among the Saracens and other unbelievers." He himself wished to become altogether like his Lord Jesus Christ, and acknowledged, evidently "out of divine dedication", that the gospel ought not to be reserved to the Christian West. Missionary activity had died out in the church in his time, for the West had become Christian. And yet Christendom was surrounded by this wall of Islam.

Thrice Francis attempted to reach the Saracen lands. His biographer writes of his first journey: "Full of fiery longing for holy martyrdom", he wished "to travel to Syria, to proclaim to the Saracens and other infidels the Christian faith".[91] But his first voyage was interrupted by a storm at sea, and the second by illness. In a third attempt, in 1219, he managed to get to Damiette, in Egypt, on board a crusader ship. The Christians had laid siege to Malek-el-Kamel, the city of the sultan, and one fine day Francis announced, "Today I go to pay the sultan a visit". Of course all attempted to dissuade him. Cardinal Pelagius, the papal delegate seeing that there was no holding him back, admonished him at least to take care not to compromise the interests of Christendom. With a single companion, Francis crossed the no-man's-land, was taken prisoner by Muslim soldiers as was to be expected, and was brought before the sultan. The sources emphasize that he was received with surprising friendliness, and that he tarried for a week, conducting several discussions on the faith. His fascinating personality, his enthusiastic witness for Christ, his scorn of the world, his spontaneous and unself-conscious love for the Muslims, all made their impression. Then he returned home. Christians could not believe their ears, so many good things did Francis have to say of their archenemy.

Now, for the first time, there had been an encounter between Islam and Christianity — on however small a scale. Until now, the sultan had seen Christians only from afar, as enemies. But now he had come to know and love one of them as his brother and a person of God. At a time when the two blocs were slamming into each other, Francis had the stroke of genius to forget all about blocs and go and talk to the people of the other bloc. Later he sent his brothers "among" (not against) the Saracens. Thus he did not challenge the mass of his partners to crave martyrdom and go in search of it, but simply to be present among the Saracens in an attitude of friendliness, and to preach Christ only when recognizing it to be God's good pleasure (see Chapter 16 of his Rule).

But his brothers seemed not to grasp this dialectical tension, and exaggerated the desire for martyrdom. Bernard and his companions had been put to death in Ceuta, Morocco, on January 16, 1220. In 1227 a larger group travelled there, under the leadership of a certain Brother Daniel. Christian merchants earnestly counselled them not to enter the Arab city, but the friars thought otherwise. After a night spent in prayer, and mutual absolution (for they felt sure of martyrdom), on Sunday, October 4, they paraded through the streets and byways of the city, cross in hand, preaching in Italian and Latin about faith in Christ and the lies of Mohammed. The people did not understand their words, but could very well interpret what all the talk was about, and they flew into a rage. They would have lynched the friars on the spot had the latter not been arrested by soldiers. Brought before the cadi, they declared through an interpreter that no one could be saved without faith in Christ. They were cast into prison, where they remained without food or drink for a week.

Brother Daniel expounded, in a letter, his theology of martyrdom: "Go, and preach the gospel to every creature. Fear not those who kill the body; God has guided our feet for the salvation of those who believe and for the damnation of those who do not. In any case we have been able to confess Christ before the cadi and his councillors, and proclaim that outside Christ is no salvation".

The following Sunday, October 11, they were offered a choice between accepting the religion of Mohammed and living in honour, or dying. To an old man who had had the goodwill to try to save them from death they declared, "Hardened in evil, you! How long will you remain in the snares of Satan? Your Mohammed was the Devil's servant too, and is the cause of the eternal death of his followers".

Condemned to be beheaded, they rejoiced: "You [Christ] have fulfilled our longings to suffer for your name, and gain martyrdom's palm. Why should we hesitate now to pass through heaven's portal." The executioner dragged them through the street and beheaded them in the presence of the people. They were canonized in 1516.[92]

The friars ought to have known from their founder's directives that their task consisted in a peaceable, simple presence, and not in combating error, or the erring, by dialectic. And it certainly did not consist in *challenging* unbelievers. Their assignment had been to allow the divine seal on Christianity to shine forth in a genuinely Christian life, and so to live among others that the others would have to take account of their manner of thinking, feeling, and behaving, and ask themselves what manner of persons these might be. *Then* they could proclaim that they were Christians. This would be Franciscan presence.[93]

The effect of their proclamation should be joy, friendship, and perhaps the conversion of the others — but not their hatred. Basically "every martyrdom represents something almost like moral bankruptcy on the part of the martyr, the collapse of his or her pedagogical efforts".[94] The first goal of the Christian proclamation is not a halo for the martyr but evangelical hope in the hearer. Of course it should never be forgotten that Jesus was put to death on account of his proclamation.

§26 *Prejudice and its Confirmation*

At the turn of the sixteenth century, the world stage underwent an unprecedented broadening. New continents suddenly came within view and within reach. Europe was ready with its preconceptions. Theology had done its work well, and the Old World knew how to regard its new neighbours, those nonwhite peoples. The interaction between prejudice and confirmation functioned just as it was desired to. Again the division

102

of the world could be tested: here was Christendom, and there were the others. Here were men and women of culture, there were the barbarians and their savagery. Here, salvation and heaven; there, damnation and hell. Here, truth; there, falsehood. The woods echo what you cry into them, and for four centuries travellers and missionaries confirmed in their reports that the situation was exactly as they had always known it to be. The only novelty was that their knowledge became spicier and more concrete through new information. Let us take Africa as our example, and limit ourselves to the religious aspect especially.[95]

Duarte Lopez, a seafarer who travelled in Africa from 1578 to 1587, reported to Pigafetta his many experiences and impressions. The latter published them in 1591 in a book that became what today would be called a bestseller. It saw several editions — Latin, Dutch, English, French, and German — and made a substantial contribution to the Western image of black Africa. "Each man there", we read, "honours and takes for his god whatever he pleases, without any proportion, rule, or order". Thus for example Lopez saw "a great heap of carved images of devils, of manifold and frightful aspect. Many worshipped winged dragons, which they kept in their houses, giving them their best and most costly food to eat. Others held serpents of rare form to be gods; others rams, others tigers, or other horrible and obscene beasts. The more unsightly, hideous, and ugly, the more highly they are held and esteemed."

A bare hundred years later, Dutch geographer O. Dapper contributed a great deal to our knowledge of the New World by his thick volumes on the three new continents. Without hesitation he passes a judgment such as this: "The Kaffirs acknowledge no worship of gods or idols. They know nothing whatever of God, and live like cattle". Of the Benin people he confidently reports that "as far as their worship of the gods, or rather of idols is concerned, it consists in the honour and worship of the Devil, to whom they offer humans and beasts. " Of the people of Senegal he says, "They are all lewd, thievish, deceitful, mendacious, and outrageous gluttons. In fact they do not *eat*; they *feed*, like animals". The people of Upper Nigeria come out better: "They used to honour a god they called Guighime, the Lord of Heaven. Later they became Christians, then Muslims".

From the same seventeenth century another traveller expresses his African experience: "No one, however carefully he may have investigated, has ever been able to discern the faintest trace of religion, or any evidence whatever of reverence for God, among all the Kaffirs, Hottentots, or dwellers of the coast".

The year 1645 marked the inauguration of the famous Italian Capuchin mission in the Congo. These poor, ascetic missioners wrote an astonishing number of reports to Europe,[96] in the style of their time. Recently an African layman, Professor Mudimbe, conducted a study of these reports. He calls our attention to the descriptions of the Africans "with their bizarre usages, their satanic morals, and their blocked intelligence that makes them like unto beasts". Into this world "of disorder and insanity, with its diabolical illusions, would have to be brought order, truth, and the eternal norms". These peoples had "to be led from a state of brutes to that of human beings, from barbarism to urbanity, from the deceits of sorcery and the worship of idols to the light of reason and faith".[97]

From the eighteenth century onward the idea gained currency that blacks, as the descendants of Ham, fell under Ham's curse. Of course this had already been proposed by Martin Luther in his commentary on the Book of Genesis. This was supposed to be the reason for their viciousness, as well as for their condition of subordination to "whites". With Christian compassion the old missionaries bent down to these "accursed children of Ham". The great pioneer bishop Augouard of Brazzaville (d. 1921) filled his letters with requests for prayers "for the black race, that the curse of Ham may soon be lifted from them". With less perspicacity than brass he maintains that "the black race is Ham's race, one feels it — the race God cursed. The blacks are lazy, greedy, given to every vice". At Vatican Council I, seventy bishops signed a petition to have priests sent to Central Africa, where "the wretched necks of those Hamites are more and more weighed down by the oldest of all curses. . . In spite of all the endeavours of mother church, the miserable race of the blacks still stands within the terrible kingdom of Satan".[98]

This diabolical interpretation of all paganism even penetrated Christian religious instruction in Africa. Father Willibald Wanger's adult catechism of 1912 is a typical example. The author was surely at pains to make a most thorough study of Zulu customs, and concretely to integrate Christian teaching with their environment. This is no penny catechism, but a 543-page textbook. Yet not even he managed to overcome the prejudice of all the missionaries. Of paganism he writes: "What error! How can humankind wander so far astray as to abandon the true God and worship what is not God? . . . This terrible error, called paganism, is from the Devil, who wishes to be as God, and from the stupidity of humans who, deceived by the Devil, pass on to their children the lies of their fathers".[99]

Of course there are other voices. The founders of the Holy Ghost Fathers and of the White Fathers — Father Libermann and Cardinal Lavigerie — for example, admonished their missioners to study African culture and religion and hold them in high esteem. But this did not prevent the attitudes we have been examining from continuing to affect the mentality of most missionaries and mission literature until well into our own century. The lowlier, the more pitiable, the unhappier the blacks were portrayed, the more touched the good benefactors back home were, and the more money they gave to "ransom" poor "pagan babies". One can understand why Africans today place the missions under indictment.[100] To our very day many educated Africans still see no harmonizing African and Christian missionary spirituality.[101]

The only serious attempts to enter into dialogue with another religion and culture were those of Father Matteo Ricci in China and Father de Nobili in India. Their basic appeal was to the famous document of the Sacred Congregation for the Propagation of the Faith in 1659, which stated:

> What could be more absurd than to transplant France, Spain, Italy, or another European land to China? Not this, but the faith is what you are to introduce. The faith scorns or offends no people's rites and usages, as long as they are not peverse. It should accept and confirm them.[102]

Yet wishing to translate such a generous mandate into practice encountered the opposition not only of certain narrow-minded fellow workers in the vineyard, but often even that of Roman authority, which seemed frightened at its own courage.

Malcolm Hay has undertaken a new investigation of Ricci's "Chinese rites" based on the documents in the Roman archives. He comes to a depressing conclusion. It was the moral rigorism of the Roman Curia, its administrative and substantive incompetence, which were principally at fault in the rupture of the friendly relations with China that the Jesuits had initiated at the end of the sixteenth century. Ricci's experiment, Hay says, can rank as one of the most significant cultural enterprises in history. He surpassed the exploit of Columbus — he discovered the real "New World". The experiment failed not because of the evil of the world without, but because of the evil world within the church. Rome failed to recognize the signs of the time, and condemned those who did. It was a case of authority without competence.

In his bull *Ex Illa Die* of March 19, 1715, Pope Clement XI definitively condemned the method of the Jesuits, "in order that God be glorified in perfect oneness of thought and speech". When Emperor Kang Hsi told the papal legate that it was not the place of Rome to condemn the Chinese rites, the legate responded that the pope was possessed of the assistance of the Holy Spirit. History recognizes that emperor as one of the wisest rulers who ever lived, but in the Roman documents he is just another "idolatrous prince". Again, the melancholy story of an opportunity gone by.[103]

Only in 1940 were Christians allowed to practise the Confucian rites, after it had been established that they had lost their religious significance and now had only a civil character.[104] Again, what a real tragedy that we are unable to deal with a living religion. We come to terms only with its dead, secularized remains.

In the conviction that paganism is of the Devil, and that therefore pagans very probably go to hell, missionaries through the centuries reached an unparalleled pitch of zeal, driven by the motivation of saving souls. The whole of missionary hagiography should be systematically investigated from the standpoint of this phenomenon. Here a few typical examples will have to suffice. In citing them we have not the least wish to derogate from the greatness of these missionaries. They were children of their time. But we can regret that the church of their time thought as it did.

Da mihi animas, ceterum tolle, are words ascribed to various saints: "Give me souls; take all else away".[105] St. Francis Xavier's thirst for souls became proverbial. He was convinced that pagans were in a basically unsalvific situation. Even on the way to India he conducted a discussion with a learned Muslim, in East African Malinde, in which he maintained that the true God could not dwell among infidels or hear their prayers. Not that he managed to convince his interlocutor.

Once in India, he repeatedly expressed the view that the idols of the pagans were devils' images, which should be destroyed at the first opportunity. For him, all those non-Christian idol-worshippers are Devil-worshippers. And so he calls for more priests. He would like to disturb the conscience of all the university professors of Europe, and cries out to them how many souls miss the glory of heaven and go to hell on account of their remissness. Instead of coming out and saving souls, our professors are over there competing for honours, riches and episcopal sees.

In his leave-taking sermon delivered in his home parish of Hitzkirch, in Switzerland, in 1841, Anastasius Hartmann, later bishop of Patna and Bombay, solemnly declared:

> God is calling me from the fatherland to a land beyond the sea, a foreign one and an unknown, among savage peoples who sit in darkness and in the shadow of death, to make known the gospel unto them ... If I leave you, it is for this reason alone: to snatch them from eternal destruction by the light and grace of the gospel, and thus to save their souls.

Pierre-Louis-Marie Chanel, the mission pioneer of Oceania, who was killed in 1841 and canonized in 1954, suffers the same distress at the thought of the innocent souls who, for want of missionaries, are not baptized and therefore not saved. In his letters he wrote:

> For the salvation of so many souls, we have come here too late. How many adults, to my grief, must I watch die without being able to teach them the truths necessary for them to go to heaven. With children in danger of death I have been more fortunate — for them, baptism itself suffices, and I had the consolation of opening the gates of heaven for a goodly number of them ... They ask me about the loss of their departed ones. How dismayed

they are when I tell them that only the baptized go to heaven, or those who have had the sincere desire to be baptized.

Finally, let us glance at one more case, a similar one, this time from Africa. The great Irish missioner and pioneer in Southern Nigeria, Bishop Shanahan, came to Rome in 1913 to beg Pope Pius X, with tears, for more priests. The pope replied that he should apply to his superior general in the name of the pope. But the general replied that many other missionary bishops had made the same request, and that he could send no new missionaries. Thus the European trip had yielded nothing, and the bishop had this thought:

> It came over my soul like a paralysis. I thought of the millions of thrones that go unoccupied in heaven forever for the lamentable lack of human instruments. The thought weighed on me like an incubus, casting me headlong into a temptation to bitterness. I fell to my knees, and begged the eternal Father to break me like his son on the cross, but not to let the poor blacks lose everlasting life.[106]

For hundreds of years, then, we have constrained God's free and generous promise of salvation. We have institutionalized it, made it dependent upon the human efforts of the baptizing missioners and of the pagans who had themselves baptized. We have made ourselves more important than God. We have fettered the giving hand of God. It required a mighty labour of aggiornamento, during the Second Vatican Council and after, to comprehend the grandeur of God's salvific plan, the importance of the other religions for salvation history, and the church in its relationship to the kingdom of God (see Part Four, §§5-21).

§28 The Hallmark of the Present Time

The expressions "heathen, idolators, those who do not know God, those who languish under Satan's domination", were used not only in popular literature but in papal documents as well. By Pius XII's reign they had almost disappeared, and John XXIII eliminated them entirely — although Angelo Roncalli still used this accustomed style in his diary as a young priest, and then as a papal nuncio. Whose is the credit to have helped him to his new insight? I asked this question of Archbishop Loris F. Capovilla, his private secretary in the early days, His ready answer: once Roncalli was apostolic delegate in Turkey, and observed Muslims at prayer and spoke with them, he could no longer speak of "pagans", but only of "brothers and sisters in one God and Father". The case typifies how we can judge others at a distance, and with a bias, for a long time, until suddenly, through better knowledge and personal contact, the scales fall from our eyes, a new image of the world comes to light, and discoveries are made on both sides that constitute the hallmark of the present time.

Once more it was the Second Vatican Council that brought about the official transition, through the Declaration on the Relation of the Church to the Non-Christian Religions, *Nostra Aetate*.[107] On Pentecost 1964, Pope Paul VI took another step, establishing the new Secretariat for Non-Christians. The inspiration for his initiative was the council's concern for unity and understanding "among all believers", Paul said (previously the expression had been "unbelievers", *infideles*), and its purpose would be to strive for mutual understanding, sincere encounter, and cooperation in all possible areas. How often ignorance, prejudices, and even a more or less conscious bad faith, have disfigured both of us, wrote the pope. We saw only vices, on both sides, when a glance that was more loving could have discovered so much natural virtue.

The pope emphasized that the main task of the secretariat was to be performed out on the frontiers, in concrete situations, with real persons.[108] His words had the effect of the olive branch, announcing reconciliation and the end of a long, destructive flood.

Incredibly much has occurred by way of mutual discovery and appreciation. Today the word "pagan" feels uncomfortable on our lips. It is too heavily laden with pejorative connotation: from Old Testament times, when all who did not belong to the chosen people were called *goyim*, "peoples, nations, Gentiles", and considered as reprobate; from Hellenistic times, when all non-Greeks were despised as *barbaroi*, "barbarians", tribespeople, savages; from the post-Constantinian era, when "pagans" meant country folk, primitive forest-dwellers; from Islam, when everyone else was designated as *kafir*, "infidel", whence the proper name Kaffir; and from the Middle Ages, when all peoples outside Christendom were *a priori* branded heathen and savage.[109]

Today we should even be cautious of speaking of "non-Christians". The very use of the expression immediately labels persons as second-class religious believers, not up to the norm of Christianity. But one cannot simply apply a norm taken from the Christian faith to persons of another faith, without thereby implying an insult. We should simply call them by their names: Muslims, Hindus, Buddhists, and so on.

K. M. Panikkar's book *Asien und die Herrschaft des Westens* (Asia and the Hegemony of the West), published in 1955, ushered in an era when whites no longer write their own history on other continents from their own viewpoint, and when Asians and Africans have begun to view these continents' histories in another light. Whites will now suddenly see themselves differently in this mirror. It now appears that the traditional missionary was simply exclusivist, intolerant, and aggressive in his or her judgment of "the others".[110] But this era is coming to an end as well. Henceforth Africans and Asians must alter their judgment of whites, just as whites have altered their judgment of them.

The Other Races

§29 *First Contacts*

Not only where religion was concerned, but in the matter of race as well, the "chosen people", white Christians, were severely prejudiced. They could not have been expected to have a scientific explanation for the origin of the different races — the divisions of humankind possessing traits transmissible by descent and sufficient to characterize them as distinct human types, such as the white race, the black race, and so forth. To this day there is no generally accepted theory as to the origins of race.

However, Christians at least had religious and theological grounds for proclaiming the unity and equality of all human beings as creatures of God. Instead, from their very first contacts with other races to the present century, the white race overwhelming represented itself as superior. Whites have terribly humiliated the other races, considering and treating their members as children, savages, "born slaves".[111]

These other races at first looked upon whites as supraterrestrial beings, and offered them their customary hospitality in shy reverence. But their guests' anything but peaceful intentions soon betrayed themselves. Whites were after gold, slaves, and territory. They occupied land on the simple principle of *jus primi occupantis*, or right of first possession, as if the land had previously belonged to no one. At best the newcomers offered unfair contracts, occupying huge tracts for mere trinkets, a few weapons, or a little money or alcohol.

Having already considered the case of the Africans (§26, above), we shall limit ourselves here to a few observations about the Indians (Americans) and Asians.

Old sources inform us, "Indians eat human flesh. They are worse sodomists than any other folk. They have no sense of justice, they are stupid and obtuse, ungrateful, and fickle. They eat lice, spiders, and worms, raw. They are nothing more than wild animals. Never had God created a race so full of vices and bestiality, without a glimmer of goodness and culture".

To be sure, whites could not close their eyes to the Aztec, Incan, and Mayan culture, but in the conception of those times these "heathen" things had to be eradicated. And indeed by the end of the sixteenth century almost nothing was left of these peoples' ancient documents and sanctuaries. Religious zeal and inhuman cruelty went hand in hand for decades in this work of annihilation. Cardinal Höffner of Cologne has written that "the cruelty of the New World's slavery and extermination of human beings is enough to make one's blood run cold". Cultural historian A. Rüstow says of G. Frederici's two-volume *Der Charakter der Entdeckung und Eroberung Amerikas durch die Europäer* (The Character of the Discovery and Conquest of America by the Europeans,

Stuttgart, 1925-1936): "It is far and away the cruellest and bloodiest chapter in recorded world history before 1933." He thinks the need is urgent for like studies of the other colonial regions of the globe, and predicts that things will turn out to have been just as shameful for Europe there as well.[112]

We need not go into the more benign position, represented especially by Bartolomeo de las Casas and brought into service at the "Battle of Valladolid" in 1550, according to which the Indians were born equal.[113] Nor need we detail the romantic movement of a Jean Jacques Rousseau, who spoke of "the noble savage", not "the barbarian".[114] All of the endeavours of this kind were powerless to transform Western benightedness or to determine the de facto course of history. The latter continued to go its heartless way, to the point where, in 1762, Abbé G. J. Raynal wrote that it would have been better not to have discovered America. That event was a catastrophic one, Raynal held,[115] and this is scarcely an exaggeration if one thinks not of the white immigrants but of the indigenous Americans, who were not only robbed of their lands, but almost exterminated by the "chosen people".

Practically the same regrettable story could be written about the East Indians, the Chinese, and the Japanese. Echoing the spirit of his time, Francis Xavier writes that "the inhabitants of India have no culture at all. It is hard to live among a people that knows not God, nor hears its own reason, because its life is so steeped in sin." Three centuries later the party line was the same: Bishop Anastasius Hartmann wrote, "The people are on the lowest rung of breeding and development, and steeped in the rawest idolatry. They lack the most primitive qualities of social life — namely, constancy, veracity, and enterprise. And we heard this from one end of India to the other".

A missionary in China in 1870 wrote: "The religions of China are ugly and absurd, the most ridiculous in the world. Their art has no rules, nor expression, nor aesthetics. Their only music is a satanic-sounding one. They have no idea of the beautiful. Their literature is stupid and childish, with neither thought nor feeling — sentences that make one want to vomit." Such was still the tenor of the language used by L. Kervyn as late as 1911 in his comprehensive work on the apostolate in modern China. The competent specialist, J. Beckmann, remarks, "Works like this one are not typical simply of this Belgian missioner, nor of the missionary society to which he belonged, nor indeed of the Catholic missions. They are typical of Europeans in general."[116]

Withal, there is no denying the good that came about through the presence of the whites on these continents. But for our purposes there is no point in underscoring it. There has always been plenty of that. What we need to face is the seamy side.

One has to smile today to discover that the Chinese and Japanese of those days, for their part, called the whites the "barbarians from the

South" (inasmuch as that is the direction from which they came), and commiserated with them for not having been born in their country. Appropriately, their artists caricatured the exotic strangers with a pale face and a long nose.[117]

§30 The Blacks of the U.S.A.

With Vatican II a very definite turn for the better came for the church's associates in history considered above — but not, in general, for the nonwhite races as such. In this sphere there are still two enormous problem areas to which we must briefly call the reader's attention: the racial problem in the U.S.A. and that in South Africa.

The blacks of the United States — as well as those of the other New World countries, where they have been to a certain extent integrated into society — are all descendants of slaves. Today it is estimated that some nine and a half million slaves reached the Americas, with perhaps the same number dying upon being captured, during the march to the coast, or on the voyage across the sea. Slavery raised no basic moral or religious questions at the time. On the contrary, Aristotle and the established thinking of the Middle Ages held that there are certain human beings who cannot properly manage their lives without strong direction by others. In order to shield the less suited American Indian from forced labour, the Catholic Bartolomeo de las Casas urged the introduction of black slaves from Africa.

Protestant Bishop Thomas Wilson (1663-1755) wrote, in a catechism that saw at least twenty-six English editions and was translated into other languages as well, that the black slaves had come from a land where there was neither law nor order, and where no one lived in security except those few violent persons who overpowered or killed the others. The blacks of America ought therefore to welcome the opportunity to live among civilized human beings, even as slaves. Wilson supports his contention by pointing out that even the Bible had cursed the descendants of Ham and destined them to slavery. They now had the good fortune to be baptized, and a just God would richly recompense, in the world to come, anything the "Negroes" had to bear here by way of privation and suffering, as long as they patiently accepted their lot.[118]

Slavery was abolished in the United States in 1868. According to the American Constitution all persons are endowed with the same rights. But politicians, as well as the churches, have done far too little to translate this into the reality of everyday life. Only the Quakers took up the cause of the blacks as early as the eighteenth century. Today it is particularly the free churches, the "sects", with their little centres on the city streets, that offer blacks genuine community, and afford them the opportunity of a spontaneous religious expression.

Without overlooking the various undertakings of the Christian churches, one cannot escape the fact that they have not come out radically enough in favour of the blacks, and that their behaviour has given cause for the very God they profess to see them as racists.[119] B. Chénu concludes his description of the situation "with a sense of the impotence of the Christian gospel":

> This gospel drives no wedge, it brings no new element into dialogue with the prevailing racist ideology. Of course the churches speak of the equality of all human beings, but this is mostly limited to religion. They feel more compassion than respect for the black person.[120]

The blacks have themselves taken action, out of the power of the gospel. They have taken a new stance, and have made for themselves another Christianity. They are on the point of living a far more radical Christianity.

On August 28, 1963, Martin Luther King, Jr., made his prophetic speech to the quarter of a million blacks marching on Washington:

> I have a dream! We shall be able to speed the day when all God's children, black and white, Jew and Gentile, Catholic and Protestant, shall take one another by the hand and sing, as in the old Negro spiritual, "Free at last!"

On April 4, 1968, he was shot to death. Have we the courage to go on believing in his dream anyway?

§31 The Blacks of South Africa

The situation of the blacks in South Africa would seem more hopeless still. Here racial discrimination is practised not in spite of laws but because of them.

Anyone who travels in South Africa loves this land, with its pleasant climate, its beautiful cities and coasts, its blooming agriculture, its developed industry, its efficient administration. South Africa has greater reserves of precious stones and minerals than the United States and Canada together. It could be a near-paradise, if it were not so cruelly scarred by original sin. Blacks, who constitute the majority of the population (with around twenty-five million, as compared with some four-and-one-half million whites), are daily humiliated in dozens of ways — in segregated bars, cinemas, buses, trains, and waiting rooms. The whole economy, as well, is geared to the welfare of the whites alone, who "need" the labour of the blacks. Seventeen percent of the white population consume seventy percent of the goods of the country. The blacks, and the "coloureds" (those of racially mixed parentage) have to be content with the rest. Forced to live in miserable slums, or in artificial box-house cities, or in the squalid "homelands" where they have only a pseudo-independence, they have nothing to say about the destiny of their own country.

112

Once they had conquered the country, its rulers managed to enslave the blacks and make them believe that they were worth nothing, so that they all became ashamed of their colour, their history, and their culture. They were made strangers in their own land.

> But now we have seen through your game. We have discovered that the great lie was woven through the whole fabric of life, even the writing of history, the sciences, and religion. The sciences, together with religion, were venal and meretricious, and served only for the upbuilding of the myth of a master race. Well, we are about to dismantle its foundations. We are about to tear down the great lie layer by layer until the truth comes to light. From now on we write our own history. Just your calling Kaffirs, natives, Bantus, non-whites, as if we were not fully human, typifies the whole gamut of your insults. But now there is black-power consciousness. And thanks to that, blackness has become something positive.[121]

So writes one of South Africa's black authors and theologians.

The situation in South Africa no longer concerns that land alone. It concerns the world. It could well happen that after Vietnam, Iran, and the Middle East, the next powder keg of world politics could be South Africa. The United States knows this, and is exerting pressure on the South African regime — not so much out of interest in the black majority as out of self-interest, for if the abolition of racial discrimination does not come from within will it come from without? That is, will it not come with the help of the Soviet Union? One can see the approaching catastrophe. The fight for Mozambique and Angola, which led to a victory for the black majority, began twenty years ago. Five years ago the same script was played out in Rhodesia, and there again the outcome was positive. Does anyone think this movement will call a halt at the gates of South Africa?

Russia has every reason for wanting to sweep into this land on the coat tails of the freedom fighters, and gain control of the world's gold, the world's diamonds, and the bulk of the world's uranium and chromium (used for the alloying of steel, hence for armaments), as well as control of all the traffic around the Cape. Should it succeed, it could throw an economic blockade around the Western world that would force it to its knees without having to resort to military action.[122]

This whole unhealthy situation is once more the fruit of a "chosen people" ideology. As the Boers undertook the long trek to the interior of the country, the Calvinist Church formed an indivisible unity with the people. The Boers felt like the chosen people of the exodus, in the desert on the way to a promised land. They carried the Bible in one hand and a rifle in the other. Black heathen tribes represented the Canaanite enemy, against whom the whites believed they had divine right on their side. To the Ham theory was now joined the Calvinist doctrine of predestination. At first the Boers were willing to admit baptized blacks into their own community; but soon the line of demarcation was no longer drawn between Christian and heathen, but between white and black — including white Christian and black Christian.

On the day before the decisive battle at Buffalo River on December 16, 1838, the Boers made a solemn vow, a kind of covenant with God. They numbered 470 men. The Zulus had 12,500. If God would give the Boers victory, they and their descendants would remember this day forever and build a church to honour it. More than three thousand Zulus fell under the guns of the Boers. From that day forward Buffalo River was called Blood River, and Covenant Day entered South African history. It is still celebrated every year, on December 16, with a divine service, speeches, and popular amusements. The nation's presidents, from Kruger to Vorster, seldom neglected the opportunity of referring to "the mighty works of God in history", and to emphasize the task of the whites as the outpost of Christian culture. The idea of the land, too, as in ancient Israel (see Part One, §20), exercises a powerful fascination.[123]

Today scepticism has crept in even here, it is true. The Afrikaner "Broederbond" ("brotherhood") — a secret society — is still in existence. Its thousands of dedicated members form the ideological backbone of the Dutch Reformed Church and the National Party. They cherish the old messianism and bolster the hard line. But other white South Africans see through their ideology and ask themselves whether Covenant Day honours Christ or Baal, and whether it is not time for a new covenant, one that would not play off the two races against each other but would embrace everyone in a covenant with God.[124]

The churches have made repeated public declarations, and have condemned the politics of apartheid. The National Conference of Catholic Bishops reacted very sharply in February 1977, after the rioting in Soweto[125] — although black priests have told me that the declaration was later very much watered down and has remained a dead letter. In 1978 a committee of the bishops' conference wrote President Vorster: "You are concerned about the threat of communism. But the best remedy for communism is not repression, but justice".

The Christian Council of Churches has shown even more courage and concreteness. From July 5 to 15, 1979, a meeting was held under its auspices with six thousand participants, half of them white and half of them black, for the purpose of praying, thinking, and working in common. One speaker, Ronald Sider, said:

> When a system is unjust, all who live and profit from the system are guilty. God is on the side of the poor. Thus, the people of God must also be in solidarity with the poor. Otherwise it will not be the people of God, however strong its experience of God, however orthodox its faith. One must emphasise this biblical truth as much as Christ's resurrection.

On July 27 that year the Christian Council informed the press that it now lent its moral support to all who break the race laws, inasmuch as such laws are not binding on the Christian conscience.

The government knows the seriousness of the situation. From sheer necessity it would like to change it from the inside. But its party is not so broad. One hears of a "peaceful transition", but black priests and lay persons comment that the accent is on the *peaceful*, not on the *transition*.

No one can foretell what is going to happen in South Africa. Race expert Egon von Eichstedt coined the saying, "Racial lunacy came from ignorance of race, not from knowledge of it." Another scientist, Albert Einstein, thought it easier to smash an atom than to smash a prejudice.[126] And yet it is still to be hoped that, even in South Africa — and wherever minorities or majorities are disadvantaged on account of their race, religion, or any other criterion — knowledge will triumph over ignorance, and freedom over violence. For this is where the current of our times is flowing.

Latter-day Antagonists

§32 The Modern Enlightenment

The first purpose of the title of §32 is to catch the reader's attention. But it is also intended as an umbrella for all ideas and movements that have this in common: they are not recognized or appreciated by the church in their legitimate aims, but instead (not entirely without fault on their own part) are condemned, and declared to be adversaries.

During the last century, men and women comprising the "Modern Enlightenment" came of age. They attempted to gain their freedom from the theocratic constraints imposed by the church. The church, feeling itself threatened on all sides, resolutely took arms. Its most important defence document was Pius IX's *Syllabus of Errors*, dated December 8, 1864. Pius hailed to the defendants' bench a long list of real or imagined enemies: pantheism, naturalism, rationalism, liberalism, socialism, communism, Freemasonry, the Bible societies, and even "those who hold the secular power of the pope to be difficult to reconcile with his spiritual task" and who thought the church would be happier and freer if it renounced earthly might.[127] Eighty propositions, or positions, were condemned.

Another document from Pius IX speaks even more frankly of the "artful, detestable Bible societies."[128] Pius's immediate predecessor, Gregory XVI, and his learned successor, Leo XIII, energetically rejected the notion that freedom of thought, writing, teaching, or religion were rights bestowed on men and women along with their human nature.[129]

The apostolic zeal behind all these condemnations is unmistakable. It should not be overlooked that all these modern movements — especially in Italy — were very radical and anticlerical. But they contained truth as well as error, and the church should have cracked the shell to get at the kernel, the legitimate aspirations of these movements. But the church showed itself to be just as radical as they. It was radically unable to give up its old schemata, radically unable to adapt to modern times. Unshakably self-sure, the church rejected values and aims that were deeply human and evangelical. It rejected movements that had acquired their anticlerical stripe precisely because the church itself (equated with the hierarchy) had goaded them to self-defence instead of to dialogue.

One wonders why these popes were so deprived of advisers who would have been capable of a more prophetic view of the new realities. All thinking was done in black and white. The church has the truth and so is always in the right. The others live in error and therefore what they fight for must be wicked.

It took the church a hundred years to discover that Bible societies do not go around wickedly falsifying the Bible, but act out of a genuinely evangelical spirit. Today cooperation with them is not only allowed but recommended (see §17, above). It took the church a hundred years to discover that freedom and religion and conscience, correctly understood, is indeed a basic human right (see DH). It took the church a hundred years to discover that Freemasonry, condemned by some two hundred papal documents, varies widely from country to country, and basically pursues humanitarian goals, and hence that Catholics should not be under a blanket prohibition from taking part in it. And indeed a letter of the Congregation for the Faith, dated July 19, 1974, virtually rescinds Canon 2335, which excommunicates Catholic Freemasons.

On September 20, 1970, the hundredth anniversary of the capture of Rome by Piedmontese troops, Pope Paul VI and President Saragat of Italy issued joint declarations, officially marking the demise of anti-clericalism and of the ecclesiastical sclerosis it had occasioned. Let us no longer look back, they said. Let us master the present, together.[130] Pope John Paul II used the occasion of the hundredth anniversary of the birthday of Albert Einstein, November 11, 1979, to make a public admission that Galileo had been unjustly dealt with, and to declare that henceforth the way was open "to a fruitful accord between science and faith, between church and world".[131]

Depending on the extent to which these official pronouncements are applied in practice, the men and women of contemporary learning and culture will no longer need to think of our theology as a joke. And what is more important, we will no longer need to think of them as a joke.

§33 Communism

Of the eight proclaimed enemies in the *Syllabus*, there is one that has since enjoyed an unprecedented development. Today it threatens not only the church but the whole world. That enemy is communism. With giant strides, its sphere of influence and power has expanded nearly everywhere. It began in Russia in 1917. Other European states fell to it in 1945, followed by China in 1949, Southeast Asia in 1973, and Mozambique and a series of other African countries since 1974. Today about forty percent of humankind lives under a communist regime.

How sad, how tragic, that such a towering messianic idea, which began by filling the masses with new hope for justice and equal opportunity, ended by making an alliance with brute force — the very sin with which Marx reproached the church! After that, communism no longer moved men and women toward their utopia; it imposed itself upon them by might, and forced them into a system that most of them would flee if they could. And so out goes the flame. "The expectation of a future paradise has often become a fanaticism that abuses and mishandles the human beings of the present", admits Milan Machovec, himself a Marxist.[132]

Unfortunately the religion Karl Marx knew did in fact attempt to palliate frustration and self-alienation in a bourgeois society. Feuerbach had posited religion's point of departure in unfulfilled individuality. Marx went further, citing the frustrating social situation as well. He set himself the goal of altering this situation, and of course this would render religion, the opium of the people, superfluous. One cannot deny that religion actually did exercise this soothing, and thereby alienating, function in Russia, precommunist Mozambique, Ethiopia, and elsewhere. And so before we throw any stones at communism, we have reason to strike our own breast, and ask ourselves how far we ourselves are responsible for communism's progress.

Thus communism became not merely an economic system, but a materialistic ideology as well. Today the two facets are so interlinked that no wedge may any longer be driven between them, or so Gustav Wetter claims. Any hope of a surrender of its atheistic ideology is either a heresy for Soviet philosophy to repudiate, or a temporary accommodation tolerated for certain practical advantages, but ruthlessly to be eliminated at the proper moment.[133]

Still, we should take cognizance of an extremely well documented study by J. P. Miranda according to which Marx would not be that hard atheist, but rather a "Christian humanist", whose ideas were deeply in harmony with the Bible. For he insisted much on the dignity of the human being, on moral conscience; he condemned the mentality of the capitalists as the "idolatry of Mammon, of Baal" ("Not only with their lips do they pray to this idol, but with all the forces of their body and soul"); he was convinced of the immanent meaning of history, and that at last "humanity will be delivered, once for all, from all exploitation and all oppression", eschatological texts reminiscent of the Old Testament prophets. True, he called himself an atheist, but there are also texts in which, for example, he professes "that shrewd Spirit that continually

117

manifests himself in all these contradictions". In any case, Miranda concludes that Marx would not have allowed today's Marxism to be taught in school, because it has become an ideology.[134] In other words as Nestorius was not a Nestorian (cf. note 10, above), Marx can be said not to have been a Marxist; and as Christians must always reorientate and renew themselves on the model of Christ, so Marxists would do well to follow the authentic Marx more closely.

Of course, the church could have no sympathy for the system as it was in fact presented. Pope Pius XI declared war on two fronts in the same week: on March 14, 1937, he published the encyclical *Mit brennender Sorge* against Nazism, and on March 19 *Divini Redemptoris* against communism. "Communism", the pope declares tersely, "is evil in its innermost essence, and no one who wishes to save Christian culture will cooperate with it in any area".[135]

This hardly says the last word. In spite of popes, communism fascinated not only the labouring masses but some of the best minds and spirits in the church. They believed that such a phenomenon could not simply be ignored, and thereby isolated. In France, a "Paris Mission" endeavoured to approach the great mass of persons who no longer darkened a church door because they believed they would find nothing inside but " a gathering of pious believers making use of God for their own ends, and shutting themselves up in transcendental selfishness". These masses were no longer called "de-Christianized". Now it was realized that they had never been Christian in the first place. The Mission also initiated conversations with workers and their communist leaders. Rome had very little liking for that. One of the guiding spirits of the Mission, Y. Daniel, reports Cardinal Ottaviani's question to him, "So you meet with communists here and there?" And his answer: "When you send missionaries to Africa, you have to expect them to meet with blacks here and there."[136]

In Germany and Austria, the *Paulusgesellschaft* was formed. It organised conversations with Marxists in Salzburg in 1965 and Marienbad in 1967, and published the *Internationale Dialog-Zeitschrift* ("International Periodical for Dialogue"). The purpose of both the conferences and the periodical was to subject the conceptions and intentions of both sides to a mutual review. Both the Catholics and the Marxists had ideas and aims for a more humane shaping of the world. Some of these ideas were held in common, and others were peculiar to one side. The hope was that the convergencies would be identified, sterile polemics would be overcome, and the way would be paved for maximal cooperation.[137] The project did not get very far. The periodical ceased publication in 1974, and the conversations were not resumed, principally because the Marxist interlocutors did not represent the "proper" Marxism and were disavowed, or even outright ejected, by their respective political parties. Heretics, we see, still burn.

Rome did not stick fast in the position of Pius XI. Even in the reign of Pius XII there was a group, led by Monsignor Cawlina, Cardinal Bea, and others, who believed the church could no longer safeguard its interests against Marxism merely by standing on its rights. What was communism basically striving for? Was there not a genuinely human value there, in spite of the ideology, in spite of the violence?

Then, through the keen initiative of pastoral Pope John XXIII, what had been going on in the wings came on stage. His encyclical *Pacem in Terris* (1963), the first to be addressed not only to the bishops but "to all human beings of goodwill", teaches that even if a person espouses social or political errors, he or she is not necessarily wicked as a person. Hence it is permissible to foster community with persons who do not believe in Christ. Prudence alone can determine whether and to what degree this is indicated in particular cases.[138]

It is said that this move, accented by the visit of Khrushchev's son-in-law Adzhubei, cost the Christian Democrats a million votes. But at the same time it finally overcame a bloc-mentality of the sort that set Christendom against Islam in the Middle Ages (see §25, above). It is not with an "anti" mentality that one should vie for votes, but with positive moves.

Along the same lines, Paul VI established the Secretariat for the non-believers in 1965. Its assignment was to get at the deeper causes of atheism, and to pave the way for a dialogue with atheists no matter what the difficulties might be. The council had already taken a basic step when it attempted to give atheism a new interpretation in *Gaudium et Spes* (GS 19-21, 92). Then came the new curial organs, one by one, keeping pace with the official church's step-by-step openness to "outsiders" — the laity, other Christians, and non-Christians. Now, with this latest secretariat, sights were fixed on the "furthest out" of all. The secretariat cannot boast great accomplishments, for a variety of reasons. But it is there, as a symbol and sign of good will and of hope.[139]

Now the question arises whether the term "nonbelievers" is still the right one. We have had to rename the "pagans", and the "non-Christians" (see §28, above); perhaps we should no longer define "nonbelievers" in terms of a "none". It is not the Christian faith that is the obvious norm and standard, with unbelief constituting the deviation. The case is really the other way around: unbelief is normal, and the Christian view of life is the great surprise. Like the first Christians, we must once more give an accounting of the hope we have (1 Peter 3:15). To speak in a perfectly balanced way, we would have to describe Christian faith today as "non-unbelief".

But there is something else, something even more important. Those outside the church who are at ground zero as far as faith is concerned are linked with us in some way. If they are not our partners in dialogue, at least they are our associates in human nature. They must be taken very seriously.[140] Christians need not necessarily "preach" to them, but ought to be gentle light shining into their lives, a sacramental sign that there is more going on in those lives than the persons who live them are willing to admit (see Part Four, §§19, 29).

Dialogue between blocs will always be difficult. No matter how necessity may force it to do business with another system, a system will still see itself as someone's adversary. But conversation person to person is never hopeless. It is striking how Pope John Paul II does not as a rule condemn a system — neither communism nor capitalism nor the national-security ideology that is evident in Latin America, as well as elsewhere. He does not forbid the Puebla bishops to place the last-named system under indictment,[141] but he himself goes another road. He scores transgressions of human rights wherever they occur; this is true. But for the rest, he seeks to keep up a good relationship with the persons who suffer in the systems — wraps them in sympathy, as it were, so that the systems may improve gradually from within.

Capitalism can still surely not be called an ideal system, but it is much better today than it was a hundred years ago. On the basis of its own insight that the factory runs better when workers are happy, and as a result of pressure from labour unions, it has changed for the good. Can one not have the same hope for the other systems? One hopes that this legitimate and prophetic view may be attended with success.

Thus from the very nature of the matter, the dialogue between Christians and Marxists has its own optimistic side. The Marxist can never escape his or her own shadow. Even Marxists carry around with them life's ultimate questions, always and necessarily. To boot, the ideal to which they commit themselves exists only as a postulate, and thereby constitutes all the more reason why they can never be satisfied with their lives.[142] It is unfortunate that there are as yet no rebellions against the interior Marxist state of mind. There probably will be none, as long as the system holds firm. Marxism seeks systematically to make person-to-person dialogue impossible, by requiring Marxists never to appear alone, but at least in pairs so that they can be checked on.

A priest from Poland declared in a meeting that at most five percent of the people in his country were Marxists — if they were Marxists. Some day, when the Marxists have finished striving in vain to do away with religion as frustrating and alienating, perhaps it may come to light how much frustration and alienation there is in Marxism.

We only stand on the threshold of a confrontation with Marxism. What we have been practising is sterile anticommunism. That is no suitable politics. That is no politics at all. It is only an alibi for a lack of politics. In the discussion just around the corner we must keep in mind that there is no longer any such thing as simply "communism", just as there is no longer any such thing as "Christianity". Christianity exists in its Catholic, Orthodox, and Protestant forms. Even within the Catholic

120

Church there are various directions it can take. Similarly, communism exists in different Russian, Polish, Albanian editions. In fact, there is European, African, and Chinese communism. The Kremlin, and certain Roman circles, liked the old monolith, the old bloc. But life, and history, are stronger than ideologies, and so today we must study concrete communism, and take care not to fall into generalizations. The example of China demonstrates that changes are possible from the inside.[143]

The gauntlet has been flung down. Hope has dawned. Every means must be atttempted to approach Marxists. The Vatican's East European politics is hotly disputed, but H. Stehle places it in its broader context of history and sounds an optimistic note:

> The East European politics of the Vatican is part of a great historical panorama, reaching back two thousand years. Popes went into banishment and emperors to Canossa. Saints were martyred and heretics burned. New doctrines were rejected, and then accepted when the time was right. And the earth is still turning.[144]

There are those whose one great interest is in the existing "order" of things — *their* order. Anyone who rattles this order a bit by coming out for the rights of the poor is immediately labelled a "communist", and the most brutal methods stand ready for bringing them into line. This is no better than what the communists do themselves. In Brazil recently, a 357-page secret document "pointed out" the infiltration of that country's clergy, and the Vatican, by communists. Paul VI himself was analyzed as being procommunist. The proof lay in the church's systematic consciousness-raising of the poor classes, in its rejection of capitalism, in its defence of priests who had been accused of subversive activities. The church's lack of order and authority was much deplored.[145]

This is the rightist anticommunist mentality that could assault Bishop Adriano Hyppolito in 1976 and splash him with red paint; or murder Archbishop Oscar A. Romero on March 25, 1980, as he was celebrating Mass; or threaten the Jesuits and other missioners in El Salvador and Guatemala, and kill a number of them — all of these outrages for one reason: the victims had come out in favour of a more just order. And so they were decried as "communists". History will tell us whether or not communism will prevail precisely as a result of this kind of sterile anticommunism.

There is another kind of anticommunism, and it is just as anachronistic, uncritical, and unevangelical as the first. Anyone may have his or her good political, economic, or religious reasons for not being a communist. But why see communism as the embodiment of all evil, and resurrect the medieval "lump thinking"? As Vatican II was opening, a book was distributed to all the conciliar fathers. The distribution had the approval of certain Italian cardinals, who live in

121

panic at the thought of new ideas in the church. The book was by a certain M. Pinay, and it called for a new crusade, against the Jews, the Freemasons, and the communists.[146]

This "anti mentality" is still very much at work in certain minds. For some, all actions and initiatives of the "others", whether they be Freemasons, radicals, socialists, communists, or what have you, are automatically suspect, wicked, and a simple camouflage for dangerous intent. But is it really true that *we* always act from ideal motives, but the "others" sadly lack our purity of intention?

Finally, we should mention those movements and periodicals that take for themselves very Christian and churchly names, but brand everything that does not fit their preconciliar concepts as antichurch, heretical, and communistic. These rightist coteries occasion a polarization. They bring the "cold war" into the church. They refuse to acknowledge a legitimate pluriformity of opinions and attitudes. They reject all thought of unity in diversity, of mutual understanding and Christian tolerance (see §§16, 19, above).

The more we listen to ourselves alone, the narrower and more limited we become. On the other hand the more we are open to the Spirit of Jesus, the more we open up to all human beings as well. We no longer set up battlefronts against those outside the church, and surely not against our sisters and brothers within the church. Only the self-righteous, who looked down on others and sought to lay unbearable legal burdens upon them (Matt. 23:4), could not depend on Jesus' mercy. One ought to learn something from the gospel, as well as from the long history we have here reviewed.

Chapter Six

Final Considerations

§34 A Feeling of Anxiety

We have taken six slices of history, lengthwise, and have examined how the church dealt or misdealt with its six groups of associates in history. Now we may feel a certain depression, or a certain humility. We certainly cannot simply draw a glad breath and thank God for this history. No, we go our way pensively, with a feeling of anxiety. Why did things have to be that way? Why did the church so often talk past its partners, talk against them, condemn them without having heard them? The only thing we both did together was fight. In that fight it was we, the church, who were the more clever — and thanks to our alliance with worldly might, unfortunately also the stronger, for a long time.

The way of the church through time is surely the way of the cross, as Jesus foretold (Matt. 16:24, Luke 21:12). But it was not often the church that carried the cross. The church thrust the cross, and its stigma, onto the shoulders of others. For them (the "not chosen people"), the presence of Christians (the "chosen people") rarely had the effect of blessing and salvation, but of curse and trouble. The church itself went its way in triumph. It did all it could to bring to fulfilment its petition in the Litany of the Saints, "That thou wouldst humble the enemies of holy church" — and not through the impotence of God on the cross, but through the might of Christendom, in whose museums to this very day are displayed countless paintings of its battles and sieges. One really has to wonder what the Christians of those times were thinking of when they read the Bible and then did exactly the opposite of what Jesus had intended them to.

History speaks an honest language, and in our case a hard one. We may not allow ourselves to gild it, or shrug it off, or drown it out with apologetics. It is a heavy mortgage, and we have to assume it. It is part of the "sin of the world" — doubtless the Lamb of God will take it away, but first it has to be confessed and repented. The Second Vatican Council did something in this direction — for example, in *Dignitatis Humanae*, when it admits that, in the history of the church, "now and then a manner of action occurred that little corresponded to the spirit of the gospel, indeed was even opposed to it" (12). Sins of weakness are easily forgiven. But sins of might — a self-assurance that does others injustice, authority that violates others' rights and personhood — have deep roots, and a change of heart is required before they can be forgiven.

Our survey of this history of unsalvation has been in broad strokes, like the view from an overpassing satellite. Were we to resurrect the details from the archives, the reader would shudder, scarcely able to believe the facts of history. Thus any discomfort our pages may have occasioned here and there in their presentation of these facts is only the faintest echo of the furious indignation of those whom the church has persecuted and humiliated.

It is true, I repeat (see §1, above), that our concern here had been only with the outward aspect of the church. And even from this aspect we have to admit, in order to be fair, that there have been better times too, times of more understanding, and a better side, the side characterized by charity and constructive work. I likewise wish to repeat that the purpose of Part Two has not been the indictment of the men and women of times gone by. In their place we probably would have thought and acted as they did, for their times were feudal, colonial, preconciliar. But we do have responsibility for one thing: it is up to us that this attitude be not prolonged. It is up to us not to repeat the mistakes of the past. Perhaps these pages may serve as a shock therapy to this end.

§35 *An Ideology of Election*

At the root of the unsalvation history we have just portrayed is not the theology of election, but what became of it: an ideology of election. It was an ideology of election that allied itself with might, generating a mentality of supremacy, exclusivism, and intolerance, with devastating consequences. True, intolerance can seem all too closely bound up with revelation and prophetic speech. The prophet speaks and acts by God's commission. Whoever opposes him or her opposes God. Then, in the Catholic Church, the authority of the prophets was transferred to the church as an institution, and magnified to such an extent that Martin Luther was partially justified in flying against it with such passion. It is also true that he himself laid claim to this prophetical authority and right of intolerance no less passionately.[147]

We have to go back and question all the "convictions" that led to such absurdities. We must subject them to a critique based on the biblical grounds they claim, and much will have to be demythologized. This is what we shall be doing in Part Four. But as we close Part Two it will not be out of place to take cognizance of certain voices raised in judgment of this ideology of election; they support the analysis that will come later.

Arnold Toynbee:

> It is a painful irony of human history that the acknowledgment of one sole God, and the concept that all human beings are brothers and sisters before

124

God, should at the same time have brought with it intolerance and persecution. The explanation naturally lies in the fact that the concept of the unity of all believers drives the protagonists of this concept to feel their goal so important that they utilize every means to translate it into reality... Hence, the influence of the concept of unity on a religion seems to lead to spiritual monstrosity. The persecution of the "wrong" religion by the self-styled "right" one is a self-contradiction, for by the very fact of such persecution the "right" or "true" religion places itself in the wrong, pulls the rug out from under its own feet ... The concept of unity attained its highest and crudest expression in church government when the church allowed spiritual supremacy fully to coincide with the supreme secular power. The papacy offers perhaps the most outstanding example of the disastrous influence of a self-intoxicated conqueror.[148]

Jürgen Moltmann:

The pusillanimous mind-set, the "mentality of little faith", generally presents itself in the mentality of an orthodoxy feeling threatened, hence particularly stiff and rigid. It presents itself when the immorality of the present age is opposed to a so-called Christian morality, and penal law is imposed instead of the gospel of creative love for the forsaken ... Where the Christian church is penetrated by a "religion of fear", faith is raped and strangled by the very persons who consider themselves its best guardians. Instead of confidence and freedom, they disseminate anxiety and apathy . . . The representatives of this attitude wall themselves up defensively within their ghetto and apocalyptically call themselves the "little flock" or the "faithful remnant", delivering the world without to the very godlessness and immorality they are deploring.[149]

F. Heer:

There is no world religion, and no human society, that has again and again amassed in its bosom the quantity of dynamite that "Christian society" has . . . Again and again it has manufactured its "deadly enemies" and its scapegoats. The church constituted itself the permanent pyre for the burning of "heretics" of right and left.

Heer goes on to speak of the self-enclosure of the church as a pathological social structure, and concludes: "Christianity is guilty of depriving the world of hope".[150]

Last, let us hear the voice of a New World black, Frantz Fanon:

This Europe, which has never stopped talking about "human beings", which has never ceased crying that it cares only for human beings! Today we know the suffering with which humanity has paid for every one of the victories of the European spirit. Up, mates, Europe is played out, and for good! We shall have to find something else.[151]

Yes, the church, by its exclusivism, has made itself into a kind of sect. Instead of proclaiming the oneness of all the men and women of God, and then living by its own model, it has exalted itself and condemned the

125

others. This simply cannot continue. This is the direction in which things have been going, but thank God, they can go no further.

§36 New Horizons

During the last twenty years, we have suddenly been transported onto a new landscape. There is a new wind, a new panorama, new horizons. And this time it is no mirage, but experiential reality.

In place of an un-Christian anti-Semitism, we see Christian-Jewish groups and commissions and a common interest in Jesus. In place of an inhumane heretic-hunting, we have ecumenical conversations and hope for union in the future. In place of a diabolical "heathenism", we have a new theology of the non-Christian religions, and a confluence at all levels. In place of a white racist hegemony even in the church, there are African and Asian bishops and cardinals. In place of a dozen imaginary enemies, we enjoy conversation and cooperation with the Bible societies, with the Masons, and with communists. Depressing as it may have been to make our six slices lengthwise through history, the depression was always equalled by the surprise that came at the end. In each case there was a "happy ending" — and not just the manufactured happy ending of a wishful dream or novel, but the reality of de facto historical development.

This general relaxation of tension is due to good Pope John XXIII and his council. They have led the church onto a new path, they have opened new horizons on history. The council's "new start" may not have kept all its promises, and many today have become weary and discouraged. And there is no minimizing the disintegration occurring today within the church itself. Nevertheless I am convinced that as far as the outward aspect of the church is concerned, we are living in a new, promising, and privileged phase of history that is impossible to overprize. It should be exploited by every means. It is true that we live within the Christian dialectic between the "already" and the "not yet", and we still see so much that is "not yet". But this is no cause for us to blind ourselves to what is already.

This historical survey (Part Two), hence, has had not just the effect of a shock therapy, but perhaps that of a brand-new start as well. The church's behaviour, its attitudes, and thereby its opportunities vis-à-vis its partners in history, are incomparably better today than they have ever been since the conversion of Constantine. Tomorrow's historiography will be astonished at this new turn.

But now we stand on the threshold of an important, broader Part Three. Now that we have spoken at such length of our own view of the others, the "not chosen peoples", the moment has come to investigate how these other peoples look upon themselves. Human individuals and peoples are not first and foremost what *others* think of them, but what *they* think of themselves. Long before they came into contact with us, these others were living their own history. They already possessed their own identity. Cautiously, and without prejudice, let us go in search of it.

Notes to Part Two

1   *Il trionfo della Santa Sede e della Chiesa contro gli assalti dei novatori.* See H. Fries, "Wandel des Kirchenbildes," MS 4/1:269-72.
2   H. Stinimann and L. Vischer, *Papsttum und Petrusdienst: Kritische Erwägungen* (Frankfurt, 1975); M. Kehl, *Kirche als Institution* (Frankfurt, 1976), pp. 106-9, "Ekklesiologie unter Ideologieverdacht"; I. Hermann, *Die Christen und ihre Konflikte.*
3   F. Châtelet and G. Mairet, eds., *Storia delle ideologie,* 2 vols. (Milan, 1978).
4   See Rahner, *Das freie Wort in der Kirche.*
5   Caprile, *Il Concilio Vaticano II,* 2:240ff.
6   Conzemius, *Propheten und Vorläufer,* pp. 136-58.
7   See H. Jedin, "Kirchengeschichte als Theologie," *Seminarium* 13:39-58 (Rome, 1973); V. Conzemius, "Kirchengeschichte als 'nicht-theologische Disziplin,'" in Haag and Kasper, *Relevanz der Geschichte,* pp. 187-97. In this same connection I have had conversations with Prof. F. Kempf of Rome and Prof. V. Conzemius of Lucerne.
8   Conzemius, *Propheten,* p. 196.
9   H. Fries, "Wandel," pp. 223-85, esp. 235-49; Jedin, *Handbuch,* passim, esp. 3/1:97-110, "Vom Regnum Francorum zum Imperium christianum," and 497-506, "Die abendländische Christenheit" (F. Kempf); P. Friolet, "Chiesa e cristianità," in Châtelet, *Storia delle ideologie,* pp. 293-308; H. Tüchle, "Mittelalter," LThK 7:494-97.
10 Fries, "Wandel," p. 249.
11 See J. Daniélou, *Théologie du Judéo-Christianisme* (Tournai, 1958).
12 Schelkle, *Israel un die Kirche im Neuen Testament;* Heer, F., *Gottes erste Liebe. 2000 Jahre Judentum und Christentum* (Munich, 1967); Kühner, H., *Der Antisemitismus der Kirche* (Zurich, 1976); Lichtenberg, J.P., *From the First to the Last of the Justs* (Jerusalem, 1971); Talmage, F.E., *Disputation and Dialogue: Readings in the Jewish-Christian Encounter* (New York, 1975); Pfammatter, J., and Furger, F., eds., *Judentum und Kirche: Volk Gottes* (Einsiedeln, 1974).
13 Talmage, *Disputation,* pp. 5-18.
14 E. Iserloh, "Die Juden in der Christenheit des Mittelalters," Jedin, *Handbuch* 3/2:717-28.
15 Küng, *Christsein,* p. 160 (with copious references).
16 Kühner, *Der Antisemitismus,* p. 191.
17 Katz, *Exclusiveness and Tolerance,* emphasizes this aspect.
18 Heer, *Gottes erste Liebe,* pp. 465ff.; Pinchas Lapide, cited in Loth, *Christentum im Spiegel,* pp. 189ff.; HK, March 1980, p. 143. See also the book by R. Ruether.
19 Hammerstein, *Von Vorurteil zum Verständnis,* pp. 7ff.
20 Consider for instance the books on Jesus by Jewish authors J. Glausner, D. Flusser, P. Lapide, Schlomo ben Chomi. For this data I am grateful to the Rev. Jorge Mejía, secretary of the Roman Commission for the Jews.
21 E. Berkovits, "Judaism in the Post-Christian Era," in Talmage, *Disputation,* pp. 284-95.

²² G. Koch, "Judentum in Gespräch. Interview mit Prof. J. Petuchowski," HK, October 1978, pp. 501ff.

²³ See Hasenhüttl;. *Ketzerbewältigung*, pp. 13-18; Goldstein, *Paulinische Gemeinde*, pp. 87-90; Papa, *Tensioni e unità*.

²⁴ Schmitz, *Frühkatholizismus*, pp. 25ff., 200, 213.

²⁵ R. Leys and L. Abramowski, in LThK 7:885-89; Grillmeier, *Mit ihm und in ihm*, pp. 219-24, "Häresie und Wahrheit: Eine häresiologische Studie als Beitrag zu einem ökumenischen Problem heute."

²⁶ See Denzinger-Schönmetzer, *Enchiridion Symbolorum*.

²⁷ J. Cabaud, *Simone Weil* (Paris, 1968); W. Nigg, *Das Buch der Büsser* (Olten, 1970), pp. 219-42.

²⁸ AAS, 1962, pp. 286-795.

²⁹ See: Grundmann, H., *Ketzergeschichte des Mittelalters* (Gottingen, 1963); *Bibliographie zur Ketzergeschichte des Mittelalters* (Rome, 1967); Nigg, W., *Das Buch der Ketzer* (Zurich, 1949); Böhm, A., ed., *Häresien der Zeit* (Freiburg, 1961); Hasenhüttl, G., *Herrschaftsfreie Kirche. Sozio-theologische Grundlegung* (Düsseldorf, 1974). Cf. also Jedin, *Handbuch* 3/2:263-73; L. Sala-Molins, "La polizia della fede: l'inquisizione," in Châtelet, Storia delle ideologie 1:371-83.

³⁰ Besides the references in note 29, see P. Mikat, in LThK 5:698-702.

³¹ Thus, for example, A. Heim, *Weltbild eines Naturforschers* (Zurich, 1942). See the response by J.B. Villiger, "Kirche und Inquisition," in F. Dessauer, ed., *Wissen und Bekenntnis* (Oelten, 1944), pp. 202-25.

³² *Der Prozess Jeanne d'Arc: Akten und Protokolle* (Munich, 1961). Printed in Hasenhüttl, *Formen kirchlicher Ketzerbewältigung*, p. 54, and in J. Lecler, *Toleration and the Reformation* (New York and London, 1960), 2:475ff.

³³ H. Grundmann, *Ketzergeschichte des Mittelalters; Bibliographie zur Ketzergeschichte des Mittelalters*.

³⁴ A. Rotzetter, *Die Funktion der franziskanischen Bewegung in der Kirche* (Schwyz, 1977), pp. 294ff.

³⁵ Nigg, *Das Buch der Ketzer*, pp. 9-21.

³⁶ Along with Jedin, *Handbuch* 4:3-446. see especially Lortz, *Die Reformation in Deutschland*, 2 vols.

³⁷ Lortz, *Reformation* 1:84ff., 75.

³⁸ Lohse, *Epochen der Dogmengeschichte*, p. 194.

³⁹ See Fernando da Riese, *Un "lavatore delle scudelle" a corte d'Asburgo* (Padua, 1972); Fiorenze S. Cuman, *L'apporto di Fra Tommaso da Olera per la difesa della fede* (Rome, 1980; doctoral dissertation at the Urbanianum College).

⁴⁰ Lortz, *Reformation* 1:381-437; Beyna, *Das katholische Lutherbild*.

⁴¹ OR, November 16, 1956.

⁴² Lortz, *Reformation*, pp. 410ff., 424.

⁴³ OR, May 21, 1925.

⁴⁴ Brown, *The Ecumenical Revolution*, pp. 4-8, 90-103; P. Barrett, *Religious Liberty and the American Presidency* (New York, 1963).

⁴⁵ See the secretariat's regular *Information Service*, Rome.

⁴⁶ Thus Pope John Paul II on repeated occasions, e.g., OR, October 18, 1978, and December 20, 1978, as well as in *Redemptor Hominis*, No. 5.

⁴⁷ H. Mühlen, *Morgen wird Einheit sein: Das kommende Konzil aller Christen*.

⁴⁸ UR 1; AG 6.

⁴⁹ K.S. Latourette, *A History of the Expansion of Christianity*, 7 vols. (New York, 1937-45).

⁵⁰ Bühlmann, *Wo der Glaube lebt*, pp. 171-81 (English edition: *The Coming of the Third Church*); "Ökumenismus in Afrika," *Evangelisches Missionsmagazin* 114:118-43 (Basel, 1970); *Missionsprozess*, pp. 92-95 (English edition: *The Missions on Trial*, St Paul Publications, Slough/Orbis Books, Maryknoll, N.Y.); J. Beckmann, ed., *Die Heilige Schrift in den katholischen Missionen* (Schöneck, 1966).

⁵¹ R. Aubert, "Die modernistische Krise," in Jedin, *Handbuch* 4/2:435-506; J.

Schmidlin, *Papstgeschichte der neuesten Zeit* 3:138-78 (Munich, 1936).
52 E. Poulat, *Catholicisme, démocratie et socialisme: Le mouvement catholique et Mgr. Benigni.*
53 Trevor, *Prophets and Guardians*, pp. 204ff.; Capovilla, *X anniversario*, pp. 38-42.
54 Schmidlin, *Papstgeschichte*, pp. 139, 165, 169.
55 E. Buonaiuti, *Pellegrino a Roma*, p. 107.
56 Rahner, "Was ist Häresie?" *Schriften* 5:527-76.
57 Internationale Theologen-Kommission, *Die Einheit des Glaubens und der theologische Pluralismus* (Einsiedeln, 1973), with literature cited there.
58 This type of behaviour appears as a constant element. See H. Fries and G. Schwaiger, *Katholische Theologen im 19. Jahrhundert*, 3 vols. (Munich, 1975).
59 Caprile, *Il Concilio* 3:212.
60 Köhler, *Bewusstseinsstörungen*, p. 30. Cf Schroeder's *Aufbruch und Missverständnis*, also written out of disappointment. See also K. Rahner, "Glaubenskongregation und Theologen-Kommission," *Schriften* 10:338-57.
61 *Annuarium Statisticum Ecclesiae* (Rome, 1979). Cf. Bühlmann, *Wo der Glaube lebt*, pp. 28-32 (English edition: *The Coming of the Third Church*).
62 See B. Häring, "Reflexionen zur Erklärung der Glaubenskongregation über einige Fragen der Sexualethik," *Theologische-praktische Quartalschrift* 1976:115-26 (Linz).
63 Bas van Iersel, "Um den Rechtsschutz im römischen Lehrprüfungsverfahren," ORI 1980:42-45, 52-56.
64 Nigg, *Ketzer*, p. 513.
65 W. de Vries, *Rom und die Patriarchate ded Ostens*, pp. 183-423; "Die Päpste von Avignon und der christliche Osten," *Orientalia Christiana Periodica* 30:85-128 (Rome, 1964).
66 De Vries, "Avignon," p. 86.
67 Jedin, *Handbuch* 3/2:699-711.
68 Maximos IV, ed., *The Eastern Churches*, pp. 48-52.
69 See for example the conclusions of the recent work by J. Spitteris, *La critica Bizantina del Primato Romano.*
70 See de Vries, *Rom und die Patriarchate*, pp. 183, 218. A similar statement is to be found in G. Mojoli, *Attività ligurgica della S.C.P.F. per il rito orientale 1862-1892* (Vicenza, 1972) and *1893-1917* (Vicenza, 1979), where it is asserted in the Foreword that the principal purpose of the publication of the documents was to demonstrate that the Holy See always (!) had the intention, and carried it out in practice, not to latinize the Eastern churches, but to preserve them in their original purity (2:5).
71 The whole Decree *Orientalium Ecclesiarum*; cf. LG 15, 23; UR 14-18.
72 AAS. 1966, p. 21.
73 See Bühlmann, *Wo der Glaube lebt*, pp. 66ff. (English edition: *The Coming of the Third Church*); *Alle haben denselben Gott*, pp. 143.58 (English edition: *All have the same God*, St Paul Publications, Slough; *The Search for God*, Orbis Books, Maryknoll, N.Y.).
74 See Jedin, *Handbuch* 1:187-211, 245-480; Schlette, *Die Religionen*, pp. 22-27; H. Chadwick, *Early Christian Thought and the Classical Tradition* (Oxford, 1966).
75 *Stromata I* (Migne, *Patrologia Graeca* 8:718). Cf. Gal. 3:24ff.
76 M. Schmaus, *Katholische Dogmatik*, vol. 3, part 1 (Munich, 1958), pp. 820-29; J. Beumer, LThK 3:1320ff.
77 "Ita ergo se res habebat: jacebat in malis, vel etiam volvebatur, et de malis in mala praecipitabatur totius humani generis massa damnata; et adjuncta parti eorum qui peccaverant angelorum, luebat impiae desertionis dignissimas poenas" (*Enchiridion ad Laurentium* [Migne, *Patrologia Latine* 40:245]). Cf. Lohse, *Dogmengeschichte*, pp. 115-21, "Augustinus"; Rahner, *Heilswille Gottes*, in SM 2:656-64.
78 *De Civitate Dei* 18:47. For this whole area see Y. Congar, "Ecclesia ab Abel," in M. Reding, ed., *Abhandlungen über Theologie und Kirche* (Düsseldorf, 1952), pp. 29-108.
79 In the new Divine Office, for the Consecration of the Lateran Basilica, November 9.
80 Denzinger-Schönmetzer, *Enchiridion*, no. 1351.

129

81 Meyer, *Geschichte der Kreuzzüge*, esp. pp. 256-65.
82 Daniel-Rops, *Histoire de l'Eglise du Christ* 3:479-83.
83 E. Benz, *Ideen zu einer Theologie der Religionswissenschaft* (Wiesbaden, 1960), p. 21. For this whole matter see Hoheisel, *Das Christentum*, p. 387; M. Grabmann, *Die Geschichte der katholischen Theologie seit dem Ausgang der Väterzeit* (Darmstadt, 1961), pp. 49-53.
84 *Orthodoxae Fidei Lumini, Haereticorum Vindici, in Virtute Sanctissimi Nominis Turcarum Fulmini*. For another typical example of the attitude with which one gave one's life with joy for God and the church in those days "in the struggle against the heathen, Mohammedans, Jews, Heretics, and godless," see the book by M. Tanner, *Societas Jesu usque ad Sanguinis et Vitae Profusionem Militans, in Europa, Africa, Asia et America, contra Gentiles, Mahometanos, Judaeos, Haereticos, pro Deo, Fide, Ecclesia, Pietate sive Vita, et Mors eorum qui ex Societate Jesu in Causa Fidei et Virtutis Propugnatae, Violenta Morte Toto Orbe Sublati Sunt* (Prague, 1675).
85 Beumann, *Heidenmission und Kreuzzugsgedanke*, esp. pp. 138ff., 177-274.
86 For a typical case see Waldenfels, *Denn ich bin bei euch*, pp. 155-60 (Father Charles Orazio di Castorano's *Brevis Apparatus et Modus Agendi ac Disputandi cum Mahometanis*, a debate manual for use against Muslims in China, presented by A. Camps.
87 Schedl, *Muhammed und Jesus*, esp. pp. 5ff., 556-66- Cf. Schumann, *Der Christus der Muslime*.
88 Jedin, *Handbuch* 1:334-36; H. von Campenhausen, "Das Martyrium in der Mission," in Frohnes, *Kirchengeschichte* 1:71-85.
89 H. Rahner, *Die Martyrerakten*, pp. 18-20, 42ff., 72.
90 Mulders, *Missionsgeschichte*, pp 116-23; H. Löwe, "Pirmin, Willibrord und Bonifatius: Ihre Bedeutung fur die Missionsgeschichte ihrer Zeit," in Frohnes, *Kirchengeschichte* 2:192-226. It is significant that C. Raabe, ed., *Sankt Bonifatius: Gedenkgabe zum 1200. Todestag* (Fulda, 1954), has nothing whatever in its 686 pages about this aspect of his preaching and his death.
91 1 Celano, 55:42. See P. Oktavian, "Das Leiden Christi im Leben des heiligen Franziskus von Assisi," in *Collectanea Franciscana* 30:353-97 (Rome, 1960) esp. pp. 365-79, "Die Sehnsucht des heiligen Franziskus nach dem Martyrium." Cf. also L. Iriarte, "Die missionarisch-franziskanische Spiritualität," in Bühlmann, *Ein Missionsorden*, pp. 63-82.
92 F. Russo, *I protomartiri francescani* (Padua, 1948); D. Zangari, *I sette santi Frati francescani martirizzati a Ceuta* (Naples, 1926).
93 Iriarte, "Spirualität," p. 74.
94 Von Campenhausen, "Martyrium," p. 83.
95 Bühlmann, *Kirche unter den Völkern, Afrika*, pp. 11-17. See also: Bitterli, U., *Die "Wilden" und die "Zivilisierten". Grundzüge einer Geistes- und Kulturgeschichte der europäischen und überseeischen Begegnungen* (Munich, 1976); *Die Entdeckung des schwarzen Afrikaners. Bersuch einer Geistesgeschichte der europäisch-afrikanischen Beziehungen* (Zurich, 1970); Friedli, R., *Fremdheit als Heimat. Auf der Suche nach einem kriterium für den Dialog zwischen den Religionen* (Fribourg, 1974); Hammer, K., *Weltmission und Kolonialismus. Sendungsideen des 19. Jahrhunderts im Konflickt* (Munich, 1966); Jahn, J., *Wir nannten sie Wilde. Aus alten und neuen Reiseschreibungen* (Munich, 1964); as well as our treatment of the question (more from the standpoint of racism) in §§29-31, immediately below.
96 T. Filesi and Isidoro de Villapadierna, *La "Missio antiqua" dei cappuccini nel Congo (1645-1835): Studio preliminare e guida delle fonti* (Rome, 1978).
97 Mudimbe-Boyi Mbulamwanza, *Testi e immagini: La missione del Congo nelle relazioni dei cappuccini italiani 1645-1700* (Lubumbashi, 1977; thesis).
98 P. Chiocchetta, "Il 'Postulatum pro Nigris Africae centralis' al Concilio Vaticano I e i suoi precedenti," in *Euntes Docete* (Rome, 1960), pp. 408-47; Msgr. Augouard, *Vingt-huit années au Congo* (Evreux, 1934), 1:77.
99 L.A. Mettler, *Christliche Terminologie und Katechismus-Gestaltung in der*

Mariannhiller-Mission 1910-1920 (Schöneck, 1967), p. 213.

[100] Bühlmann, *Missionsprozess* (English edition: *The Missions on Trial*); *Wo der Glaube lebt*, pp. 140-43 (English edition: *The Coming of the Third Church*).

[101] Fashole-Luke, *Christianity in Independent Africa*, pp. 542ff., 426-42. Cf. the earlier analysis by S. Hertlein, *Christentum und Mission im Urteil der neoafrikanischen prosaliteratur* (Münster-Schwarzach, 1962).

[102] *Collectanea S.C.P.F.* (Rome, 1907), 1:42ff. For the whole problem of the quarrel over the rites see LThK 8:1322-24.

[103] M. Hay, *Failure in the Far East*, pp. viii ff., 6, 97, 147, 152.

[104] AAS, 1940, pp. 24-26. Cf. Agenzia Fides, March 3, 1976.

[105] The text is originally from Gen. 14:21, and has a totally different sense here: the besieged king of Sodom says to Abraham, "Give me only the people, but take the goods for yourself."

[106] J. Broderick, *Saint François Xavier* (Paris, 1954), pp. 110-13, 137, 159ff.; W. Bühlmann, *Pionier der Einheit: Anastasius Hartmann* (Zurich, 1966), p. 54; C. Nicolet, *Vita del Beato Luigi Maria Chanel* (Rome, 1889), pp. 240, 243; J.P. Jordan, *Bishop Shanahan of Southern Nigeria* (Dublin, 1948), pp. 120ff.

[107] For the odd history of the declaration see Bühlmann, *Alle haben denselben Gott*, pp. 26-39 (English edition: *All have the same God / The Search for God*). This book also describes the contacts that have since occurred at all levels.

[108] OR, May 21, 1964.

[109] Further information is provided in W. Bühlmann, *Die christliche Terminologie als missionsmethodisches Problem* (Schöneck, 1950), pp. 274-77.

[110] Loth, *Christentum im Spiegel*, pp. 199ff., 323ff. Cf. the earlier T. Ohm, *Asiens Nein und Ja zum westlichen Christentum;* Bühlmann, *Missionsprozess* (English edition: *The Missions on Trial*).

[111] See Bitterli, U., *Die "Wilden" und die "Zivilisierten." Grundzüge einer Geistes- und Kulturgeschichte der europäischen und überseeischen Begegnungen* (Munich, 1976); ibid., *Die Entdeckung des schwarzen Afrikaners. Versuch einer Geistesgeschichte der europäisch-afrikanischen Beziehungen* (Zurich, 1970); Höffner, J., *Christentum und Menschenwürde. Das Anliegen der spanischen Kolonialpolitik im Goldenen Zeitalter* (Trier, 1947); ibid., *Pastoral der Kirchenfremden* (Bonn, 1979); Bühlmann, W., "Die Rechte der Person und der Nation und ihre Bedeutung für die Mission," NZM 1957:192-207, 241-55; H. Clastres, "Selvaggi e civili nel Settecento," in Châtelet, *Storia delle ideologie* 2:159-73.

[112] See documents in Bühlmann, ibid., pp. 192-203.

[113] L. Hanke, *All Mankind is One: A Study of the Disputation between Bartolemeo de las Casas and Juan Ginés de Sepúlveda on the Religious and Intellectual Capacity of the American Indians* (Northern Illinois Univ. Press, 1974). Cf. E. Dussel, "Dall'indio 'rude' al 'buon selvaggio,'" *Concilium* 10:83-97.

[114] J.J. Rousseau, *Discours sur l'origine et les fondemens* [sic] *de l'inégelité parmi les hommes* (Amsterdam, 1759).

[115] G.T. Raynal, *Histoire philosophique et politique des établissements et du commerce des Européens dans les deux Indes* (Paris, 1762). Cf. Bitterli, *Die "Wilden,"* pp. 433, 270-88.

[116] See documents in Bühlmann, *Alle haben denselben Gott*, pp. 20-22 (English edition: *All have the Same God / The Search for God*).

[117] D.J. Roginski, "Arts of the East: The Exotic White Man," *Philippine Airlines, Wingtips,* July-Sept. 1977, pp. 5-9.

[118] A.B. Ziegler, *Thomas Wilson, Bischof von Sodor und Man: Ein Beitrag zur Geschichte der englischen Literatur des 18. Jahrhunderts* (Fribourg, 1972). For material on the various myths concerning the blacks, see M.J. Herskovitz, *Myth of the Negro Past;* G. Fitzhugh, *Sociology of the South,* 1847; D. Curtin, *The Atlantic Slave Trade* (Madison, 1969).

[119] W.R. Jones, *Is God a White Racist?* (New York, 1973).

120 Chenu, *Dieu est noir*, p. 117; Jordan, *White over Black*.
121 Nosipho Majeko, *The Role of the Missionaries* (see the Foreword); cf. Sundermeier.
122 D. Rees, *Soviet Strategic Penetration of Africa* (London, 1977); R. Nixon, *The Real War* (New York, 1980).
123 See Müller, A., ed., *Missionare im Lernprozess. Zehn Jahre Seminararbeit der Missionszentrale der Franziskaner* (Mettingen, 1979); Marquard, L., *The Peoples and Policies of South Africa* (Oxford, 1962); Beckmann, *Rasse*, pp. 158-87; H.M. Grosse-Oetringhaus, "Kirche in Südafrika: Theologie der Herrschaft — Theologie der Befreiung," ZMR 1978:52-72; M. Weber, "Die protestantische Ethik und der Geist des Kapitalismus," *Gesammelte Aufsätze*, vol. 1 (Tübingen, 1972), pp. 17-206; idem, "Die israelitische Eidgenossenschaft und Jahwe," ibid. 3:1-280. For the concept of the land see G.H. Calpin, *At Last We Have Got Our Country Back* (Capetown, 1968); K. Schoeman, *Promised Land* (London, 1979).
124 Wilkins and Strydom, *The Super-Afrikaners*; R. Meyer and B. Naunde, *Gelofdedag: Christus fees of Baals fees?* (Braamfontein, 1971).
125 *Catholic Commitment on Social Justice* (Pretoria, 1977).
126 Kattmann, *Rassen*, p. 9 L. Harding, *Die Südafrika Politik der UNO und der Kirchen: Studie zum Konflikt im südlichen Afrika* (Munich, 1977); B. Himwood, *Race: The Reflection of a Theologian* (Rome, 1964); see the annual survey of race relations by the South African Institute of Race Relations, Johannesburg.
127 Denzinger-Schönmetzer, *Enchiridion*, nos. 2901-80.
128 Ibid., no. 2784.
129 Ibid., nos. 2731, 2979, 3252.
130 On the whole question see R.F. Esposito's books, *Le buone opere dei laici; Pio IX; La Massoneria e l'Italia del 1800 ai nostri giorni*. See also Esposito's address in *Rivista Massonica* 14:66-84 (Rome, 1979).
131 OR, November 12 and 13, 1979.
132 Machovec, *Jesus für Atheisten*, p. 27.
133 Wetter, *Der dialektische Materialismus*, pp. 301-12, 625-41.
134 J.P. Miranda, *Marx against the marxists. The christian humanism of Karl Marx*, Maryknoll, 1980.
135 AAS, 1937, p. 96.
136 Daniel, *Aux frontières*, pp. 56, 83.
137 *Internationale Dialog-Zeitschrift*, Freiburg, 1968 seq.; Garaudy, Metz, and Rahner, *Der Dialog, oder: Ändert sich das Verhältnis zwischen Katholizismus und Marxismus?* (Hamburg, 1966).
138 AAS, 1963, pp. 299ff.
139 Some of this information has come to me thanks to Father Balbo Andrea, of the Secretariat for Non-Believers. On the whole matter see G. Girardi (ed.), *L'ateismo contemporaneo*, 4 vols. (Rome, 1967-69). See also Hebblethwaite, P., *Mehr Christentum oder mehr Marxismus?* (Frankfurt, 1977); Morra, A., *Marxismo e religione* (Milan, 1967).
140 Jacquemont, *Le temps de la patience*, pp. 98-110.
141 Cf. Pueble, nos. 402-12.
142 Rolfes, *Der Sinn des lebens im marxistischen Denken*.
143 Cf. Bühlmann, *Alle haben*, pp. 143-58 (English edition: *All have the same God / The Search for God*); *Concilium*, vol. 6 (1979).
144 Stehle, *Ostpolitik*, p. 404.
145 HK, 1979:287ff.
146 M. Pinay, *Complotto contro la Chiesa* (Madrid, 1962). Cf. Heer, *Gottes erste Liebe*, pp. 20, 509ff.
147 Kühn, *Toleranz und Offenbarung*, pp. 72-83, 453-73. Cf. Schultz.
148 Toynbee, *Studie zur Weltgeschichte*, pp. 303ff., 334ff.
149 Moltmann, *Der gekreuzigte Gott*, p. 24.

[150] Liebe, pp. 520ff. See the books by Mirgeler, Hebga, Schmitz; also Rüstow, *Ortsbestimmung der Gegenwart*, 1:152-54.

[151] F. Fanon, "Die Verdammten dieser Erdeo," *RoRoRo aktuell*, pp. 239, 1209-10.

Part Three

The Other Peoples' Self-Image

A Study in Comparative Religion

Chapter Seven

The God of the Peoples

§1 *Preliminary Methodological Observations*

In Part One we concentrated our attention on the people of the old covenant, then on the people of the new. In Part Two we asked how the new covenant people viewed itself vis-à-vis its associates throughout the course of history and how it acted toward them. Now in Part Three the question before us is whether a covenant god is the monopoly of the Jewish and Christian experience. For if we were to discover that not only Jews and Christians but other peoples as well know and honour a kind of covenant god, we should have to take this discovery very seriously. We should be obliged to consider what this might mean for our understanding of the world history.

We shall not be examining all the categories of associates we looked at in Part Two, but shall attend to one only: the so-called pagans. For the pagans are the "nonpeople" of the Bible (see Part One, §36, 38), whereas Jews, heretics, and schismatics, in spite of all the friction, are part of the Old or New Testament people. This pagan "nonpeople" — innumerable peoples, really — will be well worth our attention: it constitutes two-thirds of humanity!

But before we embark upon this sea of non-Christian humanity, let us set our sights. That is, we must make certain preliminary methodological observations. We have no illusions. We are not the first to have ventured this crossing. In addition to monographs and collections in comparative religion, which present the non-Christian religions in themselves,[1] there are a considerable number of writings that compare them with Christianity from various viewpoints — with the express or implied apologetical aim of demonstrating the correctness and superiority of Christianity.[2] But it is not really our concern to go into the ethnology of non-Christian peoples in order to defend Christianity. Christianity has not the slightest need. Rather, what we are aiming at is the validation of these peoples' religions themselves. Our awareness of the fact that they have been too long despised and neglected will not, we warrant, place an obstacle in the path of our absolute impartiality; but no one can impute to us anything but the human and evangelical aspiration to bring these marginal religions "home." Our standpoint will be altogether limited and specific: God and his people. There is as yet not a single systematic study in this area.

Of course, we are not going to get all yes and no answers. Christianity's strength, as well as its weakness, at least from the Middle Ages on, has been its pronounced intellectualism. By contrast, these pagan peoples have written no theological *summas*, and have built no truth systems to locate and classify everything in the universe. Their devotees do not so much ponder religion as live it. Their religion gravitates not so much to religious knowledge as to religious experience. Now, religious experience is transmitted in ritual and myth — which are marked by intuition, fantasy, and naiveté of the good sort, and not by critique or analysis. It requires a great capacity for empathy to get at their meaning, and the savants of comparative religion do a great deal of disputing about them.

It is also important to make a distinction between popular religion and official religion. The ancient Greek peoples practised polytheism, although their best philosophers postulated a monotheism. The case would seem to be similar with Hinduism — and to a certain extent even with Christianity, where, for some persons, certain saints — real or imagined — have more practical importance than has God.

Comparative religion and ethnology today overwhelmingly prefer particular cases to great syntheses or summaries. But we shall not be able to pursue our study without certain generalizations. Naturally we shall be careful to base these interpretations upon a sufficient number of individual cases.

For my presentation of the religion of the Pygmies and the shepherd peoples of Africa I rely greatly on Professor W. Schmidt's twelve-volume *Ursprung der Gottesidee* (Origin of the Notion of God). But this in no way implies that I join him in his battle against the ideas of so many other savants, or that I always subscribe to his positions on the age, origin, and interrelationships of the religions of the various peoples. With Schmidt, one has to distinguish between religious material that still has validity today, and religio-historical interpretations or constructs from which one may do very well to dissociate oneself. But even after all the surgery, Professor Schmidt is a giant in his field. We are greatly in his debt.[3]

138

Africa

The Working Hypothesis

§2 *A Kind of Covenant*

With luck, the right books fall into our hands and our question whether pagan peoples know a kind of covenant with God, or feel themselves to be a kind of "chosen people", might seem to call for a quick answer, at least as a working hypothesis. "Yes, of course", we may be inclined to answer.

But it will not pay to be overeager. Let us examine some of the apparent evidence to this effect, in the historical order of its occurrence. Even in ancient times, Diodore of Sicily was saying that the Ethiopians considered themselves to be the first to have been taught to honour the gods with rites and festivals, and that consequently it must be their own religion that was now known everywhere and by all. They were also convinced, according to Diodore, that their sacrifices were most pleasing to heaven.[4]

Among the many reports written by the seventeenth-century Italian Capuchins in the Congo, the detailed chronicle of Father Antonio Cavazzi da Montecuccolo is unique. In contrast with his confreres' numerous statements about the shortcomings of every African religion (see Part Two, §26), Father Antonio had discovered among his Congolese not just another religion, but practically a monotheistic faith, along with the consciousness of being the one God's altogether special people. Unhappily — child of his time! — to him this appears as simple arrogance. He writes:

> The populations of the Congo have a stubborn opinion concerning their origin, which they represent to be the most noble and most eminent of all the world. . . They imagine their territory to be not merely the broadest, but also the luckiest, richest, and most beautiful part of the world . . . and it is their constant contention that, when he created the universe, God assigned the constitution of the remainder of the world to his angels and other loyal minions, but reserved unto himself the formation of the Ethiopian lands, and most especially the kingdoms of the Congo, after his sublime conception and taste. Puffed up by the excellence of these supposed principles of theirs, they presume themselves to be the world's first human beings.[5]

In 1910, M. Merker wrote about the Masai shepherds of East Africa:

139

The most salient characteristic of the Masai is their national pride, based on their religious notion that they are the chosen people of God. God is supposed to have created the world and all that is in it for them alone. All non-Masai are considered to be inferior to the Masai. This is the explanation for the pride and deep scorn with which they regard the sedentary black peoples — who do not know Ngai, the Masai supreme being, and hence have no right to any of the good things created by him. Thus these latter are condemned to wring their daily sustenance from the earth in the sweat of their toil; God cares for the Masai, on the other hand, as for his own children.[6]

Hence, Merker continues, the Masai think they have the right to assault and plunder the other tribes. Not the most attractive picture of a "chosen people"!

Of another shepherd people, the Tutsi of Rwanda and Burundi, J. P. Hallet reported in 1966 their belief that

their region is not only the greatest and most civilized on earth, but the centre of the universe itself. They take their own propaganda very seriously, and consider themselves the "chosen people" — the descendants of the Ybimanuka, or first human beings, who fell to earth through a hole in the sky and were chosen to rule the world forever and ever.[7]

Three more general assertions are worthy of note. H. W. Debrunner insists that Christ was no newcomer in Ghana — that with the missioners he had come "as into his own house". Even the notion of covenant was present, says Debrunner, and he thinks the religions of Ghana are most strikingly like that of the Old Testament.[8]

In the conclusion of his lengthy study on African religions, D. Zahan goes so far as to say that this continent is the seat not only of an ethics but of a mysticism, a certain oneness and intimacy with God as creator, "a kind of covenant, based on trust and self-surrender".[9] And there are collective features about this mysticism, says Zahan, which he describes in such a way as would seem to identify a people that has entirely given itself over to its god.

L. V. Thomas summarizes his assessment of the traditional African religions in similar terms. They can be "defined anthropologically, in their substance and in their expressions, as a religion of covenant".[10]

Welcome as these testimonials may be, we must not allow ourselves to overestimate them. On the contrary, there is a special caution to be observed with all of them. Our last three authors are using "covenant" only in a very general way, and they adduce no concrete texts in support of their contention. The other assertions, concerning "chosen peoples", are testimonies *about* the Masai, the Tutsi, and the Congolese, not *by* these peoples themselves. We must therefore subject our working hypothesis to a very thorough testing.

140

If we were to proceed with absolute scientific exactitude, we should have to study a whole series of monographs on individual peoples, from each culture as well as from each cultural area.[11]. But here we shall have to content ourselves with an indispensable minimum. We shall, however, distinguish among three groups: the Pygmies, the shepherds, and the farmers and hunters.

Verification?

The Pygmies

§3 *Basic Religious Beliefs*

The study of the Pygmies from the viewpoint of ethnology and comparative religion has close ties with the search for "religionless peoples", which was all the rage at the turn of the century. Various scholars were applying the doctrine of evolution to religion, and they held that monotheism was the penultimate stage in humanity's religious development. Men and women were supposed to have progressed from a prereligious state in hordelike prehistoric humanity, to animism, totemism, and manism, then through polytheism to monotheism — which last, in its turn, is to be superseded by the religionless condition of enlightened scientific humanity.

This is where Professor Schmidt stepped in. Collecting all available materials on the oldest peoples accessible today, among them the short-statured Pygmies, he put his confreres — Gusinda, Schebesta, Koppers — on their trail. The result was that Schmidt could triumphantly proclaim in his lectures (I was a student of his in the 1940s in Fribourg, Switzerland): "The 'religionless peoples' category has been struck from the apparatus of modern ethnology".[12]

There are still Pygmies living today, in small, scattered groups, driven back into the rain forests by the advent of newer tribes, and living the hand-to-mouth life of hunters and gatherers. A more primitive life is impossible to imagine, but they are happy with it, and consider themselves great in every way. H. Trill reports the West Equatorial Pygmies' view of the world:

> Our little people would point their fingers to the immense expanse of blue,

141

the Milky Way, enthroned among the sparkling stars and ruling everyone and everything, lives God — the creator of all, invisible but not inaccessible, active and present, busily engaged in the care of his creatures — though less now than in the past.[13]

Kmvum is his name, but he is also called "Lord of All", "Sun Lord", "Ancient One", and "Father". Various creation myths recount how all things arose in the beginning. There is a hymn the people sing, "Beast runs, fish swims, bird flies, people eat. Kmvum, you have created us". Once upon a time a Pygmy complained that he was too small. God answered:

> Rejoice rather, and be content in your heart, for you are lord and chieftain. I have given you cunning, and you shall be the most cunning. I have given you the fruits of the forest, and all the beasts that walk and fly. I have given you everything, and hunger shall never be in your life. You shall hide yourself in the wood, and the wood will hide you. You shall be the smallest — but you shall be free and happy.

There is also the concept of a sinful fall. On its account God has withdrawn from the company of human beings, but he remains in active association with them. Aroused by a cry for help, he gave them the gift of fire, and so they sing:

> No more fear have we,
>   Thou Mighty!
> No more suffer we the cold,
>   Thou Mighty!
> No more suffer we hunger,
>   Thou Mighty!
> To Thee, O Mighty One, we say:
>   This is good!

God wishes human beings well. The rainbow is a sign of his goodness and his nearness. In various circumstances of life, prayers are made and sacrifices offered. At the birth of a child the chieftain says, "To thee the creator, to thee the mighty, I offer these plants — this new fruit of an old tree. You are the Lord, we are your children". In strife and battle with other tribes, the Pygmies invoke Kmvum, for he is the defender of what is right. In the puberty rites, young persons are initiated into the morality of the tribe and anyone failing to observe it can count on God's punishment.

Similar data are reported by Ratheer Schebesta in regard to the Ituri Pygmies of Central Africa, in particular the Bambuti.[14] Their faith in a supreme being is more explicit. He is called Kalisia, the one from whom all good gifts come. He is offered the first fruits in sacrifice. He goes hunting with the little people and guides their arrows. He shows them where to find honey and fruit. He goes ahead of them on their way and blazes their trail. If the eldest has a dream that they should break camp, they all move to another place, which Kalisia shows them. Their god is even called "Our Father". In the puberty ceremony God's voice is believed to be heard in the bull-roarer (a wooden spatula whirled about on a string) and other instruments.

When a certain Father Schuhmacher wished to study the East Kivu Batwa Pygmoids, he encountered great difficulties at first. The people were friendly enough, but they kept their secrets to themselves. They had a dozen excuses. Only when he had acquired their confidence — in fact, had been proclaimed a chieftain — did they finally open their hearts to him.[15] He discovered an unquestioning faith in a god "Imana", whom the people invoked with childlike naiveté. Imana, he learned, has all power. Everything good comes from him, he knows all things, he is the guardian of morality. Beneath him are the *bazimu*, the spirits, who control life's concrete details. Sacrifices are offered to them, and not to Imana. An ancient of the tribe shared with Father Schuhmacher this psalmlike prayer:

> When we sally into the forest
> and tread upon the lion asleep,
> on the viper in the earth that bites
> if Imana is for us then,
> he protects us from all these monsters.
> But if Imana is against one,
> all this can kill a person.
> Even the gold-monkey can.
> But when one is with Imana,
> no beast is any match,
> nor *bazimu*,
> nor any other thing.

Compare this with Psalm 91. Sheltered in God's protection! There is a favourite prayer of intercession in the spirituality of this people: "Imana be with me, Imana be with me!"

There is no need to delve into the other elements of Pygmy religion, its magic, spiritism, and so on, which often yield a vague and contradictory image of God.

Shepherd Peoples

§4 *The Galla*

After the Pygmies, it is the nomadic herding peoples of Asia and Africa that are of the greatest interest for religion. They drive their flocks over very extensive regions, and feel themselves to be rulers of the world, with a vocation to bring order among the other tribes and lord it over them. They are intelligent, energetic, and proud. In Africa they have been driven from their original territories in the East toward the south, and have subdued the farming peoples of those lands, such as in Rwanda and Burundi, and move among them as the upper class. They have a markedly explicit belief in a highest god, who determines both their life and their self-image.

Typical of the shepherds are the Galla of southern Ethiopia.[16] They call their highest being "Waka", God, or, often, "dear God", and his name is ever on their lips. They even call him their father. They offer him the first fruits, for he has made heaven and earth, and all good things come from him. He is the guardian of morality:

> God demands an accounting from the wind of the haystack it has overturned, and God will demand an accounting from the sinner of the smallest faults . . . The evil that lurks in the bowels' depths is night to the human gaze, but it is day to the eye of God.

Instead of a decalogue, the Galla have a kind of hexalogue. The first three commandments of the decalogue are missing, for they are thought to be self-evident.

Waka is not thought of as just a national god, as distinguished from the deities of other nations, but as the god who created heaven and earth and humankind, therefore as the sole God of all peoples. Hence the Galla practise a double standard in dealing with other peoples: if their religion is monotheistic, the Galla identify their god with Waka. But they feel superior to polytheistic peoples, and look down on them as of little worth. They feel themselves called to vanquish them, and either lead them to faith in Waka or exterminate them.

The Galla are known for their beautiful prayers. We cite three examples:

Morning Prayer

O God,
in peace hast thou given me to pass the night;
in peace give me as well to pass this day.
Where'er my way may lead,
which thou in peace madest for me,
guide thou, O God, my steps aright.
In speech take falsehood from me,
in hunger take murmuring from me,
in satiety take complacency from me.
I pass the day invoking thee,
O lordless Lord!

144

Evening Prayer

O God,
in peace hast thou given me to pass the day;
in peace give me as well to pass this night.
O Lord, who knowest no lord,
beside thee there is no might;
Thou alone art unconstrained.
Under hand of thine pass I the day,
under hand of thine pass I the night.
Thou art my Mother,
Thou art my Father.

Prayer of Intercession and Praise

O God, O Master,
O Lord who knowest no lord,
O Rich who knowest no poverty,
All-Knowing, whose knowledge is not by acquisition,
King of throne unrivalled,
God of my land, my Lord,
above me,
beneath me —
when misfortune strikes,
as trees protect me from the sun
do thou keep far from me this woe.
Be thou, O Lord, my very shadow.

O God my Lord, thou Sun of thirty beams,
at the enemy's approach
permit not this worm of thine to die on the ground.
For when we see a worm on the earth,
if we wish we crush him
and if we wish we spare him.
Wakayo,
who walk with good and evil in thy hand,
my Lord, let us not be killed;
for we thy worms have besought thee!

It would not be difficult for us to take such prayers as these upon our own lips, and pray together with "pagans" such as these to our common God (See Part Four, §33).

There is a great deal more that we could say about the shepherd peoples — for instance, about the many prayers of the Masai for peace, and in time of war, in which they often tenderly refer to their god Ngai as "Sister", "Brother", or "Bridegroom".[17] Or we could study the Nuer in the Sudan, who call God "Grandfather", feel themselves to be totally dependent on him and, because he does all things in goodness and power, trust him almost to the point of abandon.[18]

But we must dwell a bit on the Tutsi, whose religion is well known through White Fathers B. Zuure and D. Nothomb,[19] as well as through the many publications of the African priest A. Kagame.

Nothomb is of the opinion that a whole theodicy could be put together out of Tutsi proverbs, which represent God not only as existing and powerful, but as the giver of all good gifts, the provident God who helps us. "When God has built the house, no wind can upset it". "The enemy digs you a pitfall; but God lifts you out." "God brings famine, and shows you where to find food".

Perhaps the same could be said for the Tutsi theophoric names, the names whose suffix is *-immana*, or "God". They have been known from time immemorial, and today they are taken by Christian converts. There are at least three hundred of them — for example, *Bizimmana* ("God knows it"), *Habimmana* ("Only God is important"), *Nsengimmana* ("I worship God"), and *Ngirimmana* ("God is with me").

Names like these are common to all regions of Africa. The Centre for Ethnological Studies in Bandundu, Zaire, has published a book containing more than eight hundred of them, collected by a group of missioners and African priests from twelve West African peoples.[20]

Farmer and Hunter Peoples

§6 *Faith in God: An Undeniable Fact*

The great majority of the African tribes are farmers and hunters. For our purposes there is no way out of having to reduce their differences to a common denominator; otherwise we should have to summarise hundreds of monographs.

The fact of faith in God among most of the peoples of Africa can no longer be seriously disputed. True, there are no temples, no statues, no creeds. But it is enough to observe the daily life of the people, and get acquainted with it from the inside. This is something that white observers were long in no position to do. They saw only "idols", "witchcraft", "amusing rituals", and wrote everything off as "stupid". For us outsiders, the God of the Africans long remained the Great Unknown.

But missioners and other researchers have succeeded in discovering more and more of him. His are a hundred names — the Ibo call him Chukwa, the Ashanti, Nyame, the Ila, Leza. The Luo call him Nyasi. The Yoruba name for him is Olodumare. In East Africa the name Mungu, or Mulungu, has great currency. In Zaire it is Nzambi. From Lake Victoria to Rhodesia we find forms such as Olumbe, Lubumba, Kiumbi, Mumbi, and so on. In most cases the meaning of the word itself is disputed, which shows how old it is.

The principal source for studies on African notions of God are the creation myths. These were never committed to writing within the tribe, but were simply transmitted orally from generation to generation, since ancient times. The old and the wise were the "ark of the covenant" of this "Torah", the repository of the myths. M. Griaule recounts his sensational discovery after fifteen years of research among the Dogon, one of the most primitive, and resistant, tribes in what was then French Africa. He had finally managed to locate an old man named Ogotemmeli, blind like Homer, and had won his confidence. For thirty-three days Ogotemmeli imparted to Griaule his secrets, the myths of his people and their view of the world. Griaule published the whole account, remarking: "These people live by a cosmogony, a metaphysics, and a religion to rival those of the ancients, and deserving the closest attention of every christologist".[21] Another ancient sage like Ogotemmeli was Tierne Bokar, introduced to the world by T. Monod in 1950, since called "man of God", "God's interpreter", "Francis of Assisi in Mali", and the like.[22]

These French scholars were preceded in their work by the German africologist H. Baumann, who collected and analyzed some two thousand creation myths, from all over Africa. Among his conclusions:

> In far the greater part of Africa, spread throughout all ethnic groups, we find a supreme deity as the exclusive force of creation . . . The facts speak very emphatically in favour of an ancient notion of a supreme deity in nearly all the regions of Africa . . . Among Africans, a people without a supreme divinity is nowhere to be found.[23]

It is recounted in most of the creation myths that God, often through the intermediary of other beings, first created the world, then lowered human beings from heaven by a kind of rope, or called them forth from the water, or formed them from clay. There was, we are told, a very ancient time when God lived with human beings, and in those days human beings lived in luxury, knowing neither sickness nor death. But then they fell. Content with neither sun nor rain nor anything else, not even with a feast given by God himself, they simply murmured at everything. Or else a woman, bidden by God to take a sealed box to a determined place, was overcome by curiosity on the way, opened the box, and out came a serpent. And God withdrew. From then on, need, sickness, and death held sway.

Of course, this does not mean that God cares no more about his human creatures. He is at once the Far One and the Near, the Absent and the Present, or, to use theological terminology, the transcendent and the immanent. But formulas such as these — categories of omnipotence, omniscience, ubiquity — should not be projected onto African myths. J. Goetz, who took up this theme of the "God far and near", holds that God's withdrawal is not simply the mythological etiology of original sin (see Part One, §7), but also, and more positively, a means of explaining the freedom and responsibility of human beings. God hands everything over to them. But he is always at hand in time of need.[24] He reigns over a whole hierarchy of nature spirits, ancestor spirits, and good and evil powers, and in some localities even minor divinities. But there is no doubt who is in charge: the One, the Mighty, the one some call "Father", who sends his children rain and sunshine, fruitful families, herds and fields, peace and harmony.

But it is not only in their creation myths that the West has gradually discovered the African concept of God. It is also in their prayer. We outsiders long thought that this "God afar" had no care for human beings — and that therefore human beings had no care for him or prayed to him, but honoured spirits only. Monsignor A. de Clercq's famous pastoral manual of 1930 says, "The Luba neither prays to God nor invokes him. His prayers and invocations are addressed only to his ancestors, and it is on their assistance alone that he relies". Thirty years later the African Franciscan Father M. Lufuluabo wrote:

> At the time when that statement was being written, my parents were teaching me to pray, to go without the first fish, and to say, "O God, Supreme Being, thou Sun with the beams of fire, upon whom one cannot gaze without being burned up by thy flame, thou Shield upon which all might shatters — this fish is for thee. The next will be for me."

We have learned more about African prayer.[25]

In my first year as a missioner in Tanganyika, in 1951, I had a beautiful experience of this total self-surrender to the one God. There were no missionary sisters at Mchombe station in those days, nor any African medical personnel either, and I had to be on call for the sick two days a week. I handled from fifty to eighty patients on those days, doing what I could for their everyday African ailments. One day there stood before me a youth of about twenty, tall and very thin, with a cough and a fever. I asked him what I could do for him. "Can't you see?" he replied. I soon determined that he was in the advanced stages of tuberculosis, and that there was simply nothing I could do for him. He was a "pagan" as they say in the books, and had come to our remote mission station for the first time, lodging with acquaintances in the vicinity. I gave him a tonic and promised to come to see him in a few days at the farmstead.

I did go to see him, and brought him more tonic and a small quantity of snuff. I took the occasion to attempt to prepare him for baptism. But before I began to instruct him I wanted to know what he knew about God. "Risasi ya Ngombe, what do you think — how many gods are there?" He answered unhesitatingly, "There can only be one God. There is only one God." Next I asked, "And what do you think, what does God do?" Risasi ya Ngombe thought a moment, then replied, "*Anatuangalia. He looks at us.*"

What a beautiful answer. Few Christians could have given such an answer. This "pagan", then, exhausted, fatally ill, and hunched at the door of his hut, lived in the gaze of God, in the presence of God. "Your answer is very beautiful, Risasi ya Ngombe", I said. "This God you know and honour is my God too, the God of the Christians, the God of all men and women. He has done things for human beings that you do not yet know", and I began to tell him about Jesus. He listened to me, was astonished, and believed.

But above and beyond such an individual spirituality, there is, as we have already stated, a community spirituality as well. There in the community of the clan and of the tribe one feels sheltered, united, strengthened — not only through the celebrations and needs of the community, but in faith in a common vital force that comes from God, flows through the generations of one's ancestors to the generation of today, is augmented by the good we do, is diminished by evil, and is to be transmitted by those living today to those who come after.

This vital force accumulates in the person of the chieftain, especially in tribes with a strongly developed monarchy. These figures are accorded a God-given authority that today's democracies would like to be able to imitate. In the rites of passage — birth, puberty, marriage, death — this vital force is stamped into one's consciousness again and again, and not through any theoretical instruction, but in myths and songs, festivals and celebrations, and the experiences and undertakings of life.[26]

All this implies, even if it cannot be found expressed in so many words, that God is in a kind of covenantal relationship with his people — that he walks with them, lives with them, and makes history with them. No matter that the central focus of African history is not the future but the past, the beginning, the primordial age, when God dwelt with humanity — the model age we yearn for, and which God will cause to be again.

§7 *Interpretation of this Faith*

This general picture of divine faith in Africa will have to be verified, and nuanced, for each individual case The possibility cannot be excluded that there are some tribes who live more or less just for the day, honouring perhaps only the ancestors of the clan, from whom they have received their blood and their homeland. And we certainly have to say that the religion of all Africans is a this-worldly religion, not an other-worldly one, especially in the case of farmers. It is not eschatological but historical, not theocentric but anthropocentric — or better perhaps, sociocentric, revolving around the community of the living and the dead.[27] It is not out of a theoretical interest in God that Africans speculate about God. It is because God turns toward human beings. Africans are chiefly concerned with life and health, but this has to do with God. The whole outlook is highly reminiscent of the biblical perspective.

Now let us take our question a bit deeper, and suddenly it becomes a more radical one. What is to be our interpretation of this divine faith? Is this faith to be accepted or rejected? Endorsed or refuted? In other words, is it true or false? There are authors, Marxist and non-Marxist, black and white, who are convinced that all religion, African or not, rests on illusion, and that it is currently in its last spasm, and will soon expire of itself.[28]

Similarly there are ethnologists who maintain *a priori* that any myths about creation and the like must be but symbolic solutions to social questions and problems that religion cannot otherwise answer — and furthermore that these myths really have nothing to do with religion as such in the first place. Levi-Strauss is their spokesman: "The fact that persons attach a few vague longings to their myths does not mean that [the myths] indicate any penchant for the transcendent."[29] This is not the place to discuss this sort of apriorism. Its protagonists are not on our wavelength, and we are not on theirs — not to mention any question of opposed ideologies. They are talking science, we are talking faith, and no purpose will be served by our simply talking past each other.

But there is a more serious objection. It is alleged that these notions of a supreme deity were, originally, impersonal forces, or at best some manner of first ancestors, and developed into their current forms only later, perhaps even under the influence of Christianity. It is only out of chauvinism, it is alleged, that African bishops and theologians vaunt and defend "their religion" — that is, the native religion of their compatriots — and that in point of fact a great chasm separates their views from those of professional anthropologists.[30]

This objection contains a great oversimplification. We by no means appeal only to Africans — Mbiti, Mulago, Idowu, Lufuluabo, and others. We have cited recognised experts on West Africa as well, Baumann, Rattray, Griaule, Mitchell, Doke, Goetz, Zahan, Thomas.[31] Thus even if we have to leave open the question of the origin and meaning of African divine faith, we are nevertheless on solid ground for our own position as we have stated it. Occasional reference to God as "Father" or "Grandfather" is surely no indication of an origin in an ancestor cult.

This is simply a matter of analogous concepts, names that are taken from human relationships but are also appropriately applied to God. Besides, we must not forget that even the Hebrew Yahweh/Elohim — both the names and the faith — have a long history of evolution (see Part One, §16; Part Four, §§13, 14). Yet this certainly does not diminish their religious value. It just means that a religion, like a people, can take a long time in developing.

Conclusion

§8 *Authentic Religion*

We have considered the religious concepts of three African cultural classes — Pygmies, shepherds, and farmers and hunters. One conclusion is evident: this is authentic religion, profound and spontaneous, permeating the whole life of a human being. To be sure, the variety of its concrete images is very great, but in most cases they constitute a hierarchy, culminating in a pinnacle, which is God — who was before human beings, who created human beings, and who in mysterious ways dwells with his human beings. This picture is clearest in the case of the Pygmies and shepherd peoples, but it is true for the farmers and hunters as well:

> The African is incurably religious . . . His or her view of the world is incomprehensible without the presence of him who stands above and beyond the world, and who nevertheless composes all things in unity.[32]

> Anyone denying God as the cause of all things would, in sub-Saharan Africa, be looked upon as an abnormal being.[33]

It is thanks to the ancestors of these peoples, to their reason and insight, that African religion, with its roots deep in prehistory, came to be. And this corresponds very well with what the creation myths emphasise: that God dealt familiarly with human beings. Theologically there is nothing at all to be said against such a primordial revelation to these pagan peoples outside the framework of the Bible. On the contrary — and we shall return to this question later (in Part Four, §§5-9). But this religion of Africa has scarcely been retrieved from the dark shadows of history when it threatens to pale and die in the glaring light of modern science and secularisation. We shall have to come back to this, as well (in Part Four, §23).

Our working hypothesis, however, according to which God has struck a real covenant with these peoples, with a resultant special consciousness of election in the African cultures, has not found the support they require, not even if we leave open the doubtful cases we mentioned. The texts that led us to formulate our hypothesis (§2, above) have not found corroboration.

Nevertheless we can say that a covenant *is* present, noncategorically and implicitly, when a people feels itself to be a people of God, sheltered in the harmony of the clan, of nature, and of an invisible world. Their religious and sociological group consciousness, developing along with an express ethnocentrism (see §§25-26, below), force us to conclude that the African peoples live the covenant of creation, in all its intensity (see Part One, §§6-9), even if they have no consciousness of any further, explicit covenant, such as that with Abraham or Moses, or in Jesus.

It is not surprising, then, that the three "Bantu Bibles" so far published detail a cosmic creation, the creation of human beings, and a sinful fall, thereby indicating that these are essential to African tradition — but that there is nothing about a new redemption, or a new history of salvation based on a new covenant.[34] (It is remarkable how African catechists can expatiate at great length, and with fantastic imagination, in filling in the details of the history of creation!) It is a discovery of considerable weight to be able to assert that the Africans, quite consciously, have stood in the presence of a creating God and have found in him an ultimate meaning for their lives.

§9 *Consequences for Missionary Methods*

This insight ought to have various consequences for missionary methods. Unhappily, applications have been long in materialising. Until a few decades ago, most missionaries' opinion of African paganism had remained unchanged since its first encounter by Europeans (see Part Two, §§26-27). They judged it without knowing it. Ethnologists rightly complained that their research meant nothing to missionaries, that missionaries were at no pains whatever to incorporate values of African culture into Christianity.

New insights have since been gained. But the discovery that Western Christianity's history has not been the only salvation history, nor its religion the only true religion, has, as F. Klöster writes, precipitated a crisis in the missions. The hope of Christendom, says Köster, lies in an African Christianity that has not yet taken shape.[35]

Nor is there any clear sign of it. Vatican Council II, it is true, recommended a much more radical model of the incarnation of the gospel in different cultures than the traditional, purely external, "accommodation". The council called for a genuine pluriformity in liturgy, theology, and spirituality to whatever extent might be legitimate.[36] Then, ten years later, the 1974 Synod of Bishops, along with *Evangelii Nuntiandi* (1975), gave still more pointed expression to this thinking (especially EN 63). And just after that synod, the African bishops made a joint declaration to the effect that the theology of accommodation had run its course and that the order of the day was now the theology and praxis of incarnation.[37] Many an address and workshop have since been held to find paths to this praxis — for example, the international colloquium held in Kinshasa in 1978, where Cardinal Malula said in his keynote address, "Our problem and our task is to strip Christ's message of its Western raiment, that it may shine in its original beauty as Christ's true religion".

Consequently it was astounding, and totally disheartening, when the competent Roman congregation, in its official message to this colloquium, abounded in anxiety and warnings, conceding in conclusion that one could, "within the framework of the irreplaceable worth of the *philosophia perennis* and patristic theology, undertake necessary adaptations"![38] Just as in "the good old 'thirties". But Africa is heading for A.D. 2000.

Asia

The Aborigines

§10 *Pygmies*

With Asia, we are starting down the most important midway of the "World Expo". This is the greatest of the continents, not only in area, and not only in the variety of its religion, but in sheer human mass. With fifty-six percent of the world's population, it outweighs all the other continents together.And so in Asia in particular we must rely on a satellite view if we hope to make a meaningful survey.

"Aborigines", for our purpose, will denote simply those religious groups that arose before the classic Asian high religions and have resisted conversion to them. Here too, as in Africa, we can distinguish three great classes, and again the first is that of a remnant group of Pygmies.

The Pygmies became known in the West in gradual stages as research progressed. For instance, those of the Andaman Islands in Southeast Asia, a Negrito tribe, were at first considered to represent a typical case of religionlessness. Then it happened that an English colonial official named E. H. Man settled among them. He lived with them for eleven years, studied their language, and got to know them as an insider. Then, in 1883, he published his sensational report.

The Andaman Pygmies, he revealed, know a supreme being, Puluga. Puluga was never born, and will never die. It was he who called into being the whole world with all its inanimate and animate creatures, and then created men and women. Puluga knows all things, even the secret thoughts of the heart. He is offended by sin — falsehood, theft, murder, adultery. The winds are his breath, the thunder his snarling, bolts of lightning are the expression of his anger. He feels compassion toward those whose heart is sad, and comes to their assistance. Like any animate being he has a wife, and children. He is invoked in need, but without ritualism, traditional prayers, feasts or ceremonies.[39]

A. Lang caused no less a sensation with his account of the aborigines of Australia, who likewise acknowledge a supreme being as orderer, guardian, and rewarder and punisher of behaviour — and not in this life alone but in the next as well. God, say the aborigines, used to live on earth, and humans then did not fall ill, or had they to die. Now, however, he lives beyond the blue sky, and observes what is going on on earth from there. He is good and benevolent. The elders and chieftains of certain tribes appeal to an authority from God, and it is also believed that certain bards, a kind of prophet, are inspired by him.

The various tribes have different names for God: the Wotjobaluk call him "Our Father", and among the Mukjawaraint he is the "Father of the Whole People". The Kurnai, indeed, simply know no other name for him than "Our Father". The Euahlai invoke him in their secret ceremonies as "Father of all things, whose laws all tribes obey". They have initiation celebrations in which all their knowledge of the Supreme Being is divulged, and good behaviour is expected to follow. In the terrifying howling and whistling of the bull-roarer, it is believed the voice of God can be discerned.[40]

Thus, once more, we have one God, far away and yet near, who walks with his people and stands by them. In other words we have a God who has struck a "covenant" with his people.

The case is the same with the Samang Pygmies in the rain forests of Malaysia, the Negritos of the Philippines, and so on. But we shall have to be satisfied with the two examples we have already examined.

§11 Shepherd Peoples

The ancient shepherd peoples, as well, who inhabited a huge expanse from Siberia across Mongolia all the way to China, are of special interest. The Altai Tatars of southern Siberia have preserved their ancient belief practically intact, whereas the Turkish peoples have adopted Islam or Orthodox Christianity. The Altai have a complicated cosmology. In the uppermost stratum of the sky dwells the "Gracious Lord Heaven", Tengere Kaira Kan, and there rules the destiny of the universe. From him, by emanation, other deities came to be. The Altai myths contain the scenario of a temptation and fall, with a forbidden food, a serpent, and human beings who grew ashamed and hid themselves behind a tree. There follows the curse of the human beings and of the devil. Then God withdraws. This account, ethnologically very old, is of course strikingly like that of the Book of Genesis. The "Gracious Lord Heaven" is also called "Father", and even "Father and Mother of the race of human beings". He is the creator of the universe, disposes all things with might, and has a fatherly care for his human creatures. He watches over their moral behaviour, and admonishes them to exercise kindness toward weak beings, especially children, calves, and lambs. He encourages his people to make confident prayer: "When you call upon me, I shall set you in my lap". A proverb says, "The human hand is helpful; God's is mighty". And another: "No sand, no river; no God, no people."[41]

We likewise have very old reports concerning the Abakan Tatars, the Huns, and the Kirgish. In 176 B.C. the Great Khan Motun wrote to the Emperor of China that Heaven had raised him, Motun, up to his throne, so that it was by Heaven's blessing and the excellence of his armies that he had gained victory over a series of peoples and united them into one family. From this and similar texts it is clear that it is to this "Heaven" that the conducting of the kingdom is ascribed, and that Heaven makes its plans in advance and carries them out through human instrumentality at the appointed time. Its dispositions demand obedience of human beings; otherwise they fall into misfortune. These texts testify to a Heaven that wills and thinks, and whose personal nature hence is beyond doubt. Prayers and sacrifices are offered to Heaven, as well as to the spirits. In the seventh century B.C. there were potentates who spoke of themselves in terms such as these:

> I the godlike. Heaven's appointed sage. . . God's anointed. . . By the grace of Heaven have I ordered and organised my people. . . We did battle, and Heaven was gracious to us: with two thousand we laid low their six thousand. The enemy was not aware of our presence — Heaven must have struck them with blindness for us. . . I am a poor and simple Tatar. My one prayer is that, as long as it may please Heaven to keep me among the living, I may be led to do my best for my people.

Thus the Lord Heaven clearly has a social function to perform — the safety and guidance of the Khan and his people.[42] He could be said to be the covenant god of his people.

The famous Genghis Khan, who unified the Mongols between 1206 and 1227 and invaded China, constantly appealed to a mission from Heaven, and to Heaven's favour and support. Before he marched on China he stirred up his armies with these words:

> Heaven has granted me the victory over every adversary, and has given me to ascend to the highest step of fortune. If you fight bravely, this same Heaven will grant us a glorious triumph over China; the Mongols will attain to the highest condition of weal, and our name will never die out among the nations.

Thus Genghis Khan acknowledged Heaven as lord of all peoples, especially of his own people. He recognised Heaven to be the guardian of good and evil, and the Lord of life and death. He was so sure of his heavenly mission that he counted any opposition to his plans for supremacy as an outrage against Heaven, to be put down with ruthless force. Between 1211 and 1223 B.C. he and his armies killed some eighteen million persons in China. He is said to have destroyed some thirty million persons in his lifetime, although these figures, like biblical statistics, may be greatly exaggerated.

His second successor, Kuyuk (1246-1258), made answer to the question of papal delegate John of Plano Carpini as to why they had killed so many persons including Christians:

> Genghis Khan and Kagan have only carried out the plan of God. Those peoples had showed themselves arrogant. They put our emissaries to death. It was, then, the eternal God who punished and annihilated those peoples. It is in the power of God that all regions have been delivered unto us, from the rising sun even unto its going down. How can anyone have accomplished such things but by the command of God?

One could think one were reading the Old Testament.

The Mongols also used prayers, sacrifices, and spring and autumn festivals to Heaven's honour.

In his response to the delegate, Kuyuk added:

> You have written in your letter that it would be a good thing if I were to receive baptism and become a Christian. And you have invited me to do so. We have not understood this invitation of yours.

Rome was to learn that the conversion of the Mongols and the Chinese was not going to be easy![43]

Summing up the whole matter, Professor Schmidt interprets the creation myths of the Asian shepherd peoples as "the canticle of a victorious optimism, with which these peoples, the future rulers of world history, viewed world events from their first beginnings."[44]

Naturally — and here we confront the whole complexus of problems presented by religious thought narrowed to nationalistic proportions — the Chinese emperors understood things just as Genghis Khan did, especially beginning with the Church Dynasty in the thirteenth century. They too understood their religion very much in a political and nationalistic sense, and entertained a strong aversion for anything foreign. The emphasis was on faith in Heaven and the deities, who, through the emperor, "the true Son of Heaven", bestowed unity and peace upon the people. This thinking perdured to our own century, when first in the democratic, then in the communist revolutions, it was replaced by a secular messianism.[45]

We must speak briefly of a third group, roughly comparable to the African farmers and hunters. Formerly these groups were thought to be simple primitives, aboriginal animists, in the matter of religion. For centuries, indeed for millennia, they had shielded themselves from the great religions of the peoples around them, holding to their own particular beliefs. They knew no temples, sacred books, or eminent founders, and hence were considered to be not really up to par where religion was concerned.

An example would be the Bihl people of India, the group among whom Father Charles de Ploemeur finally enjoyed such missionary success,[46] or the Jorai of the high plateau of Vietnam, who — with all their faults — were so dear to God and other peoples that P. J. Dournes called his book about them *God Loves the Pagans*.[47] Unlike followers of the great religions, these groups are very open to evangelisation, and it is from them that most Asian Christians have come.

Here we shall consider but one instance. Our example has a clear analogy with Africa. It is the case of the Toba-Batak people of northern Sumatra. Wedged in among Muslim tribes, they kept their primitive religion until recently, when a majority embraced Protestant or Catholic Christianity. One of the members of the Toba-Batak, A. B. Sinaga, who became prefect apostolic of Sibolga, wrote his doctoral dissertation on the faith of his forbears in a supreme deity.[48] They had a great number of creation myths, explains Sinaga, and these testify to "Mulajadi na Bolon" as creator. He never began, and he will never die; "in the beginning" he made the earth and all that exists; there are other deities, but it is Mulajdi who has made them. The first human beings came forth from an egg. Humans lived in a happy land at first, with a River of Life and a Tree of Life, and God was close to them; but then they prayed no longer, showed themselves to be prideful, and God withdrew; still, he watches over their moral conduct just as before. The whole *adat* — the system of traditional folkloric prescriptions — is sacred ordinance. God is especially near in the moment of need, bestowing health, fertility, and succour in all difficulties. "When God helps, the dewdrop becomes food". "When God helps, the old once more become young". The Toba-Batak have a great number of festivals and ceremonies, including a kind of baptism in which a name is bestowed. Members attempted to regain their primordial state through the exercise of their religion.

Hinduism

§13 *Sacred Books*

Concerning the African religions, we remarked that it is difficult for non-Africans fully to appreciate them, or even to interpret them correctly. This is even more true of the religions of Asia. One can read a five-hundred-page book on Hinduism and come away not "understanding" much more than before. One must live, breathe, pray, and be still in these religions — and gradually learn what is meant by them.

Hinduism, professed by eighty percent of the more than six hundred million inhabitants of India, stands before us not in the manner of a stark monument, but as a mysterious, alluring shape — not as a pedagogical system, but as a way of life, a jungle in which only initiates can find fullness of life, a volcano perpetually bubbling and seething. Accordingly, we here renounce any intention of giving a description of Hinduism in itself. What we shall attempt to do is merely to call attention to the fact that here, too, the mystery of God, and the people of God, converge.[49]

Like Judaism, Hinduism is distinguished by a whole series of sacred books. The oldest collection is that of the Vedas, which were composed between 1500 and 1200 B.C. (or, as some say, between 1200 and 600 B.C.), but consigned to writing generally only much later. The Vedas in turn are divided into four groups, the Rig-Vedas, the Yajur-Vedas, the Sama-Vedas, and the Atharva-Vedas. The Rig-Vedas form the foundation piece. The other collections resume them, with extensive elaboration, developing them for use in sacrificial cult and daily necessity alike. They consist of over a thousand psalmlike hymns, of which it is said that they were not "composed" by "authors" but "contemplated" by "singers".

R. Panikkar, a Catholic priest who by dint of much study and practical experience became one of Hinduism's foremost specialists, composed an anthology of the Vedas of nearly a thousand pages. His intention was to offer modern readers a bouquet of Vedic experience. For Panikkar, the Vedas are a monument not only of broad religious significance, but of deeply human meaning as well. Some see the Vedas as the expression of a primitive spirit. Others see them as the highest manifestation of truth, the definitive revelation never to be surpassed.[50] In any case they make up not only the earliest religious composition, but the earliest document of any kind in India.

Later the Vedanta were added — divided into three collections, mostly in prose, written in the form of generally difficult conversations. They deal with human nature, immortality, blessedness, mysticism, and suffering. The Upanishads are concerned mostly with wisdom or faith; the Brahma Sutra with logic or the formulation of knowledge; and the Bhagavadgita ("The Song of the Lord") with discipline, the religious life. The last-named ranks as the most popular of the books, and is a kind of compendium of Hinduism, somewhat as the four gospels (with abundant differences, as we shall see later, in Part Four, §§10-12) are considered to contain the essentials of Christianity. In the Bhagavadgita

God's personal love for human beings is set forth graphically and tangibly. Today it belongs to world literature — to the works that a formed and educated person must have read. It appeared in the second (some say the fifth or the eighth) century of our era.

It is not difficult to understand why such effusive praise has been lavished by the Hindus on the Bhagavadgita. Here are endless songs of death and life, good and evil, truth and error, corruption and blessedness — and withal, God's omnipresence and universal activity:

> I am the world's beginning, and its end. There is nothing higher — all is threaded on me like pearls on a necklace. I am the taste in water, the light in the moon and in the sun; I am the sound in the upper air, and the humanness in human beings. I am the scent in the earth, the brightness in fire, the breath of life in every animate being. Know me as the eternal seed of all existences: I am the judgment of the judicious, the brilliance of the brilliant, the strength of the mighty. . . With me is the All shot through, with my hidden nature. All beings live within me — but I do not live within them. . . As the breeze stirs in the air, so are all beings within me. . . I am the father of this world, and its mother, and its vessel. I am its goal, its bearer, its Lord, its witness, its dwelling, its refuge, and its friend. I am the beginning and the end, the bed, the foundation, the inaccessible kernel. I am immortality, and death as well. I am Being and Non-Being [VII, 4-11; IX, 4-6, 16-19].

Never officially recognised by any "church" after the fashion of the Old or New Testament, these books are all nevertheless accounted as holy writ, as the word of God to human beings, and they are read — or rather, sung and listened to — with a reverence in accord with this status. The collection is not considered necessarily closed, and more recent texts, such as those of philosopher-president S. Radhakrishnan, are reckoned as part of the Vedanta. We Christians may well take very seriously the word of God in these scriptures (see Part Four, §§10-12).

§14 The Concept of God

In order to begin to grasp the much discussed idea of God in Hinduism, we must start with the historical background. Some six thousand years before Christ (as Indian authors say), or perhaps only one or two thousand years (most European authors hold), India was penetrated by the Aryans, a people related by blood and language to the ancient Greeks, Romans, and Germans. The Aryans destroyed the ancient Indus civilisation, which had attained a level comparable to that of Mesopotamia, and Hinduism emerged — of a gradual intermingling of the Aryan cult of the God of heaven with the sacrificial worship of the deities of the Dravidian culture.

It has been said of Hindu polytheism that one can distinguish from 33 to 3,339 representations of God. These, we are informed, antedate the transition from henotheism (the acknowledgment of a supreme god without denying the existence of others) to monotheism. But this conception is no longer much in vogue, and the tendency today is to hold that Hinduism was monotheistic from its very beginning, and that the many names and forms of the gods are but the expression of the many activities and manifestations of one God. This, of course, is theology; there is no denying the many deities that came to be present in popular religion. A. C. Bose has introduced the expression "Advaitic", or "Vedic" theism to denote this peculiar brand of monotheism. However this may be, today's educated Hindus entertain no doubt of either the reality or the supremacy of one universal Spirit, whose stillness and mystery they seek to attain. And all the while they wisely tolerate the "plain folk", who look to the gods in hope and prayer.[51]

One piece of evidence for the primitive origin of Hindu monotheism is in these passages from the Rig-Veda: "Manifoldly to name what is but one, this do the poets" (I, 164:46); or again, "Neither being nor not-being, neither air nor firmament, neither death nor immortality, neither day nor night were. The One breathed peacefully, reposing upon Itself, and there was nothing there but It" (X, 129).

Is this "One" a personal God? Or is it some manner of impersonal prime matter? S. Radhakrishnan explains the synthesis of both aspects in this way:

> The suprapersonal and the personal conception of the Real [i.e., God] represent, respectively, the absolute and relative ways of expressing Its single reality. When we emphasise the Reality [Itself], we speak of the absolute Brahman. When we wish to stress Its relationship to us human beings, we speak of the personal Bhagavan, the exalted personal God.[52]

This eternal First Principle, Brahman, manifested Itself in three deities, which have been styled the "Hindu Trinity": Brahma, Vishnu, and Shiva. They perform, respectively, the functions of creating, sustaining, and annihilating the universe, but taken together they are one god. Depending on the region or the community, one or other of these gods comes to the fore. Thus often it is Vishnu who has become the highest divinity, and is called the Eternal, the Inaccessible, Creator, Saviour, Redeemer, and Friend, and who will at last assume human beings into his kingdom. His devotees pray litanies of his names — from 108 to 1,008 of them! But it is most of all in his "incarnations" (*avatara*) that Vishnu manifests his graces, making himself present to men and women in need, especially when they are in danger from evil spirits, and leading them to final liberation. The many myths about Vishnu place him in a fish, a tortoise, a boar, a dwarf, or, especially a prophet.

The most celebrated of the "incarnations" of Vishnu is in Krishna. Krishna was not born in the usual way, but issued from his mother's side, and the mountains trembled at his birth. When he grew he waged a heroic battle, destroying everything that opposed him, and returned home to the Father-God. He is not called Son of God, but God's Courier, God's Intermediary, or Bridge to God. The mighty deeds of Krishna are sung especially in the Bhagavadgita, and there are passages there in which one could substitute "Christ" for "Krishna" — keeping in mind, of course, that Krishna is not a god incarnate but a deified human being,[53] and indeed that he himself is not a historical figure but a mythological one.

§15 Hindu Way of Life

As we have said, Hinduism is a religion, not a system of thought. Hindus hold no disputations on the theological issues that might be suggested by the beautiful and contradictory expressions of the holy books; one simply lets them stand, seeking only to share the Hindu experience of God and seeking to lead the Hindu way of life.

Hinduism's central theme is the endeavour to reduce everything to its ultimate elements: to (1) the *atman*, the Self, and then ultimately to make the discovery that this immanent *atman* is one with (2) the transcendent Brahman. But this unification is not accomplished in a process of discursive thinking. Instead, one is plunged, in a certain "becoming inward", into the ocean of the divine Being, to be totally lost therein, and thereby to actualise the human ideal of the Hindus. Again it is the Bhagavadgita that sings:

> Once a man has estranged all concupiscences, and has brought his spirit altogether to rest, then he is confirmed in insight: that one is wise who is neither confused by suffering nor overweening in joy, who is free of passion, fear, and anger, without any predilection for anything at all. Neither does he rejoice on meeting unexpected luck, nor does he sorrow when misfortune befalls him, for he withraws all his senses from their objects as the tortoise withdraws its members within itself (II, 54).

One could think one were reading *The Imitation of Christ!*[54]

Hinduism, like Christianity, accords a special place to the theme of sin and forgiveness.[55] Here the operative principle is that of the good moral order, and the moral imperative embraces all of private and social life. One could call it the "theanthropocosmic totality" — all things are interrelated, all things exist within and together with one another. Whoever inserts himself or herself into this good order, does rightly. Otherwise he or she disturbs the order, augmenting the sinful condition of the world. The sinful person falls victim to darkness, and can expect punishment both here and hereafter. His or her sole hope is the mercy of God — hence the oft-repeated refrain, "May his light frighten away our sins" (Rig-Veda I, 97). One whose sin is forgiven "will wax in might, will live a hundred springs, a hundred autumns, a hundred winters" (X,

161:4). Then that person's blessing will spread out upon all the members of his or her community.

The means of obtaining this forgiveness are sacrifices, prayer, and the sacred bath. If no more sacrifices were offered, the sun would no longer rise, the rain would no longer fall from heaven, the harvest would ripen in the fields no more (VII, 34:6; X, 160:3). There are several thousand recognised places of pilgrimage and grace at which one may take the sacred bath, all along the rivers of India. But the Ganges is special. Simply pronouncing its name cleanses the individual sinners, and bathing in it, or drinking its water, purifies one's whole family retroactively for seven generations. Thus, at any given moment there are millions of Hindus on pilgrimage, and to appreciate this phenomenon one really must see the masses of humanity in Benares, men and women, old and young, descending the stairways to the Ganges before sunrise, walking into the dirty water, raising their hands and their eyes to heaven, immersing themselves, pouring the water over their bodies, and carrying away a bottle of water to take home with them — and afterward sitting in a circle, flowers and votive lamps in hand, singing songs, convinced that they are now purified, are nearer to Brahman.

The classic Hindu way of life is led by the *sanyasi*, or "monks", also called *sadhus* ("saints") or *swamis* ("lords"). Their number is estimated at between two and fifteen million. Most are constantly on their way from holy place to holy place. Some smear their bodies with ashes, or with pigments of every hue, even going completely naked, speaking not a word, and possessing literally nothing — seeking only full union with God. Others wear the saffron robe of the monk, and sit hunched by the side of a road or on the bank of a river. Others dress in elegant silk gowns, are driven about in magnificent carriages, live in palaces, and hold learned discourses on Hinduism. Most are loosely bound in community.

Initiation into the monastic life is preceded by a lengthy fast; then all hair is removed from the body, and there ensues a symbolic cremation, in which the candidate himself erects the pyre, then lies upon it. From this moment forth he has died to the world. (When he comes to die his bodily death, he is not cremated "again", but simply buried.) Now he receives, from his *guru*, or "teacher", his personal mantra (sacred syllables from the text of the scriptures), a new name, and a new garment.

If the vitality of a religion may be measured by that of its monasticism, Hinduism need have no fear for its future.[56] To be sure, secularism will have a word to say, and we shall look into this matter further on (Part Four, §23).

Now we understand what the Vatican Council meant in the Declaration on the Non-Christian Religions, when it said of Hinduism:

From earliest times even unto our days, various peoples have possessed a certain perception of that hidden power that is present to the world's course and to the occurrences of human life, and not seldom even the acknowledgment of a supreme deity, indeed of a father. This perception and acknowledgment imbue their life with a deep religious meaning. . . Thus in Hinduism men pursue the divine mystery and bring it to expression in an inexhaustible wealth of mythology and penetrating philosophical efforts, seeking, through an ascetic way of life, or deep meditation, or a vital and confident refuge in God, liberation from the narrow confines of our condition (NA 2).

By way of illustration, let us examine some texts from the Rig-Veda.[57]

Invocation

I magnify God, the Divine Fire,
the Priest, Minister of the sacrifice,
the Offerer of oblation, supreme Giver of treasure.

[I, 1:1]

Fearlessness

From that which we fear, O Lord, make us fearless.
O bounteous One, assist us with your aid.
    Drive far the malevolent, the foeman.

Indra, the generous giver, we invoke.
May we please all creatures, both two-legged and four-legged!
Let not the armies of our foes overwhelm us!
    Destroy all evil spirits!

Lead us to a wide world, O wise one,
to heavenly light, fearlessness, and blessing.
Strong are your arms, O powerful Lord.
    We resort to your infinite refuge.

May the atmosphere we breathe
breathe fearlessness into us:
fearlessness on earth
and fearlessness in heaven!
May fearlessness guard us
behind and before!
May fearlessness surround us
above and below!

May we be without fear
of friend and foe!
May we be without fear
of the known and the unknown!

May we be without fear
by night and by day!
Let all the world be my friend!

[Atharva-Veda XIX, 15]

We leave the question open whether this is a prayer to God or a magical
incantation for protection.

Prayer for the Forgiveness of Sins

Shine brightly, Agni, and chase away
our sin; beam down upon us grace.
May the Lord burn away our sin!

We make our offering to you
for fruitful fields and pleasant homes.
May the Lord burn away our sin!

May high priests spring from you, O Lord!
May we also be born again in you!
May the Lord burn away our sin!

Rescue us safely, as in a boat,
across the stream, from dark to light.
May the Lord burn away our sin!

[Rig-Veda, I, 97]

Prayer of Petition

Draw near in friendship.
Save us and help us.
Show yourself gracious, O Lord!

Be present, O Lord,
wonderful, adorned.
Shower on us treasure most precious!

Hear now our cry.
Lend us your ear.
Shield us from sin's contagion!

To you, radiant God,
we bring this prayer.
Shine on our friends in blessing!

[V, 24]

God, of All of Us the Brother

O Lord, noblest of the noble,
wisest and best mediator,
may we utter an acceptable prayer, efficacious!

Who among men is your brother?
Who offers you holy worship?
Who are you, Lord? On whom dependent?

You are of all Men the brother
and dear companion, O Lord,
the Friend whose name we may invoke for our friends!

[I, 75]

§16 *The Caste System*

One cannot speak of Hinduism without mentioning the caste system. We are struck by a marvellous openness to the world in the poetry we have just read. "Let all the world be my friend!" "O Lord, . . . you are of all Men the brother. . ." But it would be a great mistake to imagine all Hindus as one large community of brothers and sisters and friends. On the contrary, Hindus are divided into several thousand castes, whose social bounds may not be transgressed.[58]

In its historical beginnings, the notion of caste had to do with colour. The Aryans were white, the Mongols yellow, the Dravidians brown, and the aborigines nearly black. This raised a social problem for which a solution had to be found — it is a pity, but different races always put up badly with one another. Were some to be eradicated by others, as happened with the Indians in America at the hands of the white immigrants? Or subjugated, as happened in colonial Africa and Asia? Or, instead, were all to be amalgamated into an ideal society, for which there is still no historical model? Or, as a solution of necessity, must a way to separate but regulated coexistence be found, a kind of *apartheid*, as in South Africa? Ancient India chose this last formula. The original intent, formed out of a spirit of respect and tolerance, was to acknowledge the special character of each group and assign to it its own special task, but the system degenerated into intolerance and oppression.

There are four principal castes:

1. The *Brahmins* constitute the priestly caste, who devote themselves to studying and expounding the holy books, as well as to see to the performance of the sacred rites for the welfare of the people.

2. The *Kshatriya* caste is that of the soldiers and administrators, with the task of preserving the good order of the state.

3. The *Vaisya* caste comprises the merchants and farmers.

4. The *Sudra* caste is the lowest, that of the labourers and servants.

165

Each caste is subdivided into hundreds of others, all socially segregated, and subject to innumerable ritual and legal precepts. The whole of daily life — meals, work, social forms, marriage and the use of marriage, the toilet, and so on — is different for each caste. The Brahmins, all of them Aryans, feel themselves to be the master people, the privileged, the ones loved by God, the "chosen people". Beneath the lowest caste are the "outcastes", who are exposed to contempt, the imputation of impurity, and untouchability. They bear the curse of Cain. Mohandas K. Gandhi fought by every peaceful means to dismantle these walls of inhumanity. "The one God wills the brotherhood of all", he proclaimed. It is as a result of his efforts that the outcastes are termed *Harijans* today, "Children of God". The constitution of an independent India has abolished legal barriers of caste, but in practice they are still very effective. The churches had more success with the outcastes, and did much to further their social betterment, but even within the churches there still survives a good deal of caste tension and thinking.

The entire caste system is supported by the religious concept of *karma* — the matter out of which one is born, the environment in which one lives, the totality of one's own behaviour. All this determines one's destiny, and one must accept it and bear it. Every person can play with the cards of life that he or she has been dealt! Hence a deep and basic fatalism, which religion helps to enhance and sanctify: in spite of all, there is ever the hope of reaching the goal of full union with God, by the path of gradual purification in a stream of rebirths.

It is no wonder that Marxist critics of religion pillory this system, seen by them as a typical case of religious alienation. W. Ruben, for example, along with Marx, terms the caste system a "religion of self-torturing asceticism", an ideology of kings and despots, a placebo for the exploited. India's unification will be accomplished only by a secularised spirituality, says Ruben, when science has at last gained the victory over religion.[59]

It is not only the Marxists who should deplore this conception of a "chosen people", and the religious basis of the caste system. Christians should as well.

For the rest, there is no explicit Hindu concept of a covenant with God. But there is an acute awareness of God's nearness — not so much his nearness to the people as such in its history, but with the individual human person in his or her ascetic and mystical life. The sacred books of Hinduism are more like the Old Testament wisdom literature. The historical books of Moses and Kings are not there.

Buddhism

§17 *Appearance in History*

We shall have to be content with a summary sketch of Buddhism. Its appearance in history[60] dates from Siddhartha Gautama, later called the Buddha, or "Enlightened One", who lived probably between 560 and 480 B.C. Siddartha's noble parents wished to spare their only son all suffering, and to see to it that he possessed all happiness. What happened instead was the contrary. Overwhelmed by life's fleeting character, Siddhartha came to experience nothing but disgust for living. Today one would say that he was so frustrated that he "hit bottom". And so, at twenty-nine years of age, he fled his palace to seek truth as a wandering hermit.

The Buddha received his enlightenment only after seven years of the most severe mortification, at Buddh-Gava, not far from Patna. Henceforth that enlightenment was to characterize his whole life. After some hesitation he determined to share with the world the salvific truth he had discovered concerning the origin and conquest of suffering. He crisscrossed northern India for more than forty years, and won a great following. His teachings were written down in three collections, and later summarized in a sacred book called the Dhammapada, or "Poem of the Law". But it was five hundred years before the writing began, and for this reason it is very difficult to determine the original content of his teaching.

By contrast with Hinduism, with the oppressive stance of its superior Brahmins and its anxiously executed sacrificial ritualism, the Buddha strove for a community without priests, without castes, without sacrifices, and apparently even without God. In modern terms one might say that he liberated religion from its clericalism and legalism, or that he radically secularized religion. He formally refused to imagine a God who interferes in our history and upon whom we may call for protection. Here there is no mistaking a reaction against the abuses of a certain approach to divine worship in which one seeks to overpower God with a surfeit of rites and external deeds. For the Buddha, the only thing that counted was human reality, and the only way of coping with that reality was the complete renunciation of all illusory desires and passions. The Buddha preached no truths, held no doctrines, but he knew a way to liberation — which nevertheless each individual would have to traverse by his or her own personal endeavour. Benevolence and compassion for all suffering beings is of the greatest importance along this way, making Buddhism the world religion of love, fraternity, and tolerance.

At the end of the salvation journey, *nirvana* waits. We have been too quick to translate the word and concept as "nothingness", whereas it literally means "exhalation", or "blowing away", and denotes liberation, the removal of all suffering, immortality, eternity, eternal happiness. Its Buddhist synonyms are "haven of refuge", "cool cave", "the farther shore", "the unspeakable", and so on. Is it just a state? Or does the Buddha mean a "being with God"? The question remains open. In any case, *nirvana* is something transcendent, an ultimate value toward which human beings strive with all their might. More probably the so-called Buddhist atheism should be interpreted as a silence about God. To a Buddhist, our Christian discourse about God appears as almost blasphemous. It can never do justice to God. For a Buddhist, God is "unthinkable and unnamable". Only the experience of God counts. How absurd to speak of God without the experience of God! But one who has experienced God need no longer, can no longer, speak about him. For us Christians, who have written volumes on the true faith, and misunderstood, condemned, and persecuted believers of other faiths for centuries, what a salutary admonition! At the same time one should not overlook the fact that later Buddhism actually developed a kind of scholasticism itself, and formed many statements about God.

Buddhism spread, in the course of the centuries, over Sri Lanka, Southeast Asia, and even China and Japan. It was much more of a missionary religion than ever Hinduism was, and indeed has now become a world religion in the strict sense. In India itself it was all but eradicated, eventually, by Hinduism, and especially by invading Islam. But if you journey in Buddhist lands you will see the Buddha's statue a thousand times — little or great, in stone or metal, in homes and in pagodas, breathing peace, composure, detachment, and strength, and indelibly marking the spirituality of its peoples even to our own day.

§18 *Modern Resilience*

Buddhism's modern resilience is simply astonishing. In 1956, Ambedkar unleashed a veritable movement among the untouchables in India to liberate them from their humiliating social status in Hinduism. In a short time some three and a half million of them had embraced Buddhism.[61]

In postwar Japan, with its total disillusionment, then with its economic boom and the accompanying secularization, Buddhism managed to seize the moment and the means for a successful renewal. It had degenerated into something of a system of magical rites; but now suddenly it offered persons the values to which it lays such authentic claim. Under the leadership of certain prophetic figures, some four hundred "new religions" have arisen, with the general context of Buddhism, holding out to their adherents the very things they need: in a flat, anonymous society, the experience of an almost patriarchal salvation society; in the meaninglessness of daily living, new hope and expectation for the future; in an atmosphere of indifference toward both state and one's fellow human beings, new commitment to social and missionizing activity. Fifteen years ago the number of adherents of these new religions had already climbed to more than thirty-five million.

One of the most dynamic is the Soka Gakkai, founded by Makiguchi and Ikeda on the Nichirenist tradition. By contrast with the tolerance that marks most of these new Buddhistic movements, the Soka Gakkai are fanatical, almost to the point of fascism, preaching their religion as *the* means of salvation from corruption.Their many social endeavours are supported by wealthy financiers and politicians, and they recruit followers through the media, splicing modern methods with the angry, threatening language of prophets. They wage a political battle against corruption, they work for world peace, and they seek to help persons overcome the helplessness and loneliness of everyday life with an intense program of community prayer. They consider Japan as the holy land of the Buddha, and teach that the time is coming when all men and women will come there as pilgrims, to the midpoint of the earth. This chauvinist tone of eschatological propheticism has become an essential part of Nichirenism. These persons are convinced that the "Law of the Buddha" will bring salvation to the whole people and to all humanity.[62] Has this tone, this conviction, arisen of its own accord, or has it been influenced by the Judeo-Christian biblical notion of election and mission? In any case this Japanese movement presents an interesting parallel with the Judeo-Christian faith.

Anyone with eyes to see is struck by the ubiquity and dynamism of the Asian religions in Western cities. Zen, Yoga, Transcendental Meditation, and so on, have their centres everywhere. It is true that there is a great deal of abuse and commercialism here. But this scarcely militates against the obvious fact that these enterprises must be offering something for which the secularized and computerized men and women of today entertain a secret nostalgia,[63] and which they seem singularly unable to discover in Christianity.

Islam

§19 *The Proclamation*

At least by name, the best known Asian religious document in the West is the Koran, the sacred book of the Muslims. After all, the West has been in confrontation with Islam ever since the Middle Ages, and it is the Koran that it has sought to refute.

Unlike Hinduism and Buddhism, Islam[64] is what is called a "post-Christian" religion, not only in the chronological sense (Mohammad died A.D. 632), but in its content. There were not only a fair number of Jews in Arabia in the time of Mohammad, there were Christians as well. Of course they all belonged to different "rites", and so they were always squabbling, and Mohammad could not have gathered from them much of an impression of Christian unity. But it was through them that he

169

became acquainted with certain passages of the New Testament, just as it was from the Jews that he learned something about the Old, and he borrowed quite extensively from both.

The proclamation of the Koran culminates in the confession of the one God, merciful and good. We use the term "proclamation" — not doctrine — advisedly. *Qur'an* (Koran) means not only "reading", but "address", "announcement", "preaching". In the faith of good Muslims, the Koran was delivered to Mohammad by God himself, in a series of revelations. The original, it is said, is written on a tablet lying on a table in heaven (Koran 85:21). Thus it is the word of God, God's gift, in the strictest sense. Those who take it upon their lips enter into a kind of communication with God. According to the Muslim faith it is not *man* that God has become, but *book*, and indeed it is not the Prophet who is at the centre of the Muslim faith, but the Koran. When the Koran is read aloud, its principal addressee is God, with the faithful coming second. In it God carries on a sort of conversation with himself. Hence the emphasis on reciting it only in its original language. I have met Muslim school children in East Africa who could rattle off whole *sures* without knowing a word of Arabic.

The Koran is divided into 114 *sures* or chapters. Some consist of songs of praise reminiscent of the Psalms, but most are sermons preached by Mohammad and collected and published after his death either from memory, or from the scraps of manuscript upon which his first disciples had taken down his words. Like Moses long before, Mohammad reestablished a monotheistic faith that had been suffocated in spirits and deities. Like Moses too, Mohammad spoke with the power and authority of a prophet. Allah is more transcendent than Jesus' "Father", but more merciful than Moses' Yahweh. Each *sure* opens "In the Name of the merciful and good God", and it is God's goodness that is sung again and again, along with his omnipotence and justice. The urgency of the proclamation rests on the concept of God's imminent arrival, for he is to come soon and hold court, render judgment. The lot of the elect in heaven and of the damned in hell is most graphically described:

> Catastrophe of judgment, once erupting, shall bring down what is high, exalt the plain! When earth shakes to and fro, the mountains crumble, collapse, and turn to dust, dust everywhere, then, human souls, according to your deeds of earthly life, in three sorts shall ye stand: There on the right are they that, nearest God in gardens of delight, at ease recline, in two rows facing, on couches of rich stuff shot through with gold, as lads forever youthful make their rounds with vessels brimming o'er of rarest wine and jars of fresh spring water (a mixture, this, from which the head nor aches nor spins), and great-eyed houris have they at their beck, in beauty like to pearls well-guarded — all this in balance of their deeds on earth. But on the left, writhing on coals that sear, in water seething, a thick black smoke for shade that neither cools nor comforts, they that led a life of ease erstwhile, persisting in the mighty sin of unbelief . . . The one whose

list of acts is labeled "ill", beginning from the last deed to the first, with shouts and screams, there roasts in fires of hell. Laughing he lived, nor burdened, in his time, surrounded by his blood and family, and dreamt that such would be his lot to everlasting ages. Ah, but no! His Lord did spy him out, marking too well each deed he did. Then wherefore not believe, O people, nor bend yourselves in prayer full low the while the holy book Koran you hear proclaimed? [From *Sures* 56, 84].

The true life of Islam, or "dedication to God's will", rests on five "Pillars": daily prayer, the fasts of the month of Ramadan, almsgiving (for the benefit of the poor, as well as for the needs of the holy war), the profession of faith, and a pilgrimage to Mecca at least once in one's lifetime. Anyone who has visited Islamic lands knows how seriously these matters are taken.

We shall cite two more *sures*. The very first one, which every Muslim knows by heart and recites over and over, reads:

Praise God, the Lord of men in all the world, the merciful, the good. On Judgment Day he reigns! Thee serve we, yea, and beg thine aid. Lead thou us in the righteous way, the path of those to whom thy grace is proved, of those who have not fallen 'neath thy wrath, and have not gone astray! [*Sure* 1].

The other example spells out what it means to be "merciful and good".

In God's Name, God the merciful and good. Morning, and night time too, when all is still, thy Lord doth take no leave of thee, nor does abhor thee. Thinkest thou that here below thou hast his kindness? Then but bide — beyond thou shalt his kindness prove! So richly will thy Lord give thee his gifts that thou must needs confess thyself content. Full sure, e'en here below his grace o'ershowers thee — did he not find thee orphan then, and take thee under his adoption? Did find thee straying, nor did lead thee straight? And found thee needy, nor did make thee rich? Against the orphan, then, raise not thy hand, nor drive the hungry beggar from thy door, but sing to all thy people ever more the grace thy Lord has done thee! [*Sure* 93].

We cannot take time here to go into all the vestiges of Christian doctrine in Mohammad's teaching — the Holy Spirit, for instance, or Jesus the Prophet, who was born of the Virgin Mary, or judgment and resurrection, paradise and hell. It will have to suffice to cite what the Vatican Council has to say about Islam:

The Church esteems the Muslims very highly. They adore the one sole God, living and self-existent, merciful and almighty, Creator of heaven and earth, who has spoken to human beings. They endeavour to submit even to his hidden dispositions, with all their soul, just as Abraham, to whom the Islamic faith appeals, submitted to God [NA 3; cf. LG 16].

Islam is not merely the affair of the individual believer. Above all it is the concern of the believing community, the *Umma*. Muslims make a clear distinction between the "House of Islam" (*Dar-ul-Islam*) and the "House of Unbelief" (*Dar-ul-Kufr*). Jews and Christians, while not exactly contemned, are considered inferior; polytheists, "unbelievers", are regarded with utter scorn.

Islam is not just a religion. It is a socio-political community. The people who left their land to follow Mohammad came from various tribes, and he had to mould the heterogeneous elements into a new community, based not on blood but on belief. His success in fusing them all into one great "super clan" is astonishing. Of course, he knew of the primordial community of all human beings:

> Human beings were one single community originally. Then, after they were become not-one, God caused the prophets to step forth, as heralds of the good news and as messengers of warning [*Sure* 2:213].

This primordial oneness was grounded in the religion that was given with creation:

> Now direct thy countenance toward the one true religion. This is the natural way in which God has created human beings. The way and manner in which God has created human beings cannot be altered. This is the right religion, but most human beings know it not [*Sure* 30:30].

Everything worked better in this new community. The *Umma* became the most effective remedy for traditional tribal rivalries, as well as for the corrupting individualism of the Arabs. Muslims have a proud faith in Islam's special position in the world:

> And so have we made ye unto a community [*umma*] standing in the midst, that ye may be witnesses of men and that the One Sent may be witness of you [*Sure* 2:143].

Even in our day, from West Africa to Indonesia, Islam has succeeded in amalgamating diverse races and cultures into a unity that surely far surpasses today's Christian sense of oneness.

> The great unifying power of the *Umma* seems to lie in the order of the emotions. It is experienced first in the hearts of the faithful, where it feeds on a personal and collective pride in belonging to the world of Islam. From this pride, certain forms of relationship, certain life principles, develop, making the believer feel at home in any land where the Koran is proclaimed.[65]

Of course, this unity does not exclude a powerful pluriformity. There are mighty differences between Islam in West Africa, Saudi Arabia, and Indonesia.

Orthodox Islam knows neither clergy nor professional missioners. The remarkable missionary thrust of Islam is a property of the community as such. Each Muslim simply professes his or her faith, speaks well of the community, feels a responsibility for the function of this community as a model to look to, and thereby seeks to win others to it.[66] Mohammad himself encouraged this self-concept when he exalted his people above the "People of the Book", the Jews and Christians:

> Ye believers are the best community that has arisen in humanity. Ye command what is right, ye forbid what is to be rejected, and ye believe in God. Were the People of the Book to believe even as ye, it would be better for them. Yea, there are believers among them, but most are murmurers [*Sure* 3:110; cf 3:113ff.].

Thus we have yet another example, supranational this time, of a people with an altogether special consciousness of being a "people of God", chosen, charged with a mission to all other peoples.

§21 *Force*

Islam has always understood itself as a very exclusive community, just as Christianity has. Those outside count for nothing. They are only invited to enter the "House of Islam". But no Muslim dare leave that house. This would be social death. Islam is theocratic, and religion is thereby linked to force. The Koran is civil law, too, just as was the Torah in the Old Testament.

In modern times the application of this principle varies extensively from state to state, but generally speaking, religion makes use of the civil power for its own ends. Many a one-sided and false statement has been made about the "Holy War" — *Jihad* — but no one has ever suggested that it is ineffective. True, it is not waged to compel acceptance of Islam. But it is waged to spread the hegemony of the *Umma* over non-Muslims. In certain localities, thanks to its sturdy organization and powerful consciousness of its unity, Islam has managed to establish minority rule over other populations. This has happened, for instance, in northern Nigeria, northern Cameroon, and the southern Sudan. There Islam has not only attempted to falsify statistics, but has exploited the populations and thereby aroused their resentment. Only with the coming of Christianity have these tribes finally found their self-identity.[67]

In 1947, in blood and confusion, Pakistan separated from India and part of Palestine became Israel. Since then we have witnessed a striking radicalisation of Islamic consciousness, and an equally radical awakening of political activity on the part of the states in question. The formation of OPEC in 1973 constituted a powerful self-affirmation. Member states became a new world power overnight, and dangled the West on a string of humiliating dependency. Unlike the nuclear weapon, the oil weapon can be both brandished and used in good conscience. Hence it has been tremendously effective. The whole process reached its climax in the Iranian crisis, when the Ayatollah Khomeini undertook not only to pass sentence on the former Shah, but to force the United States and the whole West to make confession of their sins.

We should approach this development with patience and understanding. It ought to be seen as the primal eruption of forces and feelings too long repressed, as the awakening of a giant who has lain too long helpless and in fetters. It is Islam's reaction to its violent reduction to the status of a Western protectorate, beginning in the time of the Crusades and continuing all the way through the colonial period. Every Islamic state, from Morocco to Indonesia (except Iran!), has been the colony of a Western power.

But political oppression was not the only thing these nations had to suffer. Even after the formal demise of colonialism the capitalist world managed to work its exploitation. Now it is feeling the counterpunch. Politically, economically, and culturally, Islam is on the move.[68] It views the success of its oil empire as an unmistakable sign of the will of God. It is paving the way for the future with its petrodollars. Richer Islamic nations help the poorer ones overcome their underdevelopment. They also finance mosques and Islamic centres in the West, giving the impression there that the world's up-and-coming religion is Islam.

One must not allow oneself to be deceived, however. There is no dissimulating the deep rift down the centre of world Islam. The Muslim elite, issuing from the portals of the universities of the world, are looking for modernisation, even secularisation. The masses, mostly under uneducated leaders, cling to tradition. Modern nations such as Tunisia, where women enjoy equal rights and polygamy is against the law, are ridiculed in conservative circles as "lands of unbelief". On the other hand it should not be forgotten that Iran's Shiites who were generally more hierarchical, more authoritarian, and more integralist than are the Sunnis, by no means constitute a majority in Islam.

Thus the current Islamic "great leap forward" is principally on the level of politics, economics, and culture. There is no accompanying religious *aggiornamento*. Islam lacks the outstanding theologians and mystics it would have to have in order to preserve its kernel but renew its form, and thus adapt to modern times. Islam will not get by without a radical crisis. But this is no cause for Christian glee; rather it means hope for an interconfessional dialogue, and for motivation on both sides to cooperate in the search for a pathway to tomorrow (see Part Two, §24; Part Four, §23).

The reader will understand that we cannot present all the other Asian religions, such as Taoism, Confucianism, or Jainism.

America

§22 *History*

When and how the Indians came to the western hemisphere is still the subject of unproved working hypotheses. Their history in the recorded sense began October 12, 1492, the day they were discovered by Christopher Columbus. Columbus, like the others of the *Conquista*, lived and acted out of a strong Christian faith. He based his own peculiar consciousness of mission on a mystique of discovery: he hoped to find kingdoms whose wealth would enable him to regain the Holy Land. And he believed that by proclaiming the gospel in the New World he was hastening the Second Coming of Christ. Columbus has rarely met his match in seeing his mission as the fulfilment of a biblical promise.[69] And it is notorious that Hernando Cortes, foremost of the Conquistadores and vanquisher of Mexico, was very pious, bearing on his person the image of the Mother of God at every moment, and assisting at Mass daily — but that for the rest he gave full vent to his passions, and knew no scruple in his political life.

This Spaniard met with a very ancient culture among the Maya, Inca, Aztec, and other Indian tribes. Let us dwell for a moment on the Aztecs of Mexico.[70] But a generation before Cortes landed, there reigned a king — a gem of Mexican culture by the name of Nezahualcoyotl. The king had no son, and had invoked various divinities without success. Reflecting on the apparent powerlessness of the gods to come to his assistance, he arrived at the insight that but one god was almighty and good. Thereupon he went into retreat, and prayed and fasted for forty days. At the end of this time a herald arrived bringing him news of victory over the enemy and of the birth of his son. Nezahualcoyotl then built a temple to this god, "the Unknown God", the cause of all causes.

Of course, the common people knew and honoured a plethora of deities, among whom the God of War, Huitzilopochitl, held the highest place. The Aztecs, with their highly developed economy — they used irrigation — and urban culture, and with their tightly regimented military administration, were also deeply religious. They practised a kind of sacrificial communion, a kind of confession, a kind of baptism by which the newborn child was cleansed from a primordial sin. A well organised and deeply revered hierarchical priesthood carried out the various rites, to the accompaniment of the singing of psalmlike hymns. Murder, adultery, and sacrilege were punished by death.

The Aztecs believed in eternal life, with a heaven and a hell. They were sure they had gained their land by God's disposition, hence a symbol of God was preserved in a sort of ark of the covenant, and no contracts were entered into without consulting him. (One would think one were examining a replica of the Old Testament!) Finally, they awaited the day of the return of the mythological god Quetzalcoatl, who would bring back the golden days of the primordial age. When Cortes appeared with his Spaniards, the Aztecs thought they must be sons or brothers of this god, hence the very friendly welcome they accorded him.

The Mayas, and other tribes as well, had a similar eschatological expectation. It is reported of various tribes that they had wandered for centuries in the hope of finding a land of rest and peace. As late as 1912 the Guarani people of São Paulo still danced for days and nights on end — until they collapsed with exhaustion — in the hope of being able to dance their way into the lost paradise.[71]

In all of this abounding religious wealth the Spanish conquerors, as well as the majority of missionaries, saw only superstition, idolatry, and diabolical mimicry. After all, they had come from the land of the Inquisition, and in the time of the Counter-Reformation. They would strike no false compromise. It was believed that one could please God by destroying the idols and building the churches out of the stones of the temples they had destroyed — on the ruins of the Devil's religion.

§23 *Today*

But Indian religion has survived much longer than we thought — at least where Indians survived. Even *today*, and even among tribes that have been Catholic for four centuries, such as the Aymara of Peru's high plateau, who are one of the largest — numbering two million — we discover that the old religion determines the thinking of the people even more than does Christianity.[72] The foreign Catholic priest baptizes the children, confers the other sacraments, and teaches a doctrine; this goes without saying. But it is the traditional "priests" who perform the initiation that really counts, dealing with the Divinity in all the concrete details of life, and duly maintaining the purity of the sacral order, with its many rites of sowing and harvest, birth and death.

Non-Christian Indian tribes generally survive only as remnants. Again it is Professor W. Schmidt who has gathered the material. The Lenni Lenape[73] all believe in a "Great Spirit", whom they also called "Our Father". He is said to be "all light, robed with brightest day, a day of many years". The rainbow is the hem of his garment. After creation he dwelt with human beings on earth in intimate community. He had instructed them in all things, imposed upon them the precepts of morality, and commanded the sacred ceremonies. Then he withdrew. Still, he remains near. All good things — light, warmth, health, fertility, success in battle — are from him. The spirits, the *manitowak*, occupy the foreground, but this does not preclude the interior relationship these peoples feel with their "Father ". His great feast is the yearly Thanksgiving, twelve days and twelve nights to his honour. The next world is called "the Land of Life", and is pictured as an island of the most ravishing loveliness.

Only 150 members of the Siyot, or Wishosk,[74] were still alive in 1910, but they could give an account of their sacred tradition. Of Gudatrigakwitl, the supreme being and creator, they said: " He works not with his hands. Whatever he thinks, comes to be". Humans died because they were evil. God admonishes his people:

> When you celebrate a festivity, call upon me. If some do not love what I say, let them go their own way. But those who accept my instruction, and hand it on to their children, they shall live well. Whenever it goes ill with you, call upon me. As long as human beings live, when an elder recounts my story to his son, it is as if I myself were there.

The Wintun[75] are convinced that their God, Olelbis, the "One Who Dwells Above", sees everything on earth, and that he is closer to his tribe than are the deities of other tribes. His is the first place in the thinking of the people. Life without him would be unimaginable. The myths of creation and of the primordial age transmit teachings for the people of today. It is recounted how once there was a rainfall after a prolonged drought. Olelbis gave drink first to an old man, who had suffered the most from thirst, and then to the others. He himself drank only last of all. Anyone can see what is meant.

The Indians of Tierra del Fuego were among the peoples who for so long had a reputation for being religionless. Eventually, however, like every other primitive folk, they were subjected to a thoroughgoing scientific investigation.[76] One of their tribes, the Yamana, is the most southerly people of the world. They call the supreme being Watauinewa, "Utterly Ancient One", but he is also often called "My Father". All of life's happenings are seen in relationship to him. His is the supreme power. He is lawgiver, and guardian of morality. He is good, and helpful, but inexorable in his punishments. In the puberty rite the young are admonished, very concretely, to devote themselves to altruistic behaviour, based on an appeal to the Utterly Ancient One.[77]

Among the Arapaho, the Algonquin tribe, the master of the seven-day sun-dance makes the following prayer:

> My Father, Man up there, Creator, Food-Giver, hear! Be near us poor beings who have need of blessings spiritual and bodily. May the people gathered here in this tent be blessed. My Father, have mercy on us. Remember we are your children, from the time when you created sky and earth. My Grandfather, Light of the Earth, please look down here, on your poor, needy people, so that whatever they do for your sake may please you. Our Father, Man up there, here is the pipe you have given us as a sign of your great love. Grant that we may better love one another. Have mercy on us all, and let us rise up now in safety and security. Especially, give the nation increase, that your holy ceremonies can continue. May we fight with evil, and conquer. We ask you to keep us.

Then the pipe is passed among the priests, to be smoked by them.
Many tribes share the belief that the Great Spirit is to return at the end
of the ages, accompanied by the spirits of all the dead. Then all human
beings will live together, all things will be made right, and happiness will
reign everywhere.[78]

Conclusion

§24 *The God of All the Peoples*

Religion cannot be described; it must be observed, in living human
beings. Above all, it must be experienced. A summary, then, is even more
difficult. It will always remain purely ancillary. Still, this third survey of
ours has made one thing clear: what we found in Africa (§8, above) is
repeated and confirmed in Asia and America. People after people
everywhere, on continent after continent, lift heart and hands to heaven,
and see to it that their children do the same. Everywhere, among the
most divergent cultural strata, we meet with the consciousness of a
primary mystery and ultimate reality, a more or less clearly recognised
supreme being, God. This God is far and yet near, mysterious and yet the
most self-evident being in the world, cloaked in awe and yet invoked as
"Father".

Among the Pygmies, shepherds, and farmers and hunters of all three
continents, in spite of all their differences, we discover similarities that
are absolutely striking. Religion is the ground and meaning of life,
morality, and happiness. The stress is on this present life. There is no
question of some "consolation in the world to come". The high religions,
which have lost something of their almost naive primitive thinking, have
deepened the idea of this highest reality, but they have complicated and
abstracted it as well. Here a concern with the next world comes much
more into the limelight, and religious peoples are consumed with waiting
for another stage of life.

Thus one's personal religious experience, along with the reflections of
philosophy and theology, find *a posteriori* corroboration in the discovery
that all peoples are religious — that therefore religion has something to
do with human beings as such, that it is something given with their
nature, and that this is why it leaves them no peace. True, there are
questions to be asked about the validity of these religions, as well as
about their future. These are questions that will occupy us in Part Four.
For the moment, we have only been examining these religions in
themselves — subjecting the God of the peoples to the methods of
comparative religion.

The origin of the high religions is often a matter of record. By contrast, the first beginnings of the primitive religions are lost in the shadows of prehistory. Primitive religions go back to primitive times. Their myths assert that God's relationship with human beings began with their very first creation. Naturally, there is no empirical demonstration that this is the "way it was" — that God actually came to these peoples in the moment of creation. But neither can we prove the contrary. One thing is certain, that as far back into the dark corridors of human existence as history's light can shine, God was always there, as God of the peoples. There is no people that has not sought him and found him, no people to whom he has not revealed himself.

"God of the peoples" and "peoples of God" are correlative concepts. In what way, precisely, did the peoples think of themselves as *God's* peoples? Ancient horizons were narrow, both literally and figuratively. One worried little about how *our* God got along with the divinities of other tribes. It was enough to know that he is *our* God, that he has created *us*, that he is close to *us*. Thus for all practical purposes God was a tribal god, who therefore accorded this people of his a preferred place among all peoples. One lived with him in an unwritten covenantal relationship (see §8, above).

Wherever we find an explicit covenant consciousness we usually find an unattractive exclusivist side as well, or even a spirit of aggressiveness, with rueful effects on the "others" — who are not equally the peoples of God. We saw it among the Masai (§2, above) and the Galla (§4) in Africa, we saw it in the Tatars and Huns in Asia (§11), and we saw it in the Hindu Brahmins (§16) and the Islamic *Umma* (§20). In the following chapter we shall venture further down this trail, and we shall see how the notion of people of God is overgrown with so much that is human, and false — just as the peoples' picture of God himself is not so clear and distinct as our abbreviated presentation may have made it appear.

Chapter Eight

The Peoples of God

§25 *Ethnocentrism*

As we have just seen, God has proved to be, in varying degrees of clarity and explicitation, the God of the peoples of all ages and all places. For their own part, human beings therefore feel themselves to be God's peoples. Of course there is a great deal of the human here, and even of the ungodly, in this so godly view of a world.

It is one's own self that is the point of departure, and the measure, of love for others. "Love your neighbour as yourself" (Mark 12:31), Jesus said, quoting the Old Testament. So it is with peoples, too. A people's point of reference for its attitude toward other peoples is always necessarily itself. But a people's self-appreciation, even its normal self-appreciation, admits of varying degrees. Then there are further degrees — abnormal or unhealthy ones. In its healthy form this self-appreciation is called patriotism. But patriotism has a tendency to inflate itself into a blind admiration for one's own people, and a corresponding underestimation of other peoples. Then it is called "chauvinism". Chauvinism is such a common thing in the world that "nation " has been defined as " a group of people united in a common error concerning their ancestry and a common undervaluation of their neighbours". Chauvinism, in turn, can be accentuated to the point of the sickness called "xenophobia", actual hatred of foreigners. All three forms of a people's self appreciation — patriotism, chauvinism, and xenophobia — go by the generic name of "ethnocentrism". For our purposes of investigating and reflecting on the "chosen peoples", we owe ethnocentrism some special attention.[79]

Ethnocentrism can be defined as that attitude of mind in which a group of human beings takes itself for the centre of everything, and judges and categorises other peoples only with reference to themselves. In the concrete, it occurs mainly as positive prejudice toward one's own group, coupled with negative prejudice toward any foreign group or groups. We hold ourselves and our own people to be more capable, more industrious, and more honest than the others — simply superior to them in every respect. In our own group, we feel "at home"; when we are among others we feel "abroad", and we keep our distance. This is plainly the vestige of an irrational herding instinct. One observes a similar behaviour in animals: an unknown environment automatically registers as dangerous. The foreigner becomes the enemy and, according to circumstances, we make ready for fight or flight.

But the entire phenomenon has even deeper roots than this. After all, one's very identity is a function of a contraposition to others — to strangers. Were all human beings equally open toward one another, they would suddenly live in an anonymous mass, not in any kind of an "at home" atmosphere. One cannot shift into all gears at once.

> Thus ethnocentrism is a basic structure of human behaviour. Without the foreign, there would be no domestic. Without what is strange, there would be no "one's own" . . . Social problems arising out of a mutual strangeness remain constitutive of a society's integration. They cannot be removed, they can merely be eased.[80]

Religion plays a very special role in all this. It represents the highest stage of a person's self-identity, hence also of a people's self-identity. What is tragic is that often — very often, almost always — instead of unifying peoples under the God of the peoples, religion is abused, placed at the service of an exaggerated ethnocentrism. This is one of the most important conclusions of the first three parts of this book, and an indictment of religion as such.

In Part One we saw how the Jews, in Yahweh's name, believed they had the obligation of ruthlessly exterminating the peoples of Canaan (§22). The depressing outcome of Part Two was that the church as the "chosen people" was by and large averse to, or aggressive toward, the "others" (§34). We have come to a similar conclusion in Part Three (§24). Even today an essential element of the national identity of a people is often its religion, even its confessional religion, such as Islam for Pakistan, Hinduism for India, Buddhism for Thailand, Catholicism for Poland, or Calvinism for South Africa.[81] Religion has very often functioned, and still functions, as a force of national unity but at the same time it is a leaven of tension and division. There must be a genuine change of heart before we can do justice to the true meaning of religion and the intention of the God of the peoples.

The whole affair is to a large extent a problem in communication: the stranger is a stranger because we know too little about him or her. And it is a problem of reflection: we have thought a good deal about ourselves, and about our own people, but very little about others. With multiplied contacts and better communication, we are now in a position to overcome the unhealthy forms of ethnocentrism — by relativizing our own values, on both sides, and integrating them into the greater whole. The furtherance of this process is the purpose of this book.

Meanwhile, however, we must concretize our general considerations on ethnocentrism. We shall begin with the southern peoples. Our geographical terminology is an attempt to circumvent unpleasant appellations such as "nature peoples" or "primitive peoples". Generally we mean the non-Christian peoples of the southern hemisphere.

Here, wherever we look we see tribal thinking. Some tribes even call themselves simply "human beings", to distinguish themselves from their neighbours.[82] Yes, it can go that far. Thus the fearsome archers of the remote regions of Cameroon call themselves the *Wute* ("human beings"). The *Khoi-Khoi* ("human beings as such") people of southern Africa refers to its neighbours as "Hottentots", or "stammerers". A group of Hamite immigrants in East Africa calls itself the *Hadendoa*, or "master people". One finds this everywhere, in America, in Africa, in Asia — for example, in Irian Jaya (Indonesia) there are peoples who call themselves *jakai, asmat,* or *kaeti* — all expressions meaning "human beings".

"Human beings". This is the term we use to distinguish ourselves from the vegetable kingdom and the animal kingdom. It is also, it would seem, the term we may use to distinguish ourselves from our neighbours. What we single out is not our human nature, which is common, but the differences — the things that separate. It is not only the Jews and the Greeks who contemptuously called everybody else *goyim* or *barbaroi*. The Chinese do the same — all foreigners are *daszy*, "barbarians". The Dinka refer to a neighbouring tribe as the *Niam-Niam*, or "Big Eaters". The Algonquin called the Eskimos "those who eat meat raw". Many tribes of Indians call their neighbours simply the "enemy".

For many, if not all, cultures, "human beings" stop where the village, the language, or the tribe stops. All others are the object of derision and contempt, and count as thieves, drunkards, sluggards, lechers, murderers, and cannibals. Of course, the feeling is mutual.

Every tribe thinks it lives at the centre of the world. After all, it is only its own history, played on the turntable of the world, that it knows anything about. Everything else lies "outside", is less important. Many East Indians refer to their own homes as standing "at the centre of the world". But it is especially the temple that is seen in this way — the locus of convergence, the navel of the universe, the meeting point of the human and the divine. In the Church of the Holy Sepulchre in Jerusalem there is a stone with the inscription in Greek, "Here is the navel of the world." In Java, princes are called *Paku Alam*, or *Paku Buwono* — "Nature's Nail", "Nail of the World" [83] The prince is the highest manifestation of the divine, and therefore the one who holds the community together.

The sacred community of the tribe, along with its ties to ancestors and to God, is erected and guaranteed through the whole ritual of tribal usage. Nonmembers stand outside this circulatory system. They have other blood, another land, other customs, another tongue. Two separate worlds are built, however neighbouring they might happen to be. Each tribe feels itself to be the people of God. What the condition of the others might be is none of one's business.

In this connection it would be interesting to write a chapter on the "saviour" — that brilliant messianic figure who provides a given tribe's ethnocentrism with concrete form and confirmation. Mythological cultural heroes brought the people (*this* people) important information for practical living — for hunting, farming, the use of weapons, and so on. Historical saviours unleash a so-called mob psychology, usually with an appeal to the Old Testament exodus account with its prophetic visions and promises — and in this case they make express use of the concept of a covenant with God. Finally, if they are still awaited in a future time, the expectation throws the population into a messianic frenzy. There would be abundant instances for us to study, but we shall have to rest content with simply having referred to the phenomenon,[84] and mentioning only two examples, the Mau-Mau movement in Kenya, and Kimbangism in Zaire.[85]

Jomo Kenyatta was hailed as God's chosen prophet, as the Moses who would lead his people out of the slavery of colonialism. With Kenyatta a new covenant was struck between God and "his" people. "God told Kenyatta in a vision that he would multiply his progeny as the stars in the sky, and that all nations would be blessed in him. Kenyatta believed, and God swore it to him by his omnipotence." After a period of imprisonment Kenyatta became the first president of an independent Kenya.

Similarly in Zaire, the church of the prophet Simon Kimbangu in its documents and declarations refers to the alliance with Moses, and to the promises of Christ as fulfilled in Simon Kimbangu in 1921. Kimbangu is said to be the "other paraclete" whom Jesus promised to send. Today the members of this church number more than three million, with a consciousness of election and mission that is colossal. In 1969 the church was admitted to the World Council of Churches.

§27 *The Western Peoples*

We find similar instances of an uncritical overestimation of one's own political and religious community in the history (including the current history) of the western peoples — by which we mean, by and large, the Christian peoples. Here we have time only for a "strobe-lamp" approach.

183

Behind all the eruption of modern imperialism and nationalism is an extraordinary, religiously enhanced and often expressly biblical, sense of mission.[86] A typical instance is to be found in late Portuguese colonialism under Antonio Salazar. Here we watched the blossoming of an outright mystique of colonialism. Newspapers wrote:

> We must ever preserve in the Portuguese people the dream, the consciousness, the pride of empire. Africa is more than a region to be developed; it is our moral justification, our *raison d'être* as a power. Without Africa, we would be a little nation. With Africa, we are a great power.

In his speeches, Salazar stated the reasons for challenging his people to a life of sacrifice in lands beyond the sea: "Our readiness for heroism stands on the noble knowledge of our mission as a chosen people, an evangelizing people". A bishop encouraged Portuguese soldiers:

> No people since the Jews has manifested so clear a sign of a divine vocation, to be realized in history, as has Portugal. The subjugation of overseas territories was the fulfilment of her destiny. It was not undertaken out of mere political motives, but out of the specifically Christian intention of propagating the faith.[87]

The Italy of the Risorgimento, the nineteenth-century unification and liberation movement, had a typical spokesman in priest, philosopher, and statesman V. Gioberti (1801-1852). One of his principal writings concerned the "moral and civil precedence of the Italians", in which he gave expression to his dream and hope that a united Italy would step forward as a "leader nation", to enlighten the world's darkness with the light of its Christian faith. Divine providence, he announced, had chosen the city of Romulus to be the navel of the world. In the Old Testament it had been the Levitical class who were to charge themselves with priestly service to God on the people's behalf. Now it was to be the Italians who, in supernatural wise, had been chosen to become the salvation of the other peoples, through the religion Italy had by right of blood. Italy was to prepare the way for Christianity. Gioberti was quite aware that such a self-concept was scarcely calculated to be pleasing to the other peoples of the earth, but he justified it on the grounds that Italy's primacy would redound to the good of all other nations. Finally, he developed an outright Isaian vision of a united Italy, at whose pinnacle, in his natural and supernatural commission as lord of the world, would stand the pope.[88]

These ideas were taken up and developed by fascism — but now no longer as a dream. This time, it was seen as reality in the process of accomplishment:

> Italy's new generation has an ethics of its own, a faith of its own, a religion of its own, and its own totalitarian credo: a profession of faith in the

nation ... We are no longer merely lovable larks. We are eager for justice, thirsty for righteousness, happy to unleash a storm of collective heroism, to bring to the world the triumph of all our ideals. We know now that the future of the other peoples depends on us alone.[89]

All this was to be effected through the person of the *duce* — in every respect the model man. It was he who would bless the world through Italian colonization, and thereby reestablish the old Roman empire. He loved to be compared with Moses, leading his people forth from their humiliation; with Francis of Assisi, the "new human being", who tamed the wolf of Gubbio; and even with Jesus, the children's friend, benefactor of the whole of humankind.[90] The Italian people, and the Italian church, identified so well with the *duce's* great plan that neither of them saw anything shocking in the fall of Abyssinia. On October 28, 1935, Cardinal Schuster proclaimed in the cathedral of Milan: "By its blood, our nation's army has opened the portals of Abyssinia to the Catholic faith and Italian civilization". [91]

This confounding of missions — religious, cultural, political — also stood behind all Great Britain's colonial undertakings. K. Hammer, who researched these interconnections, made it his central thesis that British consciousness of mission had its direct or indirect roots in the Bible, in the Old and New Testament belief in election.[92] All through nineteenth-century English literature the refrain recurs: England was the ark of liberty, and hence its Anglican faith, free of Catholic superstition, had been chosen by heaven to lord it over others.

Like notions made the rounds in Germany. On July 27, 1900, Kaiser Wilhelm II dispatched a German troop on a punitive expedition against the Chinese for the murder of an ambassador, and seized the occasion to develop an Old Testament theology of battle. Two days later, to strengthen his soldiers' colonial commitment, he spoke of Moses' victory over the Amalekites.

The same theology lesson was taught during World War I. This time, both sides spoke of a "last judgment" upon the enemy.[93] It happened all over again in World War II. The *Führer* had mapped out his geopolitics carefully, and made his plans for the world from the viewpoint of the interests of the "Aryan people". Then as the new war broke out (for it "must"), the churches supported political decisions with religious motivations, and called upon soldiers to render obedience to the *Führer*. The victories over Poland and France were each celebrated by the long pealing of church bells. Even as late as 1944, episcopal declarations referred to German soldiers as "martyrs" who were fighting "godless Bolshevism".[94] Thus a nation was held prisoner by its own ethnocentric mentality: " our people is the people of God, our war is just, our borders are sacred, our government acts with God's authority". Citizens had not yet arrived at the point of being able to take a critical distance from their regime, as do many churches today in Latin America and elsewhere.

A chosen-people ideology likewise provided a moral thrust for many American immigrants. They saw a new "land of promise" on that beckoning continent, a New Canaan, the New Jerusalem, given by God's hand to "his" people, whom he would lead as they crossed the sea, leaving their poverty behind them. *Magnalia Christi Americana*, "Christ's Mighty Deeds in America", was the title of a book by seventeenth-century minister Cotton Mather.[95] More recently a book with the meaningful title, *The Almost Chosen People*, makes another presentation of this ideology, which found its classic expression in Abraham Lincoln.[96] Once more the consciousness of being a chosen people was confined to the parameters of a single people. Of course, it was only the WASPs, the "White Anglo-Saxon Protestants", who possessed it in its fulness. A quite recent work summarizes it all retrospectively:

> The founders of the American nation were not looking for an easy faith; it was this biblical tradition on which they drew for inspiration. The new republic would be no merely secular social compact, but the bearer of eternal values; not just an agreement among men, but a new covenant with God. For America was the New Israel, the promised land to which God had led his people, an Elect Nation, set apart by Divine Providence. A single symbolic tradition linked the prophets Isaiah and Amos, Jesus and Abraham Lincoln. Certainly, there was no conflict here between one's civic and religious obligations: patriotism blended with piety, civic duty with obedience to God. But the religion of the new nation should not be dismissed as some thinly disguised self-worship. At its best it represented a people's attempt to make explicit the ideals they were committed to live by, the standards of humanity they would strive to maintain, the yardstick against which they would measure the quality of national life. And they were exacting standards. If they were a chosen nation, they were also a nation under divine judgment. The covenant with God was both a guarantee of God's blessing and a reminder of God's command.[97]

It was in this same spirit that American presidents, believing Christians, looked upon their nations's intervention in World War II, and formulated American postwar policy.[98]

We could go on and on, with people after people. We could speak of the chauvinism of the French — after all, they coined the word, and well before the time of de Gaulle! We could recall even little Switzerland, which loved to hear Hilty saying, "Except for that of the Israelites, no history shows how the happiness or unhappiness of peoples depends on the acknowledgment of eternal moral imperatives as clearly as does the history of Switzerland".

One could point out how Catholicism forms an essential component of Poland's national consciousness, fusing its people to a single unity and kindling in them the fire of their centuries-long struggle against Turks, Russians, Prussians, and communists.[99] We could call attention to the ideology of "people of God", "divine order", and "Christian civilization" as they are abused by the "national security" system of so many Latin American states, the more easily to justify itself to a "believing people".[100] And of couse one may not overlook the messianism of old "Holy Russia", cunningly employed all over again in these latter days by the communist regime in order to contrast the "Soviet patriotism of the great Russian people" with the "reactionary ideology of American imperialism". Newer biographies of Karl Marx allege his captivation by a Jewish consciousness of mission; even Marxist messianism, we are told, has its roots in Old Testament prophecy.[101]

§28 Conclusions

But we cannot go into all that at length. Nor need we. What we wanted to establish lies crystal clear before us, and not as an *a priori* hypothesis but as a rigidly demonstrated thesis. The conclusions of Parts One, Two, and Three of this study may be summed up as follows.

Most peoples, on all continents, nourish and foster a marked ethnocentrism, generally accentuated and supported by religion. They acknowledge a deity as the ultimate foundation of their identity as a people. Consequently, they live in a kind of covenant with God. They see themselves as an altogether special people — as the people of God, and hence explicitly or implicitly, a chosen people.

It suddenly strikes us that the notion of election by God, or covenant with God, has nothing exclusively, or even originally, to do with Israel. There were older peoples than those nomadic tribes of the Sinai who believed themselves to be especially close to God. Instructed by our insights and conclusions it would behoove us to rethink the theology of covenant[102] — especially in view of the fact that until now the consciousness of election has generally been understood in a very narrow and exclusivistic way, often to the detriment of others, and hence in an inhuman and ungodly fashion (see §§24-27, above). Such convictions of special election ought to be unmasked and, along with their "divine foundation", subjected to a thoroughgoing *reductio ad absurdum*. A genuine theology of election, on the other hand, could argue its appeal to God validly, and could offer today's humanity a new prototype of its greatness and oneness.

Every people has been thinking of itself as *the* star in the sky. It is time to stand in admiration of the beauty of all the stars together, in all their different degrees of brightness, and thus to discover the glory of a single universe.

Notes to Part Three

1   For example, C.M. Schröder, *Die Religionen der Menschheit; Homo religiosus: L'expression sacré dans les grandes religions* (Louvain, 1978 seq.); H.C. Puech, *Histoire des religions* (Bibliography).

2   See W. Schneider, *Die Religion der afrikanischen Naturvölker* (Münster, 1891); C. Tesch, *Gott und Götter* (Freiburg, 1890); H. Schell, *Apologie des Christentums: Religionen und Offenbarung* (Paderborn, 1901); A. Le Roy, *La religion des primitifs* (Paris, 1909); P.V. Cathrein, *Die Einheit des sittlichen Bewusstseins der Menschheit*, 3 vols. (Freiburg, 1914); J. Riem, *Die Sintflut in Sage und Wissenschaft* (Hamburg, 1925).

3   See the most recent appreciation, S. Pajak, *Urmonotheismus und Uroffenbarung bei W. Schmidt* (St. Augustin, 1978). See also J. Henninger, "P.W. Schmidt: 25 Jahre nach seinem Tod," *Anthropos* 74:1-5 (Fribourg, 1979). I am happy to acknowledge the help it was to me in Part Three to be able to use the library of the Anthropos Institute in St. Augustin, near Bonn, and to speak with members of the institute.

4   Cited by F. Snowdon, *Black in Antiquity: Ethiopians in the Graeco-Roman Experience* (Cambridge, 1970), p. 146.

5   Padre Giovanni Antonio Cavazzi da Montecucculo, *Istorica descrizione dei tre Regni Congo, Matamba et Angola situati nell'Etiopia inferiore occidentale* (Bologna, 1687), vol. 1, n. 156.

6   In Schmidt, *Ursprung*, 7:324. "Chosen peoples" finally appears in the Index in vol. 7 — never to recur. Its eleven entries all refer to the East African shepherds!

7   Hallet, *Afrika Kitabu*, p. 117.

8   Debrunner, *A History of Christianity in Ghana*, 1:5ff.

9   Zahan, in Puech, *Histoire des religions*, 3:646ff.

10   In *Colloque International de Kinshasa 1978*, p. 88.

11   See Baumann, in H. Baumann, R. Thurnwald, and D. Westermann, *Völkerkunde von Afrika* (Essen, 1940).

12   See W. Schmidt, *Handbuch der vergleichenden Religionsgeschichte* (Münster, 1930), p. 56. See also *Ursprung*, vols. 2-6.

13   Schmidt, ibid. 4:17-219. Trilles' testimony is to be admitted with caution, inasmuch as he seems to have fabricated certain things: see K. Piskaty in *Anthropos*, 1957:33-48.

14   Schmidt, *Ursprung* 4:220-302.

15   Ibid., pp. 336-404.

16   Ibid. 7:11-162.

17   Ibid., pp. 321-431, esp. 427.

18   Ibid. 8:1-93, esp. 30.

19   Nothomb, *Un humanisme africain*, esp. pp. 89-98; B. Zuure, *L'âme du Murundi* (Paris, 1932).

20   C.E.E.B., *Noms théophoriques d'Afrique* (Bandundu, 1977). But see the reservations with which R. Friedli approaches these theophoric names, in Waldenfels, *Festschrift Glazik*, pp. 261-71. In §6, below, we shall return to the thorny question of belief in a highest god.

21   Grialue, *Schwarze Genesis*, p. 10.

22   Dieterlen, *Textes sacrés*, p. 7.

23   Baumann, *Schöpfung und Urzeit*, pp. 97, 162ff.

24   J. Goetz, *Dieu lointain et puissances proches*, pp. 21-55.

25   Lufuluabo, in *African Ecclesiastical Review* 1962:250. See also: Mbiti, J.S., *African Religions and Philosophy* (London, 1969); *New Testament Eschatology in an African Background* (Oxford, 1971); and Part Four, note 102.

26   See: Tempels, P., *La philosophie bantoue* (Paris, 1949); Mulago, V., *Un visage africain du christianisme. L'union vitale bantu face à l'unité vitale ecclésiale* (Paris, 1962); Lufuluabo, F., *Valeur des religions africaines selon la Bible et selon Vatican II*

(Kinshasa, 1968). See also, as one example of the many books on the sacred kingdom in Africa, Irstam Tor, *The King of Ganda* (Stockholm, 1944).

27 Thiel, *Ahnen*, pp. 175ff.

28 Typical of this attitude is Okot p'Bitek, *African Religions in Western Scholarship* (Nairobi, 1970); see the treatment of this book in Bühlmann, *Missionsprozess*, pp. 27-31 (English edition: *The Missions on Trial*); also B.I. Sharevskaya, cited in *Des africanistes russes parlent de l'Afrique* (Paris, 1960), pp. 109-27.

29 See the discussion of M. Oppitz's book on structural anthropology by R. Rahmann in *Anthropos* 73:602ff.

30 Singleton, *Ancêtres, adolescents et l'absolu*.

31 See Baumann, H., *Schöpfung und Urzeit des Menschen im Mythus der afrikanischen Völker* (Berlin, 1936); Doke, C.M., *The Lambas of Northern Rhodesia* (London, 1931); Goetz, J., "Dieu lontain et puissances proches," in *Missionalia* 21:21-55 (Rome, 1972); Griaule, M., *Schwarze Genesis. Ein afrikanischer Schöpfungsbericht* (Freiburg, 1970); Idowu, E.B., *Olodumare. God in Yoruba Belief* (London, 1962); Lufuluabo, F., *Valeur des religions africaines selon la Bible et selon Vatican II* (Kinshasa, 1968); Mbiti, J.S., *African Religions and Philosophy* (London, 1969); ibid., *New Testament Eschatology in an African Background* (Oxford, 1971); Mitchell, R.C., *African Primal Religions* (Niles [Illinois], 1977); Mulago, V., *Un visage africain du christianisme. L'union vitale bantu face à l'unité vitale ecclésiale* (Paris, 1962); Rattray, R.S., *Religion and Art in Ashanti* (Oxford, 1927); Thomas, L.V. and Luneau, R. *La terre africaine et ses religions* (Paris, 1975).

32 Thomas and Luneau, *Les sages*, p. 144.

33 Amadou Hampaté Ba, in Dieterlen, *Textes sacrés*, p. 9.

34 See Fourche, T. and Morlinghem, M., *Une Bible noire* (Brussels, 1973); Griaule, M., *Schwarze Genesis. Ein afrikanischer Schopfungsbericht* (Freiburg, 1970); Schlosser, K., *Die Bantubibel. Schöpfungsberichte der Zulu* (Kiel, 1977).

35 Köster, *Afrikanisches Christsein*, pp. 50, 400.

36 LG 73; AG 10; SC 37-40. See Bühlmann, *Wo der Glaube lebt*, pp. 224-33 (English edition: *The Coming of the Third Church*).

37 AIF, Nov. 16, 1974. See the books by Butturini and Zago; also Shorter, *African Christian Theology;* Bühlmann, *Ein Missionsorden*, pp. 39-59, "Missionstheologie vom Vatican II zu Evangelii nuntiandi."

38 *Colloque International de Kinshasa 1978*, pp. 19 (Cardinal Malula), 300 (Cardinal Rossi).

39 Schmidt, *Ursprung* 1:160-63.

40 Ibid. 143-60, 334-487; 3:565-1114.

41 Ibid. 9:71-141.

42 Ibid. 3-67.

43 Ibid. 11-39.

44 Ibid. 157ff.

45 Yang, *Religion in Chinese Society*, pp. 104-26, 378-404. Wing-tsit-chan, *Religiöses Leben im heutigen China* (Munich, 1955); W. Eichhorn, *Die Religionen Chinas*.

46 Father François-Régis de Lascuet, *La trouée: Le Père Charles* (Paris, 1947).

47 J. Dournes, *Dieu aime les païens*.

48 Sinaga, *The Toba-Batak High-God* (Louvain, dissertation).

49 Because we are using no diacritical marks for our few Indian expressions, we must at least note that the *sh* corresponds to the German *sch*, and the *dg* to *dsch*. Panikar, *The Vedic Experience*, pp. 4, 10.

50 For this whole paragraph see: Klostermaier, K., *Hinduism* (Cologne, 1956); Rahdakrishnan, S., The Hindu View of Life (London, 17th ed., 1974); Zaehner, *Hinduism* (Oxford, 1966); *Inde, Israël, Islam, religions mystiques et révélations prophétiques* (Paris, 1965); von Glasenapp, H., *Die Religionen Indiens* (Stuttgart, 1955); Parrinder, G., *Le Upanishad, la Gita e la Bibbia* (Rome, 1964). I also acknowledge the information and help of Patrick Crasts, from India, a student of Hinduism.

189

[51] This is what Radhakrishnan reports in his *The Hindu View of Life*, pp. 20, 25; as well as A.C. Bose, *The Call of the Vedas* (Bombay, 1954), pp. 32-35; T. Panikkar, *Vedic Experience*, pp. 11, 790. See J. Daniélou, *Hindu Polytheism* (London, 1964).

[52] See Mensching, *Buddha*, p. 275.

[53] M. Dhavamony, "Hindu Incarnations," *Studia Missionalia* 21:127-69 (Rome, 1972).

[54] Klostermeier, *Hinduismus*, pp. 171-84, 311.

[55] See Sequeira, *Sin and Forgiveness in the Early Vedic Period.*

[56] Klostereier, *Hinduismus*, pp. 361-74.

[57] As given in Panikkar, *Vedic Experience.*

[58] Radhakrishnan, *Hindu View*, pp. 67-72; M. Dhavamony, "La cristianità e le società basate sul sistema delle caste," *Concilium* 10:134-44.

[59] Ruben, *Die Entwicklung der Religion im alten Indien*, pp. 4, 41, 239ff.

[60] See the book by Siegmund; also von Glasenapp, *Die Religionen Indiens*, pp. 206-80; "Buddismo e cristianesimo," *Concilium* 6 (1978), esp. the articles by M. Dhavamony, D. Dubarle, Mervin Fernando; C. Regamey, in LThK 2:752-56.

[61] Wilkinson, *Ambedhar and the Neo-Buddhist Movement.*

[62] Dumoulin, *Buddhismus der Gegenwart*, pp. 166-87; H.B. Earhart, *The New Religions of Japan: A Bibliography* (Tokyo, 1970); E. Benz, *Neue Religionen* (Stuttgart, 1971); H. Biezais, *New Religions* (Stockholm, 1975).

[63] Cox, *Licht aus Asien;* Bühlmann, *All haben denselben Gott*, pp. 188-92 (English edition: *All have the same God / The Search for God*).

[64] See von Paret, *Der Koran;* Gardet, *L'Islam*, pp. 41-51; T. Fahd, "Naissance de l'Islam," in Puech, *Histoire des réligions* 2:646-94; J. Henninger, *Spuren christlicher Glaubenswahrheiten im Koran* (Schöneck, 1951). In this section I am grateful for the good information I have from Professor Ary A. Roest Crollius, of the Gregorian University, Rome.

[65] Gardet, *L'Islam*, p. 281. See L. Gardet, *La cité musulmane* (Paris, 1961).

[66] Ary A. Roest Crollius, "Mission and Morality: The Communitarian and Missionary Dimensions of the Qur'anic Ethics," *Studia Missionalia* 27:257-83 (Rome, 1978); P. Antes, "'Mission' im Islam," in Waldenfels, *Festschrift Glazik*, pp. 375-81.

[67] See J. Henninger, "Über den Beitrag der Laien bei der Ausbreitung des Islams," in J. Specker and W. Bühlmann, *Das Laienapostolat in den Missionen* (Schöneck, 1961), pp. 345-71; R. Paret, "Toleranz und Intoleranz im Islam," *Saeculum* 21:344-65 (Freiburg, 1970); U. Schoen, *Determination und Freiheit im arabischen Denken heute;* M. Mintjes, *Social Justice in Islam.*

[68] Ary A. Roest Crollius, "Il risveglio dell'Islam in un mondo pluralista," *Civiltà Cattolica* 1980:117-32; *The Journal*, Muslim World League (Mecca, 1977 seq.); "Le dialogue islamo.chrétien des dix dernières années," *PMV-Bulletin*, Sept.- Oct., 1978.

[69] L. Kolafa, *Das Sendungsbewusstsein des Christoph Kolumbus* (Munich, 1974). See NZM 1976:129. The same considerations later drove the missionaries to China: see J. Beckmann, "China im Blickfeld der mexikanischen Bettelorden des 16. Jahrhunderts," NZM 1963:81-92, 195-214. 1964:27-41. 89-108.

[70] Ricard, "La conquête spirituelle," pp. 25-52; Braden, *Religious Aspects of the Conquest of Mexico*, pp. 20-75.

[71] M. Eliade, *La nostalgie des origines*, pp. 203ff.

[72] The assertion of Father R. Cadorette, a missionary among the Aymara. See *Boletín*, Instituto de Estudios Aymaras (Puno, 1978 seq.); and similar assertions concerning the Catholic Mapuche in Chile in E. Böning, *Der Pillanbegriff der Mapuche* (ST. Augustin, 1974).

[73] Schmidt, *Ursprung* 2:408-48; 5:475-521; 6:53-55.

[74] Ibid. 2:36-41.

[75] Ibid., pp. 73-101.

[76] Ibid., pp. 873-1033.

[77] Ibid., pp. 680-756.

[78] Ibid., pp. 354, 367, 371; 5:413.

79 Nouilhac, *La peur de l'autre:* Friedli, *Fremdheit als Heimat,* pp. 127-29; Deutsch, *Nationalism;* G.M. Murdock, "Ethnocentrism," *Enclyclopaedia of the Social Sciences* (New York, 1948), 5:613ff.; D. Bidney, "Cultural Relativism," in D.L. Sills, ed., *International Encyclopaedia of the Social Sciences* 3:543-47; P. Heinth, "Soziale Vorurteile," *Wörterbuch der Soziologie* (Stuttgart, 1969), pp. 996ff.

80 Ohle, *Das Ich und das Andere,* p. 97.

81 Von der Mehden, *Religion and Nationalism.*

82 Plischke, *Völkerkundliches zur Entstehung von Stammes- und Völkernamen;* C. Levi-Strauss, *Rasse und Geschichte* (Frankfurt, 1972), pp. 16-23.

83 On this whole matter see M. Eliade, *Centre du monde.* For the information on Indonesia I am grateful to Prof. Jan Boelaerts, who refers to Stoehr and Zoetmulder, *Die Religionen Indonesiens* (Stuttgart, 1965).

84 See the most important literature: M. Hermann, *Die Erlöser und Heilbringer der Tibeter;* H. Mynarek, "Religionen und Utopien der Hoffnung," in Erharter, *Hoffnung für alle,* pp. 36-69; H. Schär, *Erlösungsvorstellungen und ihre psychologischen Aspecte;* R. Guardini, *Der Heilbringer in Mythos, Offenbarung und Politik* (Zurich, 1946); Guariglia, *Prophetismus und Heilserwartungen,* pp. 254-77; M.I. Pereira de Queiroz, *O messianismo no Brasil e no mundo* (São Paulo, 1965); B.D.M. Sundkler, *Bantu Prophets in South Africa* (London, 1961); D.A. Barrett, *Schism and Renewal in Africa.*

85 R. Buijtenhuijs, *Le mouvement Mau-Mau* (Paris, 1971), pp. 300-313; Sinda, *Le messianisme congolais,* pp. 141-47; P. Raymaekers, *L'Eglise de Jésus-Christ sur la terre par le prophète S. Kimbangu* (Kinshasa, 1975); W. Heintze-Fad, *L'Eglise Kimbanguiste, une Eglise qui chante et prie* (Leiden, 1978).

86 "Die Ursachen des neuen Imperialismus," in Gola Mann, *Propyläen-Weltgeschichte,* vol. 8/2 (Frankfurt, 1976), pp. 713-19.

87 J. Duffy, *Portuguese Africa* (Cambridge, 1959), pp. 268-88; Semaine de Missiologie de Louvain 1972, p. 98.

88 V. Gioberti, *Primato morale e civile degli Italiani,* esp. 1:45-50, 64, 81; 3:107, 260-63.

89 Mirko Ardemagni, *Supremazia di Mussolini* (Milan, 1936), pp. 101ff. Similarly E. Bodrero, *La fine di un'epoca* (Bologna, 1933), pp. 73-89; A. Aquarone and M. Vernassa, *Il regime fascista* (Bologna, 1974), pp. 413-33.

90 A communication from A. Hasler, who is engaged in a major study of the Führer/Duce cult in Italian Fascism and German National Socialism.

91 M. Gall, *L'affaire d'Ethiopie: Aux origines de la guerre mondiale* (Paris, 1967), p. 229.

92 Hammer, *Weltmission,* p. 15.

93 Ibid., pp. 309-31.

94 The items in Heer, *Gottes erste Liebe,* pp. 416ff., 440ff.; G. Lewy, *Die katholische Kirche und das Dritte Reich* (Munich, 1965); H. Missalla, *Für Volk und Vaterland: Die kirchliche Kriegshilfe im Zweiten Weltkrieg* (Königstein-Taunus, 1978); HK, March 1980 , pp. 138-44.

95 See Amery, *Das Ende der Vorsehung,* pp. 99-111; M. Koriuman, "Le ideologie del territorio," in Châtelet, *Storia delle ideologie* 2:175-93.

96 Wolf, *The Almost Chosen People* (Garden City, 1959).

97 Marstin, *Beyond Our Tribal Gods,* p. 75.

98 See Bühlmann, *Wo der Glaube lebt,* pp. 69ff. (English edition: *The Coming of the Third Church);* D.D. Eisenhower, *Kreuzzug in Europa,* 1948.

99 Mechtenberg, "Kultur und National bewusstsein in Polen," ORI 1980/1:9-12.

100 J. Comblin, *The Church and the National Security State.*

101 Bluhm, *Ideologies,* pp. 320-35, "Soviet Nationalism"; G. Guariglia, *Il Messianismo russo,* (Rome, 1956).

102 R.R. Ruether, "Towards a New Covenantal Theology," in Talmage, *Disputation,* pp. 320-29.

Part Four

Our New Understanding
of the Peoples

A Theological Interpretation

Chapter Nine

The Challenge

§1 *Resumption of Postponed Questions*

We have come to the last part of our book. We shall find it the most important and the most difficult part. Everything we have been doing so far comes under the heading of collection of data. For the rest of the book we shall be elaborating these data. And we hope to arrive at a fresh, new view of things as a result.

In Part One it became clear that God has chosen for himself a special people, first in the Old Testament and then in the New, in order to create, with them, "his" history. In Part Two we had to confront the fact that that chosen people, in the new covenant as in the old covenant before, understood itself in a very exclusivist sense, with the result that they were perceived by the other, the "nonchosen", peoples as more of a terror than a blessing. Then in Part Three we made the discovery that most peoples think ethnocentrically, and on profane as well as religious grounds consider themselves a special people, a people of God. Expressly or implicitly, the nations all think of themselves as "chosen peoples".

In all three foregoing parts, we postponed consideration of questions that arose, or could have arisen, at the end of each part. But now we can no longer allow ourselves to do so. Nor do we wish to any longer, for the more strident the questions, the more engaging the dialogue, and the questions we postponed are just the ones we need to ask in order to break out of our deadlock and gain a new outlook. The time has come to ask these critical questions.

§2 *The New Situation in the World*

The challenge to do new thinking arises not just from scientific reflection, but first and foremost from the world's new situation. Of course one has to be careful when speaking of "new situations". "Nothing new under the sun", said Qoheleth in the Old Testament (Eccles. 1:10). Human beings of all times thought they stood at the centre of history and the pinnacle of development. Nevertheless, surveying the world of the postwar decades, there are several respects in which we can speak of a genuinely new and first-time situation.

Transportation technology lays the world of the other continents at our doorstep. They used to be so far away! Now international tourism beckons, and in seven hours (three and one-half on the Concorde) you can fly from Europe to America, Africa, or Asia. Communications technology has reduced temporal distance to zero. At the same moment as the president of the United States or the pope is delivering a major address, or the Olympic Games or a world championship are under way, they can be seen and heard in all the living rooms of the world. In such a world we cannot continue to live as we did before — without any relationships, or even as enemies. The new world situation has pushed us right to the brink of conversation and brotherhood. The younger generation certainly feels it. Youth travels everywhere and feels at home.

At the same time, not only has the white claim to superiority and hegemony, so long uncontested, met with its sudden demise in decolonialization, but white humankind itself is in the throes of a deep political identity crisis and a fierce culture shock. Long creation's crown, lord of the earth, sole depository of divine revelation, author of the only worthwhile culture, Western humanity suddenly discovers it has the same kind of skin as do all other human beings, and is like them all in its greatness and smallness.

The truth of change obtrudes painfully on the consciousness of white humankind in manifold ways. It is displaced as majoritarian element in the United Nations by the Afro-Asian bloc. It is driven into a humiliating dependency by the oil countries. It can no longer handle its own problems: with the economy, which is suffering from inflation and unemployment; with the cities, which it wishes it could flee, and where the old masterpieces hanging on the palace walls are being eaten away by exhaust fumes; with the waters of the earth, where the fish die and swimming is no longer safe; with the pills and drugs and artificial foods, which it comes to depend on despite all warnings of the dire consequences; with the terrorism and criminality that threatens to increase beyond all bounds.

At the top of this mountain of threats there lurks the question of questions: to be or not to be. The Southern peoples may be threatened by the hunger bomb; but the Western and Eastern peoples are threatened by the atom bomb, that supreme achievement of human intelligence, and brutal betrayer of the cloven nature of contemporary human existence.[1]

We are becoming more and more conscious of the interconnections of our mutual, planetary dependency and output, our common hope and terror. We look for bonds with others. Divisive barricades are torn down. Privileges are silently given up. All humankind feels held together by the universal destiny it faces.

This is where we wish religion could construct a new Archimedean device, with which we could lift the world right off its hinges and change the structures that are raping the human race.

§3 *The New Situation in the Church*

The situation in the church is altogether similar. Here too a constrained coexistence pushes us forward, out of our aversion and separation from one another, toward tolerance, dialogue, and new religious syntheses. The great challenge of current history lies in the task of bringing humankind to religious encounter — to the recognition of God's all-embracing leadership, to the community of all God's peoples.[2] This is the thought expressed by the Vatican Council in the opening lines of the *Constitution on the Church:*

> The circumstances of our present time endow with a special urgency this task of the church to be a sign of unification with God and of the unity of all humanity, so that all human beings, bound together today by so many and varied social, technical, and cultural bonds, may attain also to full oneness in Christ.

This eruption from medieval *Christianitas* (see Part Two, §4), this irruption into the world community, is favoured by crises. After all, the human being, as history teaches, is generally ready to adopt new behaviour only under pressure rather than as a result of personal insight. Now not only the Western world but the Western church is in grave crisis — crisis of faith and credibility, crisis of authority and vocation, crisis of the missions and ecclesiastical institutions. Those who know the situation put it gloomily indeed in their public addresses and private conversations: "The church in our country is at the end of its rope . . . Regional weather report: low-pressure system over city and countryside alike, on the parish, diocesan, and episcopal-conference levels; no life, no ardour; no longer any young persons who wish to identify with this church . . . The ecclesiastical apparatus is functioning better than ever. It will survive the crisis, and not even notice that in the meantime the members of the church have left . . . The only thing remaining for Christianity in our country is the shroud. But hidden in the shroud is Easter hope".

The root of the malaise is not just the heavy weight of the church's present, but also the collapse of its glorious past. The church is finally being subjected to the critical gaze of history (see Part Two). The ground we were so sure of has been snatched from beneath our feet. Ranged alongside Christianity we suddenly discover a whole row of religions that take themselves just as seriously as we take ourselves.

The cautious P. Rohner writes:

> Today it has become stylish to speak of "the misery of Christianity", and how sorely the church is betraying its mission today, as it did in the past— how instead of setting an example for the community by its praxis, it has become a scandal. I shall not join this choir. But I cannot deny or gloss over the fact. I admit that as a Christian I can think of the church only with shame and grief.[3]

And he adds that the church nevertheless has the courage to go right on presenting the ideal picture of the human being according to the gospel, and to hold it before humanity's eyes as sure salvation; and that this is its great accomplishment.

Likewise J. Ratzinger, a thinker beyond suspicion:

> For modern consciousness, the certainty that God's mercy transcends the bounds of the lawfully established church is an evidence of such elementary force that there really is no longer any problem with it at all; and this renders all the more questionable a church that for a millennium and a half, not only tolerated its own claim to be the unique way to salvation, but has elevated it to an essential element of its self-understanding, and seems to have made it part of its very faith.[4]

This "certainty that God's mercy transcends the bounds of the church", with all the attendant consequences, is of course by no means obvious to all Christians. For many it is a scandal instead. Here we must reckon with the principle of nonsimultaneity: it is not given to everyone to "see the light" at the same time and in the same degree. If modern mass communication destroys even the *general* worldview of so many persons, deprives them of their serenity, depresses them, generates within them the psychology of the "person without a country", and unleashes frustration, fear, and panic in the face of the vacuum, as the experts tell us[5] — then how much more radical are the consequences of such a process when what is called into question is one's precious *religious* worldview.[6]

Instead of wailing painfully in the crisis, or trying to laugh our way out of it with gallows humour, or just waiting it out somehow with gloom and pessimism, we will do better to understand it as a growth crisis — as a normal phase of life — and to master it accordingly. "Primitive" peoples celebrate such phases — birth, maturity, marriage, death — with rites of passage. Could one not also make the attempt to celebrate the present crisis in the church with a "rite of passage"? It might switch on some new lights. We might try to recognize that while the vases of our certainty are bursting in shards, God is preparing a new, and greater, future for his church.[7]

We have been glued to old schemata for such a long time. After Galileo and Copernicus the biblical worldview no longer held; but at least one could count on the medieval image of the church, straitjacketed by the principles of hierarchy and exclusivity. Theologians who sought to break out of the mould were made to feel the consequences (Part Two, §19). And so scholastic theology, from the seventeenth century to the middle of the nineteenth, underwent little change, making it easy for priests to deal with the *adversarii* of the past, but hard for them to come to terms with the ideas of modern times and bring the faith forward into today.[8]

Meanwhile, however, modern thought with its wider horizon had long been driving wedges into our system. Arnold Toynbee, an exponent of modern thought — and a believer — confesses that as a historian he is suspicious, *a priori*, of any thesis that asserts that God has deemed only one people worthy of one revelation at only one time in history. This would constitute an unacceptable constriction of the truth that God is the God of all of his creatures. Logically, why should we suppose that the "chosen people", if there ever was such a thing, was Israel and not, for example, the Chinese? "Is not any creature guilty of a great illusion if it believes that God, through a covenant that he strikes with one or several of his creatures at a certain point in space and time, can descend so low as to make this one encounter the crown of his creation's history?"[9]

Even if it is not the place of a historian to make commentaries on the divine decrees, still Toynbee's reflections are worth thinking about. He even speaks of a heresy of religious ideas and institutions. Nothing is more repugnant to today's thinker than the position that "over here is all right and truth, over there is all wrong and error" — entirely apart from the fact that this is not the way to solve today's religious questions in any case.

§4 *New Opportunity*

But can the church tender random discipleship to "modern thought" like this? Has the church not its own standpoint to represent? Of course it has. But it cannot therefore ignore the new realities. We distinguished above between a "christology from within" and a "christology from without" (Part One, §27). In a similar vein there is an "ecology of theology" being talked about today,[10] meaning the conditions of the environment by which theology has been, and is, more profoundly influenced than it imagines. But then it becomes clear at once that today's theology can be on the lookout for a high-voltage charge from the non-Christian religions, and that the church will see a new opportunity here — the opportunity to speak a new prophetic word to non-Christians, who constitute two-thirds of humankind,[11] and who have become our new neighbours. Christianity will no longer be thinking of itself as a bloc in confrontation with other blocs, but as their inspirer and interpreter. Thus the church could offer new, burning ideas, new ideals and driving motives, to human beings so involved with one another, but so at odds with one another as well.

If the church, according to its own favourite definition, is a "universal sacrament of salvation", or a "sign of salvation for all" (see below, §§19, 28), then it must first of all think of its partners, which it so long has confronted as adversaries (Part Two), and send them a new word of salvation. The church must now understand its own mission with these "others" in mind. Not only in economics but in religion too, north-south polarization portrays the basic structure of the coming world.[12] Neither the political West nor the Christian West has yet finished with its role, but now that role must be played with much more of an eye on the others, who constitute with the West one sole humanity. This is the way the "old" West could outgrow itself, and find the fountain of youth in genuine community with the "young" world.

To speak this new word, no new revelation is needed. What is needed is a new interpretation of revelation, a new stage of Christian maturity. To put it in modern terms, what is needed is a new rocket stage. We do not deny that there have been theologians, especially in the very early centuries (see Part Two, §23) and again in the sixteenth and the nineteenth, who had the vision to anticipate this new insight. But these pioneers[13] found scant audience in their time; just as the "Parliament of Religions" in Chicago in 1893, which convened in the conviction that "never before has Christianity come into such intimate, open, and decisive contact with the other religions of the world", had no further repercussions.[14]

But then the Second Vatican Council opened the sluices and out came the dammed-up ideas. Not that it spoke the last word on many questions, but it lent the freedom and courage to speak new words. Karl Rahner observed of this council that it was a "council at the beginning of a new time, and so it is the beginning of the beginning that the postconciliar church must make".[15] What he said was especially true for our questions in this book. Here postconciliar theology has done a great deal of work. The church has already seized astonishing initiatives in the dialogue with the other religions,[16] although of course in respect to only a small portion of the great masses. But it is not enough for a few theologians and specialists to be busy with the non-Christian majority of humanity. It is the church as such that must build its new understanding of the non-Christians into its own self-understanding and thereby into its proclamation. The church cannot leave the "enlightenment" to the anthropologists and the tourists. They will never do justice to the depths of the mystery.[17]

Worst of all, nothing would be more untimely and unsalutary than to wish to "hit the brakes" at this point — to fall back into the "little remnant" mystique, to become a sect of introverted, fundamentalist, fanatical Christians, as we were for too long in history and ought to be no longer. The ecumenical movement within Christianity, the Catholic openness to non-Catholics, when seen against the horizon of the world religions, suddenly looks like a side issue that ought to be definitively resolved as speedily as possible, in order to be able to cry the announcement of salvation all the louder for being able to cry it in common.

In this new interpretation the role of the church is not so much that of tradition's guardian as of tradition's maker. This is consonant with its

200

innermost essence.[18] One cannot accept that tradition, which was always most creative in the most vital times of the church, should suddenly grow numb in its present situation. Especially in a dynamic world like today's, Christ has bequeathed us the gospel not as a stone but as a loaf — ever to bless, break, distribute anew, and multiply in the distribution. M. Pomilio points up the vitality of our gospel in his book *The Fifth Gospel*. In days gone by, the four evangelists, and with them the first Christians, handed on the good news, of course — but they always gave it new nuances and promulgation, according to the milieu. So today, each Christian generation ought to write "its" gospel, and carry it to the men and women of its time.[19] Then the gospel of today's Christian generation will be an unconditional message of joy to all the peoples of the world. We shall elaborate on this further as Part Four proceeds.

European bishops have always taken care to hold their conferences in traditionally Catholic places such as Fulda, Lourdes, Einsiedeln, or Rome — not that this meant they were withdrawing from the world and dealing only with internal church problems. But in the future we shall have to raise to the second power our involvement with the world, with humanity, with the religions, and with the structures of economics and politics, and see all our own problems from this new outlook. So why could we not expect (utopian though it might sound) that in the near or remote future the bishops might go to Fortaleza or Kinshasa or Benares or Kyoto? Not just as individuals, but in regional or (in small countries) national bishops' conferences, they could repair to these centres of non-Christian humanity as a sign that every local church, on the parish, diocesan, or national level, is not a darkroom where one studies x-rays, but a watchtower on the world and a sign for the world.

Let us now take up the matter of the world religions in more thoroughgoing fashion. But before we do, I should like to make two observations.

First, when I compare the Koran and the Bible here and there as sacred writings, or Mohammad and Christ as religious figures, or Yahweh and Allah as deities, and so on, I am fully conscious of the fact that I am not dealing with identical quantities. But after having so long emphasized what distinguishes and separates, is it not high time we made ourselves aware of what is common and connecting?

Second, I should like to emphasize most urgently that the confrontation of the religions with secularization and with a threatened human race must stand as a constant horizon before our eyes. This is not constantly stated in what follows, but is handled only later, in the interests of orderliness, in its own special section (§§23, 24, below).

201

Chapter Ten

The Other Religions

Revelation in Other Religions?

§5 *The Basic Attitude of Fundamental Theology Today*

Many of our subtitles under "The Religions" will have question marks. Nor is this just a matter of style. The questions are intended to reflect a basic attitude of fundamental theology today.[20] When believers have no questions, they expect no information. And even where faith gives an answer, other questions remain. The church as "guardian of the full truth" was too ready to express itself in exclamations, when it should have been seeking its point of departure in believers' questions. Young persons who live in a certain very Catholic city told me, "The church gives us prefabricated answers to questions we didn't ask, and doesn't even bother with our real questions".

Meanwhile, many a doctrinal statement that our ancestors never dared to doubt has become a question. Today it goes against the grain to have to accept infallible books, to render unconditional obedience to men who claim to speak in the name of God, to believe the divine revelation has been packaged up in the confines of the Bible, or that it closed with the death of the Apostles. The theology of revelation, which has already produced such a great variety of models in the course of the centuries, must undertake yet another radical adaptation in our own day.[21]

The "apologetics" that was so cocksure, with its classics by F.S. Hettinger, A.M. Weiss, or H. Felder, who established the credibility of revelation, the divinity of Christ, and the divine character of the church all too surely with their texts from Scripture, prophecies, and miracles that only a tiny hope of personal faith remained — this kind of apologetics has been laid to rest, and without hope of resurrection. Its heir, "fundamental theology", is of far more modest pretenses — but not because it is unimportant. On the contrary, after the long hegemony of dogmatic and moral theology, and then of exegesis, fundamental theology is the theological discipline most in demand today.

Today's critical men and women are looking not so much for precise pronouncements of faith, especially not on points of controversy between Catholics and Protestants, but for the ultimate foundations of faith itself, for God's reality in the face of the overwhelming reality of the world, for the divinity of Christ in the face of a person's own doubt. *Theologia perennis* is no longer of much help to this person.

Significantly, no classic work on fundamental theology exists even today. Only appendages, only *quaestiones disputatae*. Every fundamental theologian must go his or her own way.[22] The individual Christian, as well, must make his or her way of faith to a large extent alone. The mere authority of the church no longer so simply helps us out of all our difficulties of faith. The church used to be the voice that taught and the lighthouse that showed the way. Today it is the church itself that is called into question, from without as well as from within. No less an authority than Pope Paul VI, in *Evangelii Nuntiandi*, made this very realistic observation: "Today the faith is nearly always confronted with secularism, indeed even with militant atheism. In this way it becomes as faith subjected to many trials, a threatened faith — indeed, a surrounded and besieged faith" (EN 54).

What actually threatens and pressures the believer today is no longer exposure to a polemic calling for passionate counterattack, as in times gone by. Today the threat is that religion is considered to have succumbed to science and community structures, so that it is simply no longer attacked. It is left to live out its brief remaining moment in silence and then sink into the grave.

In this situation the Christian no longer allows faith to be prescribed by authority. Faith now has to be offered as a meaningful interpretation of life through the credible witness of the believing Christian community. The believer wants a faith that is not the antithesis of science but its obverse. The old catechism formulas are not much good any more for the practical implementation of the faith, and this goes for the dogmas too. Our contemporaries prefer the inductive style. They prefer mystagogy — the cautious initiation into mystery.

This would not prevent us from eventually compiling the essential assertions, in contemporary language, in a "compendium of faith".[23] On the contrary, it could be very useful. But our compendium will no longer look like a timetable giving exact data on all trains. It will be more like a compass to help us keep from losing our orientation during our passage over a broad ocean. After all, not even the Apostles believed from the very beginning. For three years they walked with Jesus, heard what he taught, saw how he lived, and were astounded at what he did. But even they long "understood nothing", they "remained unbelieving", and Jesus had his loving trouble with them (Mark 8:21, 9:19). So we have to be cautious in speaking about the faith, among ourselves and especially with non-Christians, lest we merely speak in formulas. Otherwise it would be better to go and learn from Buddhism how to be silent about God (see Part Three, §17).

§6 Does Religion Come from Revelation?

Now we come to the heart of the matter. Is religion, is God, the invention of human beings, our projection of ourselves into heaven — a self-deification, as Feuerbach and Barth would have it? Or a pacification and solace, à la Marx? Or a castle in the air, the compensation the human being manufactures for a heart never satisfied, as Freud thought? Or, instead, does religion stem from the initiative of a real God — from what we call "revelation"?[24]

No statement of proof can be made in answer to this question; only a statement of faith. Most human beings have believed, and believe, that their life does not bear its meaning within itself as in a closed shell, but opens out beyond, grasping for an ultimate mystery, and that it is only through this mystery that a human being comes to his or her own fulfilment. Human beings further believe that this primal mystery, which they term God, factually exists — that it was there before they were, that it has made them and called them, and they respond by giving themselves over to it in prayers and rituals and in the whole direction and ordering of their lives.

But what was self-evident for the traditional human being has for the modern, questioning human being, become a problem. And the most self-evident becomes the most incomprehensible. Yet even modern men and women, who in their questioning have missed the forest for the trees and have been foundering in their existential vacuum, are now beginning to turn in a different direction. They are once again on the lookout for the ultimate meaning of life. They cannot be without God. They may write God off, but they are not written off by God. They may term themselves "godless", but they do not thereby rid themselves of God. They bear God's image within them!

Karl Marx sneered at philosophers who "only interpret" the world, whereas communists go about changing it. But Czech philosopher Vitêzlav Gardavsky drew a different conclusion from our new situation. The world must be changed, of course, but that does not solve the problem. Set the world on its ear and it will still have to be interpreted, unless it is to sink to its ruin. Worn and weary, the human person is once more on the lookout for an ultimate goal, and demands the right to surrender, in a final act of trust, to the One who created it so small and so divinely great.[25]

How this mysterious God reveals himself to us — how the Silence speaks — remains, however much one may wish to deny it, a profound mystery. We need not deny the actuality of an external, miraculous intervention of God — his appearance and his speech — in a revelation

204

"driven into the world like a wedge", as F. Rosenzweig put it. But neither must we unconditionally accept it.[26] God has his ways of making himself understood without giving away his mystery. Persons can suddenly come to know something in an interior insight that becomes more certain for them than an external observation. Thus from one viewpoint it is "their insight". But God is not only transcendent, he is also immanent, and hence he is always concurring in our activity. And so he brings it about that every insight of ours is at the same time "his inspiration" — raised to a superior order by grace, because in the present order of salvation nothing humanly good is ever outside the field of grace, outside the field of God's free self-communication.

The short-lived "God is dead" theology and the heyday of secularization suddenly gave way to a new tendency: the experience of God, which totally altered the foreground of the public religious scene and has become a central theme of theology.[27] Once more it has become easier to accept that the experience of God constitutes a greater happening than the whole external course of human history. (This is not to say that we can now breathe a sigh of relief and let the critique of religion die in peace. Our God-experiences would have to be naive — uncritical and precritical indeed — to encourage such a conclusion, and would afford the world more amusement than witness.)

A concrete instance from modern history can help us see how revelation can come. In his *Diary of a Soul*, Pope John XXIII writes, as the last entry during his retreat at the opening of the Second Vatican Council, that he had had two great graces to especially thank God for in his life. First, that he had been able to accept the pontificate with inner peace. And second, that he had always been able to follow the good inspirations (*ispirazioni*) of the Lord with simplicity and honesty. And he reveals a concrete instance of the latter: when he announced the council, on January 25, 1959, the person most surprised was himself.[28] The idea had come over him as a sudden inspiration. From experiences like these, and surely from similar personal ones, each of us can better understand the phenomenon of biblical revelation.

But this example tells us something about the content of revelation, too. Revelation does not simply communicate truths in propositions, truths of which one can speak. It also gives impulses and thrusts by whose power one can act. Revelation not only lays out a system of truths, it forms the course of history, and interprets it as meaningful.

Furthermore, it is to be noted that revelation does not simply deliver new truths. In connection with creation and covenant (Part One, §§7, 21) we have already seen that Israel drew most of the content of its revelation from neighbouring peoples, but saw it in a new light and placed it unambiguously within the scope of the lordship of the one Yahweh.

Finally, and supremely, revelation means that above and beyond all truths and impulses, it is God himself who is its content, communicating himself (DV 2, 6) as companion God of the covenant, and Father of our Lord Jesus Christ.

§7 Inspiration

The search for the certitude of revelation, and for the inerrancy of the sacred writings that contain that revelation, involves the concept of inspiration.[29] Certain criteria of person, content, and effect have been established to help determine the authenticity of a private revelation.[30] Still more clarity is required in the matter of public revelation. In the Old Testament a special assistance of the spirit of God was repeatedly attributed to its authors, especially to the prophets who spoke in the name of God (Hos. 9:7; Mic. 3:8; Ezek. 2:2, 11:5). In the New Testament, this developed into the notion that its compositions had been "written by the Holy Spirit" (Heb. 3:7, 2 Pet. 1:21). This in turn led to the view, beginning in the fifth century, that the primary author of holy writ was God. Finally, scholasticism then forced this doctrine to the extreme with the notion of literal inspiration, holding that every word bore the stamp of divine authority almost as if the human author had merely taken God's dictation.

This last view does not accord well with the historical facts. In the first place, the history of the canon of the sacred books is one of great uncertainty, in Old Testament times as well as for the first few centuries of the Christian era. One never knew exactly which books belonged to Holy Scripture. Secondly, the editorial development of the sacred books, a centuries-long process in most cases, raises many questions (see Part One, §5). What today is a single book — Genesis, for instance — can evince a variety of authorship. Now, who was inspired? The original authors? Or the editor who collected their texts and compiled the book as we have it today? Was it the prophets who were inspired as they were speaking, or was it their pupils who wrote down what they said? Or, instead, was it the editors who published these texts centuries later, often expanding and adapting them? The situation is the same with the Psalms. Finally, does not Holy Scripture contain so many inconsistencies and extreme divergencies of concept that harmony and inerrancy can be spoken of only in respect of some comparison, or balance, of them? There is no end of questions.

Karl Rahner had the courage to take up these prickly questions even before Vatican II. In 1958 he started the series of volumes called *Theological Investigations*, which open with the question of the inspiration of Scripture. In his Introduction, Rahner emphasizes that the task of theology is not simply to look back and repeat, but to further the living process of tradition — to ask new questions and give new answers.

His interpretation of inspiration, which follows, is still an acceptable basic explanation today.

God led his people and communicated his truth to them from the very beginning. It is not so much that he "inspired" the first author or the last compiler, but that he guided the whole origin and development of Scripture. Then God willed and created his church; and in doing so he established the primitive church as the foundation and norm of all ecclesiality, of all church. Inasmuch as the primitive church received the writings of the Old and New Testaments as "the word of God", and integrated them into its own self-understanding as a constitutive element, it posited a view behind which one cannot go without calling into question the church as such.

This wipes out a significant part of the scholastic explanation, but it saves the essential. For me as a believing Christian, in Scripture as a whole, (1) truth is communicated, without substantial error; (2) the most correct image of God, which reached its perfection in Jesus Christ, is presented, though we can never fully comprehend God; and (3) the Spirit of God is personally at work, "inspiring" me and making it clear to me that his leadership of old can still be taken as type and model of his leadership today.

§8 Revelation and Inspiration Today?

And this leads us to a new question. Is there, or can there be, revelation and inspiration still today? It was never in doubt that private revelations, and private divine inspirations, can be granted to individuals, such as John XXIII. But are they on the same level as the revelation contained in Holy Scripture? If not, what is the difference, exactly, other than that the church recognizes the one officially and not the other?

Perhaps it would be better to avoid dividing revelation up with theological concepts like "more" and "less", or "special" and "general", and leave the matter to God's free disposition. Surely in Jesus Christ God's self-communication has reached a point that it is unthinkable for other revelations ever to surpass or even equal. There cannot be a more-than-Christ. In him the last age, the final time, has already begun. "Whence the Christian order of salvation, the new and definitive covenant, is insurpassable, and no new public revelation may be expected before the appearance of our Lord Jesus Christ in glory" (DV 4).

But this should not lead us to think that the God who revealed himself in former times has now retreated into silence. He is continuously at work within us by way of development of and commentary on the Jesus-revelation, through his Spirit, who "will lead us into all truth" (John 16:13). The Judaeo-Christian revelation can be credible only as a special instance of the revelation of God that is at work everywhere and always.

207

A God who manifested himself in days of yore, but then broke off his conversation with human beings, would not be a historical God, or a real God.

This assumption of a general phenomenon of revelation is a healthy *via media* between two extreme positions. One maintains that the only revelation was in the Old and New Testaments. The other maintains that there was never any revelation at all; the only news God has left us is that there is no news.[31] Our position lies between the two. The general phenomenon of revelation provides the matrix for the special instance. Gabriel Moran's two books are a clear statement of this new viewpoint. In 1966 he draws the conclusion from biblical revelation that there must be revelation today as well. In 1972 he begins instead with today's revelation and concludes to the special nature of biblical revelation. He goes so far as to claim that if Jeremiah and Jesus came back today they would not say "Read what I said", but "Look at today's events and try to crack them open and get at their meaning".[32]

"Today's revelation" as it occurs within the church is circumscribed by the technical expressions of church tradition. Hence this tradition, in order to be recognized as "revelation", must not be understood in a simple retrospective and conservative spirit but as a constant and vital process of development. Granted, revelation can be designated as definitively closed with Jesus Christ. But it is just as true to say that it was definitively opened with him. The dynamic (or, to use the New Testament expression, "pneumatic") thing about the gospel is precisely that it does not express itself as an isolated historical quantity of the past, but renders the revealing Lord ever present in his church and in all human history.[33]

§9 *Revelation in Other Religions?*

These preliminary considerations and clarifications have prepared us for the answer to the question about revelation in other religions. If God is a God revealing himself at all times, then he must also reveal himself in all places, to all peoples — and in all religions. Peoples and religions are coextensive (see Part Three). If God wishes to reveal himself to peoples, he does so in and through their religions.[34]

The problem is a new one in theology. It is a consequence of the broadening of our horizons to include the other religions. As late as twenty years ago most manuals and monographs considered themselves well acquitted to make an ecclesiocentric presentation of the Judaeo-Christian revelation and be done with the matter.[35] In this respect the science of comparative religions was far in advance of theology. Writing at the turn of the century, M. Mueller considered it "the worst heresy" to hold that God had revealed himself to one people alone, to the Jews.[36] God would have had to ignore and despise non-Jews and non-Christians, who have constituted the major portion of humanity from the very beginning. Is that really something to expect from God?

Today it is permissible to hold that secular history and salvation history are coextensive in time and space. Wherever men and women seek to form their lives meaningfully and strive for a better human existence, wherever they live according to their conscience and thereby according to their religion, this is where salvation occurs. Even the seeking comes from the God of creation and revelation. God always takes the first initiative. The human being's action is reaction, response to God's word. Thus, salvation history and revelation history are coincident, coextensive. And so there are salvific experiences before, during, and after the Judaeo-Christian era; and it is a matter of simple fact that all religions have had their elders, seers, prophets, and messengers of God who had been enlightened in a special manner and interpreted life from a religious viewpoint, seeking to insure that this religious viewpoint be handed down after them from generation to generation.

Naturally God's revelation in the various religions occurred in various stages of development, and in increasing clarity, from unexpressed surmises about the ultimate meaning of life, to the express words of a "prophet", to the religious rites of a people, to the Old Testament revelation and the unique self-communication of God in Jesus Christ and its perfection in the Parousia.

We can still make the conceptual distinction between natural and supernatural revelation. But no longer can we say, in such cut-and-dried fashion (as if it were self-evident), that Jews or Christians (depending on the author) had a monopoly on the historical, the supernatural, the categorical revelation, leaving the pagans "only" the cosmic, the natural, the transcendental. Today when we distinguish between biblical and nonbiblical revelation — which P. Rossano suggests we call "revelation" and "illumination" respectively[37] — we can no longer deny *a priori* a historical, supernatural, categorical revelation in the non-Christian religions.

These insights have to break away from theology and penetrate the realm of pastoral practice. In the newer churches they seem to have done so already to a considerable extent. For my paper "The New Theology of Religions and Catechesis" at the International Congress of Missiology at the Urbanianum in 1975, I wrote to eight university-level catechetical centres, four in Africa and four in Asia, and asked two questions. As of twenty years ago, did catechisms in your country mention the non-Christian religions? If so, in what tone? In three cases the answer was yes, but only in a polemical tone. In the other five cases they were not mentioned at all; Christianity was presented to catechumens as having appeared on a religious *tabula rasa*. The second question asked whether the non-Christian religions are mentioned in today's catechisms, and if so, in what tone? In one case no. In the other seven yes, and in a positive tone, inasmuch as the pre-Christian religious experience of catechumens is taken as a point of departure for the journey to Christian fullness.

In the Western churches, too, young Christians should be invited to open their eyes to the wondrous works of God in other religions. Comparative religion should be integrated into religion courses. Resources are already available.[38]

The discovery of revelation in other religions can be treated as a great event in church history. Until now we Christians have just been listening to our own fiddle — and have not even noticed that it has been hired as first violin in the glorious fullness and rich variety of a whole orchestra. To be sure, this orchestra's beauty will become fully apparent only when it no longer plays "music for music's sake" — when religion is no longer satisfied simply with beautiful interpretations of the world, but supplies the tempo and dynamics for concrete measures to change the world.

The Old Testament and Other Sacred Books

§10 *Preliminary Questions*

Let us open our consideration of this topic by asking some preliminary questions. Our discussion is primarily concerned with the "book religions". So we have to keep in mind the relativity of scriptures to oral tradition. With respect to both time and meaning, it is tradition that has priority. There is no scripture without oral tradition. Most scriptural authors have not written "their" message. Rather, they have compiled oral traditions — often centuries after the fact, in the Old Testament, and decades in the case of the New — and have given them permanent form in the written word. Religions that possess no sacred books because their founders were not literate are deserving of no less reverence than the book religions.

In making our comparison between the Christian Scriptures and those of the other world religions, we shall limit ourselves, as far as the former are concerned, to the Old Testament. The Old Testament, like the other religions, is teacher and precursor of Christ (see Part Two, §23). As a book the New Testament is like all the other sacred books; its unique position derives from its content (see §§15-17, below).

We must avoid setting up the Old Testament in opposition to other holy books. Probably the greater part of the Old Testament originated in other sacred writings, or in pre-Judaic and extra-Judaic oral tradition, which are no longer extant. M. Smith caused a sensation thirty years ago when he discovered, in the ancient texts of neighbours of Israel, a single god emerging from the multitude of gods and goddesses and being accorded special reverence; then this god's activity in nature, and the history of his people, receiving prominence; this god being lauded as just and gracious, rewarding good and punishing evil; his relations with human beings resting on some manner of agreement or covenant; and his sending his prophets to announce reward or judgment in his name.[39]

This is not to say that the religion of the Old Testament is nothing more than a footnote to that of the Babylonians. It does mean that the religions of other peoples were incorporated into the Old Testament:

> [This is one of the] most audacious religious ideas in human history. The polytheism of patriarchal times is not condemned or rejected as such, but is transformed and assimilated as prelude, first beginnings, and prehistory of the Yahweh religion. From their deepened understanding of the living God, it was clear to the primitive interpreters of history that this same living God had "spoken in sundry and various ways to the fathers" (Heb. 1:1). It had been the true religion, in embryo.[40]

We might graphically represent the action of Yahweh in all religions, and his influence on Israel through the other religions, as in Figure 1.[41]

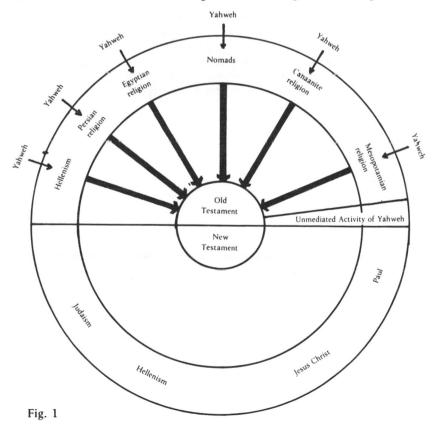

Fig. 1

211

Explanation of Figure 1: This schema shows that, quantitatively speaking, the greater part of the Old Testament's myths and laws had been taken over from other religions. Of course, they were seen in the new light of the covenant with Yahweh, and placed in new relationships, so that they became the Old Testament's specific property. The Jews of old vaguely discerned what we today see more clearly — that the same Yahweh who had become the God of Israel also stood in the shadows of the other religions, and was with their peoples too (see below, §14). Thus all religious meaning in the world derives directly or indirectly from him.

In our concern to acknowledge the worth of religions we so long ignored, let us take note once and for all that just as it was a mistake to damn them, so it would be a mistake to exalt them to hagiographic and triumphalistic heights. We have become critical of our own Christianity; let us not be uncritical where the other religions are concerned. Just as there are pages in the Old Testament we wish we had never seen, which we can only explain by their "literary genre" (see Part One, §22), there is much that is comical, much that is devious, and much that is downright loathsome. Just as there is so much unfaithfulness and sin, so much that is false and warped, in the life and practice of the people of Israel (Part One, §§17, 23, 24), so we should not be astonished to find a good deal of the human and diabolical in the other religions and in their popular piety. God appears throughout as supremely tolerant. At bottom, though, he is seen to be all the more radical for knowing how to make salvation history out of a world going to the devil.

§11 A Variety of Standpoints

There are various standpoints from which one can make a comparison between the Old Testament and other sacred books. As outsiders, we shall scarcely be capable of doing full justice to the sacred writings of Asia. This demands an unusual talent and empathy for the language, thought, and feelings of the people in question. The generations of Christians and priests of Asia who were so ignorant of their own lands' native religions and were on their guard against them, have given way to a new generation of Christian specialists, who know Hinduism, for instance, from the inside and can evaluate it accordingly. I have in mind persons such as R. Panikkar or the Jeevadhara periodicals group (in Alleppey), and Vidya Iyoti (Delhi). There is much hope for the religious encounter.

Our own comparison can take place on either of two levels. We could take a purely phenomenological approach, and either compare the different books from the standpoint of literature and comparative religion, investigating their stylistic devices, their vocabulary, their prosody, and the like; or compare them thematically, studying God, the soul, salvation, and so on, in each of the various books respectively. [42] As long as all of this remained in the area of pure data there would be nothing objectionable about it. But there is also not very much helpful in it. Science leaves the heart cold. But as soon as one begins to formulate value judgments, and to compare relative worth, and says for instance that the Koran or the Upanishads contain many wearisome and meaningless passages, and that the Old Testament is therefore superior in this respect, one touches a tender nerve and invites resentment and contradiction.

The situation is even more delicate when the comparison is made on the religious plane. Nothing is closer to persons that their religion. They do not like it tampered with. And this is a good thing. From the point of view of the efficacy of religion, one cannot easily prove that the Bible has shone with a brighter light on Christians than have the other sacred writings on their devotees.

Ultimately it comes down to each one's faith options, and they are admittedly conditioned, in part, by the cultural roots of the various religions. The Christians may believe that in Jesus Christ salvation history has reached a pinnacle never to be surpassed. The Muslim may believe that the last and highest revelation came only in Mohammad. Fanaticism is no longer the road to travel. Each of us must recognize the other's standpoint as his or her options of faith, in mutual respect, and seek a synthesis by broadening our own view (see §§14, 34, below).

With all these reservations in mind, then, let us examine some value judgments. Perhaps we shall be able to compare them.

An Old Testament professor in Rome: "The Old Testament is both comparable to the other religions, and at the same time incomparably superior to them. *Toto caelo differunt.*"

An Indian student in Rome: "Honestly speaking, it is very simple to contrast the Rigveda with the Old Testament. For instance, with respect to forgiveness of sin it is the Rigveda that has the richer, broader view".

A professor of ethnology in Rome: "The old Africans were convinced they were a superior people, and their tradition has withstood the test of time. When we closely examine their whole conception of life, we have to say, 'This is the Old Testament exactly'. Only, the Africans, thank God, did not have to offer those hecatombs that the God of the Old Testament seemed to demand. The Africans live a religion of the Easter Mystery without Christ. One does not find death and resurrection in the Old Testament as it is celebrated in African rites of initiation. The Old Testament was long in coming to the idea of resurrection; Africans always knew that the dead live mysteriously on, in the community — that one is always in the hand of God, even in death and after death. This is why Africa so easily found the road to Christianity".

213

As we see, many questions will remain open! But in them all, one thing is undeniable: that the Old Testament can perform the function of a model for many purposes of comparison. The other religions may be bearers of revelation, channels of grace, providential routes in God's plan of salvation[43] — but the Old Testament is clearly something more. Except for Islam, which the Bible partly inspired, no other religion rallied to monotheism in a manner so theologically unambiguous, and so morally demanding, and heralded monotheism as the coming form of human religion, as did the Old Testament (see §§13-15, below).[44]

A further advantage of the Old Testament is the deep-dyed mark of its messianic expectation — beginning with the journey of Abraham, reaching its highest expression in the prophets, and finally, according to Christian belief, fulfilled in Jesus Christ. Of course, hope of liberation from evil, and the expectation of salvation — utopias — are essential categories of all religions. The whole history of religion is a demonstration of the fact that nothing can charge life with more tension than can the hope of a better future.[45] But along with the hope, many religions taught their adherents an attitude of acquiescence and passivity, of addiction to miracles and wonders, and thus estranged their own expectations (see below, §23). The Asiatic religions were by and large the prisoners of cyclic thought; the African religions looked for a return to the primordial. Neither, therefore, had any concept of a clear eruption into a new, coming, time.

J.S. Mbiti says that it was only with Christianity and the arrival of modern civilization that African time acquired a future dimension. "This is perhaps the most dynamic, and at the same time the most dangerous, discovery of the African peoples in the twentieth century. Their hopes have been prodded to life and are heading for the future."[46] The Old Testament, on the other hand, bears the stamp of future expectation from the very start. "The Old Testament can only be read as a book of increasing expectation of something vast and momentous. For this cause alone the Old Testament must be assigned a special position in the framework of the general history of religion."[47]

Thus the particular privilege and *raison d'être* of the Old Testament is to be found in its conviction that its history would lead to the Messiah. In him, Jesus Christ, it found its fulfilment, and its limitation (see Part One, §32). The Christians called Israel's scriptures "Old". But this made them new. Now their new dimension was discovered: they were signposts pointing to Christ. They had not been the last word. The new, the last, word was to come in God's Word, the Logos. Through its "relativization" to Christ, the Old Testament became the model, valid absolutely and for all times, of God's providential dealings. By coming to an end as the religion of one people, the Old Testament became universal. Its problems and its expectations turned out to be the problems and expectations of all humanity. Now, in retrospect, so much of it became new and definitive.

Christianity is not grafted onto Judaism as a new religion. It is the new reading of the scripture of Israel. In Christianity the religion of Israel achieves its own truth.[48] Thus while the Old Testament's "uniqueness" is undergoing today's broad demythologization, it nevertheless retains its altogether specific function in regard to other religions, for whose sake it was that God, "in special wise", placed himself at the source of Israel's scriptures and of the history they celebrate (see §7, above).

Now let us continue this course of thought. Must there not be a parallel situation in the case of the other sacred books? Do not all sacred books bear within themselves an implicit openness to a new interpretation in the light of the fact of Christ?

Those who do not believe in Christ cannot answer this question in the affirmative. But the Christians of a given land can have the inspiration to read and interpret the sacred books of their people as a kind of Old Testament. They can give many statements a new meaning that would not occur to a Hindu or a Buddhist. And indeed today Christians of Hindu origin frequently seek to read the Gitas as Christians. Thereby they gain many a new insight into the Gitas — and thereby they also better understand the Bible.[49] Just as gentile Christians could receive the Old Testament with love because they discovered Christ hidden everywhere, so too, and more so, the Christians of India can do the same with the sacred books of their people.

Now we understand how the best theologians of India could come together in 1974 in a carefully prepared congress in Bangalore to ask themselves what position and function the sacred writings of India could have in the church. Perhaps their most beautiful passages could find a place in the Christian liturgy — not in place of the Old Testament, but as a complement to it — to make Christians aware that God is a God of all peoples, that he has also spoken to the fathers of ancient India, and that today he wishes to bring the peoples of those lands to fuller truth in Christ. It should be the decision of the local church — thought the members of the congress — to what extent such scriptures can also be considered the word of God.

The time was ripe, and these ideas were published in a 700-page report. But Rome, instead of examining them, answered with a categorical no. A number of the Indian bishops, as well, had come out against them. From the very nature of things the magisterium of the church has to be several steps behind the thinking of theologians, and even behind the ordinary members of the church, who are not so far ahead as the theologians.

Still, the ideas are blowing in the wind. They keep developing. The time will come when the saving works of God will be perceived and acknowledged in their whole breadth.[50] Such eruptions usually occur in moments of difficulty, and in the face of opposition, as did the transition from the Jewish to the gentile church in New Testament times (Part One, §§33, 36).

Yahweh and the Other Deities

§13 *From Tribal God to God of the Peoples*

During the thousands of centuries when humanity led a nomadic life, with each group spatially separated from the others, every people had "its" god or gods. The gods were part of the essence of each group's self-concept. They brought fortune or inflicted punishment. They were offered prayers and sacrifices. And they were generally at war with the neighbouring gods, for generally a state of war existed between each group of persons and its neighbours. One considered oneself better than one's neighbours, and one's god better than their gods. Pure-culture ethnocentrism! (See Part Three, §§25, 26).

Then, some 3,200 years ago — quite a late point in time if you consider the whole time frame — an important event occurred in salvation history. God revealed himself to Moses as Yahweh — the Midianites' name for God — and sent him to lead the tribe of Joseph out of the land of Egypt. As a result of the project's success, Moses was able to prevail upon the people to acknowledge Yahweh as their own God, and they solemnized their acknowledgment at the foot of Mount Sinai.

They were not rejecting the "God of their fathers". They recognized that he was basically identical with Yahweh (Exod. 3:6). Later a similar identification enabled them to accept the Canaanites' god El, and to transfer to Yahweh the attributes of Baal as god of rain and weather (see Part One, §4). Thus in a tension-filled process that is not altogether clear (there is a kind of evolution going on here, too), Yahweh was promoted from an insignificant tribal god to the God of the peoples. And so it is relatively quite recent in the history of religions that the movement in the direction of monotheism began.

At the beginning of that history, at the striking of the covenant at the foot of Mount Sinai, Yahweh presented himself in terms of exclusive demand: "I am the Lord, your God, who has led you out of the land of Egypt, the house of servitude. You shall have no other gods but me! . . . For I, the Lord your God, am a jealous God" (Exod. 20:2-5).

Now there was a first phase in which Yahweh developed as the national god of the Jews. One after another, the tribes attached themselves to this god. And when the people, time and again, succumbed to the temptation to invoke other gods, time and again their leaders and prophets recalled them to the one Yahweh. "All the gods of the nations are but idols", sang David in his hymn of thanksgiving (1 Chron. 16:26), and "all the gods of the pagans are devils", the psalmist echoes (Ps. 95:5). Wherefore "they ought to fall backward covered with shame, who trust in idols — those who say to cast images, 'You are our gods'" Isaiah preached (Isa. 42:17).

But then there was a second step, in which this mighty national god was recognized to be at the same time the God of all peoples. "All peoples, all islands" are called upon to sing to Yahweh. Yahweh is the God who can elect peoples and reject them (Isa. 41:1-7), and who therefore cries out to the ends of the earth to abandon their idols and turn unto him (Isa. 45:20-25. 51:4).

Herein lies the almost irresistible tension of this religion — that the national god of the Israelites was also to be made known as the God of the whole world; or, more accurately, that the God of the world wished to be the national god of the Jews in a special manner. We have already seen that the tension did not so easily find a happy balance, and that a contest of power was nearly always under way between "the people and the peoples" (see Part One, §§25, 26). But eventually, thanks to the Christians, Yahweh came more and more to be recognized by the peoples as the one and only God.

§14 *Are Other Deities Identical with Yahweh?*

Is there not still another conclusion to be drawn today from this history of the evolution of a religion? An insignificant Yahweh managed to have himself acknowledged as God to the point of annihilating or absorbing all the other gods. Demythologized, must this fact not demonstrate that the one and only true God had always been hidden, not only behind Yahweh, but behind all the other deities as well? Must it not mean that this one, true God had always been present and active, everywhere and under a hundred names — but that now, at this late moment of history, he wished to reveal himself as Yahweh in order at last to extract the nations from their isolation and enmity and come together to form a single humanity?

Surely in the God of Adam, in the God of Noah, in Melchizedek's God, in the God of the fathers, in the Midianites' God, in all peoples' God, it was ever the true God who had spoken, and who now revealed himself in his identity. Surely we must now bring this process to its logical conclusion and explain all deities of the many peoples as identical with Yahweh, and subsumed into Yahweh.

In reality there cannot be "gods". There can only be many names and representations for the one true God. There is only one transcendence, one primordial reason why human beings are so constructed that they are always on the lookout for God, the ultimate End and Fulfilment toward which they unflaggingly strive, the mysterious Grace that stands

217

benevolently at their side on their journey through time. This is ever the one and only God, the Mighty One, the Gracious One. The nations, peeping out from the prison cells of their troubled existence, all saw the same sky, even if they all thought it was only theirs because they were cut off from one another by space and enmity.

Is it not the time, then, to proclaim that Yahweh is interchangeable with the Arabs' Allah, with the Africans' Mungu and Nzambi, and with the Asians' Brahman and Kami? May we not surely say that all names denote the same God, and that the God of the Christians has no intention of eliminating the other deities, but only of leading them back to their common denominator and genuine greatness? The saying "all have the same God" can be a false one; but it can also be true. On the phenomenological level, as an interpretation of the average consciousness of believers, it is wrong; hence the uneasiness of some persons with this expression is justifiable. But on the reflective, theological level, it is correct — with the reservation that we shall make in §15 — and it is our task and duty to place these considerations at the service of every man and woman.[51]

It is unfortunate that we have practised not only a cultural, but also a theological colonialism in history. We have sought to force upon the Indians, the Africans, the Asians, "our" God — the God of the colonizer — instead of interpreting "their" god as Yahweh everywhere present and active. How many inner tensions and conflicts of conscience, how many outward struggles and wars, could have been spared if only we had had this new, broad, true, divine view! Our traditional, narrow, human view was un-Christian and anti-Christian. So let us begin today, and acknowledge their God — while making known to them that this God of theirs has done much of which they as yet have no knowledge.

Of course in the last analysis the correct view of God will not come to us so much from the past as from the future. The many human names that the nations have given God without ever exhausting his nature are not identical. The identity has to be brought about. The identity of the one divine Being experienced by all human beings, and variously named by them, has yet to be consciously integrated. It is a process of becoming. And Christians have a special role of leadership and witness to perform.

The whole course of our considerations demonstrates that there are different stages in the knowledge of God. "All have the same God" can be false. When an African Pygmy, an Asian Hindu, a European Christian, say "God", they mean, it is true, numerically one and the same God according to our theological interpretation. But at the same time each names a very different God from the viewpoint of content. Even an ordinary Christian and a grace-flooded mystic mean different things when they say "God". The name and the concept plumb far different depths. And even the mystic is only part way there, and is pained that he or she can never attain God. For "our knowledge is patchwork" (1 Cor. 13:9).

The Vatican Council's *Declaration on the Non-Christian Religions* had this to say of the different stages on the way to the knowledge of God:

> From the most ancient times to our own days, the various peoples have enjoyed a certain perception of that hidden force that is present to the course of the world and the events of human life, and not infrequently even the recognition of a highest deity, or even of a father [NA 2].

Hence, impersonal force (or ultimate value toward which one directs one's life), supreme God, Father — these are different steps in the explicitation of what God wants to be for human beings. And Christians are called ever "to progress in the knowledge of God" (Col. 1:10), to be "ever more filled up to the whole fullness of God" (Eph. 3:19), and then to communicate this higher image, and deeper experience, of God to other human beings.

Jesus Christ and Other Salvation Expectations

§15 *The Central Question*

Our data-gathering treks across the religious landscape of our planet have already yielded several different pieces of knowledge:

1. Most peoples direct their lives according to religious values, and reverence a more or less clearly recognized supreme deity (Part Three).

2. Many peoples live in the unshakable hope of some ultimate salvation, and often have vague notions of a saviour sent by God (Part Three, esp. §26).

3. For Christians, Jesus Christ is the closing and fulfillment of the Old Testament, and the head of his church, a church drawn from among all peoples (Part One, §§27-32).

All this places us before the central question: What relation does Jesus bear to the various religions? Does he enter the scene as one of their many saviours and redeemers ? Does he come as their end and fulfillment? Does he fly into a passion, as he did in Jerusalem long ago, to cleanse their temple of so much superstition and "religious" selfishness? Or does he reveal himself as a mystery that was always present and active in them?

We have evaluated the religions from many points of view, and in doing so have somehow been compelled to see Christianity in a place apart in its exclusive historical value for salvation. A church that exists for the salvation of all peoples can only rejoice to see all these religions to be much more brightly illumined by salvation's light than was previously thought. But we must not go to the other extreme and simply place Jesus cn the same level as everyone and everything else. This would be to do humanity a disservice.

Still — is it perhaps just our own imagination that seems to compel us to put Christ in a very special position? Could it simply be the instinct of our traditional Western Christian provincialism, and our need to have the upper hand?

We sense the urgency and delicacy of such questions instantly. For Christian thought, must Jesus Christ be the only All Holy, so that the other religions only stand in the courtyard waiting to be summoned? Or does such an interpretation somehow clash with reality? Here we must repeat what we said above (§§5, 6): this is a question about which we can prove nothing. We can only make a profession of faith, live according to this faith, and thereby demonstrate it to be worthy of belief. No one has the right to take it amiss that it is our faith, just as we can lay it to no one's charge if he or she cannot (yet) accept this faith. Here we are in touch with the deepest mysteries of the liberty of God and the human being, which, since the Vatican Council's *Declaration on Freedom of Conscience* (DH), we take more seriously than we did before.

§16 *Profession of Faith in Jesus Christ*

Thus our profession of faith in Jesus Christ, in terms of the viewpoints under consideration, can be formulated as follows[52] (see also Part One, §31):

I believe in Jesus of Nazareth, in whom Yahweh has given himself a human countenance, a visible and audible historical presence, and has revealed himself totally, hence unsurpassably, as Father of our Lord Jesus Christ. This Christ, the Son of God, through his life, death, and resurrection, has performed deeds of salvation that have fundamentally, as well as retroactively to the beginnings of human history, altered humanity's situation to the good. In him the way to the Father now stands open to every human being. In him every hidden hope is not only guaranteed but surpassed. On his account we can be sure that our longing for ultimate fulfilment is not a lifelong illusion, to be snuffed out in the stillness of death, but a justifiable certitude, for we have truly been assumed into God, in life, in death, and thereafter.

Through his Spirit, Jesus Christ ever inspired the founders and prophets of the religions. He is spiritually present in their scriptures. He fills with his ardour and confidence the hearts of all who seek and believe. Whenever missionaries came to other folds, he was there before them, already insuring that these human beings could attain to salvation. He has entered into one and the same relationship with all human beings, especially with the lowly — whence distinctions of race, religion, and social status become meaningless. In him the whole creation receives its centre, upon which all is concentrated, and its Omega point, toward which everything courses outward.

The more fully human beings achieve their self-identity, in history as in the future, the further they will penetrate history's deepest mystery — and see themselves in Jesus Christ, to the glory of God the Father. Amen.

§17 *Similar Incarnations in Other Religions?*

Such a profession of faith is not a point of departure, it is the point of arrival. It presupposes a lengthy road, and a long Christian experience. It is not to be memorized and recited as a formula. It is only to be gratefully repeated by one who feels a readiness for it in the Spirit. By those of other faiths it will be perceived as the faith that I take care to observe and guard or, at most, that I attest to as the expression of my own faith and sign of my own trust.

But what do I say when followers of other faiths state that there has been a like incarnation of God in their own religions? We have already spoken of such avatars in connection with Hinduism (Part Three, §14). But it is not only Hindus, but some Catholic theologians of India as well who are of the view that it is simplistic to think that all religions are for the sake of Christ. They hold that God willed these religions for their *own* sake, and not simply in view of Christ. They reproach theologians of the West with a "provincialism" in their thought, with a lack of catholicity, and accuse them of "theologizing in a primitive ignorance of the other religious traditions", of not taking seriously enough the coming pluralism in theology.[53]

In Africa, too, we hear the repeated cry for a "black Messiah" to come and free the people at long last from Western religious tutelage. Certain civil leaders have already laid claim to such messiahship, until their ignominious ends all too soon disclosed the falsehood of their ambitions.

Altogether apart from the possibility of different manners of theophany in the various religions, one can also ask the question whether it would be possible without intrinsic theological contradiction for God to have become incarnate both in Palestine in Jesus Christ and also elsewhere and at other times in other forms, in order to communicate himself fully to other tribes and peoples as well.

Here there can be various replies. The Christian faith acknowledges only one incarnation. The celebrated incarnation of Vishnu in Krishna cannot be placed in the same category, for Jesus' incarnation was historical whereas Krishna's is mythological.

There are also intrinsic reasons against the possibility of a variety of actual incarnations of God. In Asian cyclic thought, to be sure, there can be nothing against it; but in Western, Christian thought, history is of far greater significance. Every historical occurrence is unique, and thereby attains to an irreplaceable, unrepeatable, somehow absolute value.

221

More especially, God's total self-communication in Jesus cannot simply be multiplied, for this would yield more than one absolute, and history as a whole, including the Parousia, would be split in two, whereas the one and only God has initiated a movement toward monotheism in his manifestation in Yahweh, a movement toward the gathering of all human beings under one God (see §§13, 14, above). This suggests all the more reason why he would wish to unite humanity through his unique and unsurpassable entry into history in Jesus Christ and not splinter humanity through other, similar incarnations.

The Prophet Ezekiel announced that the Messiah would bring the tribes of Israel together and unite the two kingdoms. In fact Jesus did much more. He had to die "not only for his people alone, but in order to lead back to unity all God's scattered children" (John 11:49-52). It is precisely in order to avoid this splintering among peoples that God brings about, on the one hand, a single incarnation with universal meaning (and not in one of the great peoples of the ancient world, by human standards, but in the least of them), and an incarnation in every person on the other. In Jesus Christ both are accomplished, inasmuch as now, on his account, all human beings reached by the word of God "are gods" (Ps. 82:6, John 10:34ff.), and he gives to all who accept him the full power "to become sons of God" (John 1:12).

§18 *Salvific Value of Other Religions*

In sum: for my faith, the Christ event is not simply a quantitative improvement in the religious development of humanity, not simply a blossom of surpassing beauty in the bountiful garden of religion, but an initiative and a revelation of God of absolute qualitative novelty, a unique event in salvation history. This is a claim we must continue to make throughout all the course of our efforts to reconcile the religions in unity.

Now that we have made this reservation concerning the mysterious presence and activity of the Logos in all religions we are in a position to consider the salvation value of these religions[54] — not just the individual non-Christian's possibility of salvation, perhaps "in spite of" his or her religion, but precisely the question of what function the religions themselves may have, as institutions, in God's plan of salvation.

Our consideration could proceed in the following manner. Daily experience demonstrates that the human being is a religious being. In all the painful marginal situations of life — illness, failure, death; and even in gladness, which is never full and never lasts — we look out beyond ourselves, questioning and hoping, and are gripped by an ultimate mystery in our life.

This same human being is by constitution a social being. He or she will therefore exteriorize religious feelings and strivings in religious activity.

222

This activity, in turn, will concretize within the clan or tribal unit in set prayers, rites, and exercises. If, in order to achieve salvation, a human being must follow his or her conscience, and that conscience directs them to these ancestral rites — hence to a religion — it follows immediately that this human being is obligated to live a life of fidelity to this religion. But then, if we are logical, this religion must have been foreseen and willed in God's salvation plan, and this human being will be saved in and by practising it.

It is illogical to object that this person is accepted by God in view of this inner faith, and not on account of this religion. This would not be consonant with a reasonable anthropology; and then we would logically have to say likewise that one is not justified through the sacraments but only through one's inner faith, which is at once true and false. We must therefore conclude that the religions, too, perform a God-given function. They are stepping stones to the church — taking "church" analogically, in the sense of that religious space in which God, the one and only God, dwells, and works the salvation he destined for the totality of humankind in Jesus Christ.

In this conception of things, one can look at non-Christian humanity and speak of a general history of salvation that has to be taken very seriously. It began with the "creation covenant", and is by no means devalued by the fact that a special salvation history began in the people of Israel and the church of Christ. These two stages of salvation history are not mutually exclusive but inclusive. They are ordered to each other. Together they form God's single plan of salvation, and reveal the continuity of his salvation activity.

Our traditional pessimism about salvation (see Part Two, §§26, 27) has, especially since Vatican Council II, happily and justifiably yielded to an optimism about salvation. It was for the sake of his salvation plan that God created the world, humanity, and the inmost striving after happiness by which all human beings seek happiness even in sin. If we take that God and his plan of salvation seriously, we can scarcely assume that life for a considerable portion of humanity will end in dark night and final damnation.

Granted, there are no sure declarations we can make on this question. The salvation of all human beings is not among things knowable but among things to be hoped for. But Christian hope does give us the right and duty to expect the salvation of all, notwithstanding the indeterminacy of our last end, which justifies our discourse on the dreadful possibility of hell. The possibility of hell does not oblige us by our faith to assume the absolute rejection of some human beings. The hope is incomparably more solidly grounded that salvation for every human being is not only attainable, but that, as the gracious gift of God, it will actually be attained.[55]

Everything we have been saying applies not only to those men and women who lead a religious life, but to those as well who live their lives in ideologies and atheism, to the extent that they follow their conscience, And we can by no means maintain *a priori* that they do not. This is the reach of God's salvation. This is how seriously God takes human beings and their consciences.

§19 *The Church and the Kingdom of God*

In this context of Christ's salvation in and through the other religions, there immediately arises the question of the church. Is that notorious and ominous declaration true that outside the church there is no salvation? (see Part Two, §23).

Instead of interpreting our way out of this exclusivistic principle to the effect that one can be justified outside the church anyway, let us abide by that other declaration by which the church described itself in Vatican Council II, saying that the church understands itself as a "universal sacrament of salvation" or "as the sacrament of salvation for all" (LG 48, 1, 9; GS 45; AG 1, 5) — hence no longer as the exclusive ark of salvation for the privileged within it, but as sacrament, as sign and cause, of salvation for all without exception.

And this brings us to the relationship between the church and the kingdom of God.[56] Jesus has announced that kingdom as God's free and all-embracing offer, inclusive of everything God in his goodness has in store for humanity. Humanity can only joyfully receive it — enlist in it, come round to it, "be converted" to it.

Jesus revealed the kingdom through his word and works: "Go tell John what you hear and see" (Matt. 11:4). He wishes his disciples, too, to make known the kingdom of God in all they do and say, in order to give persons confidence and awaken their hope (Part One, §28). The church as community stands just as the church building stands in the village — as a sign that this village, this humanity, is Jesus Christ's. The visible church was willed by Jesus as seed, as sign, as pledge of the kingdom. He willed it as the community of those who believe in the kingdom of God, bear witness to it, wait for it, hope for it for themselves and for everyone.

The church, then, stands as part for whole, as anticipation for actuality, as human imperfection for divine completion, as temporal precursor for the eternal and definitive. The church must interpret the whole of history as the history of salvation, to be revealed and perfected in the kingdom of God. Church and kingdom are therefore not coextensive. They are not coextensive in time, for the centre of gravity of the church is in history, while that of the kingdom is in the future. And they are not coextensive in space, because the church is ever but a smaller or larger minority group, which, however, awaits the kingdom in the name of all.

224

All persons of goodwill, following their conscience and practising their religion — even atheists, who reject God or a particular image of God but who devote their lives to the highest values, such as loyalty, dedication, and justice for all — all these persons, while not living within the church, are nevertheless journeying with the church toward the kingdom of God. At the proper time their eyes will be opened, and they will realize — not that they are naked and sinful (Gen. 3:7), but that God has done great things for them too (Luke 1:49).

A vision like this, which is altogether consonant with the gospel as the glad tidings, the "good news", broadens our horizon, and shows us the church in a new light. We no longer see the church as the exclusive community of those who await salvation, but as the vanguard of all humanity on its way to salvation. We see it no longer as preacher of judgment and hell, but as herald of God's universal salvific will. We see it no longer as defender of its own rights and privileges, but as servant of humanity and sign of salvation to all.

This universalist view of the cosmic Christ, and of the kingdom of God he has brought us, has to be defended not only with the members of other religions (which we can only do in faith, as we have abundantly stated) , but even with certain practising members of the church who in their narrow purview cannot imagine Jesus as elsewhere than in their church. No, for the church to wish to shrink Jesus down to its own size would be to lay violent hands on him, to assault him. His presence in the church is sign and warranty that he is bound in mysterious covenant with all religions.

A beautiful text from the Latin American Bishops' Conference at Puebla in 1979 summarizes the matter:

> The midpoint of the message of Jesus is the proclamation of the kingdom, which comes, and is present, in himself. This kingdom, it is true, is not a reality separable from the church (LG 8). Still, it overflows its visible boundaries (LG 5). It is to be found in a certain manner wherever God reigns through his grace and love, overcoming sin and helping human beings grow up to the stature of the great community that he offers them in Christ.
>
> God's activity also occurs in the hearts of those who live outside the visible scope of the church (LG 16; GS 22; RR 3). But this by no means implies that membership in the church is meaningless. Quite the contrary, it means that the church has received the mission to make known the kingdom and to establish it among all peoples (LG 5). The church is the sign of the kingdom. In the church, what God brings to pass in stillness the world over is revealed in visible form. The church is the locus where the works of the Father concentrate most intensely — that Father who in the power of the Spirit of love undeviatingly seeks out human beings in order to share with them, in his ineffable love, his own trinitarian life. The church is also the instrument that carries the kingdom to human beings in order to lead them to their last end. The church represents, still on earth,

the seed and commencement of the kingdom (LG 5) — the seed that must grow through history under the influence of the Spirit until the day when God rules all in all (1 Cor. 15:28).

Until that moment in time, the church remains in many respects in need of perfection, remains the subject of a self-evangelization, of renewed conversion and purification (LG 15). And yet the kingdom of God is already within the church. Its presence on our continent is good news. For it fulfils, even if only as a beginning, the deepest longings and hopes of our peoples. Herein consists the mystery of the church — that it is a human reality, made up of limited and miserable human beings, which is shot through nevertheless with the unfathomable presence and power of God in Trinity.

That God burns bright within it, calling together and redeeming humanity (LG 4, 8; SC 2). The church is not yet that to which it is called. It is important to keep this in account in order not to fall into a false and triumphalistic view. On the other hand it will not do to lay too much stress on the church's deficiencies; for the power of the definitive kingdom is already present and active in the church in our time.[57]

§20 *What is Specifically Christian?*

If Jesus Christ constitutes the central content of the Christian faith in such wise that on his account Christianity cannot be set up as just one religion alongside many others (because Christ himself cannot be understood as one saviour alongside many others), then the question arises: What is decisively and specifically Christian in biblical revelation?

Here we must distinguish between the content of faith and the realm of ethical behaviour. As far as the content of faith is concerned, Christians hold that their worldview has become "other". In Jesus Christ, they believe in the Father and his unshakable love for human beings, in the Spirit and his works in all human beings of goodwill, in the church and its sacraments that help maintain it as an enduring community of faith (see above, §16).[58]

With regard to ethical behaviour, the matter cannot be lightly dismissed with a reference to Jesus' declarations, "It was said of old . . . but I say to you . . ." (Matt. 5:21-48), in order triumphalistically to proclaim the superiority of the Christian moral code. In the first place we Christians — in history, as also today — have by no means always represented the model of life lived according to the gospel. But besides this, modern scholarship has established that, for instance, the ten commandments were by no means the exclusive property of the Jews, and that in other religions love of neighbour, tolerance, and love of enemies are perhaps just as well taught and practised as in Christianity. "Special morality" is repugnant today, whether it be Hinduism's sacred cows or the Catholic Church's proscription of artificial birth control. Such concepts are wide of the mark. They can lead to sectarianism, and thereby impede rather than further the general good behaviour of the world.

There has been a good deal of reflection, especially since the Congress of the International Association for Theological Ethics in Lund in 1966, on what is specific in Christian ethics. The question is among the most complex in theology today, especially inasmuch as it must not be considered simply in view of the other religions, but with an eye to the secularizing world as well.

Doubtless one can say that with respect to content there is nothing specifically Christian that is not generically human.[59] Ethical themes do not become Christian by being discussed and proclaimed in the church. In view of the unicity of God's plan of creation and redemption, the full identity of ideal human and Christian behaviour has to be accepted. It is the human being who must be read, as he and she was willed by God as meaning and centre of creation, if we would discover God's design for humankind. God's law should not be thought of as a superstructure imposed upon human nature, a rigid system of physiological and biological principles and their corollaries erected as an afterthought and addition. Rather, human beings bear God's law within, in their conscience. Whatever guarantees the optimal development of a human being's existence, whatever enhances his worth as a person, corresponds to the will of God. Hence we must no longer say, "Doing God's will is good", but, "What is good, and human in the best sense of the word, is God's will".

What is new in the gospel is that we recognize these notions more clearly and understand them better, on grounds of our concept of creation and of God as Father. Especially, what is new in the gospel is that we have been inserted into the new relationship of the kingdom of God and his grace. And thus we have, or ought to have, more strength with regard to the responsibility and trust that God has given us, so to live as to build a better world, a world worthy of ourselves and of God.

The single special moral tenet of Christians ought to be to feel themselves challenged to better behaviour. Thus Christians can stand in solidarity with all human beings and at the same time, through their more dynamic conduct, bear the deepest foundation of their Christian hope into dialogue at the right moment.

§21 Graphic Representations

By way of conclusion, let us attempt to set forth the relationship of Christ to the religions, as we have been discussing it, in terms of some graphic representations.

We used to divide humanity into "Christians and non-Christians" — with the same humiliating results as in their division into "whites" and "nonwhites" in South Africa! But today statistical charts simply list the great religions one after the other — Christians, Jews, Muslims, Hindus, and so on. Or their distribution can be represented statically, on a map. For studies in comparative religion, that can be sufficient. One simply wants to grasp the data.[60]

If, however, we wish to entertain a theological consideration of their mutual relationships, the Christian viewpoint is customarily represented by a series of concentric circles. O. Karrer wrote in 1934: "Christ as Saviour has two halos: a nearer one, with visible borders, and a farther one, a zone where Christ is known by faithful souls and reverenced and loved as the living form of holiness, and a zone where Christ is not yet known and loved, or known and loved only in foreshadowing".[61] This model has been used by the popes, John XXIII at the opening of the Vatican Council, and Paul VI in his first encyclical, *Ecclesiam Suam*.[62] It is represented in Figure 2.

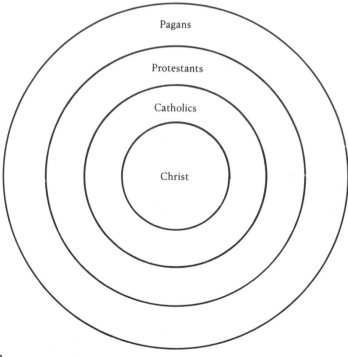

Pagans

Protestants

Catholics

Christ

Fig. 2

Comment on Figure 2. In today's way of thinking, one can no longer simply say that Protestants stand further from Christ than do Catholics. In particular cases there are Catholics who are very far from Christ and

Protestants who are very near to Christ.[63] The same can be said of the "pagans".

A more dynamic model shows the various religions on their way to the eschatological completion that has already begun in Christ: Figure 3.

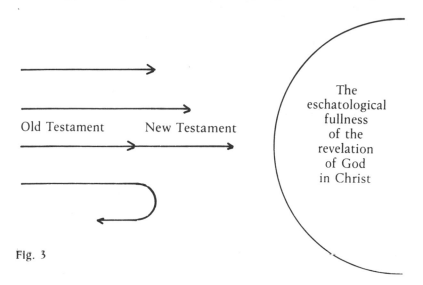

The
eschatological
fullness
of the
revelation
of God
in Christ

Fig. 3

Explanation of Figure 3. The diagram is meant to show that in the Christian understanding all religions are on the way to the fulness of God. The church has reached the messianic-eschatological time that has arrived in Christ. Other religions are further from this event or nearer to it; they can even, temporarily, turn away from it. But all will finally be subsumed and embraced by it.

In order to have a more complete picture we should note that Old and New Testament are not simply chronological categories, but existential ones as well. One can live temporally in the New Testament and still be a prisoner of the Old by living under the old law.

There is another model we might use. Professor Clemens Holzmeister sketches a cosmic sanctuary, a sort of world Holy of Holies, to represent a theological interpretation of the great religions. Figure 4 is a simplified version of it.

Explanation of Figure 4. Each of the eight most widespread religions has its own sanctuary in the diagram. From a purely phenomenological viewpoint, Christianity is one religion alongside the others. These eight halls are linked by a passageway with the central sanctuary — where one can join in common prayer. The Christian will say that this central sanctuary corresponds to the cosmic Christ, who is already mysteriously

229

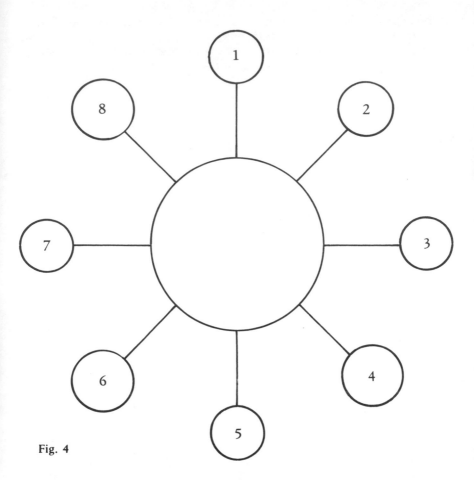

Fig. 4

present in all religions and toward whom all religions are ordered, quite like the nine-sided Bahai temple.

The final model — the simplest and best — is the elliptical one represented in Figure 5.

Explanation of Figure 5. God's self-communication reaches its highest point in the mystery of Christ who, once more, is present in humanity in two points of concentration: as the historical Jesus, around whom the Christian churches gather, and as cosmic Christ, the (unrecognized) centre of the religions and ideologies, which outweigh Christians numerically. The whole is bounded and unified in a basic creation covenant with all humanity, and in the fulfilment of the kingdom of God for all humanity.

230

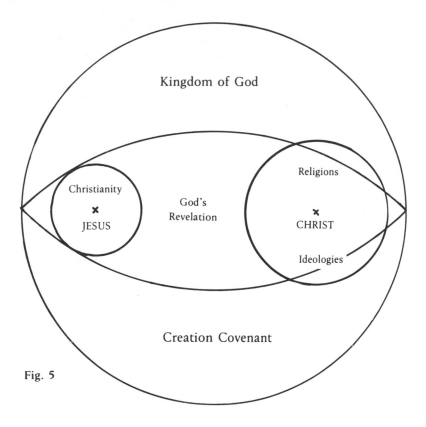

Kingdom of God

Religions

Christianity

God's
Revelation

x
JESUS

x
CHRIST

Ideologies

Creation Covenant

Fig. 5

Will Religions Survive?

§22 A Mortal Crisis

Having discovered so many common values between Christianity and the other religions, we cannot overlook the further fact that they are all of them in great danger at the present moment. The crisis of all these religious systems expresses itself in doubts of faith, the exodus of the faithful, persecutions, fear, sin, schism, and in the threats of science and secularization. What does the future hold in store?

The future of religion, like its origin, lies in the shadows of the unknown. But the market is sharply down as far as public opinion is concerned.

Christians, however, ignoring all surface indications, believe the church has its future guaranteed by Christ — if not for its own sake then for the sake of humankind that needs the church.[64] Is this future hope not applicable to the other religions too, now that we see them no longer as counterpart but as partner of the preeschatological church?

Not only the Christian but every human being is "incurably religious" and "condemned to transcendence". The human constitution includes the physiological, the intellectual, the emotional component, and the religious as well. Were any considerable part of the human race ever not only to deny this fourth dimension, but actually carry it within itself no longer, it would then no longer belong to the category of human, but to some new, posthuman race [65] (see §18, above, and Part One, §8).

Our confident commentary is by no means intended as a peaceful lullaby kiss. The churches and the great religions are today traversing a historically new phase, a mortal crisis, and disease. Yet it is "not unto death, but to the glorification of God" (John 11:4) — if only it be understood and borne as a trial and a challenge.

§23 *The Gauntlet of Secularization*

The first trial, the gauntlet of secularization, spares no religion.[66] For thousands of years, for thousands of centuries, of mythological thinking, human beings gave free rein to their religious tendencies securely and uncritically, erecting a religious tower from which to await salvation and succour. Now secularization storms across the continents like a tornado, scouring up religious might and myth by the truckload. This is the end of religion, proclaimed the ideologues. Religion will streak off like a bat in the rosy dawn of the scientific morning. And so the religions resisted the irruption of secularization as long as they could.

But the resistance has finally had to be given up. Secularization must be accepted and endured. It is time to surrender the dichotomy between sacred and profane places, persons, and modes of behaviour. It is time to surrender the hegemony of the holy. Vatican Council II recognized the autonomy of earthly realities — science, politics, economics, culture, and the like (GS 36, 56) — and *Evangelii Nuntiandi* encouraged us to discover and confess the holy as the deepest dimension of all these realities (EN 70). Persons should therefore be prudently led to new ways of thinking and speaking, as the following table of oppositions suggests.

Actually, we ought to have a third column, to indicate that, even in the age of all these secular accomplishments, *prayer* is still meaningful. First, we can pray for the strength to face the world and its tasks with confidence. Second, we can pray because no human being can plan a task in such a way as to foresee whether he or she will be alive tomorrow to carry it out, or will be called this very night. While we make our engagements and try to keep them, prayer can be very helpful for helping us meet the unknown hour of our final accomplishment.

Many Christians, priests included, have weathered secularization successfully. In the typical case they underwent a severe interior crisis and had to jettison a good deal of ballast. But then they were liberated, and now they would no longer renounce the high flights they enjoy. They

232

Religious Interpretation	Secular Accomplishment
Prayers for good weather, rogation processions	Weather forecasts, avalanche warnings, hail insurance, chemical fertilizers
Prayers for victory, thanksgiving for victory	Tactics and strategy, peace as a human task
"Evil spirits", exorcisms, witch hunts	Psychotherapy, psychology of fanaticism and aggression, behavioural experiments
Pilgrimages in time of pestilence, miraculous medals, blessing of throats, prayers for health	Vaccinations, hygiene, healthy lifestyle, medical services
"Bearing the cross of poverty", recompense in the world to come, obedience to divine-right rulers, alms giving	Economic justice, social work, democracy, taxes, government departments

no longer feel themselves children of fear and law, but of freedom and joy. Others, it is true, have had their faith shattered, and they will doubtless have long detours of experience to traverse in their mature lives before finding their way back to final religious stability and maturity.

One can say that the Western world has already survived secularization to a certain measure, and that the effect it has had on Christianity has not been lethal but purgative. The phenomenon of God is more forceful, and more intimately bound up with the human phenomenon, than before. But God is no longer a God anthropomorphically enthroned in the skies and miraculously interfering in the course of daily events (which is the God the atheists deny, and should deny), but a God who is life's ultimate mystery, the absolute future, and the ground of our courageous living and dying — the God whom even the atheists seek, and recognize in the depth of their hearts (see Part Two, §38).

233

In the case of the other religions, secularization is still charging in at top speed. In Christianity it grew from the inside out, and actually had its ultimate basis in the critical behaviour and discourse of Jesus. But in the case of the other religions it presses in from the outside like the Trojan horse, and does its deeds in a milieu far less well prepared for the conflict. In particular, the other religions lack great theologians to grasp secularization by the lapels and force it to yield up its positive power and meaning. Religious leaders, by and large, are representatives of the old, uncritical, fundamentalist ways of thinking, less well educated than either the youth growing up around them or the intelligentsia.

The mute exodus of the faithful from the other religions is even more radical than in Christianity — although it is less visible because these religions are social structures at the same time, and those who abandon them as religions remain within their social units. But the falling out between the secular and religious mentalities is more thoroughgoing in the other religions, and this will constitute their approaching crisis.

Now that Christians have more or less held up under biblical criticism and secularization, one of the greatest services that Christian specialists in non-Christian religions could render to these religions would be the cautious initiation of a similar process. Not in the brutal fashion of the old liberal biblical criticism, which shocked believers and awakened their disrespect. In this way our brothers and sisters in the other religions could be helped to see through the myth as such, while rescuing the core.

All this optimistic discourse of ours is not intended to imply that secularization has been basically altogether harmless. It has had its effect, and it is still at work, guaranteeing that in future there will be more and more "wordly" persons along with the "religious" ones, according to the disposition, grace, and mission of each one. It is not a matter of unconditionally and expressly rejecting an ultimate religious orientation. Many simply feel no more need of religious behaviour. As far as they can manage to do so, they have their God-experience in the world, in nature, and in the works of righteousness.

This has called forth a new stage in the ecumenical process. The first stage was ecumenism among Christians. The second was ecumenism with other religions. Now there is a new ecumenism with "worldly" persons[67] whom we respect and appreciate, and with whom we should be talking and working for the welfare of a unified humanity. We suddenly realize that goodness and unselfishness are qualities found in *all* human groups. We find ourselves suddenly taking account that many "worldly" values are basically evangelical values that have detached themselves from the church in the name of greater liberty.

In this connection one sometimes hears of "exploded Christianity",[68] meaning a value-flight that is bad for Christianity but good for the world. Of course it could also be put the other way around: since the

234

incarnation of Christ, all genuinely human values are also "Christian" values. Hence, the order of the day will not be competition but coexistence.

Further, Christians believe that all secular history is also salvation history, and that Jesus is now simply identified with every human being, and that this will be the great surprise of the Parousia (Matt. 25:34-46). At the Last Judgment we shall not be asked how many sacraments we have received, nor how many places of pilgrimage we have visited, but only and solely how we have related to our fellow human beings in their pernicious socio-political structures. For whenever we met them we met Jesus, cognito or incognito.

In the past, we took good care to deify everything in our own church and damn everything outside it. Now it is time to humanize all things, and glorify God in the human being.

§24 *Commitment to Integral Salvation*

The second challenge to the religions (including the church) is the commitment to integral salvation. Surely the goal of the religions is to direct human beings to the mystery of God. Their purpose is to disclose the ultimate meaning of life, and continually to remind human beings that they have a greater task before them than just to play out their few decades on the stage of daily existence. But to indicate an ultimate meaning in life, and life's definitive fulfilment in a life after life, it is not necessary to do harm to the fulness of life in the here and now. On the contrary.

Meanwhile, it will do no good to deny that religion has always been the ideological underpinning of the status quo in traditional society, and the guarantor of its authority and order. Religion has taught that humanity's division into poor and rich, ranks and castes, slave and free, was by the will of God, and sought to alleviate the worst of it with alms and mercy. The disadvantaged were consoled with the promise of a recompense in the next world. This is the religion that the Marxists — rightly — called opium. One cannot disguise the fact that in precommunist Russia, in precommunist Mozambique and Ethiopia, official religion did perform this function (which is not to say that everything was better as soon as the system was changed). The religions have had a blocking, alienating, downright devastating influence on personal, human development in many places.

In Christianity, too, we too long concentrated everything (in preaching, if not in practice) on the supernatural and on eternal salvation. Not too long ago books of spirituality and theology still asserted that salvation consisted in accepting the faith, receiving the sacraments, and hoping for eternal life. The refrain of all the mighty sermons was "Save thy soul!" The gospel salvation — *shalom* — had been disincarnated, spiritualized, eschatologized.

235

In a world in which, according to World Bank statistics, 800 million human beings live below the absolute poverty level in spite of all progress that has been made; in which catastrophes and wars root out entire populations; in which aid and assistance are hindered by the whim of authority; where corruption and exploitation at the hands of a ruling class destroy a people's hope and lead to uprisings, and new hopes, which in turn are promptly disappointed once more; where the military budget of most nations is larger than the education budget; where in many places the extreme forms of communism without freedom or capitalism without justice, and a Fourth World of refugees, oppressed minorities, and political prisoners cries out to heaven — in a word, where human beings and the human race are threatened by structures of inhumanity, injustice, and indignity — in a world like that, religious leaders may not withdraw from this unsaved world to pray in their temples, satisfied that the masses, in the midst of poverty and injustice, nevertheless remain believers. Precisely because they do take God seriously, they must also take human beings seriously, and make a commitment to their integral salvations.[69]

The Christian churches have already turned toward the world. For the Catholic Church, *Gaudium et Spes*, the 1971 Synod of Bishops, and *Evangelii Nuntiandi* have declared that commitment to justice is an essential part of evangelization itself, hence not a corollary but a constitutive of religion. The World Council of Churches has had its Uppsala, Bangkok, Nairobi, and Melbourne. Every Christian ought to know now that the following of Christ and the return to the Father leads up the path of courageous devotion to their brothers and sisters. Evangelical love can no longer be satisfied with almsgiving. It means "in the modern context, the human being's genuine progress in justice and peace" (EN 31). Bishops' conferences and the World Council of Churches have recently raised their voices like Old Testament prophets, and have unsparingly castigated the injustices they see around them. They have become the voice of the voiceless.

The Association of Third-World Theologians, an ecumenical group founded in 1976 in Dar es Salaam, has taken the idea of "contextual theology" and made of it its new departure. They want no more abstract theology — the kind you learn in a classroom and is valid always and everywhere, but never answers any real questions. They want a theology moulded in the frontlines of life, directing the light of the gospel into a particular corner of the world, and giving the people there the strength and courage to overcome their situation. They interpret history as the place where God challenges human beings. History is made, they say, not found, and they want to build a history in which the present and the coming generation will be able to experience God's salvation. "The gospel should liberate the community to prepare the New Jerusalem in this world — to cooperate in the creation of a progressive, just, free,

236

humane world, in which not the elite, but the least become the standard of merciful behaviour".[70]

But for the religions, this "return to the world" is much more difficult. For thousands of years their temples have directed the vision upward and inward, but not into the world with all its tensions and hopes. How much longer? If the religions continue to ignore the world, the world will soon begin to ignore the religions. The modern human being does not wish to lead a life torn in two. A religion that turns us away from life, instead of interpreting and altering life, no longer means anything to us.

Life is closer to us than is religion. We instinctively feel that religion should lead us out beyond humanity to God. If the religions do not grasp this challenge, they will become the affair of unworldly monks, whom the world respects at best, perhaps also laughs at, but in no case asks for information or guidance.

There are signs. There is hope. Since the World Conferences of Religions for Peace in Kyoto in 1970, in Louvain in 1974, and in Princeton in 1979, with their continental secretariats and their scientific peace research, coupled with their practical undertakings in the furtherance of peace, there is something new under way.[71] The religions are gradually becoming what they should be: not a tower, not a superstructure — but an interpretation, and a power for making life more worth living.

§25 Environmental Problems

There is one aspect of integral salvation that must be given separate and special consideration. It is the complexus of environmental problems — ecology. In the three decades immediately following the last world war, everyone dreamed of "the American way of life". What we all wanted most was to better our "standard of living". (J.W. Thompson showed in 1960 that Americans had to increase their consumption by $16 billion every year in order to maintain the rhythm of production.) We plundered the resources of the earth without a second thought.

Then we suddenly learned with horror that we were destroying the biosphere, in which we breathe and live — that we were dismantling the very raft we were riding. It was the Club of Rome that first opened our eyes to this drastic situation. If the present rate of population growth, industrialization, pollution of the environment, and waste of raw materials continues, we will soon reach the absolute limit of growth and have to undertake catastrophic retrenchments simply in order to survive.[72]

And the cries of the Cassandras have been multiplying. "If we live the next thirty years the way we have lived the last thirty, we shall be digging our children's mass grave" (R. Garaudy). "Only someone pessimistic

237

enough to recognize the size of the danger has any chance at all of cooperating in averting it" (W. Röpke). "We are waging a reckless war of supremacy with nature, and nature has been rendered defenceless. In a matter of decades we plunder what nature has taken millions of years to amass. The forests are going up in smoke, the desert is spreading in all directions, the air is poisoned, the waters have become a sewer. The human technological total victory is ending in total self-annihilation" (H. Gruhl).[73]

It takes a sense of responsibility to know that one should not build the Tower of Babel any higher, but should begin at once to dismantle the upper stories. The foundation is already atremble. But no one dares to give the order. The citizenry at its foot are too busy enjoying life. No political party can screw up the courage to jostle it out of its habits of consumption, for fear of losing votes. H. Gruhl, one of the voices crying in the desert, put this problem ahead of everything else in his life. He had been a Christian Democratic member of the Bundestag and chairman of the Environmental Protection Committee. But the party failed to take his warnings seriously, so he left it and became a founder of the "Green Party".

The day of reckoning is fast approaching. We know that at the present rate of consumption the last barrel of oil will have been sucked out of the earth in thirty years. Yet instead of diminishing, consumption increases every year. We know that we cut enough timber every year to cover Switzerland twice over, in order to obtain land for building, planting, and grazing, and to have wood for the paper industry. And we know that, at this rate, in eighty-five years the forests that store up our rainfall and renew our air will have disappeared.But this deadline is too far off to stop the plunder. We are faced with a choice. We can face up to the challenge of a moderate economic crisis in the hope of mastering it with ingenuity and research, or we can push the ecological crisis to its limits and suddenly be faced with catastrophe.

If the politicians do not have the courage to tell the truth, then the churches must. At stake is the salvation or destruction of the human race. Without religious motivation the course of things cannot be altered. Preaching and parish missions could well do less thundering against certain sins of the past, and pillory consumerism instead, encouraging a new alternative lifestyle as a necessity and virtue. "Small is beautiful." "Live otherwise, so others can live." A theology of environmental protection and self-denial must be developed.

There are still many blank areas on this part of the ethics and moral theology charts. The list of sins against body and goods must be completed with the ones against nature. The African A. Tevoedjire has written a book full of meaning, *Poverty, the Kingdom of the Peoples*.[74] Neither for Africa nor for Europe does he demand misery, but he does want a meaningful poverty, which would dismantle much of what is superfluous and enable persons to enjoy life more simply again. Several bishops' conferences have already published statements on the subject, but we must not think that this does the job.

One must have the courage to strike out for solutions that are utopic and at the same time realistic. It wrenches my heart to see the chaotic traffic of Rome (or of any other great metropolis) — long lines of cars (usually carrying only one person), traffic jams, horns honking, drivers cursing (or laughing, depending on one's natural disposition), exhaust fumes actually eating away the old masterpieces on the walls of palaces and museums, time lost by the worker trying to get home in the evening, and an absolutely irresponsible consumption of gasoline! When will the civil and ecclesiastical administration of a city begin a common campaign for bicycles, and give the example themselves by riding them to work? The automobile would still serve for emergencies, rainy days, and holidays and vacations.

Here is another suggestion. The second "Decade of Development" is now over and gone. As the first one (1960-1970) began, the United Nations listed the "twenty-five poorest nations", the ones specially in need of help to catch up. Now it would be in order to declare a decade of "de-development", and list the twenty-five richest nations, which should take special steps to lower their living standards, for three reasons:

1. For economic reasons, because the ecological plunder of the past three decades can simply no longer continue,

2. For psychological reasons: it is a proven fact that the richest countries have the highest rate of nervous breakdowns and frustrations, hence also of divorce and suicide,

3. On grounds of solidarity with the poor peoples of the world.

What else but religion can give the encouragement for a planetary change of direction like this? Pope John Paul II's bull of November 30, 1979, named Francis of Assisi as patron saint of ecology. Francis was the lovable saint who recognized nature as a gift from God, loved it, sang of it, and was so cheerful in the midst of poverty. Will Francis perhaps work the miracle of opening modern humanity's eyes and restoring to it the joy of a simple life?

Chapter Eleven

Evangelization

§26 *The Church's Special Mission to the Other Religions*

We have spoken long of the religions, recognizing the great worth there is in them. At the same time we did not underestimate the uniqueness of the Christ event (see above, §§15-17). Now we must consider the church not so much as having a special place among the religions, but as having a special mission to the other religions. As in all the rest of this book, we are investigating the church not in its interior aspect, but in its exterior aspect. What can the other religions expect and demand of the church?

Of course we could also put the question the other way around and ask what the church can expect from the other great world religions. Tribal religions have no foreign missions. They are expressly stay-at-home religions, bound to "their" gods, limited to the purview of their own ancestors. When their practitioners emigrate they cannot practise the ancestral religion, for now they are far from the tribe and from the tombs of their forebears. But the high religions, the book religions, are expressly migrating religions. They extend themselves, either by radiation and attraction in the peace-loving ways of Hinduism and Buddhism, or by prophetic preaching and explicit missionary activity as in Zoroastrianism and Islam.

Christianity too has always understood itself, on grounds of its institution and its entire history, as a missionary religion. It has spread over six continents, and more extensively than any other religion. Today, of course, it finds itself in the shade of two new "missionary" forces, science and Marxism, with their factual or ideological doctrine that has circled the globe in our day and staked out equal global claims with the religions. And now that European hegemony is no more, and the value of the world religions has been recognized, the question arises for Christianity whether its mission claims will still stand up in court. From now on, why, where, and how can and should missionary activity be carried on? To use a new, more comprehensive term — what about "evangelization"?

240

Why Evangelize?

§27 God's Salvation Plan

History has caricatured evangelization. Mass baptisms of whole tribes in the early Middle Ages, and a tight connection with colonialism and Europeanism in the modern era, have been the traits that typify it in the contemporary imagination.

Actually, evangelization is the mediation, or transmittal, of the gospel, of *shalom* (and so evangelization could be called "shalomization" just as well), of the good news, of salvation, of a hope and meaning for life. And so it needs no further justification. Such an offer speaks for itself. Every sincere man and woman will welcome it, for God himself has created the human being as a being who, unlike the brute beast, is a salvation-seeker (see §22, above).

Evangelization is not the outgrowth of the free initiative of some dynamic group of human beings. The initiative is always God's. The revelation of the Old Testament bore a universal character, even if the chosen people of those times had difficulty in recognizing it and taking it seriously. The self-revelation of the one and only true God as Yahweh represents the beginning of a process in which all religions moved toward unity (see §§13-14, above). The Christ event of the New Testament is unique in its whole concept, and hence bears an intrinsic tendency not to be reserved for privileged groups but to be made known to all humanity (Part One, 30, 35-38; Part Four, §§15-17).

From these "divine" premises the conclusion follows of itself. Precisely because God revealed himself in diverse ways to the fathers from the beginning, but later in a unique way to all humanity (Heb. 1:1ff.), it is now God's responsibility to make known the uniqueness of his saving action to humanity on its way to unity, in order to remove all inward confusion and outward division. And precisely because God "has made known to *us* the mystery of Christ according to his gracious decree", *we* have the responsibility of making known to all peoples "this superabundant richness of his grace in the approaching ages" (Eph. 1:9, 2:7).

We can take it as a firm and constitutive part of God's salvation plan that he wills to redeem all human beings, and that he actually does redeem them in Christ. But whether he wills to lead them into his socially constituted church in this historical time, or wills to manifest full unity in them only in the day the kingdom is accomplished, remains an open question. And it is a question that it is not incumbent upon us to resolve. Still, a realistic appraisal of the history of salvation until our day, with sufficient attention to the fact that two-thirds of humankind still goes the way of its own religions with no signs at present of an immediate alteration in this state of affairs, does incline one to prefer the second hypothesis. Perhaps it is more important that no human being be able to boast (Eph. 2:9), not even the church. Perhaps it is more important to safeguard the absolute freedom of God and of human beings.

The church should publish its witness to Christ most earnestly (see §28, below). But it should be equally earnest not to consider itself more important than God. It is not only through the mediating instrumentality of the church that God can lead the men and women of the world's religions to salvation. God's freedom is still his, and it is complete. His latter-day activity has already begun, when *he* is the one who saves his creatures. The church cannot wrest his salvation activity from his hand but it does have the commission of making it known:

> Special salvation history seeks to bring within itself the whole general salvation and revelation history, and present that history through itself. Thus it strives toward an identity of events and occurrences with the general history of salvation, just as with secular history, even though it knows that this identification is never achieved in history but will find its actualization only in the removal of opposites in the kingdom of God.[75]

§28 *The Church and Evangelization*

From the viewpoint of the church the motive for evangelization is just as clear. The church sees itself as the people of God in a special way. But it cannot be people of God merely for itself. This is something it has to be always *for others*, for everyone. The whole dynamic of God's salvific activity brooks no other conclusion. Neither does the whole biblical theology of vocation.

History shows us different models, or stages of development, of the mode and manner in which the church's commission "to be for others" has been actualized. In his *Models of the Church*, Avery Dulles set forth various models of the church in its inward aspect. We can sketch a similar series of models corresponding to its outward aspect.[76] Or better, let us construct two series, corresponding to (1) different currents of theological thought, and (2) different approaches in pastoral activity, as observed in the course of history.

First, let us outline the different modes of theological thinking.

The supremacist model. This model held sway during the great missionary era spanning the sixteenth to the twentieth centuries, and had its roots in the medieval spirituality of *Christianitas* (see Part Two, §4). Within the Christian pale behold faith, light, and culture; without, lo, unbelief, night, and barbarism. From within this thought pattern, a Pope Nicholas V could in 1455 accord a Christian king "liberty and plenipotentiary right to penetrate the land of the Saracen, heathen, and the other enemies of Christ and subjugate it". This is the theological presupposition of Pope Alexander VI's division of the New World

242

between Spain and Portugal in 1493, with the accompanying commission to each royal court "to subjugate those barbarous peoples and lead them to the faith" (see also Part Two, §§12-15, 23-27). And so, for centuries, out sailed the missionaries aboard the colonizers' ships — to baptize those heathen peoples, to snatch them from the jaws of hell, and to lead them into the church.

The fulfilment model. This is the model that has prevailed in more recent decades. The value of the other great religions was now recognized, along with the possibility of salvation in them. But they ranked as germinal, embryonic, auxiliary religions. They were in need of historical, or eschatological, "fulfilment" in Christ. This is the model that corresponds to the thinking of Vatican Council II (e.g., AG 9; LG 5). And it can defend itself very respectably. But it still smacks strongly of the unidirectional mentality — as if the other religions could be enriched by the church but not vice versa.

The sacramental model is not opposed to the fulfilment model, but is a further development of it. It, too, is based on Vatican Council II, and on the idea, so dear to the council, of "the church as sacrament of salvation for all" (see above, §19). Thus the church is the visible and efficacious sign of salvation for all, the instrument in the service of the kingdom of God that already embraces all men and women. The goal to strive for now is no longer unconditionally to lead all men and women into the church, but to proclaim God's salvation to all men and women and encourage them on the way to that salvation.

These three theological modes of thinking have their analogues in three distinct pastoral approaches.

The accommodation model corresponds to the supremacy model, and was taught and practised in varying degrees from the early prophets of adaptation to the missiologists of recent times. This model is represented graphically in Figure 6.

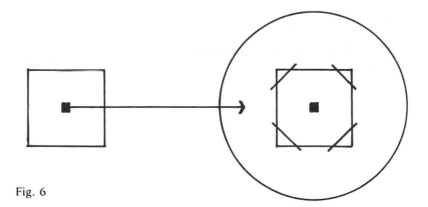

Fig. 6

Explanation of Figure 6. Around the essential core of the gospel the West has developed a plethora of rites, traditions, and laws. The missionaries transported this whole Western form of Christianity to the New World. Certain exceptions were allowed, largely for tactical reasons, in external matters such as dress and singing.

The incarnational model accompanies the fulfilment model. It has had more influence on theory than on practice (see Part Three, §9). It is represented in Figure 7.

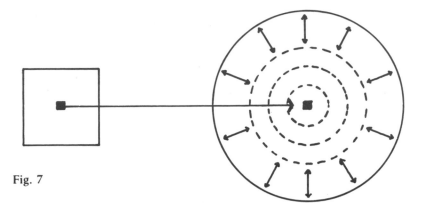

Fig. 7

Explanation of Figure 7. Instead of carting to the field the whole apparatus of Western usage, missionaries bring only "the essential core of the gospel" (EN 63). Of course they well realize that the full meaning of the gospel can never be grasped as a "core" divorced from culture, so they allow the gospel full rein to create a new body for itself, to make its own history among these new peoples. The tremendous opposition that this model has met whenever its proponents have attempted to implement it is a sign of the great tension within the church in our present age (see below, §§32, 33).

The interpretative model corresponds to the sacramental model. It presupposes the incarnational model, but places great additional emphasis on the church's mission to be a sign for others. Gathered around the gospel, the Christian community sees as one of its chief tasks a dialogue with the faithful of other religions and with the secular world. In this dialogue, Christians would undertake to confirm and reassure these other peoples as to the credibility of their hopes for salvation, but would also enter into a common religious life with them, endeavouring to transmit Christian values to them, while remaining on the alert to receive their own enriching values for Christian neediness.[77] The diagram indicates this with two-headed arrows. We cannot and must not aim at a universalist missionary conquest by virtue of superiority; we should practise an interpretative universalism.

244

Still, it bears repeated emphasis that our efforts must never be confined to the realm of pure interpretation. Our interpretation should go hand in hand with efforts for change. Our theory should be the vehicle of our practice, the motive of our cooperation with the resources we find in other peoples for the realization of integral salvation. Indeed, we could add a "cooperation model" to the list, but this would be a church of the future.

These, then, are the modes by which the church can and ought to fulfil its mission to the other religions. They complement and enhance one another. They model not only the church as such but each individual member of it. This was the great insight of the Synod of Bishops in 1974 — that it is impossible to divide the church into evangelizers and evangelized (youth, labour, women, and so on). No, everyone who expects to belong to the church and to participate in its mission must evangelize.[78] All who are being evangelized must evangelize, and *only* those who are being evangelized *can* evangelize!

God made Isaiah "a light of the peoples, that my salvation may reach to the end of the world" (Isa. 49:6; cf. Luke 2:32). He made Paul "the chosen instrument to bear my name before kings and peoples" (Acts 9:15). But as my whole line of argumentation has shown, these figures are not monopolists of their calling. They are models and prototypes. Every Christian, and every Christian community, is called to the same task. Even the genuinely unique case — Jesus — is at the same time everyone's model, for we are called to imitate his example and follow in his footsteps (1 Pet. 2:21). We are all *called* children of God, and *are* (1 John 3:1).

Baptism in the church does not first and foremost mean salvation. The unbaptized can be saved. Baptism in the church means, first and foremost, that we are called to be a part of the church's sacramental witness — to be witnesses to the fact that forgiveness of sins is announced in Jesus' name to all peoples (Luke 24:47ff.).

The evangelization assignment that each Christian, as also the Christian community, has received can proceed by stages. One need not crash through the door and tumble into the house, seeking to convert the others and baptize them at once. This was, and is, the tendency of tribal religions. But the great religions of Asia, which is the home of the great mass of non-Christian humanity, have a lesson to teach us — in five hundred years of missionary history with minimal results — and it is that theology, not strategy, will indicate the right moment for the firing of the following "rocket stages".

Live and think as a representative. Whatever Christian communities do, they should do as Jesus did — not for himself but for others. "Vocation for" and "mission to" are basic categories of every biblical calling. This does not necessarily always mean "going to", but it surely does involve "thinking of". Even mere Christian existence must be understood as service to others. Jesus has made himself "sin" for all (2 Cor. 5:21) and "has sanctified himself" for all (John 17:19). Especially our Sunday Eucharist should always be celebrated as a divine service "for all".[79]

Give Christian testimony in the manner of one's life. This is more important than proclaiming the word. What good is it to teach catechism when Christian individuals, communities, and peoples are a scandal to the gospel? After all, evangelization is not just the proclamation of a message, but the actualization of a new and better life. Like the communities of Jerusalem and Antioch (Acts 2:42-47, 4:32-37, 13:1-3), all Christian communities should be question marks and exclamation points for others. Their alternative lifestyles should ask questions and give answers!

Foster dialogue. Muslims, Hindus, even atheists live and work side by side with us. The first problem this raises is a social one. The religious problem follows. One's first task in their regard is not spiritual ministry but social concern. Then of course we should also enter into conversation and dialogue with them. However, our conversation will not seek to obtrude our "conversion" upon them, but will simply endeavour to make the acquaintance of fellow human beings out of respect for their values, convictions, and freedom. This will prepare us not only to instruct them, but also to listen. Thus we shall be mutually enriched and come nearer to each other. Not that dialogue will consist in mere conversation. It will be an exchange in which we are genuinely engaged, and thereby it will constitute our witness.

Leave conversion to God. "The Lord increased the number of those being saved" (Acts 2:47). It is contrary to the spirit of the gospel feverishly to run after mass conversions, to wish to keep pace with the population explosion. This is what "evangelical" groups do in their pessimism about salvation.[80] Eagerness for quantitative growth is not the real goal to be striven after. Rather it is to be considered a consequence of authentic Christian behaviour, as well as a basis from which to render service to others in their search for salvation. The new springboard to evangelization is no longer fear of hell (see Part Two, §§23-27), but love for God and human beings — a motive more worthy of both.

One of the main tasks of an up-to-date pastoral practice is the "conversion" of our own Christians, who are so often introverted and self-centred, and use the church only for the satisfaction of their own religious needs. They have to be turned around, redirected "for others".

Where Evangelize?

§29 A Church on Six Continents

Until recently the world was divided, ecclesially speaking, in two: the church and the missions. And this seemed to present no problem. The church was the centre, the missions were its periphery. We had the model over here, the copy over there. The rich, teaching, giving church was over here, and the poor, learning, receiving missions were over there. This was not a very good way to build a relationship of equality and brotherhood; instead it led to dependency, humiliation, and inward opposition.

One could make many statements about the present situation in the church, but few more significant than these two: the church is a church on six continents, and the missions are missions on six continents.

This fact is, in the first instance, a simple finding of the sociology of religion. Counting the Americas as two, the church today is on six continents. In the course of our present generation, Christendom's centre of gravity has shifted from the Western world to the Southern world.[81] At the turn of the century eighty-five percent af all Christians lived in the West. At century's end this figure will be forty-two percent — of Catholics, only thirty percent. Thus the great majority of Christians will be Latin Americans, Africans, and Asians.

In retrospect one can pinpoint the moment of transition from Western church to world church during the pontificate of Paul VI. The scales tipped in 1970 (see Part Two, §19). And this was the pope who systematically named native bishops, so that today in Asia nearly all the bishops, and in Africa some seventy-five percent, are native born.

The Synod of Bishops in 1974 was a very special event in church history, in the sense that, whereas the council and the first three synods were still frankly the work of Western bishops and theologians, the fourth synod was just as frankly the work of the bishops and theologians of the Third World, and the pope expressly cited their contribution twice in the closing document (EN 30,31). The journeys, too, of Paul VI must be seen in this light. No pope had ever left Europe since the first one, Peter, came there. Paul VI opened his pontificate by visiting all six continents, to show that the church is indeed on six continents.

By the same token Vatican Council II had laid the theological groundwork for the existence of the many local churches, which together make up the one church of Christ, but each one of which enjoys a relative autonomy and a legitimate pluriformity (LG 13, 23; SC 37-40; EN 63). For "local church" is not just a topological concept; it is also an ecclesiological concept. The local church is the place where the gospel is incarnated, proclaimed, and lived here and now — the place where locally conditioned new forms and experiments are encouraged, and when they work, are endorsed and approved. A plethora of conciliar and postconciliar books and dissertations have brought all this into sharp focus.

§30 *Missions on Six Continents*

The missions did not simply vanish into thin air the moment the church was everywhere established. Missionary activity is defined as the first proclamation of the gospel to persons still far from Christ (AG 6; EN 51). Consequently there are missionary situations wherever the church is established. This is why we can speak today of missions on six continents.

In the case of the old mission lands, the truth of this statement is evident. Even if there are local churches everywhere, they are usually minoritarian churches, which, as Vatican II expressly states, are now no longer simply the object of missionary activity, but are themselves the agents of that activity. They have the obligation to proclaim the gospel to the many who are far from Christ in their own land (AG 20). Doubtless they will need the help of their fellow churches in this work for a long time to come. But it is they who bear its primary responsibility.

However, it may strike the reader as strange that traditional Christian countries should now be called missions again. H. Godin and Y. Daniel made this statement as early as 1943, on grounds of an analysis of conditions in France,[82] and of course they aroused a good deal of protest. Karl Rahner had much the same thesis in mind when he spoke of Christianity's "diaspora situation". Today one is no longer a Christian by birth, but only by choice. Christianity itself consists of minority groups of these Christians by conviction who, instead of walling themselves up in ghettos, ought to spread out and be a leaven of presence. That is, they ought to be missionary.[83]

The expression "missions on six continents" was coined by the World Council of Churches in its plenary congress in Mexico City in 1963. The meaning was that the spirit and deeds of the gospel are so little in evidence in the universities, in the suburbs, in the centres of the world's activities, that they have to be "missionized" again.

Catholic circles long rejected this thinking. But we have finally had to accept it. And no less than a Pope John Paul II declared to the Council of European Bishops' Conferences that Europe was on the point of becoming a missionary continent once more — adding that this was not to be understood as grounds for pessimism, but as a challenge.[84]

We need only take an objective look at reality to become aware of this new situation. In the "Catholic city" of Vienna, ten percent of the population go to church, ninety percent are alienated. In "Catholic Munich", in 1974, fifty-two percent of the marriages in which both partners were Catholic were celebrated outside the church; forty-two percent of the children born that year were not baptized; and more persons (6,079) left the church than there were baptisms in it. In France three to five percent of suburbanites go to church. In the United States there are eighty million "unchurched" persons. There is only one way to view the state of affairs: we are in a missionary situation.

This does not mean that all these persons alienated from the church are also alienated from Christ, or that they are "irreligious". They still carry their religious questions around with them. Only they try to solve them themselves. They could be called "religious nomads", and there are as many of them among non-Christians as among Christians. They have exchanged their sedentary religious structures for the life of the wanderer. They go their own ways now.

The phenomenon of the "unchurched" has been noticed for several years now, and it has aroused an outcry.[85] Pastoral action is demanded, new initiatives — missionaries are to go not only to Africa and Asia but out beyond the boundaries of the Christian community at home, "with new methods and a new language" (EN 56), in an organized and systematic way, to try to bring the one who is far from Christ near to him again. What has been done in the United States in recent years[86] could be an inspiration for other churches.

§31 Consequences for the Church

In the light of this new situation there are conclusions to be drawn for the church.

First, we ought to stop speaking and thinking of "the missions" — and especially of "our missions". That was the way it was for a long time. Certain regions of the world, by "right of commission", were entrusted to a missionary order. That order would send missionaries, and money, to those regions, and take upon itself the total responsibility for the establishment of a local church there. The *jus commissionis* was abrogated by an Instruction of the Sacred Congregation for Evangelization of Peoples on February 24, 1969. This is indicative of the mind of the church. It is also striking that Pope Paul VI in *Evangelii Nuntiandi* used the expression "the missions" only twice, in all his long discussion of missionary activity — that is, of the first proclamation of the gospel to those who are far from Christ — and he used it only very incidentally (EN 69, 73). It is somehow anachronistic — and it is downright offensive to the Christians who live there — to still be speaking of "the missions", to be taking up collections for "the missions", instead of simply entering into association with our fellow churches abroad and lending them our church-to-church assistance. "The missions", as a historical form, as served by "foreign missionaries", are seeing their last days. But the "mission" as first proclamation, on the contrary, is in the ascendant — with its primary responsibility being taken over by the local churches, often with the assistance of foreign churches.

Not everyone likes to hear about the "end of the missions". But it takes an ostrich to miss the turn of historical events. From 1968 to 1979 the number of American missionaries decreased fromn 9,655 to 6,455 — almost exactly one-third. Statistics on the age of German missionaries are easy to interpret: nearly one-third (30.94%) of the 7,845 men and women are over seventy years of age; 27.56% are between the ages of sixty and seventy; and only a good third, or 41.5% are between twenty and sixty.[87] It is therefore a simple matter of historical fact that the *missiones ad partes exteriores* are rapidly on the wane.

They leave no vacuum behind them. They leave the local church in their wake, and the local church is itself busy with missionary activity. Until now the only missionary work was by one continent to another. But today the churches of all six continents are developing their missionary activity, and this multiplies it by six. The "crisis of the missions" we hear about is expressly a Western phenomenon; as a whole, the church is more missionary than ever before.

But the question arises: What is the task of missionary congregations now? We might answer somewhat as follows.

The specialized missionary orders and congregations have completed the historical task for which they were founded some hundred years ago. In those days they went forth to an ecclesial no man's land; today, they see the fruit of their labours — the local churches. Now they should continue their service to the young local churches, for such time and in whatever measure they are still needed and welcome as missionaries. But it is to be expected that within ten or twenty years many countries will no longer issue visas for foreign missionaries; and the local churches themselves, at any rate in the majority of instances, will likely have no more need.

The new function of the missionary congregations is therefore to become the "missionary conscience" of the church. Any church, young or old, can run the risk of "going the way of the stereotype pastor" — of beginning to attend only to those who are already its members. And any local church can run the risk of being *only* a local church, instead of seeing itself ever bound up with the church universal. Until now, "missionary assistance" has been a one-way street. But this one-way street is opening up another lane, under the auspices of *koinonia*, or interchurch assistance, as expressed in mutual prayer, mutual interest, mutual pastoral inspiration, and mutual aid. And the missionary congregations are the conscience of *koinonia*. They should seek new missionary commitments only where there is still need of the first proclamation. And they should not forget to return the missionary thrust to the church of their native land; they must not forget to bring the "missionary situation" of their own country into sharp focus.[88]

In view of the political and psychological developments of the twenty years since *Ad Gentes*, one could ask whether the time has perhaps come for "the missions, those special undertakings . . . in areas designated by the Holy See" (AG 6) to be handed over to the general administration of the church. Then if the Curia itself were to be reformed and decentralized, so that the national bishops' conferences and the continental associations of bishops' conferences actually enjoyed a certain competency, the Roman central office for evangelization would acquire a new, dynamic task — that of being the missionary conscience of the entire church. Its new task would be to investigate the missionary situations on all continents, supply the needed impulse to the local churches, and solicit and channel interchurch assistance in the form of personnel and financial aid. The "double church" has for all practical purposes given Europe and North America an alibi: missionaries have gone to Africa and Asia, but failed, or nearly failed, to care for the men and women who are far from Christ in their own lands. A central office for evangelization will therefore always be necessary, to study, program, and animate the church's activity *ad extra*, which is the first proclamation to the not-yet-Christian and the no-longer-Christian.

How Evangelize?

§32 *Warning Signals*

The right and duty to evangelize and be evangelized — to proclaim one's religion as well as to change one's religion — are beyond question. They are based on the gospel, as well as on today's understanding of human rights, which include religious freedom. And of course one must grant religious freedom to religions other than one's own.

The only question is how. A solid, basic right can be divested of all its meaning, from the inside, by a false implementation.

Here we understand evangelization in the broadest sense — as it is to be carried out everywhere, on all six continents, by all local churches and by all who are within the church, toward all groups of persons (EN 51-56). This is a task in which the hierarchy has a special role of leadership to perform, and it has a great responsibility for its success.

It lies in the tragic nature of every supreme authority to be able easily to lose contact with its grassroots. The church is no exception. A bishop in Africa told me, with a smile, "Bishops lose their friends, get invited to too many banquets, and no longer hear the truth". Bishops have a series of reasons for often making only what the French call an *acte de présence* among their people or in their seminaries. They give a talk, but they do not sufficiently hear and feel what is being thought and said at the grassroots level. And yet it is not only the nonbishops of the church who are to abide by the mind of the hierarchy; the hierarchy, too, should abide by the mind of the other members of the church, who often better understand the signs of the times, and know what can be expected from church members today, and what cannot be expected of them, on grounds of the gospel and human dignity.

The closer one is to the base of the pyramid the more one feels obliged to build a bridge to the top. Those in contact with the grassroots feel a duty to see that the necessary information gets to the top of the pyramid and to see that the necessary and legitimate pressure is exerted, there at the top, to correct a given situation.

In Part Two, in view of the facts of history, we formulated statements about the church that were not exactly flattering to it (§§19, 39). In the present context as well, we must make certain critical remarks in view of the present. How can this be consonant with love for and dedication to the church? There are two possible attitudes. One can set the church on a shining pedestal in the firm conviction that it always does everything well (although the whole history of the church contradicts this view). But one must not take it amiss if another segment of the church membership thinks more critically — if it happens to know something about the church's history and wants to take some responsibility for the church. They only want to gain a hearing for certain justifiable desires for the improvement of the church.

In this latter spirit, we beg to be allowed to list the following six unlovely accusations as warning signals that certain roads are no longer safe to travel. This is not a digression. It is an effort to avoid false attitudes, which hinder evangelization (§32), and to foster correct attitudes, which further it (§33).

Exclusivism. In the light of all the things that history shows us happen as a result of ideological exclusivism, we surely have the right today to throw open our borders, maintain a dialogue, and renounce the wish to uproot the weeds before the harvest. We may no longer simply cut off the inconvenient disturbers of the peace; if we do, we run the risk of thrusting aside their legitimate wishes. There are many today who are alienated from the church but close to Christ (just as perhaps there are persons close to the church but far from Christ). Continuous external adherence to the church should not be the sole criterion of church membership. The door will have to swing in both directions, and be open to all the religious nomads, waverers, and border patrols, so that they will all be able to pass in both directions without much formality. Let the church be the caravans' oasis. "All or nothing" should no longer be its motto.

252

The first thing to look for is not how far "the others" are from being ideal Christians, but how much good is in them already. We have to ask ourselves "where and how we can find Christ in our brother or sister, be he or she Jew or Gentile, slave or free, white or black, yellow or red, atheist or communist. Now that God has become everyone's brother in Jesus, his church can remain vital and effective only if it binds itself, without discrimination, to all the forms of God's epiphany".[89]

Authoritarianism. There is tremendous emphasis today on obedience to the bishops. There is a tendency to neglect the fact that, before they obey, priests, theologians, religious, and lay persons have the right and duty to exercise their complementary charisms. If they did not, the church would soon become a static and sterile affair. This is all the more urgent in view of the wide chasm often separating competent church authority from those who actually sit at the desks and exercise that authority. Now that administrators have become too busy to keep up their reading and study, it becomes all the more important for them to keep in contact and in dialogue with specialists. But instead of doing so, they often manifest a rather peculiar embarrassment, if not an impolite attitude of superiority.

Anyone who thinks authority is sufficient unto itself is understandably astonished to find others thinking otherwise. Strikingly, in the new Secretariats for the Unity of Christians and for the Non-Christian Religions, one finds specialists; but in the old congregations of the Roman Curia one still finds administrators. Various commissions of specialists were called for by Vatican II and were actually established, but nobody listened to them and they never made any difference. The letter of the council's request was carried out, but not the spirit (see also Part Two, §19). And so it comes about that, instead of being inspired and coordinated by the Curia, theological and pastoral research and experimentation is carried on outside the Curia and often against it.

Legalism. The thrust of conciliar texts has to be translated into concrete living, surely. But was it really necessary for that great, open-hearted *Constitution on the Liturgy* to be constantly whittled away at by one official instruction after another? There is practically no room left for legitimate pluriformity, for the incarnation of the liturgy in various cultures, for the creative action of the Holy Spirit. If all the norms are observed, all signs point to the restoration of a one-rite church.

Instead of addressing itself to the priests who simply read out the printed page Sunday after Sunday from the first sign of the cross to the dismissal, and encouraging them to loosen up a bit, Rome calls on the carpet the ones who take pains to carry out the liturgy in a personal and communicative manner, and orders them to cease and desist, fall back, and march in step with everybody else on all six continents. Rome seems unable to summon the courage to make the leap from Romanism to Catholicism. The principle of the incarnation is acknowledged in theory, but what is actually followed in practice is the old patchwork (Part Three, §9; Part Four, §28). Rome talks about episcopal collegiality, but this turns out to mean mainly bishops' subordination to Rome and not Rome's recognition of bishops' relative independence.

Never in all the history of the church have so many instructions, executive orders, and norms been issued in the name of unity. Everything is regulated to the smallest detail, for the worldwide church. But we live in an emancipated world and an emancipated church — unity can no longer be imposed; it can only be suggested. It cannot be established in repressive uniformity, but only in generous pluriformity. It has very deep roots in the one faith, one Lord, one Spirit. The more you attempt to guarantee it by human means and laws, the greater risk the church runs of falling into a new "Judaizing" phase (see Part One, §24), where laws will pile up and observance of the law will become the measure of fidelity to God.

Time and again — at every opportunity, in fact — we have heard that the church is against divorce, against abortion, against artificial birth control, against homosexuality, and against much else. But today a large proportion of humankind no longer cares what the church says. And the condemnation is scarcely of any help to those who do care and who live in emergency situations. The patient gets no encouragement from the doctor's diagnosis of the disease as serious. What one would hope for from the church more than anything else would be not condemnation, but human understanding and an effort to alter social circumstances. In other words what is needed is pastoral help.

Institutionalism. In Vatican II the church abrogated once and for all the holy alliance of throne and altar. But now it is the church itself that threatens to become a power structure. How mighty are its offices, diocesan and national, in physical plant, in personnel, in tasks, across so many lands! Nowadays everything has to be checked, centralized, controlled. But here is where we observe the distaste and resistance of our contemporaries for everything institutional. It is good for the church to be an institution. Only an institution, not an individual, has the power to stand up to societal pressure, to pronounce social critique. But it is essential that the church be an institution without lordship, with a free following of men and women who understand the institution's decisions and have a part in them.

In spite of all the services rendered by Rome to local churches, the Roman Curia is generally perceived as a burden. It is hard to forget how the Curia was taken by surprise by Pope John XXIII when he convoked Vatican II. One had the feeling that before, during, and after the council the Curia never really came to terms with it. The schemata that were prepared in advance under curial supervision, and under curial theology, were little to the liking of the conciliar fathers and their theologians. When the council finally ended, the Curia, in brilliant, downright cunning fashion, slowly and systematically managed to get everything back in hand and regulated in the spirit of Roman centralism, clericalism, and uniformism.

The reform of the Curia remained one of the council's unfulfilled desiderata. Pope Paul VI, with *Regimini Ecclesiae Universalis*, changed a few names, redistributed a few responsibilities, and did breathe into the system a new spirit; but the system as such remained untouched. Great were the hopes laid on "the pope from faraway Poland", especially when, in November 1979, he convoked all the cardinals and asked them for suggestions on how to improve the Roman Curia's "service" to the bishops and bishops' conferences in terms of collegiality — how "a better balance" could be established between Rome and the local churches.[90] With bated breath we are still waiting for surprises.

Meanwhile the only ones who are satisfied with this church are the ones who prefer the institutional model to the sacramental model, the Word-of-God model, and the community-of-service model. They simply want to obey. They want law and order. By and large they are the older generation, hankering for the good old times.[91]

Sacralism. In the midst of our profane, evil world, we build our sacral, good world. What God has joined together, we put asunder. Why do we so fear secularization? Is secularization not the liberation of religion from the opinions and attitudes decried by the prophets and opposed by Jesus himself (see §23, above)? Did not Jesus teach that God would no longer be adored on this mountain or on that one, in this sanctuary or in that, but in the Spirit and in truth (John 4:23)? Why do we make absolute values of communion in the hand, nuns' habits, eucharistic prayers — "sacristy problems" — and thereby afford so many persons the occasion to measure obedience to the church by these things? We simply hand persons an alibi for not seeing the true problems of the world and the church.

Why are we still peddling medieval feudal titles, dividing the people of the church into the untitled (laity), the venerable (religious), the reverend (priests), the very reverend (religious superiors), Monsignors (which means "milords"), Their Most Reverend Excellencies (bishops), and Their Most Reverend Eminences and Lord Cardinals? This is the Roman Curial style, which the Curia still practises and urges, and it is still imitated in many parts of the church throughout the world. Communists call one another comrade. In some Third World countries the recognized social title for all males except the president is Brother. Instead of being glad of the chance to practise such an evangelical and fraternal custom, bishops and cardinals in these same countries continue to permit themselves to be called Excellency and Eminence! How much longer will this sacralistic, discriminatory, unevangelical speech prevail?

Clericalism. It is almost incredible how high and how low the laity have ranked in the church. In primitive Christianity there was not nearly so much emphasis upon the distinction of offices. Everyone ranked simply as "God's people" (see Part One, §§37-39). But then the term "people" (in Greek, *laos*) gradually began to be used in a belittling sense, and finally in an outright pejorative sense, so that today to be a "layman" in a specialized field means to be someone who understands nothing and has nothing to say. In *Lumen Gentium* Vatican Council II restored the people of God to their original dignity, striking at the antireformist ecclesiology of the hierarchical pyramid. In *Apostolicam Actuositatem* it emphasized that lay persons are not merely the mechanical arm of the hierarchy, but should, on the basis of their baptism and confirmation, develop their own initiatives. The document added that their new consciousness of responsibility in the church is a clear sign of the workings of the Holy Spirit (AA 1-3).

What became of this view? The laity in various countries cooperated, with new hope and full commitment. The church seemed to become more up to date, closer to life, more effective. Lay persons, living in the midst of the world, have an access — barred to clerics — to the problems of Christian living. Then panic gripped the top of the pyramid. The laity had its wings clipped. Now it could no longer fly, and it became disappointed, discouraged, resigned.

In an emergency, when there are not enough priests to go around, lay persons are permitted to perform certain liturgical functions. The discrimination against women is even stronger. Lay theologians and pastoral assistants are suffered but not sought. They are seen more as a danger than as an opportunity. The traditional concept of orders is given no chance to develop new models for this new age of mature and educated lay persons. We freeze in the conservative tradition instead of availing ourselves of the great opportunities of the creative tradition (see above, §8). The devastating dearth of priests in some countries paralyzes the priesthood, and the rejection of the help proffered by the laity paralyzes the laity.

And yet lay persons are 99.9% of the church. They could be a mighty force. They might have the Holy Spirit too! But instead of utilizing this potential, everything is done to prop up the clerical system. It ought to be evident how sorely this system has suffered in the eyes of the faithful, who are no longer willing simply to be served and cared for as "sheep of the flock" or "children of the parish". They are no longer willing to be treated as retarded members of church and society.

This "laiphobia" is but part of a more comprehensive and generalized timidity. The church at present seems to be going through a whole phase of fear, however unevangelical fear may be as an attitude. After its doughty new launching in Vatican II, Peter's bark once more succumbed to fear and cast anchor; or rather, headed for shore, where the buffeted craft's crew could scurry up on *terra firma* and play it safe.

This same fear of seeing the gospel incarnated plagues us in differing cultures and situations. According to the theology of local church, such a church, moving out from a basis in its special situation and charism, can and should carry out pastoral experiments. Then, if these experiments were to be judged successful, they could be adopted by other churches later. But instead all initiative is looked for from the top. Wherever a local church takes any concrete steps to become truly a local church it is called back in bounds in the name of unity. Of course, it is always "the wishes of the local bishops, priests, and laity" that are cited. But no one ever hears how many or how few these persons are, or what were the wishes of all the bishops, priests, and laity together.

Lastly, we are afraid of the new age. The bold outlook of Vatican II in recognizing the signs of the times as the voice of God (GS 4, 11; UR 4; AA 14; PO 9) has not been maintained. Once more the church threatens to settle down in a rigid tradition and allow the new age to go singing on by, just as happened a hundred years ago when the world was lost to the church piece by piece.

The church is a cause of suffering to many within its pale, as well as to many on the outside. Viennese psychotherapist Professor E. Ringel claims that many persons repress their religion and suffer under it because there is nowhere for them to go with their problems where they will feel understood. "For me this is strong evidence that a barricade looms between church authorities and the people." The Gallup Institute speaks in a similar vein of eighty million "unchurched" persons in the United States: sixty percent of them criticize church institutions and see in them an obstacle to living in the church; thirty-two percent admit they would go back to church if they thought there was any hope their problems and doubts would meet with the understanding of priests or communities.[92] After near two thousand years, the church is confronted with a choice: either surrender the burdensome elements of a traditional image or become a flywheel that keeps on spinning without turning anything. The church is missing its chance to arrive in the world of tomorrow. Its "isms" are holding it back and weighing it down, while Jesus and his gospel are winning ever more and more acceptance with humanity. It would be a pity for the church if the kingdom of God keeps happening more and more outside it.[93]

§33 *Recommendations for Proclaiming the Gospel*

The content of our prayer, the object of Christian hope, is the coming of the kingdom of God. Spring's yearly victory over winter can be understood as a symbol of the kingdom of God, and help us into the right mood and disposition. As the poet says, "If winter comes, can spring be far behind?" Now that we have finished with our six unlovely words for unlovely attitudes, we come now to six more beautiful, more attractive words, which can be understood as recommendations for proclaiming the gospel.

Evangelization. By evangelization we mean what we have said above (§§27ff.) — plus today's new emphasis on sacramentalization. There is no question of alternatives, only of synthesis — but even so the centre of gravity càn be shifted. Until now the church's aim, based on its strongly institutional orientation, was to recruit converts and administer baptism — in a word, to swell its ranks. But from now on we must think more of those others, the majority of humanity, whom, for God knows what reasons, we cannot christianize but whom we can evangelize. The enthusiastic and prophetic Anglican John Mott (1865-1955) proclaimed, indefatigably and everywhere, "World evangelization in this generation!"

What we are going to have to strive for is a church among all peoples, a church whose membership is drawn from all peoples — but not necessarily a church *of* all peoples.[94] Islamic and Hindu lands are a good example. In those countries the church cannot always and unconditionally be a catechumenal church, but it can be a witnessing church. It can call all to the kingdom of God, but cannot call all within itself. And indeed, what will advance the cause of that kingdom the more: breaking a few individuals out of their milieu and baptizing them, thus gaining a little direct success but alienating the community, or winning the sympathy of a great number of persons through a simple and unpretentious Christian presence, thereby bringing that milieu as a whole closer to Christ and to the church?[95]

Here a providential role falls to the communications media. Just at the moment when the mass of humanity is swelling from three to six billion in a single generation, so that one-to-one evangelization will no longer work, lo and behold technology bestows upon us the means to reach the masses and give them the gift of the good news. Suddenly we can change the world into a listening room for the gospel. What is needed now, alongside the "bush missioners" who go from hut to hut and village to village, are "media missioners" who scatter the seed over the whole territory, in the conviction that some of it, perhaps much of it, will take root. The administration of the sacraments can be decelerated a little, but evangelization should know no bounds.

It is interesting what Indonesia does in this regard. Each week twenty-five church programs are broadcast by eighty-five radio stations all over the country. And each morning *The Compass*, the nation's largest daily with a circulation of some 270,000, is flown to the thirty largest cities in the country. Both media are "Catholic" in their ownership and production. But their audience is mainly non-Christian, for their content is not just "Catholic" but includes reports and commentaries on politics, economics, culture, human rights, tolerance, fellowship, religion, commitment, and justice. Radio Veritas in Manila does something similar for all Southeast Asia, China, and Japan. An average of seven hundred letters a week come from Japanese listeners, mostly non-Christians.

These Christians are cleverer than we. A survey taken in Switzerland shows that explicitly religious broadcasts reach only one to four percent of television viewers (always the loyal churchgoers, who need them the least).[96] As a rule, this is how overtly "religious" programs will fare. Of course, there can be exceptions in the case of a personality with very special charisma, such as Archbishop Sheen in the United States, or Capuchin Father Mariano in Italy. But generally, in order not to manoeuver oneself into a media ghetto, it will be necessary to package religion with daily questions and human values as is done in Asia.

Spontaneity. Until our day, the church had at its disposition in missionary countries a hierarchically organized apostolic system. There was the bishop, the priest, and the catechist. Catechists were hired by the bishop, or the priest, as his lengthened arm, and they often played the "little king" in the parishes. But this system was replaced, on the parish level, by a group of "ministers" appointed, and paid where engaged for salary, by the parish priest. The actual life of the church no longer unfolds in the big church centres but in the outlying parishes. There, with or without a priest, the community assembles for one to three hours to pray, sing, hear the gospel and a homily, and sing some more. In these same parishes, all week long, catechumens are instructed, the sick are visited, and team action is undertaken to improve the quality of life. Today Christianity spreads spontaneously, through the radiant energy of the Christian parish.

Here we could say much about the phenomenon of the ecclesial *comunidades de base* — "base" or "basic communities" — which saw their first sensational success in Latin America. These "grassroots communities" brought a static, clerical, sacramentalist church into a phase of far-reaching renewal and evangelization. Today they are more or less common on all six continents, operating under the auspices of various international movements or simply through independent parish communities (which, taken together, are also a "movement" — the movement of the Spirit in the church). Here we no longer have a folk Christianity — an organized, often sociologically obtrusive, anonymous, encrusted quantitative unit — but a faith Christianity as a genuine movement, as spontaneous community, as credible witness. Here the Jesus-fact is lived and transmitted with a new confidence.

In the nineteenth century, the demand for universal primary education arose. Colonialism had opened up distant lands, and Spirit-filled men and women founded many religious institutes for the schools and the missions. Today, where lay maturity is in evidence and the questionable nature of certain church institutions is felt, the same Spirit is calling into being the Christian *comunidades de base*, bringing new life to the church and encouraging alternative lifestyles within it. Ronald Knox ended his long book *Enthusiasm* with the words, "The only vice is paralysis. The only virtue is enthusiasm".[97] He is right. Unfortunately, however, these *comunidades de base* are dividing up now into those that "only pray" and those that "only act" in the political arena. Both aspects are essential to the basic Christian attitude and they belong together in the actualization of integral salvation (see above, §§23, 24).

Incarnation. Christ had no fear for his status. He did not hesitate to step down from being equal to God into earthly flesh and take the form of a servant (Phil. 2:7). Nor should the Western church, therefore, fear to incarnate itself courageously on other continents and in other cultures (see above, §28). It took the church a long time to don its Western attire. Now it should accord the same right to other cultures, and not think that Roman raiment is of the essence of the gospel.

The church has become a church on six continents. Each of these continents has its own political, cultural, hence even ecclesial consciousness. But in our present configuration we are tools being used to lay out, over the whole planet, an inexorable uniform complexus of technical, economic, and political laws and structures. Will the result be a uniform culture for the whole planet? What a monstrous impoverishment this could be, and how unworthy of a creative God so rich in ideas and inspiration! And it would be equally unworthy of the creative human being. Hence we must take the contrary tack. The more we must be involved with the furtherance and challenge of a uniform society, the more we have the need and the right to live "contextually" while doing so. We must all be ourselves, and develop our own values. This is what leisure, liturgy, and play are for — not for some kind of apolitical regression, but for the gathering of new strength for the mission to the world.

In this regard we are only on the threshold of the third millennium, the millennium of the Third World and the Third Church, and we shall be seeing some more surprises (soon, we hope) in Latin American, African, and Asian theology, liturgy, and church discipline. Only a generous cultural pluralism can enable the church to transmit anything of the stature and transcendence of Christ, and thereby attain not only geographical but qualitative catholicity.[98]

For some time now there has been intensive discussion of the "Hindu Christians" in India.[99] More and more persons of that land are becoming dissatisfied with Hinduism. They attend Christian schools, but then, because they cannot change their sociological milieu, life becomes harder for them.

Must this be? Paul was altogether a Jew, and remained a Jew; but the new discovery, the new content of his thinking, had become Christ. Why, then, could these Hindus not remain altogether Hindu? Why could they not accept Christ, and gradually the church, without closing themselves up in Christian ghettos? These are our border patrols, and we should keep our doors open for them.

And the case can be reversed. There are Christians — sisters and priests — who not only live in the Hindu-style in simple ashrams, but even spend some time in Hindu monastic communities, like that of Rishikesh. If the Jews, so firmly believing in Yahweh, could esteem and incorporate all the foreign religious values they found[100] (except magic supposedly linked with God), then why could this not be possible today with the Christ-faith?

Oikoumene. We in the church lived through a long era of exclusivism, based on a false understanding of faith in election. Then we went through a relativist phase, induced by a theory of the lowest common denominator fostered by the science of comparative religion. Now we are finally arriving at a solid synthesis of both in ecumenism.

We are using the word ecumenism in its broadest meaning. Catholic *oikoumene* begins deep within the Catholic bosom itself, as contacts multiply and cooperation waxes among the various missionary orders, the indigenous religious orders of women, new movements like Focolari, and so on. All these groups used to live as in so many feudal forts. Today the moat bridges are down and the gates are open. We no longer consider ourselves to be *the* community. Today we know that all true Christians and members of religious orders are equally called to the gospel and to Vatican II, and that all are equally threatened by the same dangers. Openness and *oikoumene* follow of themselves.

Now we must move out from documents to deeds, from high-level dialogue to local praxis. We are already very much on the way. We already share discussion, prayer, and action. Interchurch theological commissions have already dismantled the old controversies piece by piece, and are finding that in certain cases there could be practically one church today. It is up to competent authority to determine when further pastoral steps would be prudent — whether believers are prepared for the unity that is coming. But one cannot escape the radical decision: are the churches to be loyal to the principles of schism, or to the task they have all received in common from Christ (see also Part Two, §§16, 17)?

The parties themselves will have to decide whether to declare a sort of "moratorium" in religious dialogue for a while and concentrate on "low christology" — presenting Jesus as the model for total union with God and total love for human beings — and get around to professing the Christ of dogmas only later. Of course this will only postpone, not solve, the dogmatic problem. Sooner or later the scandal of the cross and of Christianity must come to the fore.[101]

The Our Father is becoming more and more appropriate as the common prayer of all men and women, who all have the same God (see above, §§14, 15). This is especially evident when we recall that Luke's version, probably the original, simply says, "Father, hallowed be thy name" (Luke 11:2), and only later the church inserted the "Our," by way of interpretation. Then, the other way around, it is also meaningful for the church to know "the world's most beautiful prayers" and use them in liturgies or paraliturgies, thus experiencing a bond with the men and women of all continents. A rich selection of books is available as source material.[102]

Last — but far from least — let us realize that the spirit of ecumenism ought to hold sway not only in theological but in economic dialogue. That is, it should govern the North-South dialogue. D.S. Amalorpavadass made an observation to this effect at the Meeting on Ecumenism in Rome in November 1979. He explained that for Third World theologians many questions of scholastic theology are mere fossils of a bygone age. Today's theologians are interested in helping to bring about an intercontinental human and religious community.[103]

Indeed the unity of humankind, rooted in the Yahweh faith and the Christ event (see above, §§13-17), should not be merely a religious question. It should be a question on the level of integral human reality. All men and women, especially all believing men and women, should participate in a cooperative critique of inhumane relationships, and in a united praxis of societal forces toward a change, toward a "new creation". As long as 800 million human beings live in absolute poverty, while 450 billion dollars go for military preparedness and less than five percent of that figure for official aid to development, there is no use in talking about a meaningful world or a human *oikoumene*. The North-South Commission's president, W. Brandt, admitted that the urgency of the current state of affairs struck him only when he was preparing his report on it. L.B. Pearson said essentially the same thing as he was writing the 1969 report on the status of development in poor countries. So did Robert McNamara as he moved from his post as U.S. secretary of defence to that of director of the World Bank. When will all this knowledge become common property, so that it can provide a thrust for the concrete alteration of structures?

"Reverse Mission." This is the expression Americans used when they said that the missions today should no longer be a one-way street. There should be a mutual give-and-take. The missions used to represent the Christian activity of go-teach-baptize-heal in its purest form. It also represented give-and-be-forgiven. For centuries, an enormous investment in money, personnel, and ardour flowed from the Western churches to the missions, basically altering the future of the mission peoples.

Meanwhile two new situations have arisen. Europe has had to come down from its pedestal, and is currently in the throes of a political, economic, and ecclesial crisis (see above, §§2, 3). At the same time non-European cultures and churches are coming into their own, and are establishing their own identity. Today the watchword should be tit for tat, Even Stephen, and the two-way street. Every church has much to give, but it is also in need of much. If a church imagines it has no need of the energy, thrust, and values of other churches, then it really is imagining things. *Koinonia* is born of interchurch assistance, of mutual fruitfulness, stimulation, and enrichment. And it is born not out of diplomacy but out of real interdependence. Missionaries today are no longer mere useful labour at the service of the other churches; they are ambassadors between churches.[104]

Optimism. When we say "optimism" here we do not mean the happy disposition of those who seem always to be able to see the good side of everything — who look at the world through rose-tinted glasses — but who are not taken very seriously by their fellow human beings. We mean a certain attitude of faith, in which one remains confident in spite of everything because one agrees with God that all things are "good, very good" (Gen. 1:21, 31), and because one believes in the Risen Lord who fills world history with its ultimate meaning, though not without the cross. The church, and we within it, must mediate this confidence to the world. Constant talk of crisis paralyzes. Persons finally give up doing what they could and should. The strength and inspiration necessary for every great undertaking come only in a climate of confidence. The prophets' utopian hope — desert and wasteland shouting for joy, bursting forth in bloom, gushing with abundant streams (Isa. 41:18-20, 42:11, 43:20) — will always be just utopia for those who disbelieve that "nothing is impossible with God" (Luke 1:37).

The problem of God can be solved only in an attitude of basic trust (see above, §6). The task of the church is to see to it that human beings can have the prerequisites for such trust. The church is not permitted to leave anyone by the wayside. It is its duty to afford every person the experience of shelter and acceptance, as a child experiences it in the arms of its mother. And who, even among us adults, has no need of that? Even the most gifted artists, musicians, actors, and athletes feel their limits. They too are insecure and need to grow, and hence stand in need of the sympathy of their public and of their coach or trainer. Even "the Greatest", Muhammad Ali, admits in his autobiography how much he owed his friend and manager; without him, Ali said, he would not have become what he became.[105] Even the funniest persons in the world — the clowns, who make everyone else laugh — are, offstage, deeply afflicted. Charlie Chaplin was certainly no exception. Nor was Alighiera Noschese, the king of the mimics, who took his own life in Rome on December 3, 1979, after a long interior struggle. "You come", he once

263

said, "and are entertained. But I am always alone. And it is a torture for me to try to entertain others."

In this world of the disconsolate, the friendless, the discouraged, the sinners, the frustrated, and the hopeful, the church has the high task of facilitating the experience of basic trust — as that "incurable optimist" Pope John XXIII succeeded in doing so well, opening up a new horizon to the journey of the church and of humanity. His words struck root in the hearts of all men and women, even unbelievers, for he saw in them all "the faces of friends, the faces of brothers".[106]

This trust, based on a conviction of faith, can even gain strength from the hard facts of bitter experience. One hears a great deal of loud lament about the church's appearances of decay. But I am of the view (without simply denying the appearances) that the church is significantly better off today than it was thirty years ago. Granted, it had more power, order, and authority then. But today it is more evangelical and credible. In Part Two (§§34-36), in an examination of the exterior aspect of the church, we reviewed historical evidence that the hardened attitude of the church's being "against" everything had suddenly and almost miraculously changed to an attitude of dialogue. Here we might add a sort of geographical argument, with regard to the church in its inward aspect, to show how the church in recent times, amid difficult circumstances, has been able to win much better respect and standing. Let us briefly survey the continents.

Thirty years ago in Latin America, the church formed a part of the feudalistic, capitalist system. Today it has the courage to stand apart from the system and criticize it, to take a stand for justice and human dignity, to stop defending its own privileges and speak out for those who have no voice.

In Africa the church rode the wake of colonialism. As administrator of colonial school systems it was awash in conflict — with teachers, children, parents, and governments. Competition with the other Christian churches was fierce. Today the church is by and large free of the schools, and is working as a leaven in the mass, fostering the ecumenical spirit, and exercising vis-à-vis the governments a moral authority that even the ten Marxist-Leninist states must reckon with.

In Asia, in times gone by, Christian groups lived in frightened little ghetto minorities. Today these same minority groups are developing new dynamics, bringing the religions of their lands into dialogue not only with the church but with one another as well.

Even in the weary old West there are forces of renewal at work— if often more lumberingly than, for instance, in Brazil. And "under the table", in small groups, communities, and movements, often much more is happening than the official church knows about. In the United States, in the Gallup poll to which we have already referred, one-third of

Americans surveyed reported experiencing a "religious rebirth" in recent years.[107]

The church's situation, then, is by no means hopeless as long as we are not hopeless! From this brief world survey we can only agree with the conclusion J. Delumeau draws for France: "The God of the Christians used to be much less alive than he was thought to be, and today he is much less dead than has been reported".[108]

Chapter Twelve

The Peoples

§34 A Christian Worldview

Availing ourselves of the methodologies of the biblical, historical, ethnological, and theological sciences, we have been examining, in all four parts of our book, the theme "chosen peoples". We have focused, surveyed, and ruminated the problem from all angles. The task that remains is that of gathering the most important results of our work into a brief synthesis, a sort of Christian worldview, as far as we honestly can. Interpreting the whole of history from a Christian viewpoint, one can construct the following summary overview.

Even the nomadic groups of men and women who gradually emerged from the shadows of prehistoric times into the light of history, must from the very beginning — wherever science may place that beginning on the evolutionary chart — have been embraced and accepted with love and graciousness by their mysterious God and creator. And this in spite of all the sinfulness that comes packaged with the cloven condition of human nature. We can call this primordial God-humanity relationship the "creation covenant" (Part One, §9). This covenant forms the immovable foundation for meaningful living, and ultimate salvation, for all persons and peoples.

At a relatively quite late point in time — just some 3,200 years ago — Scripture tells us that God revealed himself under the name of Yahweh to the people called Jews. He struck a covenant with them, chose them as his special people, and totally identified himself with their history. Thereby was initiated a movement that would one day lead to the full unity of the one humanity. In this one people a prototype of all the peoples of God was set before the eyes of humanity. In this people it would be seen how very much God loves "his" people; but because God is God, he can never be the national god of just one people, and hence "his people" actually always meant all peoples. Israel would not have a monopoly on him. But Israel would be the vehicle of a historical, visible, and credible model of the great love God has for all peoples (see Part One, §§12-26; Part Four, §§13-14).

Israel's special covenant relationship with God does not of course mean that all its *saving* history was *saved* history. In the first place this people so often proved untrue (prototype yes, model no). Secondly, even a covenant God is accessible only in faith, not in the tangible experience of naked history. God does not give away his ultimate mystery in this historical time. He forces no one with external evidence. He leaves it to each individual to determine whether he or she considers life more meaningful with faith in God or without it.

Unfortunately Israel only half-fulfilled its mission as sign for all peoples. What was not accomplished in the first chosen people must be sought anew in the second people of God, founded on the life, death, and resurrection of Jesus. In this people the narrowed purview of "people" as "nation" will be blasted wide open. Its horizon will broaden to the ends of the earth. Now that first people, so suddenly brought to the foreground as with a zoom lens, had to retreat upstage to the broader background of the world — not to perish in it, but to work as sign, interpreter, and animator, and make all the peoples of the primordial creation covenant aware of the reality of election and acceptance in Jesus Christ (see Part One, §§30-31; Part Two, §§15-21).

But then human patterns of thought overcame God's plan of salvation all over again. Instead of proclaiming this election, this all-embracing love of God, affirmatively for all peoples, God's second people restricted it exclusively to the members of the church. Instead of being for others, this people worked against others. Instead of the comradely unity of all human beings, this people brought ugly schism between those within it and those without, between the ones in the ark and the ones in the flood, between the elect and the reprobate (Part Three).

Today, as our horizons open up in our new times, we belatedly discover that those other peoples, too, always considered themselves God's peoples — and they were! Of course they too were largely confined in the trammels of ethnocentrism and chauvinism, but this is understandable considering the time, for peoples still lived separated from one another (Part Three).

Today we seem to be living in a privileged phase of history. We recognize that all peoples have always had a covenant with "their god", who is the one and only God, and have experienced his leadership and his salvation even when they were not conscious of it in the same way as Israel or the church. In no case can it ever have been God's intention that such "covenants" redound to the detriment of other peoples, as they were interpreted to do in South Africa, for instance, or North America. This was to pervert theology into ideology.

Today the signs of the times show us that, with all his strategies of election and of choosing, God always aimed at only one goal: to make it clear to all peoples, and in regard to all peoples, that he had always loved all of them — that the creation covenant was not abrogated in the later covenants with Abraham, Moses, and Jesus, but confirmed, explicated, and elevated, in order always to work to the weal of all peoples.

267

Today, then, the movement toward unity comes to a kind of conclusion. It began of old when Yahweh revealed himself as the God of this people and at the same time the God of all peoples, and when Jesus Christ entered human history as a unique, unrepeatable event (see Part One, §§25-26; Part Three, §§13-14, 15-17). Today it can be said that a third phase of salvation history has begun, in which one people is no longer singled out to represent the others, but all peoples are discovering that they are a chosen people all together, that they form, in common, the "Third People of God", comprised of all humanity.Now they are all the bearers of God's promises, regardless of whether as individuals they are presently in the church, in one of the other world religions, or living a modern ideology according to their conscience. They are all well-pleasing to God, not on grounds of their own justification but by the divine good pleasure through the grace of Christ. They already live all together within sight of the kingdom of God, and it is the proper task of the church to cry this out to them, to make proclamation of this kingdom (see Part Four, §§19, 33).

Thus our path has led us from the many scattered human groups to the two chosen peoples of the old and the new covenants, and then on to the multiplicity of all chosen peoples, now no longer a disconnected mass of peoples but a "third chosen people", a community of all peoples — a historical, very imperfect but genuine, pledge and anticipation of that eschatological oneness in which, at last, "God will be all in all" (1 Cor. 5:28).[109]

§35 On the Way to a Community of Peoples

But how can such a theological interpretation be reconciled with reality? Do not the facts of our present hour cry out against such an idealistic worldview?

No, despite all the facts, and some of them are very bleak, and even though we surely have not yet achieved the ideal situation we strive for, still we may say that all signs of the times point that way — that we are truly in an altogether new and decisive phase on the way to a community of peoples. For the first time in the long history of the world, the races, religions, and confessions no longer live territorially cut off from one another, ridiculing or scorning one another in their ignorance. They stand in daily contact, in their work, their transportation, their communication. For the first time in the history of the world, all human beings are possessed by the passionate wish to have the same human rights as everyone alse, and one of their most fiery spokespersons, Eldridge Cleaver, cries this oath: "We are going to be human beings! We *are* going to be, or the world will get wiped flat with us trying to be".[110] For the first time in the history of the world, side by side with the vested lords of that world — namely, the fifty-seven founding states of the

United Nations — one hundred and ten new nations have risen up in the last thirty-five years, and now all peoples have taken their places on the modern stage of the world. For the first time in the history of the world, all these peoples come together for political, economic, cultural, and religious dialogues and meetings. For the first time in the history of the world, human beings possess the power to change the earth, to lay bare its secrets above their heads and beneath their feet. Or they have the power to destroy humanity instead.

Characteristically, in his homily on New Year's Day 1980, the day the world began the last step of the second millennium, Pope John Paul II reported that scientists had communicated to him that there were currently 50,000 atom bombs in the world, but that 200 of them would be enough to destroy the largest cities and kill 200 million persons at one blow, turning survival into a torture for the rest by poisoning the environment. For the first time in the history of the world, then, we are faced with these alternatives: either total fellowship or total annihilation, either total East-West reconciliation and total North-South equalization, or war on everyone by everyone. Thus despite all obstacles and difficulties, the world, for the first time in history, is not only *called* to unity but downright *condemned* to it. God *will* lead it to unity, one way or the other. This is biblical theology today.

Pierre Teilhard de Chardin's cherished vision was the "planetization of humanity".[111] What he saw in the offing, based on his study of the history of evolution along with his personal insight, is actually occurring before our very eyes in the history of our present day. We are no longer rocking over the billows in separate boats; we are shooting through space in the same capsule, our planet earth, all of us heading for the same fate as all the rest of us.

Our new situation has brought us to a new level of insight. It took Christians 1,850 years to realize that slavery was not just something to be softened, it was something absolutely to be condemned as irreconcilable with human dignity. It took Europe 1,950 years definitively to renounce, partly by insight and partly under duress, colonialism and hegemony. And it has taken an equal length of time to grasp today's new concept of the world religions, one more consonant with God's plan of salvation, and to start making plans to mobilize all souls in the interest of the equality and oneness of all peoples.

Here we have to recognize the dawning of a new age. We can call it the "World Age". What we have been calling world history are merely three eras of European history — ancient, medieval, modern. It is only now that we stand on the threshold of genuine *world* history. It is a simple fact. And it is a challenge.[112]

The churches and the world religions must read the signs of the times, and motivate persons to a behaviour appropriate to the times. There is no lack of resistance. Exploitation, oppression, crime, terrorism, tribalism, war — all militate against the new thrust to oneness. As persons awaken to maturity and liberty of conscience, they insist more and more on their own rights. As nations multiply, the danger of war multiplies. It has taken long centuries for Western Europe to come to the point where war can no longer be considered possible. The young nations must now be allowed time to reach the same phase. In all the tragic behaviour around us we recognize sin, human history's tragic travelling companion. But the sin of sins, the condemnation and execution of Jesus, is revealed as working to the world's salvation. This is how far the Christian interpretation of history can go!

Thus if the church had nothing meaningful to say about happenings that so often seem meaningless, it would become irrelevant and might as well disappear. The church must insert the euphoric counterpoint of its proclamation into the melancholy world concert. The church must be the prototype, as well as the workshop, of the approaching unity of the human race, and set in motion some models and examples.

Rightly do the churches today speak of "Peace, Development, and Mission" (synodal documents of Germany and Switzerland). The churches have such a longing for unity that they express the thought again and again. The World Council of Churches is even more sensitive to the lack of unity, and has worked through the problematic with greater theological depth than have the individual churches, especially in the World Conference of "Faith and Order" held in Louvain in 1971.[113] The World Council realizes that nothing spurs theological and ecclesial development more effectively than transnational attempts to meet the challenges of the world in concert.[114] We are well justified in saying that what is distinctly Christian lies not so much in creeds or the reception of sacraments as in the way and manner that Christ meets human beings, encounters humanity.[115]

In an effort to be relevant to this need, and coming as he does from a background in ethics, Pope John Paul II adopted the Council's thinking on unity (e.g., LG 1; GS 40; NA 5) from the very beginning, and became the herald not only of the Catholic Church but of the whole human race. Here are only a few of his classic statements. In his homily on the occasion of his installation: "With what awe must one utter the words, 'human being'!" In *Redemptor Hominis*: "The human being is the path of the church" (No. 16). To the United Nations, October 2, 1979: "The proper basis of my presence before this assembly and my addressing it is the human being — all human beings, all peoples of this world".

Humanity is the only community that can match, and surpass, the church in catholicity. But it has no head, no one person to speak in its behalf. Hence it is not arrogance but service when the pope steps into this breach and makes himself the representative of humanity on the road to unity.

The effort toward world unity is to be furthered by every necessary means. But it is not absolutely necessary to erect, side by side with existing structures that are still new, anything like a world government,[116] a superchurch, or a unity religion, as certain authors demand. What is needed is new thinking. What is needed is victory over all parochial, nationalistic, confessionalistic behaviour. What is needed is a readiness to accept one another's every justifiable uniqueness, a readiness to work together, a readiness not merely to be patient with one another (formal tolerance) but to accord one another full recognition (substantial tolerance).[117] What is needed is the conviction that a theology without ideology, the teachings of history, and the path the world has taken today, have all converged on one goal, and are pressing forward toward the openness, breadth, and oneness of all men and women.

The greatest need is for pioneers of unity, heroes of the new humanity, who simply go their way leaving all wooden thinking behind. Once upon a time there was a Francis of Assisi who did that. He walked out of the crusader army in Egypt straight to the sultan — the enemy — without so much as batting an eyelash, and he made a good job of it (see Part Two, §25). So did Egyptian President Anwar Sadat the day he surprised the world with his visit to Jerusalem, November 19, 1977. The road to peace is long, and it is amazing when you see anyone take the first step.[118]

The heroes of our time are no longer the ones whose statues stand in the squares of our capitals. "They served their country", the plaque usually says — which means they conquered other peoples and subjugated other lands in order to build a colonial empire around their own. But in St. Paul's Cathedral in London, among the tombs of the heroes of Waterloo, Trafalgar, and the rest, the heroes of the past, of nationalism — there lies a simple plaque inscribed: "Sir Alexander Fleming". Here was a person who lived a long, hidden life in the labour of a quest. And one day he synthesized penicillin. Penicillin was to save the lives of countless human beings. Alexander Fleming is one of the heroes of the present, one of the heroes of universalism, one of the peacemakers of the beatitudes (Matt. 5:9), who are called the children of God — who do not simply make peace speeches against meaningless wars but who actually hinder war, further life, conduct dialogue, offer hope, build unity.

Woe to humankind if this utopia remains . . . just utopia. A glance at the daily newpaper headline only confirms our anxiety:

"Fifteen percent of East Timor Population Starving: International Food Assistance Siphoned Off by Government."
"Hundreds of Thousands in Hell between Cambodia and Thailand."
"Four Million Political Refugees in Africa."
"Cubans Abandon their Island by Tens of Thousands."

271

"Covert Ties Revealed between Multinationals and Brazil's Repressive System."

"Charta '77 People Sentenced in Prague."

"Thirty Thousand Persons Disappear in Argentina — Liquidated by Government?"

In a world like this it takes courage to believe in utopia. It takes courage to undertake, whether as an ordinary citizen or as a politician, the necessary steps to bring the reality of that utopia a bit closer. Before all else the churches and the religions have to certify their heavenly utopia here on earth first. And they cannot rest satisfied with documents and interpretations. They must get their engines going. Only practical action gives anyone any justification for talking about the meaning of history. God's revelation occurs not in theory, but in the memorial and recollection of his deeds of old and in the corresponding action of our deeds today.

The validity of a christology is seen in its consequences. Only the one who follows Christ doing good, working wonders, criticizing human structures, changing society, trusting in the Father withal — only such a one knows in whom his or her trust has been placed. Through such persons, in spite of everything . . . a better world will become a reality.[119]

It was said of Jules Verne (d. 1905) that he invented the future. And indeed much of what he dreamed of in *Around the World in Eighty Days* and *Journey to the Moon* has become reality. Today we need not so much those who can further develop our doubt-shrouded technological achievements, but those who can charge today's confused circumstances with the fantasy and the energy of their new patterns for a better future, and concretely open up the way for the unification of humankind. The day of that unification is coming ever closer.

We live in the first phase of the World Age. Hence we are still beginners. We still have little experience where global living is concerned. But we shall develop. We shall learn the new lifestyle. Meanwhile, all human beings are bound up together already — for they turn out to be, in spite of their religious or ideological parochialism, citizens of one another's lands.[120] They all live for a dream, a utopia, a promise. They are all chosen men and women caught up in the same web of ultimate mystery. They will reach out their hands to one another and journey on together, coming ever closer to their homeland.

Notes to Part Four

1. See M. Eliade, *The Quest: History and Meaning*, p. 51; Mensching, *Der offene Tempel*, pp. 9-31; Pesch, *Einheit der Kirche*, pp. 10ff.; A. Toffler, *Future Shock* (New York, 1970).

2. Panikkar, *Religionen und die Religion*, pp. 10ff., 169; Mensching, *Buddha und Christus*, pp. 219-34.

3. Rahner, *Mitmenschlichkeit*, pp. 47ff.

4. Ratzinger, *Das neue Volk Gottes*, p. 339; see the whole treatment, "Kein Heil ausserhalb der Kirche?," pp. 339-61.

5. Berger, *Das Unbehaben in der Modernität*, pp. 118-21, 159-61.

6. Köster, *Afrikanisches Christsein*, p. 50.

7. See W. Bühlmann, "Die Bedeutung der Kirche der Dritten Welt für das abendländische Christentum," in Mensen, *Die Begegnung*, pp. 91-106, esp. pp. 92-95, "Die Wachstumskrise des abendländischen Christentums."

8. Wildiers, *Weltbild und Theologie*, pp. 147-292.

9. Toynbee, *Wie stehn wir zur Religion?*, pp. 170-79.

10. Prof. A. Exeler, in an address to the meeting of German-speaking pastoral theologians in Vienna, January 2-5, 1980.

11. Apparently this proportion will also hold in the future: see D. Barrett, "A.D. 2000," *International Review of Mission* (Geneva) 1970:39-54.

12. Mildenberger, *Christentum im Spiegel der Weltreligionen*, p. 16.

13. F. Kollbrunner, "Mission und Religionen bei den deutschsprachigen katholischen Theologen des 19. Jahrhunderts," NZM 1977:145-47; Klinger, *Offenbarung im Horizont der Heilsgeschichte*.

14. D.H. Bishop, "Religious Confrontation. A Case Study: The 1893 Parliament of Religions," *Numen* 16:63-76 (Leiden, 1969).

15. Rahner and Vorgrimmler, *Kleines Konzilskompendium* (Freiburg, 1966), p. 28; see K. Rahner, *Das Konzil - ein neuer Beginn* (Freiburg, 1966).

16. Bühlmann, *Alle haben denselben Gott* (English edition: *All have the same God/The Search for God*).

17. The consequences of the incomplete "enlightenment" were commented on by Father Theobald, O.F.M. Cap., at the the autumn meeting of the Union of Superiors General of religious orders at Villa Cavaletti near Rome. He suggested that if some 40,000 priests and religious have "given up" in the last ten years it is not least of all because they had not been prepared for the cultural, sociological, and theological changes that called everything into question. This is why they could not cope with the changes. Fr . Theobald said. If we see all this in the right light, he went on, if we understand it as God's challenge, we shall be able to react to it positively. Instead of feeling like a besieged fortress being pounded by cannonballs, we can live through this maturity crisis with a new, positive attitude.

18. W. Kasper, "Tradition als Erkenntnisprinzip ," in Haag, *Relevanz der Geschichte*, pp. 198-215; *Glaube und Geschichte* (Mainz, 1970).

19. M. Pomilio, *Il quinto Evangelio*.

20. Zahrnt, *Gott kann nicht sterben*, pp. 107-12.

21. Dulles, *Revelation Theology*, esp. pp. 175-77.

22. H. Fries, "Zum heutigen Stand der Fundamentaltheologie," in Fries, *Glaube und Kirche als Angebot*, pp. 175-71; P. Knauer, *Der Glaube kommt vom Hören*.

23. Rahner, *Glaubenskurs*, pp. 430-40; L. Karrer, *Der Glaube in Kurzformeln*.

24. See: Benoit, P., Rivelazione e ispirazione (Brescia, 1965); Dulles, A., *Revelation Theology* (London, 1970); *Models of the Church* (New York, 1974); Latourelle, R., *Teologia della Rivelazione* (Assisi, 1967); Mann, U., *Theologische Frage. Die*

Entwicklungsphasen des Gottesbewusstseins in der altorientalischen und biblischen Religion (Stuttgart, 1970); Das Christentum als absolute Religion (darmstadt, 3rd ed., 1974); Klinger, E., Offenbarung im Horizont der Heilsgeschichte (Einsiedeln, 1969); ed., Christentum innerhalb und ausserhalb der Kirche (Freiburg, 1976); Oberhammer, G., ed., Offenbarung, geistige Realität des Menschen (Vienna, 1974); Rahner, K., Schriften zur Theologie, 14 vols. (Einsiedeln, 1954-1980) and his other books; Ratzinger, J., Der Gott des Glaubens und der Gott der Philosophen (Munich, 1960); Das neue Volk Gottes. Entwurfe zur Ekklesiologie (Düsseldorf, 1969); ed., Dienst an der Einheit (Düsseldorf, 1978).

[25] H. Küng, Existiert Gott?, pp. 625-29; see his chapter, "Die Herausforderung des Atheismus," pp. 221-380; also V.E. Frankl, Der Mensch auf der Suche nach Sinn (Freiburg, 1972); A. Pauls, ed., Suche nach Sinn - Suche nach Gott (Graz, 1978); J.B. Lotz, Wider den Unsinn: Zinn Sinnkrise unseres Zeitalters (Frankfurt, 1977); Welte, Die Heilsbedürftigkeit des Menschen.

[26] W. Strolz, "Ein judischer Denker der Offenbarung," ORI 1979:247-50.

[27] See H. Cox, The Secular City (New York, 1965) and The Feast of Fools (Cambridge, 1969); H. Zahrnt, Gott kann nicht sterben (Munich, 1970) and Warum ich glaube: Meine Sache mit Gott (Munich, 1977). See also the abundant literature on the experience of God — e.g., the books of J. Zink; M. Legaut; L. Boros; H. Mühlen; D. Sölle, Die Hinreise: Zur religiösen Erfahrung (Stuttgart, 1975), K. Rahner, Schriften zur Theologie, vol. 12 (Theologie aus Erfahrung des Geistes).

[28] Il Giornale dell'anima (Rome, 1964), pp. 330 ff.

[29] Rahner, Über die Schrift-Inspiration; Lohfink, Das Siegeslied, pp. 44-80, "Die Irrtumslosigkeit"; Ishanand Vempeny, Inspiration in the Non-Biblical Scriptures?

[30] L. Volken, Die Offenbarung in der Kirche (Innsbruck, 1965); K. Rahner, Visionen und Prophezeiungen (Freiburg, 1958); A. Bea, "Inspiration," LThK 5:703-11.

[31] F.G. Downing, Has Christianity a Revelation? (Philadelphia, 1966). The question posed in the title is answered in the negative.

[32] G. Moran, Theology of Revelation (New York, 1966); The Present Revelation (New York, 1972), the citation on pp. 228ff.

[33] W. Kasper, "Die Welt als Ort des Evangeliums," in Glaube und Geschichte, pp. 209-23, esp. 215.

[34] Besides the books already mentioned, Revelation in Christianity and Other Religions; P. Rossano, " Y a-t-il une révélation authentique en dehors de la révélation Judéochrétienne?." Bulletin, Secretariatus pro non christianis (Rome) 1968:82-84; Rahner, Grundkurs, pp. 147-65; A. Darlap, "Heilsgeschichte," SM 2:647-56; Kraft, Christianity in Culture, pp. 169-215, 396ff.

[35] For example, the works of Benoit and Latourelle; while K. Rahner, Über die Schrift-Inspiration, p. 85, treats it as self-evident (as early as 1958) that other sacred books can indeed have their character as constitutive of community and as willed by God, as has their prime analogate, the Old Testament.

[36] M. Müller, Leben und Religion (Stuttgart, 1906), p. 159.

[37] Rossano, Il problema teologico delle religioni, p. 32.

[38] See: Tworuschka, U., and Zillessen, D., Thema Weltreligionen. Ein Diskussions- und Arbeitsbuch fur Religionspädagogen und Religionswissenschaftler (Frankfurt, 1977); Klages, G., and Heutger, N., Weltreligionen und Christentum im Gespräch (Hildesheim-New York, 1977). It is significant that newer books on faith present a comparison of Christianity with the other world religions as something that goes without saying, e.g., Küng, Christsein, pp. 81-108; Rahner, Grundkurs, pp. 303-12; Feiner and Vischer, Neues Glaubenbuch, pp. 392-409. Even in introductions to the New Testament today a presentation of the other religions is offered as a meaningful part of the whole orientation; e.g., Il Nuovo Testamento: I quattro Vangeli (Rome, 1978), pp. 14-20, P. Rossano, "Il Vangelo e i messaggi religiosi della storia."

[39] M. Smith, Ancient Near Eastern Texts Related to the Old Testament (1950). Cf. Gottwald, The Tribes of Yahwe, pp. 670-78.

40 H. Urs von Balthasar, in MS 2:42.
41 As sketched by K. Jaros.
42 For example, L. Alonso-Schökel, *Das Alte Testament als literarisches Kunstwekr*; Roest Crollius, *The Word in the Experience of Revelation in Qur'an and Hindu Scriptures.*
43 See further explanations and entries in Bühlmann, *Alle haben denselben Gott*, esp. pp. 193-214 (English edition: *All have the same God/The Search for God*).
44 Labuschagne, *The Incomparability of Yahwe.*
45 H. Mynarek, "Religionen und Utopien der Hoffnung," in Erharter, *Hoffnung für alle*, pp. 36-69.
46 Mbiti, *African Religion*, pp. 18-35, 282; M. Eliade, *La nostalgie des origines; Le mythe de l'éternal retour* (Paris, 1949). Cf. eight interesting treatments by Africans of parallels between the African and the Jewish concepts of God in von Hammerstein, *Christian-Jewish Relations*. See also the elaborations in: *Colloque International de Kinshasa 1978;* Dickson, *Biblical Revelation and African Beliefs;* Parrinder, *Le Upanishad e la Bibbia.*
47 Von Rad, *Theologie* 2:341.
48 P. Knauer, "Das Verhältnis des Neuen Testamentes zum Alten als historisches Paradigma für das Verhältnis der christlichen Botschaft zu andern Religionen und Weltanschauungen," in Oberhammer, *Offenbarung*, pp. 153-70.
49 Klostermaier, *Hinduismus*, p. 307; H. von Campenhausen, *Aus der Frühzeit des Christentums* (Tübingen, 1963), pp. 152-96, "Das Alte Testament als Bibel der Kirche."
50 Further elaborated in Bühlmann, *Alle haben denselben Gott*, pp. 99-115 (English edition: *All have the same God/The Search for God*).
51 A. Alt, "Der Gott der väter," in *Kleine Schriften zur Geschichte des Volkes Israel*, vol. 1 (Munich, 1953), pp. 1-78; de Meuter, *Your God is My God*; Rattray, *Ashanti* (Oxford, 1969), pp. 139-44 (Rattray in convinced that the supreme deity of the Ashanti is identical with the Yahweh of the Israelites); Brosnan, *The Gospel to the Birom*, pp. 155-212, 239-70, is also of the opinion that one could present Dagwi and Yahweh as interchangeable, thereby avoiding a total alienation from the old religion as part of the process of conversion to Christianity. On the whole matter see Bühlmann, *Die christliche Terminologie als missionsmethodisches Problem* (Schöneck, 1950), pp. 124-51.
52 The theological basis is expressed in Kasper, *Absolutheit des Christentums*; Dupuis, *Jesus Christ and His Spirit*; Panikkar, *The Unknown Christ of Hinduism*; Schumann, *Der Christus der Muslime*; Amalorpavadass, *Théologie du Tiers-Monde*, pp. 212-32; S. Regli, "Überlegungen zum Absolutheitsanspruch des Christentums," in *Wissenschaft und Weisheit* (Mönchengladbach, 1977), pp. 100-124; R. Latourelle, "La spécificité de la révélation chrétienne," in *Revelation in Christianity*, pp. 41-74; K. Rahner, "Jesus Christus in den nichtchristlichen Religionen," in *Schriften* 12:370-83; D. Wiederkehr, "Jesus Christus als die Erfüllung der Religionen," in Paus, *Jesus Christus und die Religionen*, pp. 161-90. See also what we have already said about the grace of Christ in connection with the creation covenant (Part One, §9), and the literature there cited; likewise the presentation of Jesus in Part One, §§27-32, and the literature there.
53 As in the congress held in Bangalore, 1974. See Bühlmann, *Alle haben denselben Gott*, pp. 104ff. (English edition: *All have the same God/The Search for God*).
54 See the lengthier treatments by Bühlmann, *Wo der Glaube lebt*, pp. 181-94 (English edition: *The Coming of the Third Church*); *Alle haben denselben Gott*, 197-205 (English edition: *All have the same God/The Search for God*); with the literature cited there, especially Rahner, Heilsbetz, Schlette, Feiner.
55 H. Urs von Balthasar, "Eschatologie," in J. Feiner, ed., *Fragen der Theologie heute* (Einsiedeln, 1960), pp. 403-22, esp. 413ff.; Rahner, Grundkurs, pp. 418-21; "Heilswille Gottes, allgemeiner," SM 2:656-64. In this connection see the fine treatment by Couto, *Hoffnung im Unglauben.*

[56] Lombardi, *Chiesa e Regno di Dio*; H. Fries, "Reich Gottes," LThK 8:1115-20; Schnackenburg, *Gottes Herrschaft und Reich.*

[57] Puebla, *Die Evangelisierung Lateinamerikas.* Unfortunately, neither the numbering nor the translation matches in the various non-Spanish versions of the Puebla documents. Our text corresponds to Nos. 226-31 of the German edition.(Ed. note: cf also Nos. 226-31 of the official English edition: *Puebla,* St Paul Publications, Slough, 1980.)

[58] See Küng, *Christsein,* pp. 109-57; H. Urs von Balthasar, *Glaubhaft ist nur die Liebe* (Einsiedeln, 1963).

[59] J. Fuchs, "Gibt es eine spezifisch christliche Moral?," *Stimmen der Zeit* 1970:99-112; Demmer, *Christlich glauben und handeln,* esp. pp. 31-54 (A. Auer, "Die Autonomie des Sittlichen nach Thomas von Aquin"), 55-57 (D. Mongillo, "Theonomie und Autonomie des Menschen ohne Gott"); Böckle, *Fundamentalmoral,* pp. 48-92.

[60] See, e.g., *Karte der Religionen und Missionen der Erde* (Stuttgart-Bern, 1960).

[61] Karrer, *Das Religiöse in der Menschheit,* p. 245.

[62] AAS 1962:793; 1964:650ff.

[63] Having seven sacraments is no guarantee of nearness to Christ either. D. Wiederkehr speaks of the pathological situation that is expressed in a belief without sacraments and in a sacramentality devoid of faith: "Der ganzheitliche Glaubensvollzug als Legitimation und Kritik der institutionellen Sacraments," in Klinger, *Christentum innerhalb und ausserhalb der Kirche,* pp. 212-31.

[64] K. Rahner, " Perspektiven für die Zukunft der Kirche," *Schriften* 9:541-57; W. Bühlmann, "La risurrezione di Gesù e il futuro della Chiesa," in Bühlmann, *Coraggio, Chiesa,* pp. 11-18 (English edition: *Forward, Church!,* St Paul Publications, Slough/*Courage Church,* Orbis Books. Maryknoll N.Y.); "Kirche der Zukunft," in Bühlmann, *Wo der Glaube lebt,* pp. 303-13 (English edition: *The Coming of the Third Church*); Schatz, *Hat Religion Zukunft?*

[65] Toynbee, "Die Zukunft der Religion," in Schatz, *Hat Religion Zukunft?,* pp. 20-45.

[66] See the books by Mühlen, *Entsakralisierung*; Cox, *The Secular City*; Baum, *God in Secular Experience*; Casiraghi, *Le nuove società.*

[67] Brown, *The Ecumenical Revolution,* pp. 396-413, "Secular Ecumenism — the Ecumenical Future."

[68] M. de Certeau and J.M. Domenach, *Le christianisme éclaté*(Paris, 1974).

[69] On the whole question see P. Bigo. *The Church and the Third World Revolution* (Maryknoll, 1978); H. Assmann, *Practical Theology of Liberation* (London, 1975); M. Bourdeaux, *The Fourth World:* Internationale Theologenkommission, *Theologie der Befreiung* (Einsiedeln, 1977); Gutierrez, *A Theology of Liberation*; Metz, *Glaube in Geschichte und Gesellschaft.*

[70] Rennstich, *Mission und wirtschaftliche Entwicklung,* pp. 260-65; *Théologies du Tiers-Monde.*

[71] See Bühlmann, *Alle haben denselben Gott,* pp. 69-80 (English edition: *All have the same God/The Search for God*).

[72] D. Meadows, *Die Grenzen des Wachstums* (Stuttgart, 1972); J.W. Botkin, ed., *No Limits to Learning: Bridging the Human Gap* (Pergamon Press, 1979).

[73] H. Gruhl, *Ein Planet wird geplündert*; G. Altner, *Sind wir noch zu reich? Schöpfungsglaube und Verantwortung für unsere Erde* (Regensburg, 1978); O.H. Steck, *Welt und Umwelt: Biblische Konfrontationen* (Stuttgart, 1978).

[74] Tévoédjiré, *La pauvreté, richesse des peuples.* Other books along the same lines: Fromm, *Haben oder Sein?*; Ancel, *Pauvreté de l'Eglise en l'an 2000*; Neal, *A Socio-Theology of Letting Go*; Sider, *Rich Christians in an Age of Hunger*; P. Lippert, *Wer sein Leben retten will: Selbstverwirklichung und Askese in einer bedrohten Welt* (Mainz, 1978); J. Moltmann, *Neuer Lebensstil* (Munich, 1977); J. Galtung, *Die tägliche Revolution: Möglichkeiten des alternativen Lebens* (Frankfurt, 1979);U. Krolzik, *Umweltkrise - Folge des Christentums?* (Stuttgart, 1979); Missionsprokura der Franziskaner, Franziskus und der neue Materialismus: Eine franziskanische

Antwort auf die Umweltkrise (Bonn, 1980).

75 A. Darlap, *"Heilsgeschichte,"* SM 2:647-56, esp. 655. See K. Rahner, "Anonymes Christentum und Missionsauftrag der Kirche," *Schriften* 9:498-515; O. Kohler, "Missionsbefehl und Missionsgeschichte," in *Gott in Welt: Festschrift K. Rahner* 2:346-71; likewise the grounds of the missionary nature of the church as expressed in the whole first chapter of *Ad Gentes*, and in Nos. 16-17 of *Lumen Gentium*.

76 A. Dulles, *Models of the Church;* I.X. Irudayaraj, "From the 'Fulfilment View' to the 'Sacramental Approach,' " *Jeevadhara* 1:200-211 (Alleppey, 1971); A. Pierris, in *Dialog* 22 (Colombo, October 1970).

77 See E. Schillebeeckx, *Intelligenza della fede: interpretazione e critica 1*(Rome, 1976). P. Tillich, *Die religiöse Deutung der Gegenwart* (Stuttgart, 1968).

78 See W. Bühlmann, "Missionstheologie vom Vaticanum II zu Evangelii nuntiandi," in Bühlmann, *Ein Missionsorden fragt nach seiner Zukunft,* pp. 39-62.

79 J. Ratzinger, "Stellvertretung," in *Handbuch theologischer Grundbegriffe,* vol. 2 (Munich, 1963), pp. 566-75; N. Klaes, *Stellvertretung und Mission* (Essen, 1968).

80 Bühlmann, *Wo der Glaube lebt,* pp. 117-22 (English edition: *The Coming of the Third Church*); F. Kollbrunner, "Kirchenwachstum — ein vernachlässigtes Ziel!," in Waldenfels, *Festschrift Glazik,* pp. 111-21; E.C. Pentecost, *Reaching the Unreached;* D.A. McGravran, *Understanding Church Growth* (Grand Rapids, 1970).

81 Bühlmann, ibid., pp. 28-33.

82 *La France, pays de Mission?* (Lyons, 1943).

83 "Theologische Bedeutung der Position des Christen in der modernen Welt," in K. Rahner, *Sendung und Gnade,* pp. 13-47; *Strukturwandel der Kirche als Aufgabe und Chance* (Freiburg, 1973), vol. 3, pp. 21-48.

84 OR, Dec. 21, 1978. See J. Glazik, "Zum Thema 'Mission in sechs Kontinenten,' " in *Ordensnachrichten* (Vienna, 1976), pp. 240-49.

85 L. Bertsch and F. Schlösser, eds., *Kirchliche und nichtkirchliche Religiosität* (Freiburg, 1978); Zulehner, *Religion ohne Kirche? Kirchlich Distanzierte* (a special edition of the periodical *Kirche in Wien* [Vienna, March, 1979]); "Entkirchlichung in der Grossstadt: München Statistik 1974," HK, Sept., 1975, pp. 428-30; K. Forster, ed., *Religiös ohne Kirche?* (Mainz, 1977); Daniel, *Aux frontières de l'Eglise;* Höffner, *Pastoral der Kirchenfremden.*

86 W. Bühlmann, "Evangelisierung der kirchlich Distanzierten: Modelle aus den U.S.A.," *Diakonia* (Vienna, 1980) pp. 210-12; The National Council of Churches of the U.S.A., *The Unchurched American,* by the *Princeton Religion Research Centre and The Gallup Organization* (Princeton, 1978); J. Russel Hale, *Who Are the Unchurched?* (Washington, D.C., 1977); J.W. Carroll, ed., *Religion in America, 1950 to the Present* (New York, 1979); D. Bohr, *Evangelization in America* (New York, 1977).

87 H. Rzepkowski, "Deutsche Missionare," in *Missio pastoral* (Aachen, 1980), pp. 33-39.

88 These thoughts are further elaborated in Bühlmann, *Ein Missionsorden fragt nach seiner Zukunft.*

89 Fmeis, *Lernprozess im Glauben,* p. 182. See J. Moltmann, *The Open Church: Invitation to a Messianic Lifestyle* (London, 1978).

90 OR, Nov. 10, 1979.

91 Dulles, *Models of the Church,* pp. 31-42; Hasenhüttl, *Herrschaftsfreie Kirche,* pp. 75ff., 116-25; *Concilium* (1979), No. 7 ("Römische Kurie und Gemeinschaft der Kirche"); cf. what I wrote about the Roman Curia some years ago: Bühlmann, *Wo der Glaube lebt,* pp. 144-60 (English edition: *The Coming of the Third Church*).

92 E. Ringel,"Religion und Neurose," HK 1978:174-82; Bühlmann, as in note 86, above.

93 See Légaut, *Meine Erfahrung mit dem Glauben,* pp. 61-95; *Der alte Glaube und die neue Kirche;* Hebga, *Emancipation d'Eglises;* Bruzzichelli, *Quale Chiesa?;* Singleton, *Let My People Go;* D. Tracy, ed., *Towards Vatican III;* Puyo, *Voyage à l'intérieur de l'Eglise.*

94 K. Stendahl, "Auf dem Wege zu einer die Welt umfassenden Gemeinschaft," in Hammerstein, *Von Vorurteilen zum Verständnis,* pp. 72-75. We touch these points

about evangelization only briefly, as they are further elaborated in my *Wo der Glaube lebt* (English edition: *The Coming of the Third Church*).

95 So thought Bishop Patrick D'Souza, and expressed himself to this effect at the mission congress in Manila in 1979 (*SEDIS-Bulletin*[Rome], March 1, 1980). Bishop H. Teissier of Oran spoke in the same vein: see "Chrétiens et non chrétiens, accueillir ensemble le règne de Dieu," *Spiritus* 75:165-80. Also note the excellent attitude of the bishops of North Africa toward the relationship of the church to non-Christians: "Chrétiens en Mahgreb," *Documentation Catholique*, Dec. 2, 1979, pp. 1032-44.

96 E. Koller, *Religion imn Fernsehen: Christliche Weltdeutung zwischen Programmauftrag, Verkundigungsanspruch und Publikumserfolg* (Zurich, 1978); W. Daniels, "Kirchliche Rundfunkarbeit in Indonesien," KM 1979:123-26; Bühlmann, *Alle haben denselben Gott*, pp. 133ff., 173ff. (English edition: *All have the same God / The Search for God*).

97 R.A. Knox, *Enthusiasm: A Chapter in the History of Religion* (Oxford, 1962). Cf. *Una Chiesa che nasce dal popolo* (Quaderni ASAL, Rome, 1975); L. Boff, *Ecclesiogenesi: Le comunità di base reinventano la Chiesa* (Rome, 1978); B. Clark, *Building Christian Communities: Strategy for Renewing the Church* (Notre Dame, Indiana, 1975); G. Hartmann, *Christliche Basisgruppen und ihre befreiende Praxis* (Mainz, 1980).

98 N. Kehl, "Kulturpluralismus und Verkündigung in biblischer Sicht," in *Ordensnachrichten* (Vienna, 1974), pp. 376-89; A. Roest-Crollius, "What Is So New About Inculturation?," *Gregorianum* (Rome, 1978), pp. 721-38; Köster, *Afrikanisches Christsein*; Shorter, *African Christian Theology*; Y. Congar, "Die Katholizität der Kirche," MS 4/1:478-502, esp. 480-87.

99 R. Panikkar,"Rtatattva: A Preface to a Hindu-Christian Theology," JEE, Jan-Feb. 1979, pp. 6-63, esp. 27; H. Staffner, *The Open Door*; Vandana, *Gurus, Asharams and Christians*.

100 See § 10, above; No. 10; also K. Jaros, *Geschichte und Vermächtnis des Königreiches Israel* (Bern, 1979), p. 108.

101 See D. Wiederkehr, in Paus, *Jesus Christus und die Religionen*, pp. 189ff.

102 C. Einiger, *Die schönsten Gebete der Welt*, 6 vols. (Munich, 1976); M. Maglione, *Le più belle preghiere del mondo* (Milan, 1978); R. Boccassino, *La preghiera*, 3 vols. (Rome, 1967); A.M. Di Nola, *La preghiera dell'uomo* (Parma, 1963); T. Ohm, *Die Gebetsgebärden der Völker und das Christentum* (Leiden, 1948); J.S. Mbiti, *The Prayers of African Religion* (London, 1975); K. Cragg, *Alive to God: Muslim and Christian Prayer* (London, 1970); A. Shorter, *Prayer in the Religious Traditions of Africa* (Nairobi, 1975); O. Bischofberger and F. Kollbrunner, *Mit afrikanischen Christen beten* (Lucerne, 1978); A. Schimmel, *Denn dein ist das Reich: Gebete aus dem Islam* (Freiburg, 1977); W. Lindenberg, *Die Menschheit betet* (Munich, 1956); I. Puthiadam and M. Kampchen, *Endlos ist die Zeit in deinen Händen: Mit den Hindus beten* (Kevelaer, 1978); G. Dieterlen, *Textes sacrés d'Afrique Noire* (Gallimard, 1965); P. Kochanek, *Gebete aus sechs Kontinenten für das Kirchenjahr* (St. Augustin, 1980).

103 See the report of G. Evers in KM 1980:49.

104 W. Bühlmann, "Die Bedeutung der Kirche der Dritten Welt für das abendländische Christentum," in Mensen, *Die Begegnung des abendländischen Christentums mit andern Völkern und Kulturen*, pp. 91-106; "Missionarische Bewusstseinsbildung für morgen," in *Ordenskorrespondenz* (Cologne, 1976), pp. 3-15; Bertsch and Schlösser, *Evangelisation: Modelle aus der Dritten Welt* (1980).

105 Muhammed Ali, *Der Grösste: Meine Geschichte* (Munich, 1977).

106 Capovilla, *Decimo anniversario*, pp. 36, 38, 49.

107 Bühlmann, as in note 86, above.

108 "Le Dieu des chrétiens était autrefois beaucoup moins vivant qu'on ne l'a cru, et il est aujourd'hui beaucoup moins mort qu'on ne le dit" (Delumeau, *Le christianisme va-t-il mourir?*, p. 149).

109 Here we have to express our thanks to Karl Rahner, who in his Christian anthropology laid the courageous and pioneering groundwork for an interpretation of the world that

is so acceptable today: K. Rahner, "Volk Gottes," SM 4:1196-1200; K.P. Fischer, *Der Mensch als Geheimnis: Die Anthropologie von K. Rahner;* G. Richard-Molard, *Le troisième peuple - héraut d'espérence* (Paris, 1977).

110 E. Cleaver, *Seele auf Eis* (Munich, 1969): our citation is from the book's back cover. Cf. F. Houtart, *Der dritte Weltkrieg hat begonnen* (Fribourg, 1972).

111 P. Teilhard de Chardin, *Der Mensch im Kosmos* (Munich, 1959), p. 245; *Die Zukunft des Menschen* (Oelten, 1963), p. 387.

112 It is on good grounds that modern world histories such as *Historia Mundi* (Bern, 1952-61) and *Saeculum Weltgeschichte* (Freiburg, 1965-71), clearly renounce the Europocentric view.

113 Consiglio Ecumenico delle Chiese, *Unità della Chiea e unità del genere umano.* Cf. Nelson and Pannenberg, *Um Einheit und Heil der Menschheit;* Ratzinger, *Dienst an der Einheit;* Mussner, *Christus, das All und die Kirche;* Ledergerber, *Geburt der Menschheit;* Pesch, *Einheit der Kirche - Einheit der Welt;* Blaser and Wolf, *Zum Thema: eine Kirche - eine Welt;* A. Auer, "Kirche und Welt," in Holböck and Sartory, *Mysterium Kirche* 2:479-570; K. Rahner, "Einheit der Menschheit," LThK 3:756ff.

114 Pesch, *Einheit,* p. 154, the final sentence.

115 "Vielleicht liegt mehr als in allen Bekenntnisformeln und Glaubenssätzen das unterscheidend Christliche in der Art, wie der Christ dem Bösen begegnet" ("Perhaps what is distinctively Christian lies, more than in all the confessional formulas and statements of the faith, in the manner in which the Christian confronts evil") — H. Haag, *Vor dem Bösen ratlos?* (Munich, 1978), p. 275 (his last sentence, as well).

116 Gruhl, *Ein Planet wird geplündert,* pp. 298-305, holds for the necessity of a world government. So does Deutsch, *Nationalism,* pp. 167-90, for overcoming world problems such as nuclear armament, feeding the world, etc. Toynbee, *Menscheit - woher, wohin?,* esp. pp. 130-50, pleads for a world state, and develops this idea in some of his other books. Pope John XXIII, too, seems to postulate such a world authority in the fourth part of *Pacem in Terris* (1963).

117 See the corresponding elaborations of Mensching, *Der offene Tempel,* pp. 249-53; *Buddha,* pp. 240-44. Cf. also LThK 10:239-46.

118 How altogether different the manner of speaking of the Ayatollah Khomeini sounds, as he cried out on Nov. 27, 1979, "We must assemble twenty million persons and train them so that each one can use a weapon. We Muslims are a billion persons! We must annihilate all our enemies! Our might rests on God and on Islam!"

119 Metz, *Glaube in Gescichte,* pp. 47-57, 136-48.

120 See Friedli, *Fremdheit als Heimat.*

Analytical Index

Bibliography

Des africanistes russes parlent de l'Afrique. Paris: Présence Africaine, 1960.

Alonso-Schökel, Luis. *Das Alte Testament als literarisches Kunstwerk.* Cologne: J. P. Bachem, 1971.

Altner, G. *Sind wir noch zu retten? Schöpfungsglaube und Verantwortung für unsere Erde.* Regensburg: 1978.

Amalorpavadass, D. S., ed. *Research Seminar on Non-Biblical Scriptures.* Bangalore: 1975.

Amery, C. *Das Ende der Vorsehung: Die gnadenlosen Folgen des Christentums.* Hamburg: 1972.

Amstutz, Josef. *Kirche der Völker: Skizze einer Theorie der Mission.* Freiburg i.B.: Herder, 1972.

Ancel, Alfred. *Pauvreté de l'Eglise en l'an 2000.* Paris: du Jour, 1973.

Ancilli, E., ed. *La mistica non cristiana.* Brescia: 1969.

Anderson, Bernhard W. *The Living Word of the Old Testament.* London: Longmans, 1971.

Anderson, James N.D. *Jesus, Krishna, Mohammed: Christentum und Welt-religionen in der Auseinandersetzung.* Wuppertal: 1972.

Antes, P.; Ruch, W.; and Uhde, B. *Islam, Hinduismus, Buddhismus: Eine Herausforderung des Christentums.* Mainz: M. Grünewald, 1973.

Aquarone, A., and Vernassa, M. *Il regime fascista.* Bologna: 1974.

Aurelius Augustinus. *Der Gottesstaat.* Salzburg: 1951/53. In English: St. Augustine. *The City of God.* Gretna, La.: Penguin, 1972.

Babel, Henry. *Le secret des grandes religions.* Neuchâtel: La Baconnière, 1975.

Balchand, A. *The Salvific Value of Non-Christian Religions according to Asian Christian Theologians.* Manila: East Asian Pastoral Institute, 1973.

Barlage, H. *Christ—Saviour of Mankind: A Christian Appreciation of Swami Akhilananda.* St. Augustin: 1977.

Barrett, David A. *Schism and Renewal in Africa: An Analysis of Six Thousand Contemporary Religious Movements.* London: Oxford University, 1968.

Baudis, A., ed. *Richte unsere Füsse auf den Weg des Friedens.* Festschrift for H. Gollwitzer. Munich: Kaiser, 1979.

Baum, Gregory. *Man Becoming: God in Secular Experience.* New York: Herder & Herder, 1970.

―――. *Religion and Alienation: A Theological Reading of Sociology.* New York: Paulist, 1975.

Baumann, Hermann. *Schöpfung und Urzeit des Menschen im Mythus der afrikanischen Völker.* Berlin: 1936.

Bäumer, R., and Dolch, H., eds. *Volk Gottes: Zum Kirchenverstädnis der katholischen, evangelischen und anglikanischen Theologie. Festschrift J. Hofer.* Freiburg i.B.: 1967.

Beaver, Robert P. *The Gospel and Frontier Peoples.* South Pasadena, Calif.: William Carey Library, 1973.

Beckmann, Klaus M., ed. *Rasse: Kirche und Humanum.* Gütersloh: Gütersloher Verlaghaus G. Mohn, 1969.

Beltz, Walter. *Gott und Götter: Biblische Mythologie.* Berlin: Aufbau, 1975.

Benoit, P. *Rivelazione e ispirazione.* Brescia: 1965.

Benz, Ernst, and Nambara, M. *Das Christentum und die nichtchristlichen Religionen: Begegnung und Ausseinandersetzung: Eine inter-nationale Bibliographie.* Leiden: 1960.

Berger, Peter L. *Das Unbehagen in der Modernitat*. Frankfurt a.M.: 1975. In English: *Facing Up to Modernity: Excursions in Society, Politics, and Religion*. New York: Basic Books, 1979.

Bertsch, L., and Schlösser, F., eds. *Kirchliche und nichtkirchliche Religiosität*. Freiburg i.B.: 1978.

Bettscheider, Heribert, ed. *Das Problem einer afrikanischen Theologie*. St. Augustin: Steyler, 1978.

Beumann, Helmut, ed. *Heidenmission und Kreuzzugspolitik in der deutschen Ostpolitik des Mittelalters*. Darmstadt: Wissenschaftliche Buchgesellschaft, 1963.

Beyna, Werner. *Das moderne katholische Lutherbild*. Essen: Ludgerus, 1969.

Bihalji-Merin O., ed. *Brücken der Welt*. Lucerne: J. Bucher, 1971.

Bitterli, Urs. *Die Entdeckung des schwarzen Afrikaners: Versuch einer Geistesgeschichte der europäisch-afrikanischen Beziehungen*. Zurich: Atlantis, 1970.

————. *Die "Wilden" und die "Zivilisierten": Grundzüge einer Geistes- und Kulturgeschichte der europäischen und überseeischen Begegnungen*. Munich: Beck, 1976.

Bläser, P., ed. *Zum Thema: Eine Kirche—Eine Menschheit*. Stuttgart: 1971. A response to: Consiglio Ecumenico delle Chiese, *Unità della Chiesa e unità del genere umano*. Bologna: 1972.

Bleeker, Claus J. *Christ in Modern Athens: The Confrontation of Christianity with Modern Culture and the Non-Christian Religions*. London: A. R. Mowbray, 1966.

————, and Widengren, George. *Historia Religionum: Handbook for the History of Religions*. Leiden: E. J. Brill, 1969–71.

Bluhm, William T. *Ideologies and Attitudes: Modern Political Culture*. Englewood Cliffs, N.J.: Prentice-Hall, 1974.

Böckle, Franz. *Fundamentalmoral*. Munich: Kösel, 1977. In English: *Fundamental Moral Theology*. New York: Pueblo, 1980.

Böhm, A., ed. *Häresien der Zeit*. Freiburg i.B.: 1961.

Borne, G. F. *Christlicher Atheismus und radikales Christentum*. Munich: 1979.

Botkin, James W., ed. *No Limits to Learning: A Report of the Club of Rome*. New York: Pergamon, 1979.

Braden, Charles S. *Religious Aspects of the Conquest of Mexico*. Durham: Duke University, 1930.

————. *Les livres sacrés de l'humanité*. Paris: 1955.

Bright, John. *Geschichte Israels*. Düsseldorf: 1966. In English: *A History of Israel*. Philadelphia: Westminster, 1972.

Brosnan, T. G. D. *The Gospel to the Biron: The Other Chosen People*. Rome: Univ. Lateranensis, 1976.

Brown, David A. *A Guide to Religions*. London: S.P.C.K., 1975.

Brown, Robert McAfee. *The Ecumenical Revolution*. New York: Doubleday, 1969.

Bruegemann, Walter. *The Land*. Philadelphia: Fortress, 1977.

Bruzzichelli, ed. *Quale Chiesa?* Assisi: Cittadella, 1970.

Bsteh, A., ed. *Universales Christentum angesichts einer pluralistischen Welt*. Mödling: St. Gabriel, 1976.

————. *Der Gott des Christentums und des Islams*. Mödling: Verlag St. Gabriel, 1978.

Bühlmann, Walbert. *Kirche unter den Völkern: Afrika*. Mainz: M. Grünewald, 1963.

————. *Missionsprozess in Addis Abeba*. Frankfurt a.M.: Knecht, 1977. In English: *The Missions on Trial: Addis Ababa 1980*. Maryknoll, N.Y.: Orbis, 1979.

————. *Alle haben denselben Gott*. Frankfurt a.M.: Knecht, 1978. In English: *The Search for God*. Maryknoll, N.Y.: Orbis, 1980.

————. *Wo der Glaube lebt: Einblicke in die Lage der Weltkirche*. 7th ed. Freiburg i.B.: Herder, 1979.

————, ed. *Ein Missionsorden fragt nach seiner Zukunft*. Münsterschwarzach, 1979. *(Un Ordine missionario si interroga sul sui avvenire*. Bologna: 1979).

Buijtenhuijs, Robert. *Le mouvement "Mau Mau."* La Haye–Paris: Mouton, 1971.

Bultmann, Rudolf. *Das Urchristentum im Rahmen der antiken Religionen.* 3rd ed. Zurich: Artemis, 1963.

Buonaiuti, E. *Pellegrino a Roma: La generazione dell'esodo.* Bari: 1964.

Bürkle, Horst. *Einführung in die Theologie der Religionen.* Darmstadt: Wissenschaftliche Buchgesellschaft, 1977.

Butturini, G., ed. *Le nuove vie del Vangelo: I vescovi africani parlano a tutta la Chiesa.* Bologna: EMI, 1975.

von Campenhausen, Hans. *Aus der Frühzeit des Christentums.* Tübingen: Mohr, 1963.

Camps, A. *Geen doodlopende weg: Lokale kerken in dialog met hun omgeving.* Baarn: 1978.

Capovilla, L. F. *Decimo anniversario della morte di Papa Giovanni.* Rome: 1973.

Caprile, Giovanni. *Il Concilio Vaticano II.* 2 vols. Rome: 1968.

Casiraghi, G. *Le nuove società afroasiatiche: secolarizzazione e sviluppo.* Bologna: 1973.

CELAM. *Puebla. Die Evangelisierung Lateinamerikas in Gegenwart und Zukunft.* Bonn: 1979. In English in: *Puebla and Beyond,* edited by John Eagleson and Philip J. Scharper. Maryknoll, N.Y.: Orbis, 1979.

Châtelet, F., and Mairet, G., eds. *Storia delle ideologie.* 2 vols. Milan: 1978.

Chenu, B. *Dieu est noir: Histoire, religion et théologie des Noirs américains.* Paris: Centurion, 1977.

Clark, Dennis E. *Jesus the Messiah (for Muslims)* Elgin, Ill.: Dove, 1979.

Colloque de Cotonou: Les religions africaines comme source de valeurs de civilisation. Paris: Présence Africaine, 1972.

Colloque International de Kinshasa 1978: Réligions africaines et christianisme. Kinshasa: 1979.

Comblin, José. *Theologie des Friedens.* Graz: 1963. Translation of: *Théologie de la Paix,* Paris, n.d.

———. *The Church and the National Security State.* Maryknoll, N.Y.: Orbis, 1979.

Congar, Yves M. J. *Eglise catholique et France moderne.* Paris: Hachette, 1978.

Conzemius, V. *Propheten und Vorläufer.* Einsiedeln: Herder, 1972.

Cornelis, Etienne. *Valeurs chrétiennes des religions non-chrétiennes.* Paris: Cerf, 1965.

Cosmao, Vincent. *Dossier nouvel ordre mondial: Les chrétiens provoqués par le développement.* Paris: Chalet, 1978.

Couto, Filipe J. *Hoffnung im Unglauben: Zur Diskussion über den allgemeinen Heilswillen Gottes.* Munich: F. Schoningh, 1973.

———. *Jesus von Nazareth—strafende Macht—Befreiung.* Hamburg: H. Reich, 1976.

Cox, Harvey. *The Secular City.* New York: Macmillan, 1965.

———. *Licht aus Asien.* Stuttgart: 1978. In English: *Turning East: The Promise and Peril of the New Orientalism.* New York: Simon and Schuster, 1977.

Cullmann, Oscar. *Heil als Geschichte.* Tübingen: Mohr, 1965. In English: *Salvation in History.* New York: Harper and Row, 1967.

Cuttat, J. A. *Asiatische Gottheit—christlicher Gott.* Einsiedeln: n.d.

Dammann, E. *Grundriss der Religionsgeschichte.* Stuttgart: 1978.

Daniel, Yvan. *Aux frontières de l'Eglise.* Paris: Cerf, 1978.

Daniélou, Jean. *Vom Heil der Völker.* Frankfurt a.M.: 1952. In English: *Salvation of the Nations.* Notre Dame, Ind.: University of Notre Dame, 1962. Translation of: *Le mystère du salut des nations.* Paris: Seuil, 1946.

———. *Le mystère de l'Avent.* Paris: Seuil, 1948. In English: *Advent.* New York: Sheed and Ward, 1950.

———. *Der Gott der Heiden, der Juden und der Christen.* Mainz: 1957.

———. *Dieu et nous.* Paris: Grasset, 1956. In English: *God and the Ways of Knowing.* New York: Meridian, 1957.

———. *Die heiligen Heiden des Alten Testamentes.* Stuttgart: 1955. Translation of: *Les saints païens de l'Ancien Testament.* Paris: Seuil, n.d. In English: *Holy Pagans of the Old Testament.* London, New York: Longmans, Green, 1977.

Dantine, Wilhelm. *Schwarze Theologie: Eine Herausforderung der Theologie der Weissen?* Vienna: Herder, 1976.

Dawe, Donald G., and Carman, J. B. eds. *Christian Faith in a Religiously Plural World.* Maryknoll, N.Y.: Orbis, 1978.

Debrunner, H. W. *A History of Christianity in Ghana.* Accra: 1967.

Delumeau, Jean. *Le christianisme va-t-il mourir?* Paris: Hachette, 1977.

De Meuter, G. *My God Is Your God.* London: Spearman, 1965.

Demmer, K., ed. *Christlich glauben und handeln.* Düsseldorf: Patmos, 1977.

Denzinger, H., and Schonmetzer, A. *Enchiridion Symbolorum: definitionum et declarationum de rebus fidei et morum.* Freiburg i.B.: Herder, 1963.

Desroche, Henri, et al. *Dieux d'hommes: Dictionnaire des messianismes et de l'ère chrétienne.* Paris: Mouton, 1969.

de Surgy, Paul, ed. *Recherches et réflexions sur libération humaine et foi.* Paris: 1975.

Deutsch, Karl W. *Nationalism and Its Alternatives.* New York: Knopf, 1969.

Dhavamony, Mariasusai. *Evangelization, Dialogue and Development.* Rome: Gregorian University, 1972.

Dickson, Kwesi A., and Ellingworth, Paul, eds. *Biblical Revelation and African Beliefs.* 3rd ed. London: Lutterworth, 1972.

Dieterlen, Germaine. *Textes sacrés d'Afrique noire.* Paris: Gallimard, 1965.

Doke, Clement M. *The Lambas of Northern Rhodesia.* Westport, Conn.: Negro Universities, 1970.

Douglass, James. *The Non-Violent Cross.* New York: Macmillan, 1968.

Dournes, J. *Gott liebt die Heiden.* Freiburg i.B.: 1966. Translation of: *Dieu aime les païens.* Paris: Aubier, 1963.

Dulles, Avery. *Revelation Theology.* New York: Herder and Herder, 1969.

———. *Models of the Church.* New York: Doubleday, 1974.

Dumoulin, Heinrich, ed. *Buddhismus der Gegenwart.* Freiburg i.B.: Herder, 1970. In English: *Buddhism in the Modern World.* New York: Macmillan, 1976.

———. *Christianity Meets Buddhism.* La Salle, Ill.: Open Court, 1974.

Dupuis, Jacques. *Jesus Christ and His Spirit.* Bangalore: 1977.

Eban, Abba. *Dies ist mein Volk: Die Geschichte der Juden.* Zurich: 1970. In English: *My People: A History of the Jews.* New York: Random House, 1968.

Eicher, Peter. "Offenbarung: Zur Präzisierung einer überstrapazierten Kategorie." In Bitter, Gottfried, ed., *Konturen heutiger Theologie,* pp. 108-34. Munich: Kösel, 1976.

Eichhorn, W. *Die Religionen Chinas.* Stuttgart: W. Kohlhammer, 1973.

Eichrodt, W. *Religionsgeschichte Israels.* Bern-Munich: 1969. In English: *Theology of the Old Testament.* 3rd ed. London: 1969.

Eissteldt, O. *Einleitung in das Alte Testament.* 3rd ed. Tübingen: 1964.

Eliade, Mircea. *The Quest: History and Meaning in Religion.* Chicago: University of Chicago, 1969. Translation of: *La nostalgie des origines.* Paris: 1971.

———. *Geschichte der religiösen Ideen.* 3 vols. Freiburg i.B.: 1978-80. In English: *A History of Religious Ideas.* Chicago: University of Chicago, 1978.

Emeis, Dieter. *Lernprozess im Glauben: Ein Arbeitsbuch für die Erwachsenenbildung.* Freiburg i.B.: Herder, 1971.

Erharter, Helmut, ed. *Hoffnung für Alle.* Vienna: Herder, 1970.

Esposito, Rosario F. *Le buone opere dei laicisti: degli anticlericali e dei framassoni.* Rome: Paoline, 1970.

———. *La massoneria e l'Italia dal 1800 ai nostri giorni.* Rome: Paoline, 1979.

———. *Pio IX: La Chiesa in conflitto col mondo.* Rome: Paoline, 1979.

Europäische Theologie herausgefordert durch die Weltökumene. Geneva: 1976.

290

Evers, Georg, *Mission, nichtchristliche Religionen, weltliche Welt.* Münster i.W.: Aschendorff, 1974.

Exeler, Adolf, and Emeis, Dieter. *Reflektierter Glaube.* Freiburg, i.B.: Herder, 1972.

Falaturi, A., ed. *Drei Wege zu dem einen Gott: Glaubenserfahrung in den monotheistischen Religionen.* Freiburg i.B.: Herder, 1976.

Fasholé-Luke, Edward. *Christianity in Independent Africa.* London: R. Collings, 1978; Bloomington: Indiana University, 1978.

Fattal, A. *Le statut légal des non-musulmans en pays d'Islam.* Beirut: Imp. Catholique, 1958.

Feiner, Johannes, and Vischar, L. *Neues Glaubensbuch.* 11th ed. Zurich: Theologischer Verlag, 1974. In English: *The Common Catechism: A Book of Christian Faith.* New York: Seabury, 1975.

Figl, J. *Atheismus als theologisches Problem.* Mainz: M. Grünewald, 1977.

Fischer, Klaus P. *Der Mensch als Geheimnis: Die Anthropologie K. Rahners.* Freiburg i.B.: Herder, 1973.

Fitzgerald, Michael, ed. *Moslems und Christen—Partner?* Graz: Styria, 1976.

Fohrer, Georg. *Einleitung in das Alte Testament.* 10th ed. Heidelberg: 1965. In English: *Introduction to the Old Testament.* Nashville: Abingdon, 1968.

Fourche, T., and Morligem, M. *Une Bible Noire.* Brussels: M. Arnold, 1973.

Frankl, V. E. *Der Mensch vor der Frage nach dem Sinn.* Munich: Piper, 1979.

Friedli, Richard. *Fremdheit als Heimat: Auf der Suche nach einem Kriterium für den Dialog zwischen den Religionen.* Fribourg: Universitätsverlag, 1974.

Fries, Heinrich. *Glaube und Kirche als Angebot.* Graz: Styria, 1976.

Frohnes, G., ed. *Kirchengeschichte als Missionsgeschichte.* 2 vols. Munich: 1974–78.

Fromm, Erich. *Haben oder Sein: Die seelischer Grundlagen einer neuen Gesellschaft.* Stuttgart: 1976. In English: *To Have or to Be?* New York: Harper & Row, 1976.

Garaudy, Roger. *Appel aux vivants.* Paris: Seuil, 1979.

Gerlitz, Peter. *Die Religionen und die neue Moral: Wirkungen einer weltweiten Säkularisation.* Munich: Claudius, 1971.

Giblet, Jean, ed. *The God of Israel, the God of Christians.* New York: Paulist, 1966.

Gioberti, Vicenzo. *Primato morale e civile degli italiani.* 3 vols. Turin: Tipografico-Torinese, 1925.

von Glasenapp, Helmut. *Die Religionen Indiens.* Stuttgart: A. Kröner, 1955.

Glazik, Josef. *Mission: der stets grossere Auftrag.* Aachen: 1979.

Goldstein, H. *Paulinische Gemeinde im Ersten Petrusbrief.* Stuttgart: 1975.

Goetz, J. "Dieu lointain et puissances proches." *Studia Missionalia,* vol. 21 (Rome: Gregorian University, 1972), pp. 21–55.

Gollwitzer, Helmut. *Krummes Holz—aufrechter Gang: Zur Frage nach dem Sinn des Lebens.* Munich: Kaiser, 1976.

Gottwald, N. K. *The Tribes of Yahweh: A Sociology of the Religion of Liberated Israel.* Maryknoll, N.Y.: Orbis, 1979.

Gravrand, H. *Dialogue avec les religions africaines.* Rome: Secretariatus pro non-christianis, 1968.

Griaule, Marcel. *Schwarze Genesis: Ein afrikanischer Schöpfungsbericht.* Freiburg i.B.: 1970.

Grillmeier, Aloys. *Mit Ihm und in Ihm: Christologische Forschungen und Perspektiven.* Freiburg i.B.: Herder, 1975. In English: *Christ in Christian Tradition.* London: Mowbrays, 1975; Atlanta: John Knox, 1975.

Gruhl, H. *Ein Planet wird geplündert: Die Schreckensbilanz unserer Politik.* 4th ed. Frankfurt a.M.: S. Fischer, 1978.

Grundmann, Herbert, *Ketzergeschichte des Mittelalters.* Göttingen: Vandenhoeck und Ruprecht, 1963.

———. *Bibliographie zur Ketzereschichte des Mittelalters.* Rome: Storia e Letturatura, 1967.

Guariglia, Guglielmo. *Il messianismo russo*. Rome: Studium, 1956.
———. *Prophetismus und Heilserwartungsbewegungen*. Vienna: F. Berger, 1959.
Gutiérrez, Gustavo. *A Theology of Liberation*. Maryknoll, N.Y.: Orbis, 1973.
Haag, Herbert. *Vor dem Bosen ratlos?* Munich: Piper, 1978.
———. *Das Buch des Bundes*. Düsseldorf: 1980.
———, ed. "Relevanz der Geschichte." *Theologische Quartalschrift,* vol. 155 (Tübingen: 1975), pp. 173–243.
Hallet, Jean-Pierre. *Afrika Kitabu: Ein Bericht*. Munich: 1966. In English: *Congo Kitabu*. New York: Random House, 1965.
Hammer, Karl. *Weltmission und Kolonialismus: Sendungsideen des 19. Jahrhunderts im Konflikt*. Munich: Kösel, 1978.
von Hammerstein, Franz. *Christian-Jewish Relations in Ecumenical Perspective*. Geneva: 1978.
———, ed. *Von Vorurteilen zum Verständnis: Dokumente zum jüdischchristlichen Dialog*. Frankfurt a.M.: Lembeck, 1976.
Hasenhüttl, G. *Herrschaftsfreie Kirche: Sozio-theologische Grundlegung*. Dusseldorf: Patmos, 1974.
———, ed. *Formen kirchlicher Ketzerbewältigung*. Dusseldorf: Patmos, 1976.
Hay, Malcolm. *Failure in the Far East*. Wetteren, Belgium: Scaldis, 1956; Philadelphia: Dufour, 1957.
Hebblethwaite, Peter. *Mehr Christentum oder mehr Marxismus?* Frankfurt a.M.: 1977. In English: *Christian-Marxist Dialogue*. New York: Paulist, 1977.
Hebga, Meinrad P. *Emancipation d'Eglises sous tutelle: Essai sur l'ère post-missionnaire*. Paris: Présence Africaine, 1976.
Heer, Friedrich. *Gottes erste Liebe: 2000 Jahre Judentum und Christentum*. Munich: Bechtle, 1967. In English: *God's First Love: Christians and Jews over Two Thousand Years:* New York: Weybright and Talley, 1970.
Heilsbetz. *Theologische Gründe der nichtchristlichen Religionen*. Freiburg i.B.: 1967.
Heinen, Wilhelm, and Schreiner, Josef, eds. *Erwartung, Verheissung, Erfüllung*. Würzburg: Echter, 1969.
Hengel, Martin. *Nachfolge und Charisma*. Berlin: A. Töpelmann, 1968.
———. *Juden, Griechen, Barbaren*. Stuttgart: KBW, 1976. In English: *Jews, Greeks and Barbarians*. Philadelphia: Fortress, 1980.
Herbst, Karl. *Was wollte Jesus selbst? Die vorkirchlichen Jesusworte in den Evangelien*. Düsseldorf: Patmos, 1979.
Herman, H. *Ketzer in Deutschland*. Cologne: 1978.
Herman, S. *Die Geschichte Israels in alttestamentlicher Zeit*. Munich: Kaiser, 1973.
Hermann, I. *Die Christen und ihre Konflikte*. Olten: Walter, 1970.
Hermans, M. *Erlöser und Heilbringer der Tibeter*. Wiesbaden: 1970.
Höffner, Joseph. *Christentum und Menschenwürde: Das Anliegen der spanischen Kolonialpolitik im Goldenen Zeitalter*. Trier: Paulinus, 1947.
———. *Pastoral der Kirchenfremden*. Bonn: 1979.
Holbock, F., and Sartory, T. *Mysterium Kirche*. 2 vols. Salzburg: 1962.
Hollenweger, W. J. *Erfahrungen der Leibhaftigkeit: Interkulturelle Theologie*. Munich: 1979.
Homo religiosus: L'expression du sacré dans les grandes religions. Louvain: 1978–.
Hoppenworth, Klaus. *Islam contra Christentum*. Bad Liebenzell: Liebenzeller Mission, 1976.
Huber, Wolfgang, and Liedke, Gerhard, eds. *Christentum und Militarismus*. Stuttgart: E. Klett, 1974.
Idowu, E. Bolaji. *Olodumare: God in Yoruba Belief*. London: 1962; New York: Praeger, 1963,
Isnanand, Vempeny. *Inspiration in All Non-Biblical Scriptures*. Bangalore: 1973.

Jacquemont, Patrick, ed. *Le temps de la patience.* Paris: Cerf, 1976.
Jahn, Jahnheinz. *Wir nannten sie Wilde: Aus alten und neuen Reisebeschreibungen.* Munich: Ehrenwirth, 1964.
Jaki, Stanley L. *The Road of Science and the Ways to God.* Chicago: University of Chicago, 1978.
Jaros, Karl. *Die Stellung des Elohisten zur Kanaanaischen Religion.* Fribourg: Universitätsverlag, 1974.
———. *Aegypten und Vorderasien.* Vienna, Stuttgart: KBW, 1976.
Jastrow, Joseph. *Storia dell'errore umano.* Verona: 1942. In English: *Story of Human Error.* New York: Appleton-Century, 1936.
Jedin, Hubert, ed. *Handbuch der Kirchengeschichte.* 6 vols. Freiburg i.B.: Herder, 1962–73.
———, and Dolan, John P., eds. *History of the Church.* New York: Seabury Press, 1980.
Jeremias, J. *Jesu Verheissung für die Völker.* Stuttgart: Kohlhammer, 1956. In English: *Jesus' Promise to the Nations.* London: SCM, 1967; Naperville, Ill.: A. R. Allenson, 1958.
Johnston, William. *The Inner Eye of Love: Mysticism and Religion.* London: 1978; New York: Harper & Row, 1978.
Jungk, Robert. *Der Jahrtausendmensch: Bericht aus den Werkstatten der neuen Gesellschaft.* Munich: C. Bertelsmann, 1973. In English: *The Everyman Project: Resources for a Humane Future.* New York: Liveright, 1977.
Jungk, R., and Mundt, H. J., eds. *Der Weg ins Jahr 2000.* Munich: 1968.
Karrer, Leo. *Der Glaube in Kurzformeln.* Mainz: M. Grünewald, 1978.
Karrer, Otto. *Das Religiöse in der Menschheit und das Christentum.* Freiburg i.B.: Herder, 1934.
———. *Religions of Mankind.* London: Sheed and Ward, 1936.
Kasper, Walter. *Glaube und Geschichte.* Mainz: M. Grünewald, 1970.
Kattmann, Ulrich, ed. *Rassen: Biologisch-sozialkundliches Arbeitsbuch.* Wuppertal: Jugenddienst, 1973.
Katz, Jacob. *Exclusiveness and Tolerance: Studies in Jewish-Gentile Relations.* New York: Greenwood, 1980.
Kaufmann, Gisbert, ed. *Tendenzen der katholischen Theologie nach dem II Vatikanischen Konzil.* Munich: Kösel, 1979.
Kaufmann, H. *Afrikas Wege in die Gegenwart.* Graz: 1963.
Keel, O., and Küchler, M. *Synoptische Texte aus der Genesis.* Fribourg: Schweizerisches Katholisches Bibelwerk, 1971.
Kehl, Medard. *Kirche als Institution.* Frankfurt a.M.: Knecht, 1976.
Klages, Günther, and Heutger, Nicolaus. *Weltreligionen und Christentum im Gesprach.* Hildesheim–New York: Olms, 1977.
Klinger, Elmar. *Offenbarung im Horizont der Heilsgeschichte.* Einsiedeln: Benziger, 1969.
———, ed. *Christentum innerhalb und ausserhalb der Kirche.* Freiburg i.B.: Herder, 1976.
Klostermaier, Klaus. *Hinduismus.* Cologne: Backem, 1965.
Knauer, Peter. *Der Glaube kommt vom Hören: Oekumenische Fundamental-theologie.* Graz: Styria, 1978.
Köhler, O. *Bewusstseinsstörungen im Katholizismus.* Frankfurt a.M.: 1972.
König, Franz, ed. *Christus und die Religionen der Erde.* 3 vols. Freiburg, i.B.: Herder, 1961.
Der Koran. Stuttgart: Kohlhammer, 1962. In English: *The Qur'an: A New Translation with a Critical Rearrangement of the Surahs.* 2 vols. New York: Attic, n.d.
Köster, Fritz. *Afrikanisches Christsein.* Einsiedeln: Benziger, 1977.

Kraft, Charles H., *Christianity in Culture: A Study in Dynamic Biblical Theologizing in Cross-Cultural Perspective*. Maryknoll, N.Y.: Orbis, 1979.

Kuhn, Helmut, ed. *Interpretation der Welt*. Würzburg: Echter, 1965.

Kühn, Johannes. *Toleranz und Offenbarung*. Leipzig: F. Meiner, 1923.

Kühner, Hans. *Der Antisemitismus der Kirche*. Zurich: Die Waage, 1976.

Kümmel, Werner G. *Theologie des Neuen Testamentes nach seinen Hauptseugen Jesus, Paulus und Johannes*. Gottingen: Vandenhoeck und Ruprecht, 1969. In English: *Theology of the New Testament*. Nashville: Abingdon, 1973.

Küng, Hans. *Christsein*. Munich: R. Piper, 1974. In English: *On Being a Christian*. New York: Doubleday, 1976.

————. *Existiert Gott? Antwort auf die Gottesfrage der neuen Zeit*. Munich: R. Piper, 1978. In English: *Does God Exist? An Answer for Today*. New York: Doubleday, 1980.

Kunnumpuram, K. *Ways of Salvation. The Salvific Meaning of Non-Christian Religions According to the Teaching of Vatican II*. Poona: 1971.

Labuschagne, C. J. *The Incomparability of Yahweh in the Old Testament*. Leiden: E. J. Brill, 1966.

Lapide, Pinchas. *Auferstehung—ein judisches Glaubenserlebnis*. Stuttgart: Calwer, 1978.

Latourelle, René. *Teologia della rivelazione*. Assisi: 1967. In English: *Theology of Revelation*. Staten Island, N.Y.: Alba House, 1966.

Leakey, Richard E., and Lewin, Roger. *Origins*. London: 1977; New York: Dutton, 1977.

Lecler, J. *Toleration and the Reformation*. 2 vols. London: 1960.

Ledergerber, Karl. *Geburt der Menschheit: Ein neues Bewusstsein entwickelt sich*. Munich: Pfeiffer, 1978.

van der Leeuw, Gerardus. *Die Bilanz des Christentums*. Zurich: 1947.

————. *Phänomenologie der Religion*. Tübingen: J. C. B. Mohr, 1956. In English: *Religion in Essence and Manifestation: A Study in Phenomenology*. New York: Harper and Row, 1963.

van den Leeuwen, Arend T. *Christentum in der Weltgeschichte*. Stuttgart: 1966. In English: *Christianity in World History*. New York: Scribner, 1966.

Légaut, Marcel. *Meine Erfahrung mit dem Glauben*. 5th ed. Freiburg i.B.: 1973.

Lehmann, Karl, ed. *Theologie der Befreiung*. Einsiedeln: 1977.

Le Saux, D. *Sagesse hindoue, Mystique chrétienne*. Paris: Centurion, 1965.

Lichtenberg, J.P. *From the First to the Last of the Just: A Study of the History of the Relations Between Jews and Christians Throughout the Centuries*. Jerusalem: Isratypeset, 1971.

Lindbeck, Georges A. *Le catholicisme a-t-il un avenir?* Paris: Casterman, 1970. In English: *The Future of Roman Catholic Theology*. Philadelphia: Fortress, 1970.

van der Linde, Hendrik, and Fiold, Hermanus. *Neue Perspektiven nach dem Ende des konventionellen Christentums*. Freiburg i.B.: Herder, 1968.

Lissner, I. *Aber Gott war da: Das Erlebnis der letzten unerforschten Wälder der Erde*. Olten: Walter, 1958.

Lohfink, Norbert. *Das Siegeslied am Schilfmeer: Christliche Auseinandersetzung mit dem Alten Testament*. Frankfurt a.M.: J. Knecht, 1965. In English: *The Christian Meaning of the Old Testament*. Milwaukee: Bruce, 1968.

Lohse, Bernhard. *Epochen der Dogmengeschichte*. Stuttgart: Kreuz, 1963. In English: *A Short History of Christian Doctrine*. Philadelphia: Fortress, 1978.

Lombardi, Riccardo. *Chiesa e Regno di Dio*. Brescia: Morcelliana, 1976.

Lonergan, Bernard. *Theologie im Pluralismus heutiger Kulturen*. Freiburg i.B.: Herder, 1975.

Lortz, Joseph. *Die Reformation in Deutschland*. 2 Vols. Freiburg i.B.: Herder, 1941.

Loth, H. J., Mildenberger, M., and Tworuschka, U. *Christentum im Spiegel der Weltreligionen*. Stuttgart: 1978.

Lotz, Johannes B. *Wider den Unsinn: Zur Sinnfrage unseres Zeitalters.* Frankfurt a.M.: Knecht, 1977.

Lufuluabo, F. *Valeur des religions africaines selon la Bible et selon Vatican II.* Kinshasa: St. Paul Afrique, 1968.

Machovec, M. *Jesus für Atheisten.* Stuttgart: Kreuz, 1972. In English: *A Marxist Looks at Jesus.* Philadelphia: Fortress, 1976.

Maloney, George A. *The Cosmic Christ: From Paul to Teilhard.* New York: Sheed and Ward, 1968.

Mann, Ulrich. *Theogonische Frage: Die Entwicklungsphasen des Gottesbewusstseins in der altorientalischen und biblischen Religion.* Stuttgart: E. Klett, 1970.

———. *Das Christentum als absolute Religion.* 3rd ed. Darmstadt: Wissenschaftliche Buchgesellschaft, 1974.

Marquard, Leopold. *The Peoples and Policies of South Africa.* London: Oxford University Press, 1962.

Marstin, Ronald. *Beyond Our Tribal Gods.* Maryknoll, N.Y.: Orbis, 1979.

Mattam, Joseph. *Land of the Trinity: A Study of Modern Christian Approaches to Hinduism.* Bangalore: Theological Publications in India, 1975.

Maurier, Henri. *The Other Covenant: A Theology of Paganism.* New York: Newman, 1968. Translation of: *Un humanisme africain.* Brussels: 1965.

Maximos IV Sayegh, ed. *The Eastern Churches and Catholic Unity.* New York: Herder & Herder, 1963.

Mbiti, John S. *African Religions and Philosophy.* London: 1969; New York: Doubleday, 1970.

———. *New Testament Eschatology in an African Background.* London: Oxford University, 1971.

McCarthy, Dennis J. *Treaty and Covenant.* Rome: 1978.

McKenzie, John L. *The Two-Edged Sword: An Interpretation of the Old Testament.* New York: Doubleday, 1966.

Meinhold, Peter. *Die Religionen der Gegenwart.* Freiburg i.B.: Herder, 1978.

Mensching, Gustav. *Toleranz und Wahrheit in den Religionen.* Heidelberg: 1955. In English: *Tolerance and Truth in Religion.* University, Ala.: University of Alabama, 1971.

———. *Der offene Tempel: Die Weltreligionen im Gespräch miteinander.* Stuttgart: Deutsche Verlags-Anstalt, 1974.

———. *Buddha und Christus, ein Vergleich.* Stuttgart: Deutsche Verlags-Anstalt, 1978.

Mensen, B., ed. *Die Begegnung des abendländischen Christentums mit andern Völkern und Kulturen.* St. Augustin: 1979.

Metz, Johannes B. *Glaube in Geschichte und Gesellschaft.* Mainz: 1977. In English: *Faith in History and Society.* New York: Seabury, 1979.

Metzger, Martin. *Grundriss der Geschichte Israels.* 4th ed. Neukirchen-Vluyn: Neukirchener, 1977.

Mildenberger, Michael. *Heil aus Asien? Hinduistische und buddhistische Bewegungen im Westen.* Stuttgart: Quell, 1974.

Mintjes, H. *Social Justice in Islam.* Amsterdam: 1977.

Mirgeler, Albert. *Kritischer Rückblick auf das abendländische Christentum.* Freiburg i.B.: 1961. In English: *Mutations of Western Christianity.* Notre Dame, Ind.: University of Notre Dame, 1968.

Mische, Gerald P., and Mische, Patricia. *Toward a Human World Order: Beyond the National Security Straitjacket.* New York: Paulist, 1977.

Mitchell, R. C. *African Primal Religions.* Niles Ill.: Argus, 1977.

Mobley, Harris W. *The Ghanaian's Image of the Missionary.* Leiden: Brill, 1970; Ann Arbor, Mich.: University Microfilms, 1974.

Les moines chrétiens face aux religions d'Asie. Vanves: 1974.

Molinski, Waldemar, ed. *Die vielen Wege zum Heil: Heilsanspruch und Heilsbedeutung der nichtchristlichen Religionen.* Munich: Pfeiffer, 1969.

Moltmann, Jürgen. *Umkehr zur Zukunft*. Munich: Siebenstern-Taschenbuch, 1970.
———. *Die ersten Freigelassenen der Schöpfung*. Munich: Kaiser, 1971. In English: *Theology and Joy*. London: SCM, 1973.
———. *Der gekreuzigte Gott*. Munich: Kaiser, 1972. In English: *The Crucified God*. New York: Harper and Row, 1974.
———. *Kirche in der Kraft des Geistes*. Munich: Kaiser, 1975. In English: *The Church in the Power of the Spirit*. New York: Harper and Row, 1977.

Monni, Piero. *ONU: Quale libertà? Trent'anni di dibattito sulla libertà religiosa*. Rome: 1979.

Morra, Gianfranco. *Marxismo e religione*. Milan: Rusconi, 1976.

Motan, G. *The Present Revelation: The Research for Religious Foundations*. New York: 1972.

Mühlen, H. *Entsakralisierung! Ein epochales Schlagwort in seiner Bedeutung für die Zukunft der christlichen Kirchen*. Paderborn: Schöningh, 1970.
———. *Morgen wird Einheit sein: Das kommende Konzil aller Christen*. Paderborn: Schöningh, 1974.

Mulago, Vincent. *Un visage africain du christianisme: L'union vitale bantue face à l'unité vitale ecclésiale*. Paris: Présence Africaine, 1962.

Mulders, Alphonsus. *Missionsgeschichte*. Regensburg: F. Pustet, 1960.

Müller, Alois, ed. *Missionare im Lernprozess: 10 Jahre Seminar-arbeit der Missionszentrale der Franziskaner*. Mettingen: 1979.

Müller-Fahrenholz, Geiko. *Heilsgeschichte zwischen Ideologie und Prophetik: Profile und Kritik heilsgeschichtlicher Theorien in der ökumenischen Bewegung zwischen 1948 und 1968*. Freiburg i.B.: Herder, 1974.

Muschalek, Hubert. *Urmensch Adam: Die Herkunft des menschlichen Leibes in naturwissenschaftlicher und theologischer Sicht*. Berlin: Morus, 1963.

Muskens, M.P.M. *Partners in Nation-Building: The Catholic Church in Indonesia*. Aachen: 1979.

Mussner, Franz. *Christus, das All und die Kirche*. Trier: Paulinus, 1968.

Nambiaparambil, A., ed. *Guidelines for Inter-Religious Dialogue*. Varanasi: 1977.

Neal, Marie Augusta. *A Socio-Theology of Letting Go: The Role of the First World Church Facing Third World Peoples*. New York: Paulist, 1977.

Nelson, J. Robert, and Pannenberg, Wolfhart, eds. *Um Einheit und Heil der Menschheit*. 2nd ed. Frankfurt a.M.: Lembeck, 1976.

Neuner, Joseph, ed. *Christian Revelation and World Religions*. London: Burns and Oates, 1967.

Nigg, Walter. *Das Buch der Ketzer*. Zurich: Artemis, 1949.

Nolan, Albert. *Jesus avant le christianisme*. Paris: Ouvrières, 1979. In English: *Jesus Before Christianity*. London: Darton, Longman, and Todd, 1977; Maryknoll, N.Y.: Orbis, 1978.

Nosipho, Majeke. *The Role of the Missionaries in Conquest*. Johannesburg: 1952.

Nothomb, Dominique. *Un humanisme africain*. Brussels: Lumen Vitae, 1965.

Nouailhae, Anne Marguerite. *La peur de l'autre: Dossier racisme*. Paris: Fleurs, 1972.

Nys, Hendrik. *Le Salut sans l'Evangile*. Paris: 1966.

Oberhammer, G., ed. *Offenbarung, geistige Realität des Menschen*. Vienna: Gerold, 1974.

Ohle, Karlheinz. *Das Ich und das Andere*. Stuttgart: Fischer, 1978.

Ohm, Thomas. *Die Liebe zu Gott in den nichtchristlichen Religionen*. Munich: 1950.
———. *Asiens Nein und Ja zum westlichen Christentum*. Munich: Kösel, 1960.

Overhage, Paul, and Rahner, Karl. *Das Problem der Hominisation*. Freiburg i.B.: Herder, 1965.

Paillard, J. *Christ unter Atheisten*. Frankfurt a.M.: 1971.

Panikkar, Raimundo. *The Unknown Christ of Hinduism*. London: Darton, Longman, and Todd, 1964.

————. *Religionen und die Religion*. Munich: Hueber 1965.

————. *The Vedic Experience: An Anthology of the Vedas for Modern Man and Contemporary Celebration*. London: 1977; Berkeley: University of California, 1977.

Papa, B. *Tensioni e unità della Chiesa*. Bari: 1976.

Parrinder, Geoffrey. *Le Upanishad, la Gita e la Biblia*. Rome: 1964. In English: *Upanishads, Gita and Bible*. New York: Harper and Row, 1972.

Paus, A., ed. *Suche nach Sinn, Suche nach Gott*. Graz: Styria, 1978.

Pentecost, Edward C. *Reaching the Unreached*. South Pasadena, Calif.: William Carey Library, 1974.

Pereira de Queiroz, M. I. *O messianismo no Brasil e no mundo*. São Paulo: 1965.

Pesch, Otto H., ed. *Einheit der Kirche, Einheit der Menschheit: Perspektiven aus Theologie, Ethik und Völkerrecht*. Freiburg i.B.: Herder, 1976.

Pestalozzi, H. A. *Nach uns die Zukunft: Von der positiven Subversion*. Bern: 1979.

Petuchowsky, Jakob J. *Melchisedech, Urgestalt der Oekumene*. Freiburg i.B.: Herder, 1979.

Pfammatter, J., and Furger, F., eds. *Judentum und Kirche: Volk Gottes*. Einsiedeln: Benziger, 1974.

Philberth, Bernhard. *Christliche Prophetie und Nuklearenergie*. Nuremberg: Glock und Lutz, 1961.

Pinay, M. *Complotto contro la Chiesa*. Madrid: 1962. In English: *The Plot Against the Catholic Church*. New York: Gordon, 1979.

Plischke. "Völkerkundliches zur Entstehung von Stammes- und Völkernamen." In Hesch, M., ed. *Kultur und Rasse*, pp. 394–407. Munich: J. F. Lehmanns, 1939.

van de Pol, Willem H. *Das Ende des konventionellen Christentums*. Freiburg i.B.: Herder, 1967. In English: *The End of Conventional Christianity*. New York: Newman, 1968.

Pomilio, Mario. *Il quinto Vangelo*. 4th ed. Milan: Rusconi, 1975.

Poulat, Emile. *Catholicisme, démocratie et socialisme: Le mouvement catholique et Mgr. Benigni*. Tournai: Casterman, 1977.

Puech, Henri Charles, ed. *Histoire des religions: Encyclopédie de la Pléjade*. 3 vols. Paris: Gallimard, 1970–76.

Puyo, Jean, and van Eersel, P. *Voyage a l'intérieur de l'Eglise catholique*. Paris: Stock, 1977.

von Rad, Gerhard. *Theologie des Alten Testamentes*. 2 vols. Munich: Kaiser, 1965–66. In English: *Old Testament Theology*. 2 vols. New York: Harper and Row, n.d.

Radhakrishnan, S. *The Hindu View of Life*. 17th ed. London: Allen and Unwin, 1974.

Rahner, Hugo, ed. *Die Märtyrerakten des zweiten Jahrhunderts*. Freiburg i.B.: Herder, 1941.

Rahner, Karl. *Schriften zur Theologie*. Vols. 1–14. Einsiedeln: Benziger, 1954–80. In English: *Theological Investigations*. Vols. 1–14. Baltimore: Helicon Press, 1961–.

————. *Das freie Wort in der Kirche*. Einsiedeln: Johannes, 1955. In English: *Free Speech in the Church*. New York: Sheed and Ward, 1960.

————. *Ueber die Schriftinspiration*. 2nd ed. Freiburg i.B.: Herder, 1958. In English: *Inspiration in the Bible*. New York: Herder and Herder, 1964.

————. *Sendung und Gnade*. 4th ed. Innsbruck: Tyrolia, 1966. In English: *Mission and Grace*. 3 vols. New York: Sheed and Ward, 1963–66.

————. *Vorfragen zu einem ökumenischen Amtsverständnis*. Freiburg i.B.: Herder, 1974.

————. *Grundkurs des Glaubens: Einführung in den Begriff des Christentums*. Freiburg i.B.: Herder, 1976. In English: *Foundations of Christian Faith*. New York: Seabury, 1978.

————, and Lehmann, K. *Marsch ins Getto? Der Weg der Katholiken in der Bundesrepublik*. Munich: Kösel, 1973.

————, and Ratzinger, J. *Das Christentum und die nichtchristlichen Religionen.* Nuremberg: 1965.

Rattray, Robert S. *Religion and Art in Ashanti.* London: Oxford University, 1980.

Ratzinger, Josef. *Der Gott des Glaubens und der Gott der Philosophen.* Munich: Schell und Steiner, 1960.

————. *Das neue Volk Gottes, Entwürfe zur Ekklesiologie.* Düsseldorf: Patmos, 1969.

————, ed. *Dienst an der Einheit.* Düsseldorf: Patmos, 1978.

Raunig, W., ed. *Schwarzafriakner: ihr Weltbild.* Innsbruck: Pinguin, 1980.

Rennstich, K. *Mission und wirtschaftliche Entwicklung.* Munich: Kaiser, 1978.

"Revelation in Christianity and Other Religions." *Studia Missionalia,* vol. 20. Rome: 1971.

Ricard, Robert. *La "conquête spirituelle" du Mexique.* Paris: Institut d'Ethnologie, 1933. In English: *The Spiritual Conquest of Mexico.* Berkeley: University of California, 1974.

Richard-Molard, George. *Le troisième peuple, héraut d'espérance.* Paris: Desclée, 1977.

Richardson, A. *An Introduction to the Theology of the New Testament.* 4th ed. London: 1969.

Riedweg, F. *Ende des Säkularismis.* Regensburg: 1978.

Roest Crollias, A. A. *The Word in the Experience of Revelation in Qur'an and Hindu Scriptures.* Rome: Gregorian University, 1974.

Rohner, Peter, ed. *Mitmenschlichkeit—eine Illusion? Die Weltreligionen im Blick zur Gemeinschaft.* Munich: Pfeiffer, 1973.

Rolfes, Helmuth. *Der Sinn des Lebens im marxistischen Denken.* Düsseldorf: Patmos, 1971.

Rossano, Pietro. *Il problema teologico delle religioni.* Rome: 1975.

Rowley, Harold H. *The Biblical Doctrine of Election.* London: Lutterworth, 1970.

Ruben, W. *Die Entwicklung der Religion im alten Indien.* Berlin: Akademie, 1971.

Ruether, Rosemary. *Nachstenliebe und Brudermord: Die theolgischen Würzeln des Antisemitismus.* Munich: Kaiser, 1978. In English: *Faith and Fratricide: The Theological Roots of Anti-Semitism.* New York: Seabury, 1974.

Rustow, A. *Ortsbestimmung der Gegenwart: Eine universalgeschichtliche Kulturkritik.* 2 vols. Erlenback: 1950–52.

Rutti, L. *Zur Theologie der Mission.* Munich-Mainz: Kaiser, 1972.

Samartha, Stanley J., ed. *Faith in the Midst of Faiths: Reflections on Dialogue in Community.* Geneva: World Council of Churches, 1977.

Sanon, A. *Tierce-Eglise, ma mère: La conversion d'une communauté païenne au Christ.* Paris: 1970.

Savramis, Demosthenes. *Religionen.* Düsseldorf: Econ-Verlag, 1972.

Schar, Hans. *Erlösungsvorstellungen und ihre psychologischen Aspekte.* Zurich: Rascher, 1950.

Schatz, O., ed. *Hat Religion Zukunft?* Graz: Styria, 1971.

Schedl, Claus. *Die Fulle der Zeit. Geschichte des Alten Testamentes.* Vol. 5. Innsbruck: Tyrolia, 1964. In English: *The Fullness of Time. History of the Old Testament.* Vol. 5. Staten Island, N.Y.: Alba House, 1973.

————. *Muhammad und Jesus: Die christologisch relevaten Texte des Korans.* Freiburg i.B.: Herder, 1978.

Schlette, Heinz R. *Die Religionen als Thema der Theologie.* Freiburg i.B.: Herder, 1964.

Schlosser, K. *Die Bantubibel: Schöpfungsberichte der Zulu.* Kiel: Kommissionsverlag Schmidt und Klaunig, 1977.

Schmid, Hans H. *Die Steine und das Wort: Fug und Unfug der biblischen Archeologie.* Zurich: Theologischer Verlag, 1975.

Schmidlin, Joseph. *Papstgeschichte der neuesten Zeit,* vol. 3. Munich: Kösel und Pustet, 1936.

Schmidt, Werner H. *Alttestamentlicher Glaube in seiner Geschichte.* 2nd ed. Neukirchen: Neukirchener, 1976.

Schmidt, W. *Der Ursprung der Gottesidee: Eine historisch-kritische und positive Studie.* 12 vols. Münster i.W.: Aschendorff, 1926–55. Parts in English: *The Origin and Growth of Religion: Facts and Theories.* Reprint of 1931 ed. Totowa, N.J.: Cooper Square, 1972.

Schmitz, Hermann J. *Frühkatholizismus bei A. von Harnack, R. Sohm und E. Käsemann.* Düsseldorf: Patmos, 1977.

Schnackenburg, Rudolf. *Gottes Herrschaft und Reich.* Freiburg i.B.: Herder, 1959. In English: *God's Rule and Kingdom.* New York: Herder and Herder, 1963.

————, ed. *Die Kirche des Anfanges: Festschrift H. Schürmann.* Freiburg i.B.: Herder, 1978.

Schoen, U. *Determination und Freiheit im arabischen Denken heute.* Göttingen: Vandenhoeck und Ruprecht, 1976.

Schoonenberg, Piet. *Covenant and Creation.* London: Sheed and Ward, 1968; Notre Dame, Ind.: University of Notre Dame, 1969.

Schröder, Christel M., ed. *Die Religionen der Menschheit.* 26 vols. Stuttgart: Kohlhammer, 1960–.

Schroeder Oskar. *Aufbruch und Missverständnis: Zur Geschichte der reformkatholischen Bewegung.* Graz: Styria, 1969.

Schult, Arthur. *Urgeschichte der Menschheit: Die biblische Schöpfungsgeschichte im Lichte der Mysterienweisheit.* Wuppertal: Henn, 1969.

Schultz, Hans J., ed. *Wer ist das eigentlich—Gott?* Munich: Kösel, 1969.

Schultz, Uwe, ed. *Toleranz: Die Krise der demokratischen Tugend und Vorschläge zu ihrer Überwindung.* Reinbeck: Rowholt, 1974.

Schumann, Olaf H. *Der Christus der Muslime: Christologische Aspekte in der arabisch-islamischen Literatur.* Gütersloh: Gütersloher, 1975.

Schwager, Raymund. *Brauchen wir einen Sündenbock? Gewalt und Erlösung in den biblischen Schriften.* Munich: Kösel 1978.

Schwarzenau, Paul. *Der grossere Gott: Christentum und die Weltreligionen.* Stuttgart: Radius, 1977.

Seale, Morris S. *The Desert Bible: Nomadic Tribal Culture and Old Testament Interpretation.* London: Wiedenfeld and Nicolson; New York: St. Martin's; 1974.

Seifart, Arnulf. *Der Gott der politischen Theologie: Die Entwicklung der Gottesdiskussion vom kämpfenden Nationalgott bis zur christlich motivierten Strategic des Guerilla-Krieges.* Einsiedeln: Benziger, 1978.

Sequeira, A. A. *Sin and Forgiveness in the Early Vedic Period.* Rome: Academia Alfonsiana, 1979.

Shorter, Aylward. *African Christian Theology. Adaptation or Incarnation?* London: 1975; Maryknoll, N.Y.: Orbis, 1977.

Sider, Ronald J. *Rich Christians in an Age of Hunger.* London: 1977; New York: Paulist, 1977.

Siegmund, Georg. *Buddhismus und Christentum.* Frankfurt a.M.: 1968. In English: *Buddhism and Christianity.* University, Ala.: University of Alabama, 1980.

de Silva, Lynn A. *Of the Self in Buddhism and Christianity.* Colombo: 1975.

Sinaga, A. B. "The Toba-Batak High-God." Dissertation. Louvain: 1975.

Sinda, Martial. *Le messianisme congolais et ses incidences politiques.* Paris: Payot, 1972.

Singleton, M. *Let My People Go: A Study of the Catholic Church in West-Nigeria.* Brussels: PMV, 1974.

————. "Ancêtres, adolescents et l'absolu: un essai de contextualisation." In *PMV Bulletin.* No. 68 (1977).

Smend, R. *Einleitung in das Alte Testament.* Neukirchen: 1978.

Smith, M. *Ancient Near Eastern Texts Relating to the Old Testament.* J. B. Pritchard, ed. Princeton: Princeton Univ., 1969.

Sperna Wiland, Jan. *Antworten: Ein Vergleich der grossen Welt-religionen in Wort und Bild.* Zurich-Cologne: Benziger, 1977.

Spitteris, J. *La critica bizantina del primato romano nel secolo XII.* Rome: 1979.
Staffner, H. *The Open Door: A Christian Approach to the World Religions.* Bangalore: 1978.
Stehle, Hanjakob. *Die Ostpolitik des Vatikans.* Munich: Piper, 1975. In English: *Eastern Politics of the Vatican, 1917–1979.* Athens: Ohio University, 1980.
Stirnimann, Hans. *Existenzgrundlagen und traditionelles Handwerk der Pangwa.* Fribourg: Universitätsverlag, 1976.
Stuhlmueller, Carroll. "God in the Witness of Israel's Election." In Matczak, S. A., ed. *God in Contemporary Thought,* pp. 349–378. New York: Learned, 1977.
Sundermeier, Theo, ed. *Christus der schwarze Befreier.* Erlangen: Ev.-Luth. Mission, 1973.
Talmage, Frank E. *Disputation and Dialogue: Readings in the Jewish-Christian Encounter.* New York: Ktav, 1975.
Tempels, P. *La philosophie bantoue.* Paris: 1949.
Tévoédjire, A. *La pauvreté richesses des peuples.* Paris: Ouvrières, 1978. In English: *Poverty: Wealth of Mankind.* New York: Pergamon, 1978.
Theissen, Gerd. *Soziologie der Jesusbewegung.* Munich: Kaiser, 1977.
Théologies du Tiers Monde: Du conformisme a l'indépendence: Le colloque de Dar-es-Salaam et ses prolongements. Paris: Harmattan, 1977. Cf.: *The Emergent Gospel.* Maryknoll, N.Y.: Orbis, 1978.
Theunis, J. M. *Buitenlandse arbeiders in Nederland.* Baarn: 1979.
Thiel, J. F. *Ahnen—Geister—Höchste Wesen: Religions-ethnologische Untersuchungen im Zaire-Kasai-Gebiet.* St. Augustin: 1977.
Thielicke, Helmut. *Wie die Welt begann: Der Mensch in der Urgeschichte der Bibel.* Stuttgart: Quell, 1963. In English: *How the World Began: Man in the First Chapter of the Bible.* Philadelphia: Fortress, 1961.
Thils, Gustave. *Propos et problèmes de la théologie des religions non-chrétiennes.* Paris: Casterman, 1966.
Thoma, Clemens. *Christliche Theologie des Judentums.* Aschaffenburg: 1978. In English: *A Christian Theology of Judaism.* New York: Paulist, 1980.
Thomas, Louis V., and Luneau, René. *La terre africaine et ses religions.* Paris: Larousse 1975.
———. *Les sages dépossédés.* Paris 1977.
Tort, Patrick, and Desalmand, P., eds. *Sciences humaines et philosophie en Afrique.* Paris: Hatier, 1978.
Toynbee, Arnold J. *Studie zur Weltgeschiehte: Wachstum und Zerfall der Zivilisationen.* Zurich: 1949. Translation of: *A Study of History.* New York: Oxford University Press, 1962–.
———. *Wie stehen wir zur Religion? Die Antwort eines Historikers.* Zurich: Europa, 1958. Translation of: *An Historian's Approach to Religion.* London, New York: Oxford University, 1956.
———. *Das Christentum und die Religionen der Welt.* Gütersloh: Gütersloher, 1959. Translation of: *Christianity among the Religions of the World.* New York: Scribner, 1957.
———. *Menschheit, woher und Wohin? Pladoyer für den Weltstaat.* Stuttgart: Kohlhammer, 1969. Translation of: *Change and Habit: The Challenge of Our Time.* London, New York: Oxford University, 1966.
———, ed. *Auf diesen Felsen: Das Christentum, Grundlagen und Weg zur Macht.* Vienna, 1970.
Tracy, David, and Küng, Hans, eds. *Towards Vatican III.* Dublin: 1978; New York: Seabury, 1978.
Trevor, Merial. *Prophets and Guardians: Renewal and Tradition of the Church.* London: Hollis and Carter, 1969.
Trutwin, Werner. *Erinnerung und Hoffnung: Eine Einführung in die Welt der Bibel.* Düsseldorf: 1977.

Tworuschka, Udo, and Zillessen, Dietrich, eds. *Thema Weltreligionen: Ein Diskussions-und Arbeitsbuch für Religionspädagogen und Religionswissenschaftler.* Frankfurt a.m.: Diesterweg, 1977.

Tyrell, Francis M. *Man: Believer and Unbeliever.* New York: Alba House, 1974.

Urs von Balthasar, Hans, et al., eds. *Absolutheit des Christentums.* Freiburg i.B.: Herder, 1977.

Vandana, S. *Gurus, Ashrams and Christians.* London: 1970.

de Vaux, Roland. *Histoire ancienne d'Israel.* 2 vols. Paris: LeCoffre 1971–73. In English: *The Early History of Israel.* Philadelphia: Westminster, 1978.

Vicedom, Georg. *Die Weltreligionen im Angriff auf die Christenheit.* Munich: Kaiser, 1957.

———. *Mission im ökumentschen Zeitalter.* Gütersloh: Gütersloher, 1967.

Vinatier, J. *Les chemins d'Emmaüs: De la religion populaire à la foi du peuple de Dieu.* Paris: Centurion, 1977.

Volz, Paul. *Das Dämonische in Jahwe.* Tübingen: C. B. Mohr, 1924.

Von der Mehden, Fred R. *Religion and Nationalism in Southeast Asia.* Madison: University of Wisconsin, 1963.

de Vries, Wilhelm. *Rom und die Patriarchate des Ostens.* Freiburg i.B.: 1963.

Waardenburg, Jacques. *Classical Approaches to the Study of Religion: Bibliography.* The Hague–Paris: Mouton, 1974.

Waldenfels, Hans. *Absolutes Nichts: Zur Grundlegung des Dialoges swischen Buddhismus und Christentums,* Freiburg i.B.: Herder, 1976. In English: *Absolute Nothingness: Foundation for a Christian-Buddhist Dialogue.* New York: Paulist, 1980.

———, ed. *"Denn ich bin bei euch": Perspektiven im christlichen Missionsbewusstsein heute: Festschrift J. Glazik und B. Willeke.* Einsiedeln: Benziger, 1978.

Welte, Paul H. *Die Heilsbedürftigkeit des Menschen.* Freiburg i.B.: Herder, 1976.

Westermann, Claus. *Theologie des Alten Testamentes in Grundzügen.* Göttingen: Vandenhoeck und Ruprecht, 1978.

Wetter, Gustav A. *Der dialektische Materialismus.* 5th ed. Freiburg i.B.: Herder, 1961. In English: *Dialectical Materialism.* New York: F. A. Praeger, 1959.

Whitaker, Benjamin, ed. *The Fourth World: Victims of Group Oppression.* London: Sidgwick and Jackson, 1972; New York: Schocken, 1973.

Wiederkehr, D. *Perspektiven der Eschatologie.* Einsiedeln: Benziger, 1974.

———. *Glaube an Erlösung: Konzepte der Soteriologie vom Neuen Testament bis heute.* Freiburg i.B.: Herder, 1976.

Wiesel, Elie. *Adam, oder das Geheimnis des Anfanges: Brüderliche Urgestalten.* Freiburg I.B.: Herder, 1980. In English: *Messengers of God: Biblical Portraits and Legends.* New York: Random House, 1976.

Wildiers, N. M. *Weltbild und Theologie.* Einsiedeln: Benziger, 1974.

Wilkinson, T. S., ed. *Ambedkar and the Neo-Buddhist Movement.* Madras: Christian Institute for the Study of Religion and Society, 1972.

Wolf, William J. *The Almost Chosen People.* New York: Doubleday, 1959.

Yang, C. K. *Religion in Chinese Society.* Berkeley: University of California, 1961.

Zaehner, Robert C. *Inde, Israel, Islam, religions mystiques et révélations prophétiques.* Paris: J. de Brouwer, 1965. In English: *At Sundry Times: An Essay in the Comparison of Religions.* London: Faber and Faber, 1958.

———. *Hinduism.* London: Oxford University, 1966.

Zago, Marcel, ed. *Semi del Vangelo. Studi e interventi dei vescovi d'Asia.* Bologna: 1975.

Zahrnt, Heinz. *Warum ich glaube: Meine Sache mit Gott.* Munich: Piper, 1977.

Zulehner, Paul M. *Religion ohne Kirche?* Freiburg i.B.: Herder, 1969.